THROUGH VALUES
TO
SOCIAL INTERPRETATION

Essays on Social Contexts, Actions,

Types, and Prospects

HOWARD BECKER

Professor of Sociology, University of Wisconsin

GREENWOOD PRESS, PUBLISHERS

NEW YORK   1968

To the memories of

PAUL JOHN BECKER

BLACKSMITH, PROSPECTOR, PIONEER

"This was a man."

AND

LETITIA STEVENSON BECKER

HOUSEWIFE, COUNSELOR, COMRADE

"She spoke of simple things and true."

. . . "misology," or hatred of theories, . . . is just like misanthropy, which arises from ignorance of the art of dealing with men. Just as the man who knows the world knows that very good men and very bad men are equally rare, so that man who knows the art of dealing with theories will not expect too much . . . but neither will he lose faith.—BURNET

. . . one must abandon any hope of completing at once the theory one is in process of building, clearly understanding that only successive approximations can bring one to the desired goal. . . . Only a presumptuous ignorance can insist on an exactness that a science of the concrete cannot attain. The terms of such a science must correspond to reality, but that is possible only within certain limits.—PARETO

No matter how important the tools of methodology and classification may be, we shall always stray into dilettantism if we make them alone, apart from the testing power of monographic research, the object of scientific thought. . . . Dilettantism, indeed, is constituted more by illusion about depth of problems than by ignorance of methods, and naïve optimism about this depth is therefore most characteristic of the dilettante. In the long run the frontiers of a science are never defined by methodological claims alone, for these bear the same relation to creative research as the mere rehashing of books does to the hand-to-hand struggle with Nature for her secrets.—RATZEL

". . . 'dingblatter' and 'gnillic,' and 'bopple,' and 'schnawp,'—are they better than the English words? . . . Why should you want to use foreign words anyhow?"
"To adorn my page. They all do it. . . . Everybody that writes elegantly. Anybody has a right to that wants to."
"I think you are mistaken . . . [but] I will let your learning remain in your report; you have as much right, I suppose, to 'adorn your page' with Zulu and Chinese and Choctaw rubbish as others of your sort have to adorn theirs with insolent odds and ends smouched from half a dozen learned tongues whose *a-b abs* they don't even know."—MARK TWAIN

". . . the vulgar error [of those to whom] . . . an unusual collocation of words, involving a juxtaposition of antiperistatical ideas, immediately suggests the notion of hyperoxysophisticated paradoxology."—PEACOCK

. . . Uncle Silas . . . preached a prayer-meeting sermon that night that gave him a rattling ruputation, because the oldest man in the world couldn't a understood it.—MARK TWAIN

EDITORIAL NOTE

ALTHOUGH the author of the essays which have been collected and revised for this volume is known primarily as a sociological theorist, he has no interest in theory as an end in itself, but writes in the belief that sociology greatly needs humanization. It must be brought "home to men's business and bosoms." If sociology is to contribute to social guidance in these confused and troubled times, it must enlighten men's choices of ends as well as means by clarifying the role of values and value-systems in human conduct. To this end it must avoid needless technicalities and be presented in as simple, clear, and direct a manner as the complex nature of the subject matter will permit. Finally, it must face frankly the controversial issues which spearhead the advance of science, confident in the faith that an unambiguous formulation of even mistaken views on important issues will in the long run further the cause of knowl-edge more than avoidance or equivocation.

Crucial among these issues is the author's position on the fundamental problem of the status of values and value-judgments in social science. "The statement 'No value-judgments in science,'" he writes, "is itself a value-judgment." Social actions are rarely if ever devoid of moral or normative content. Obligation and prohibition, acceptance and rejection, approval and disapproval, praise and blame, reward and punishment, in milder or stronger form, implicitly and covertly assumed or explicitly and overtly expressed, are of their essence. Sociological methodology must therefore provide the rational and empirical means for the treatment of human experience in its valuational aspects, and substantive sociological theory must provide the principles for their adequate interpretation.

This position requires a reappraisal of the positivistic and behavioristic[1] trends which have exercised so powerful an influence upon the development of academic sociology in America during the past four decades. They have greatly enhanced our knowledge of empirical sociological phenomena and have contributed much to the development of research techniques essential to the collection and analysis of factual data, especially in their quantitative aspects. They have checked the excessive concern with a priori speculations which sociology had acquired from its earlier intimate association with the philosophy of history and have turned the attention of sociologists towards a fresh analysis of collective human conduct as recorded in history and as observable in contemporary events.

But these trends have carried with them the defects of their virtues. Their basic assumption that science is concerned *only* with the externally observable and quantitative aspects[2] of phenomena has frustrated the development of sociology on both its theoretical and methodological sides. For as the father of sociological positivism well knew, even if his modern representatives have sometimes seemed to forget it, the preliminary assumptions which one makes concerning the nature of the data

---

[1] Behaviorism is here used in the strictly methodological sense of the term, as limiting the field of psychology to "the integrated responses of muscles and glands" (John B. Watson, *Psychology from the Standpoint of a Behaviorist*, p. 39). Unfortunately, because of the great popular vogue of the term, many psychologists have hastened to call themselves behaviorists who mean nothing more than that "psychology is the positive science of human conduct or behavior" or that the laboratory methods employed in the study of animal psychology should be pursued as far as possible in the study of the human subject. Similarly, sociologists have called their work "behavioristic" merely to indicate that they have based it upon as accurate observation of human beings in association as lay within their power. But in this sense "we are all behaviorists now," and the word ceases to have meaning except as it refers to surviving Watsonianism.

[2] It should be noted that the *defect* here referred to does not consist in the attempt to deal competently with the quantitative aspects of social phenomena, but in the methodological assumptions that would limit science *to these aspects only*. The essays are in *no* sense *anti*-quantitative. The author is in full accord with the small but growing group of colleagues who hold that theory-less quantification is as bad as uncontrolled speculation, and who are laboring effectively to bring quantitative research and workable theory together. "Constructive typology," he says, "gives ample room for relevant quantitative procedure . . . the mere fact that the uncritical are deceived by numerical halos is insufficient reason for the arrogant rejection of number as such. We should use numerical symbols, and quantitative formulation when we legitimately can" (pp. 113, 160; see also pp. 119, 219, and elsewhere).

that any given science investigates determine not only the kinds of interpretative hypotheses which can be verified, but also the rational and empirical principles and processes which must guide scientific inquiry. By determining the former, the preliminary assumptions of sociological positivism determine and limit the possible body of substantive sociological theory, and by determining the latter they likewise determine and limit its methodology. In consequence, we have accumulated an enormous mass of factual data,[3] but few significant sociological generalizations to interpret them, and have produced a large number of handbooks on fact-finding and other research *techniques*, but little *methodological* literature in the strict sense of systematic and critical analysis and organization of the basic assumptions concerning the nature of the phenomena to be investigated, of the methods of processing and reasoning about them, and of drawing inferences from them and from the conditions under which they occur in order to interpret them as accurately as possible.

It is the purpose of the essays which have been collected and revised for this volume to add to this small but slowly growing number of methodological treatises. Their author is fully aware of the importance of the perspectives of time and place in the interpretation of contemporary sociological phenomena, as the third essay, "Prospects of Social Change as Viewed by Historian and Sociologist," will bear witness. He is also aware of the importance of an intimate knowledge of the work of his predecessors and contemporaries, as every page of the text will show. But he also strongly believes that in the development of sociology as an empirical science the value of such materials is chiefly propaedeutic, and that our greatest need is now for more extensive, accurate, systematic, and direct observation and reporting of human conduct in the widest possible variety of socio-

[3] It is an unfortunate accident of history that the term *datum* (Latin, past participle of *do*, "to give") rather than *captum* (Latin, past participle of *capere*, "to take") should have come to symbolize the unit-phenomenon in science. For science deals, not with "that which has been given" by nature to the scientist but with "that which has been taken" or selected from nature by the scientist in accordance with his purpose, and to a degree even constructed out of nature by the scientist's preliminary assumptions as to which of "the things which have been given" are also to be "taken" or observed.

cultural contexts. To this end he has spent considerable time during the past quarter century in extensive travel and residence abroad. His periods of study and field work in Europe during the twenties and thirties were followed by a long overseas tour of active duty with the Office of Strategic Services as "black propagandist" in the simulation of German underground radio broadcasts during World War II. Returning to the United States, he was soon recalled as Chief of Higher Education for the state of Hesse as successor to Dr. E. Y. Hartshorne after the murder of the latter by roving Nazis in 1946. These experiences, combined with his fluent command of French and German, have enabled him to secure original data from an unusually wide range of personal as well as documentary sources. His recent book, *German Youth: Bond or Free*, has been issued in an expanded German edition and has been recognized by all German reviewers as based on a thorough knowledge of German society and culture, however much a few of them may disagree with its markedly adverse judgments of Nazi and reactionary elements in their country.

But the author also strongly believes that the gathering of sociological facts, however painstaking and comprehensive, is pertinent to science and becomes sociological research only in so far as the gathering is a part of systematic inquiry guided by sound methodological principles, and the facts themselves are given a sound theoretical orientation. Consequently, as the title of the collection indicates, the methodological problem of the nature of sociological phenomena as socially defined valuations is implicit in all the essays, and becomes the explicit theme of the opening and concluding chapters. The growth of human society occurs through the invention, transmission, and accumulation of values which become socially defined and enriched in content through communication because, as Aristotle pointed out long ago, man is a talking animal.

It is the further task of sociology as an empirical science to represent the richness and variety of these social evaluations as they appear in direct experience in a unified and orderly conceptual scheme that will permit of their prediction and control. It is with this problem of the symbolic representation of empirical data that the second, fourth, and fifth essays are primarily concerned. In the author's earlier writings he followed closely Max Weber's view that certain kinds of scientific concepts, which represent the empirical data symbolically, are "ideal types," that is, they are purely heuristic constructs whose empirical existence is plausible, but which never exist in their pure or unmixed form. The uniqueness of empirical events requires their symbolic representation within a stable structure of meanings by the use of which the empirical phenomena may then be compared, and the spatial and temporal variations they disclose or the changes they undergo noted. Thus, the "typical case" of the physician is never duplicated exactly in any patient he treats, but it is not on that account less valuable in enabling him to reach a correct diagnosis and in directing his choice of effective therapeutic measures by noting the similarities and divergences between his patient and the "typical case."

The author soon grew restive, however, under the unwarranted metaphysical and ethical assumptions which the word "ideal" evokes in many students, and finally substituted the term "constructed type" for Weber's earlier term. The author's divergence from Weber, who after all took up his basic position over forty years ago, grew with the feeling that the type should be not only plausible or possible, but basically probable. This dissatisfaction led to the development of a "constructive typology" as represented in these essays, formulated with greater care and with greater regard for probable empirical approximations and precise validation than the author had previously thought necessary.

Since the author's views on other topics have undergone a corresponding development, the original sources from which these essays have been selected and revised are cited in the "Acknowledgments." Students of the sociology of knowledge will be interested in tracing the ways in which a sensitive mind has grown through critical reflection upon the changing sociocultural context and in the stress of action.

It is with these ends in view that the essays herein contained have been selected and revised for this volume.

HOWARD E. JENSEN, *Editor*

ACKNOWLEDGMENTS

FREQUENTLY, although not always, the pages of this book have been marked, or marred, by conformity to the academic mores imposing the mock modesty of "the writer" when "I" or "me" would have been shorter and more straight-forward. In this "acknowledgments section," however, I think that it should be possible to say that I sincerely want to express my appreciation to the persons and firms hereafter named, as directly and heartily as I possibly can in cold print, dispensing with learned titles and forms of address. "Acknowledgments" and "appreciation" are poor words for this purpose; I should just like to say, "Thank you":

To Eugene Schneider, now of Carleton College, who when carrying a heavy load as instructor at the University of Wisconsin nevertheless found time to read the first revision and to offer many useful suggestions. Account was taken of nearly all of them, but of course he cannot be blamed (the fancy phrase is "bears no responsibility") for what I have done or left undone.

To Helmut Viebrock, now of the University of Cologne, who while an instructor at the University of Marburg translated all but one of these essays. His frequent conferences with me were extremely helpful in getting rid of at least some of the obscurities and ambiguities in the original text that were visible only under the cross-light of another language.

To the many graduate students, several of them now on college and university staffs (and, incidentally, every now and again showing a clean pair of heels to their former teacher), whose persistent and searching questions occasionally made me stop and think. They sometimes induced me to put in clearer form, and occasionally to correct, what I had previously written or had been spouting from the rostrum. Here I think, in particular, of Franz Adler, Samuel Bloom, Wilbur Brookover, Norman O. Brown, H. O. Dahlke, Robert Davis, Gerhard Ditz, Allan Eister, Hugo Engelmann, Regina Feiner Flesch, Roy Francis, Philip Frolich, Chester Hartwig, Gisela Mann Hinkle, Roscoe Hinkle, Richard L. Hopkins, W. L. Kolb, Elmer Luchterhand, Lowell Maechtle, Don Martindale, C. Wright Mills, Joe D. Mills, Charles Murphy, Edna Peterson, Robert Schmid, Margaret Smith Stahl, Melvin Tumin, John Useem, Ruth Hill Useem, Bonita Valien, Preston Valien, Pablo Vasquez, Arthur Wood, Milton Yinger, and many others not listed because of my faulty memory for names.

To Howard E. Jensen for sound advice about the revision of several essays, and for his willingness to take the book under his editorship even when, in 1946, my return to academic life seemed doubtful.

To Ashbel G. Brice and other members of the staff of Duke University Press whose skill, speed, and courtesy have made the final stages of the enterprise enjoyable.

To the following publishers for permission to use articles and book chapters previously published:

D. C. Heath and Company for "Values as Tools of Sociological Analysis," which, in an abridged and simplified version, appeared under the title of "Interpreting Family Life in Context" as the introductory chapter of *Family, Marriage, and Parenthood* (1948), edited by Reuben Hill and myself.

D. Appleton-Century Company for "Constructive Typology in the Social Sciences," read at the 1939 meeting of the American Sociological Society and later published as the second chapter of *Contemporary Social Theory* (1940), edited by Harry Elmer Barnes, Howard Becker, and Frances Bennett Becker, and for "Prospects of Social Change as Viewed by Historian and Sociologist," which formed the fifteenth chapter of the same work.

The Philosophical Library for "Interpretative Sociology and Constructive Typology," the first two parts of which, in abridged form, appeared in *Twentieth Century Sociology* (1945), edited by Georges Gurvitch and Wilbur E. Moore.

John Wiley and Sons for a passage from the writer's *Systematic Sociology on the Basis of the* Beziehungslehre *and* Gebildelehre *of Leopold von Wiese* (1932).

The editors of *Social Forces* for "Sacred and Secular Societies: Retrospect and Prospect," which appeared in abridged form in the May, 1950, number (XXVIII, 361-376).

The editors of the *American Sociological Review* for "Supreme Values and the Sociologist," which appeared in abridged form in the April, 1941, number (VI, 155-172).

To Doralice Colell, Hanna Kolb, and Ilse Nelson, who cheerfully and efficiently did most of the retyping under the semi-starvation conditions prevailing in Germany during 1947-48.

To Richard L. Hopkins and Joe D. Mills, who gladly prepared what we hope are useful chapter bibliographies while remaining within limits of language, etc., that would have proved irksome to academic exhibitionists.

To my daughter, Ann Hemenway Becker, who painstakingly typed the final draft of Chapter V when she might have been "teen-aging."

To my wife, Frances Bennett Becker, who wrote down from dictation the first drafts of Chapters I and III, and who not only patiently endured my reading aloud of several versions of all the essays, but also kept so wide awake that she was able to offer much salutary criticism of both form and content.

To Florian Znaniecki who, although he did not know it, has been a perpetual source of stimulation to me.

HOWARD BECKER

Madison, Wisconsin
June 14, 1950

TABLE OF CONTENTS

THROUGH VALUES
TO
SOCIAL INTERPRETATION

CHAPTER I

VALUES AS TOOLS OF
SOCIOLOGICAL ANALYSIS

I. INTERPRETATION IN CONTEXT

THE GREAT GAME of parliamentary politics, when it is unscrupulously played, includes the merry practice of taking the utterances of opponents out of context and using them to yield meanings directly opposite to those initially intended. Politics? In the good old days of sectarian controversy, devoutly religious men chose proof texts from this or that part of Holy Writ and used them in ways entirely foreign to their real meaning; the context was ignored by both the controversialists and their hearers. Religion? Even scholars and scientists have been known to wrench phrases, sentences, or paragraphs from their settings and exhibit them as appalling examples of the stupidity or sheer ignorance of someone belonging to another school of thought, whereas due heed to the context might have reduced the argument to much ado about nothing. Who shall cast the first stone?

Further, overconfidence, carelessness, or sheer inability to understand the essentials of a contrasting point of view may lead to the switching of meaning to the wrong track. For instance, the value-system of many parts of the Old Testament is radically different from a great portion of the New. Failing to recognize this, Christians have often used the Old Testament formula "The Lord watch between me and thee while we are absent one from another" as a sort of mutual benediction or joint invocation of the kindly care of a loving Heavenly Father—they have interpreted it from the standpoint of New Testament values. Actually, Laban's reference to the Mizpah formula was one showing utter distrust: Yahweh (the Lord) was called upon as avenging judge in the event of violation by Jacob of a clan marriage and boundary agreement. Old

Testament values are involved; the formula's real meaning, taken in the total context of Genesis 31, is "May the Lord lay a curse upon thee if thou breakest thy pledged word while we are absent one from another." No Christian, therefore, should ever use the Mizpah formula if he prides himself on his New Testament consistency, for it is in complete contradiction with what are supposed to be his key values. Failure to study the context has led to ludicrous misuse of an ancient threat. Here again, however, let us not cast the first stone; scholars and scientists—yes, even sociologists!—often do not take the trouble to understand what their opponents, fancied or real, actually mean, or they lack the equipment for such understanding. If they take issue with each other, then, their attacks may be quite superfluous or, more frequently, misdirected. In other words, they may discover, when they finally examine the context of each other's remarks, that they have been in agreement all the time, and didn't know it. Under less fortunate circumstances, they may be in basic disagreement, but not for the reasons they advance; failure to interpret the opponent's meaning in context leads to an assault on the wrong front.

Again, excessive concentration on insignificant detail, without polemic or argumentative intent, may lead to results equally disastrous. We all know the saying "He's not able to see the forest for the trees"; in the search for minute facts the meaningful context comes to be ignored. If some irreverent bystander asks the researcher for the significance of some cherished detail with a rude "What of it?" there may be a little stammering before even a persuasive rationalization can be offered. And many a student who has too hastily skimmed the introduction to the topic over which he is poring finds that nothing he is reading makes sense until he retraces his steps and gets his general bearings. If he does not make a determined effort to place what he is studying in context, he may go over the same passage again and again until finally he gazes at separate words which fall apart into jumbled letters, and such a combination as t h i s gives him the queer feeling that he is confronted by a language never seen before. All sense of context is lost.

Once more, ignorance of functional relations, of essential links, of interdependence, may produce curiously mistaken notions or completely block any attempt at interpretation. Aristotle long ago pointed this out when he said that a hand severed from the body to which it belongs is a hand only in an equivocal sense, for it no longer carries out the functions of a hand. If, expanding on H. G. Wells, we can imagine the invasion of the earth by creatures from another planet, we might also imagine the puzzlement of one of these creatures— a highly intelligent giant spider, let us say—when exhuming a shriveled hand after all the organisms equipped with this odd excrescence had been turned to dust in one atomic flash. Our spider would be hard put to it in determining the functional relations of such a member, for the essential context, as it were, could never be supplied.[1]

Leaving these analogies and speaking technically, in studying classes, castes, families, and so on, we run some risk of forgetting that these are all aspects of societies. As such aspects, they are functionally bound up with many other clusters of social actions. Societies composed of social action clusters can be viewed as embodiments of systems of value. These systems provide the larger contexts within which otherwise meaningless fragments of conduct become interpretable. Convenient terms for value-systems of comprehensive type are "sacred" and "secular"; these will be discussed in sections soon to follow, but also here and there throughout the entire book, and especially in Chapter V, "Sacred and Secular Societies: Retrospect and Prospect."

[1] Students of social relations for a long time tended to ignore the contexts of the "interactions" they studied, with the result that their results were either platitudinous or trivial. This situation, however, has begun to change:

"Closely related to the increased attention given to value-system analysis has been the changed emphasis in the study of sociation. Where once it was thought sufficient merely to classify and rank in order of intensity the various associative and dissociative relations, it has become increasingly evident that social interaction of every kind has so large a value-component that very little predictive utility attaches to researches which ignore it or treat it as secondary. Pairs, 'sets,' and like groupings, for example, cannot be adequately analyzed without direct heed to the value-systems in which they are incorporated" (Howard Becker, "Sociology from 1937 to 1946," in *Ten Eventful Years*, special issue of the *Encyclopaedia Britannica*, Chicago, 1947).

II. VALUES ARE INESCAPABLE

Let us start with the values that interweave to form the "sacred" and "secular" contexts to be used for interpretative[2] purposes. How do values play their part in human conduct?

Note, first of all, that man is a valuing animal. From at least the time of the ancient sages whose sayings have come down to us, and almost certainly long before then, those who have watched the doings of their fellows have taken account of the striking differences between the thin-skinned, scant-haired, two-legged creatures shivering beside the fire and the other inhabitants of the earth. The other animals, to be sure, carry out rudimentary acts of valuation, but man alone has developed the power of adequate speech.[3] Man talks, and talking, he weaves a network of symbols that simultaneously helps him to master some aspects of the world about him and to work into the very texture of his personality strands of conduct intertwined with value-objects defined as good and bad, right and wrong, helpful and harmful, useful and useless, proper and improper, holy and profane, blessed and cursed, and so on and on.[4]

The concomitants thereof are everywhere apparent: among

---

[2] See pp. 189-205.

[3] Take account of the qualification, *adequate* speech. The moot question as to whether or not animals have "language" does not here concern us, for in any case the most ardent advocate of "animal language" would grant that such language is very rudimentary indeed. When Köhler was studying anthropoid apes he found that he could isolate perhaps as many as twenty or thirty differing signals or cues. There were roars of rage and coos of sympathy, groans of distress and whines of appeal, murmurs of love, and sighs of relief which were demonstrably recognized by the other organisms as having particular signal uses. When you take as many as one hundred different sounds, however, and oppose them to the tens of thousands of sounds and sound-combinations that even the simplest human groups already possess, you find a difference in degree so great that it becomes virtually a difference in kind.

This of course says nothing about the basic difference between signals and significant symbols, but let that pass, except for reference to G. H. Mead, *Mind, Self, and Society* (Chicago, 1934), pp. 61-68.

[4] Underlying this is an epistemology: human reality is value-reality. No useful purpose would be served by going into the matter further here, but the statement should be made nevertheless. Those interested should consult Florian Znaniecki, *Cultural Reality* (Chicago, 1919); and Howard Becker, "Supreme Values and the Sociologist," *American Sociological Review*, VI (April, 1941), esp. 157-163 (see also pp. 281-305 of the present book), and "The Limits of Sociological Positivism," *Journal of Social Philosophy*, VI (July, 1941), 156-172.

all peoples are encountered cherished habits; time-honored ways of doing things; usages, customs, standards, folkways, proverbial wisdom, folklore that enshrines hallowed practices; shrewd counsel about ways of getting on in the world; laws written and unwritten; and vaguely or sharply outlined patterns for living the good life—all bearing the verbal labels affixed to them by their maker, man.[5]

Nowhere does man's ever-present tendency to develop and define his values appear more strikingly than in the family. Many other animals cluster together in little networks that may justifiably be called families, but only "man the talker" has used these networks effectively in establishing and transmitting socially defined values.

From its very beginning, of course, all life involves activity of one sort or another, and this activity flows in various channels, deep or shallow as the case may be. The shallow and vague channels in which the behavior of human beings initially flows tend to serve the "raw needs" of the organism—no amount of emphasis on culture, on what man has made by hand or tongue, should cause us to lose sight of this fact—but such needs of the human organism are not at first clearly defined. What may be termed "prepared needs,"[6] to name no

[5] The term "value" is sometimes suspect because of its supposedly supernaturalistic connotations. Even though it seems superfluous to erect defenses against such interpretations, let it be said categorically that as here presented "value" is a purely naturalistic term. Metaphysics cannot be dodged, and my metaphysical assumptions are strictly naturalistic. As Protagoras put it long ago, "Man is the measure of all things: of the things that are, that they are; of the things that are not, that they are not."

Incidentally, the statement that "Metaphysics cannot be dodged" and the labeling of naturalism as a variety of metaphysics should need no comment. It is unfortunately true, however, that many professional sociologists think that their naturalistic assumptions have nothing whatever to do with metaphysics. The remedy for this state of affairs is to be found solely in the bettering of sociological education on the topic of naturalism.

But though naturalism is here espoused, this does not mean commitment to positivism. My position, here and elsewhere, is strongly anti-positivistic. Everything of anti-positivistic bearing said by Talcott Parsons in *The Structure of Social Action* (New York, 1937) I can heartily underscore. See also my article, "The Limits of Sociological Positivism," *loc. cit.*

[6] This contrast between "raw" and "prepared" needs holds, of course, for animals other than man—in particular, for animals dependent for survival on actual physical contact with a generation which has arrived at a later stage of development and in relation to which a "matching" of needs occurs. Thus, the

others at this point, are acquired in and through processes of definition by learning, for man has no instincts sufficiently automatic or unfailing to carry him even a little way in the bustling, confusing world in which he must live out his life. The various ways in which *Homo sapiens* comes to "act like a human being" can be conveniently epitomized in five stages—always remembering, of course, that "stages" are mere devices of exposition.

The initial stage of any human activity is a more or less vague impulse, craving, or longing which manifests itself in

---

restlessness of a mammal infant manifesting its raw need for nutrition is matched by the raw need of the mammal mother for discharge of her milk supply and her accompanying restlessness (of a different type, of course). When the infant has learned to suckle at the right place and the mother has learned to offer the mammae properly, the raw needs of both become prepared needs.

Obviously, the contrast between raw and prepared needs holds only for those organisms having, at the very least, matching instinctive equipment and some necessity for learning to effect the match. When instinctive equipment is completely automatic, which can be readily seen in those instances where no physical contact with an earlier generation occurs, raw needs, in our sense, remain raw needs.

For instance, if you want to get a good example of how well instincts can work, look at the mason wasp. The female parent organism, at a given stage in its life cycle, goes to work and kills a caterpillar. It doesn't kill *any* caterpillar; it kills only a certain species, and in killing that caterpillar, if one may be paradoxical, it doesn't *kill* it at all. It simply paralyzes it. It stings it in a particular place, just one particular place, that will keep the caterpillar alive but inert. When this operation has been performed, the next task of the mason wasp is to build up around the caterpillar a little hut of mud which goes higher and higher, closing in towards the top. Just before the last few fragments are deposited, the mason wasp lays a clutch of eggs on the caterpillar, and seals the structure tightly. About three or four weeks after the death of the parent organism—which makes a clean break between generations, hence there is no preparation by learning, for there can be none—the eggs hatch and the grubs begin to consume the paralyzed caterpillar. Fresh meat hypodermically preserved, as it were, has been instinctively provided for them by the parent organism. They continue to eat until all the food has been consumed. They then break out of the enclosing mud hut, fly about, fertilize and are fertilized. The females then lay their eggs, and the cycle is repeated. As I have said, there is no possibility of learning; the continuity between generations is broken by a series of three- or four-week gaps, and yet this life cycle of the mason wasp goes on for millennium after millennium. See the striking article, about a closely related species, by George Elwood Jenks, "Marvels of Metamorphosis," *National Geographic Magazine*, LXXIV (Dec., 1938), 807-828.

The contrast pointed to by "raw" and "prepared" is partially paralleled by that between "organic" and "learned" drives. The psychologists using the "organic-learned" antithesis, however, rarely call attention to the value-components involved. Moreover, they often fail to distinguish between various kinds of learning.

restless trial-and-error seeking. The possibilities of gratifying such raw, undefined needs are manifold, and exploratory responses are made to many different stimuli; eventually the one particular kind of stimulus which gives the greatest gratification is found. A new-born infant certainly becomes hungry very soon after birth, but it is equally certain that he does not know that he is hungry. He is restless and "fussy," and he may suckle vigorously on the corner of a blanket, his fist, or whatever else comes within range of his mouth, stopping at intervals to give vent to loud wails. If he is to survive, his restlessness must be recognized as a need for food by his mother or, at the very least, by some other organism able to nourish the newcomer.[7] When the restlessness has been repeatedly stilled by feeding, the child comes to relate his hunger-feeling with food; and his vague "knowledge" that he is hungry is evidenced by the *special* kind of wailing or other sign of tension to which he gives expression.[8] His raw need has become a prepared need; his impulse has been defined. The second stage of the activity is thereby reached.

Following this, he seeks food whenever he is hungry, and frequent gratification soon instills a habit with all the qualities pointed out by Dewey:

. . . that kind of human activity which is influenced by prior activity and in that sense is acquired; which contains within itself a certain ordering or systematization of minor elements of action; which is projective, dynamic in quality, ready for overt manifestation; and which is operative in some subdued subordinate form even when not obviously dominating activity.[9]

[7] This reservation is imposed because of the possibility that some of the stories of children reared from earliest infancy by nonhuman mammals may prove to be true. "I hae ma doots," but that is another matter. It should be added, incidentally, that I am not quite so skeptical of cases where the child has acquired a whole set of prepared needs initially matched with those of human beings and only later switched to animal nurses and protectors. There seems no basic reason why Arnold Gesell's acceptance of the story of Kamala, the wolf girl, should be scoffed at as utterly "unscientific," although such scoffing has recently become popular, e.g., B. B. Evans, *The Natural History of Nonsense* (New York, 1946).

[8] Many mothers—and fathers, too, for that matter—will testify and demonstrate that they can tell the difference between an infant's characteristic cryings when angry, tired, hungry, or wet.

[9] John Dewey, *Human Nature and Conduct* (New York, 1922), pp. 40-41.

In other words, the third stage of the activity has been attained; the prepared need has become dynamic and is fully incorporated in the overt activities and latent tensions of the child. He has attitudinally defined his vague restlessness as a hunger-food situation. Habit-attitude and value-object have been successfully paired, and, through repeated pairing, they have become inseparably wedded.[10]

Habitual definition of elementary cravings, then, is part of the process by which the child *begins* to become fully human, by which the biotic individual is transformed into the social person, but only *part* of the process. It is a necessary factor, but the sufficient factor is found in that specific type of definition

[10] When interpreted for our purposes here, Ralph Barton Perry's definition of value as "any object of any interest" is quite usable (see his *General Theory of Value*, New York, 1926, *passim*). "Interest," however, must not be given connotations of "consciousness" or "awareness." "Any object of any need" is perhaps preferable.

Even raw needs may quite properly be linked with the concept of value as long as we remember that when a need is undefined (raw), then the value, as the object of that need, is likewise undefined. When the raw need has become a defined need (prepared), it follows that the value involved has become a defined value. To be sure, there are degrees of definition, and while the definition remains vague, while the need is only partially prepared, its correlated value remains a relatively vague "object." That is to say, the habits which link it with the partially prepared need lack sharpness and precision. This is certainly true where the early feeding habits of the child are concerned; he defines hunger-food situations readily enough, but his habits are still so "loose" that almost anything that seems edible may be treated as a food-object—once, at least. Oftentimes parents are appalled by the indiscriminate way in which presumably well-trained children will pick up and attempt to eat the most "repulsive" substances. Of course, there are some substances so bitter or otherwise intrinsically repellent that one experiment, and a very tentative one at that, quite suffices. In most instances, however, the child has to be told or otherwise "gesticulated" what is repulsive and what is not.

It should also be noted that the vagueness of the "food-object" as value may make it possible for a fragment of the need-gratifying activity to serve, for a time, as a substitute for the complete activity. Thus, for example, a child may be given something to suckle even when the hunger-food situation is recognized by the child as such a situation—his crying in other words, is clearly hunger-crying. The "something to suckle" may be the "sugar-tit" offered by a Cracker mother or the rubber "pacifier" provided by a middle-class New York parent of a generation ago, or the child may make use of his own thumb. It might be thought that the use of the thumb indicates that the need is still a raw need, not a prepared one, but here again reference must be made to the fact that the crying involved is food-crying; it is a signal of the specialized character linked with a prepared need. Eventually, of course, *two* prepared needs may emerge: one for actual food, the other for the thumb (when restraining mittens or the like are used) or the "pacifier." When this occurs, it will usually be found that the related crying has likewise become differentiated.

found only in "man the talker."[11] The fourth and *essential* stage is one in which social actions in the strict sense manifest themselves—actions having significance communicable by means of words or other symbols.

III. THE DIALECTIC OF ROLE-ASSUMPTION

Continuing to illustrate by reference to feeding, let us analyze a social action looking like the setting up of an almost mechanical routine but actually representing the taking over of a role, the playing of a part in a societal cast of characters, namely, the process by which a child learns to feed itself.

Suppose that a mother who is not markedly "modern" in the sense of using no corporal punishment (the reason for the qualification will appear a bit later) has a youngster named Bobby. This young man has arrived at that age—fourteen or fifteen months, let us say—where food needs already defined in terms of breast—or bottle—and spoon-feeding can justifiably be redefined. That is, he is now expected to do something himself about conveying semisolid food from his porringer to his mouth. His mother begins to tax her brains as to what the particular method of teaching Bobby will be, and one morning she sets him in his highchair with the porringer on the tray, his fist firmly clutching his new loop-handled spoon. Thinking that perhaps "imitation" will

[11] This of course should not be taken to mean that other types of symbolism cannot be used. The visual "handuage" of the seeing deaf-mute, and the pressure "handuage" of the blind, deaf, and mute Helen Keller, most certainly can make up in many respects for the absence of speech. Further, those who work with subhuman animals, and particularly with highly intelligent primates such as chimpanzees, will readily testify that there may be symbolic definition of situations and a crude kind of role-assumption among their charges. Note, however, that *it is in interaction with human beings* that Jocko learns to ride a tricycle, to respond appropriately to verbal commands, and even to manifest shame when reprimanded. Here again there is no remotest intention of denying the kinship of man with the rest of animal creation, but simply insistence on a tremendous difference in degree where the capacity for symbolic conduct is concerned.

Curiously, such insistence conjures up dissent from two otherwise widely separated camps. On the one hand are the sentimentalists who write poems to "Lassie, My Collie in Heaven," and on the other are the "hard-boiled" who systematically blind themselves to differences between man and his relatives in the belief that they will otherwise be false to evolutionary doctrine. With the sentimentalists we need not concern ourselves further, but with the true believers we must go so far as to mention the recent book by Julian Huxley, who surely is "hard-boiled" enough, entitled *Man Stands Alone* (New York, 1941), chap. i, "The Uniqueness of Man." In saying that man is unique, of course, no value-judgments are implied, one way or the other. He may be unique in his power to do evil, or he may be potentially angelic, but Huxley's focus is purely biological.

solve the problem, she sits opposite him and goes through the motions of conveying food to her own mouth. Soon, however, she discovers that Bobby, like other youngsters of this age, does not imitate in any such way—there is no infallible "instinct" to lend aid.[12] He looks at her with his mouth open and drooling slightly at the corners, bangs the spoon on the tray of the highchair, playfully flourishes it about, and finally throws it on the floor.

Briefly, not one of the mother's methods of teaching Bobby to feed himself seems to work very well. The upshot is that she gives vent to a little irritation, not being a "modern" mother, and slaps Bobby sharply on the wrist just as he is about to throw the spoon on the floor for the nth time. He looks at her, taking in the whole configuration,[13] not merely the slap but also the maternal frown and like traces of displeasure. Among these are what Mead calls "vocal gestures," for when the mother slaps Bobby's wrist she says, indulging in the usual baby talk, "Bobby, na, na."

His chin puckers up and a few tears begin to gather, but in spite of these evidences of remorse on Bobby's part, nothing happens that fits the mother's definition of the situation, for he has defined it in terms of egocentric play. The spoon is still being flung on the floor, and each time "Bobby, na, na" and the slap on the wrist are repeated, until finally she gives up in despair and starts to go about her regular household duties. Casting one fleeting look over her shoulder as she passes through the doorway, she witnesses Bobby's redefining of the situation. The spoon is brandished once more and seems on the verge of making another trip to the floor. Just as this is about to happen, however, the hand is suddenly checked almost as though the wrist had been slapped, the child is heard to mumble something which can be interpreted as "Bobby, na, na," the spoon descends into the porringer, and then begins its uncertain journey towards the waiting mouth.

[12] That vague mimicry may occur cannot be denied, but it is also true that we are not mockingbirds. Mimicry or no mimicry, "imitation" in the sense necessary to induce self-feeding in Bobby cannot be relied on. As Mead puts it:

"There is no evidence that the gesture generally tends to call out the same gesture in the other organism.

"Imitation as the mere tendency on the part of an organism to reproduce what it sees or hears other organisms doing is mechanically impossible; one cannot conceive an organism as so constructed that all the sights and sounds which reach it would arouse in the organism tendencies to reproduce what it sees and hears in those fields of experience. Such an assumption is possible only in terms of an older psychology" (G. H. Mead, *op. cit.*, p. 60).

[13] "Configuration" is here used as the most usable Anglicization of *Gestalt*. The references to stimulus and response made earlier should not be interpreted in ordinary behavioristic terms, for configurational theory is much more adequate to the facts with which we deal here.

This anecdote, for all its triviality, actually illustrates the basic conduct by means of which children acquire those definitions of needs in terms of social action—i.e., conduct assigned meanings communicable to others by means of significant symbols[14]—characteristic of genuinely *human* beings. Bobby has manifested toward his own conduct the actions (more precisely, has himself engaged in actions which, however imperfectly, reproduce the overt and covert actions) of the parent. Differently stated, he is talking to himself, symbolizing himself, as an object—"*Bobby*, na, na." Stated still differently, he represents, in himself, a value defined in the same way for himself as it is defined by someone else. Or, he is, if you will, inhibiting himself—"Bobby, *na, na*." In this self-checking action the words spoken, of course, represent only one aspect of a functioning whole (which is why the parenthetical reference to "overt and covert" was made above). Why? Because in addition to the words there are all the kinesthetic sensations attached to the sudden arrest of spoon-flourishing, with its wrist-slapping accompaniment and, perhaps, even a mind's-eye picture of the maternal frown and other evidences of nervous tension. The self-inhibition is simultaneously other-prohibition.

All in all, then, Bobby is acting towards himself, in however fragmentary and inadequate a way, as his mother was acting. He has assumed the role of the parent with regard to his own conduct. Social actions, from this standpoint, are dramatic performances in which a part is taken over, a role is assumed. Naturally, all connotations of deceit or disguise in "part-playing" or "role-assumption" are barred; the child *is* the mother, for the time that he is playing her part, with reference to his own conduct. Bobby is checking himself, disciplining himself, in maternal terms; he has manifested the actions of the mother toward his own behavior, and it thereby becomes a social action—the fourth stage of the activity.

There is not much "mere habit" or "habit as such" about this sort of action.[15] Only an organism possessing significant

[14] In G. H. Mead's very specific sense; see *op. cit.*, pp. 68-74, 117-124.
[15] There is a widespread misconception to the effect that everything ordinarily termed "habit" is "mere habit," i.e., is sheerly "mechanical." Parsons, for ex-

symbols, those of speech in particular, can redefine needs in terms of social actions. Man is an animal defining values in very special and precise ways because man is a talking animal.[16]

IV. SELVES EMERGE WHEN OTHERS EMERGE

Next in this presentation of the interrelations of needs and values is the fifth stage, the development of what may be called sociative needs ⇌ self-and-other defined values. Putting this

---

ample, repeatedly refers to habit as "a mechanism" or as "sheer automatism." Indeed, he even goes so far as to speak of "the uniformities of 'automatism,' the results of instinct, habit, etc." (Parsons, op. cit., pp. 646-647, 678). To say this flies in the face of most contemporary social psychology and psychoanalytic psychiatry, to say nothing of the recent work of Kardiner and others of the effects of feeding habits, toilet training, and the like on basic personality structure. Granted, Parsons may be right in referring to "habit as such" as "a mechanism"; but where in the world of relevant social experience can a "habit as such" be found? The argument is circular. What Parsons says, in effect, is this: "Show me a habit as such and I will show you a mere mechanism, for I have defined a habit as such as a mere mechanism."

Let us carry this a little further. The gratifying of prepared needs certainly provides a basis for so-called mechanical habits, but very few if any needs remain at the prepared level. Would anyone say that the learned inter-organismic matching of the male and female genitals, which fits the definition of prepared needs ⇌ defined values, would long remain at a level short of habitual needs ⇌ attitudinally defined values? Even though Dewey's use of habit as a term including attitudes, social actions, and explicitly normative patterns unquestionably goes too far, there can be no denying the evidence he has brought to show that habits come to provide their own "drives." Habits, in other words, partake of the nature of "prime movers"; they are not sheer automatisms deriving all their power from some other source.

Moreover, when habits (or attitudes, which may be the preferable term) are redefined in terms of social actions, they may acquire a heavy normative content, a "Thou shalt" or "Thou shalt not" emphasis, even though this emphasis is indirect rather than direct. The way in which Bobby learns to feed himself lends his feeding habits a definite element of the approved and disapproved, the permitted and the forbidden. The transition from this to moral codes and ethical precepts is gradual; no sharp line can be drawn, empirically.

The fact that habits are dynamic, not static, or that attitudes are "arrested activities," means that frustration or thwarting is not the simple blocking of a "mere mechanism." When frustration occurs, "upset" feelings may arise that are in no way distinguishable, except in degree and extent of verbalization, from "moral indignation." To maintain otherwise is to remove the study of norms to a realm where naturalistic considerations are inapplicable.

These remarks are not incidental, for the later discussion of certain sacred phenomena will hinge, in part, on the normative content of some action patterns.

[16] Manifestly a large part of what has been said about the crucial importance of speech in human actions derives from Mead, op. cit., and elsewhere. Nevertheless, I do not wish to limit the range of symbolism in specifically human conduct; see Suzanne Langer, *Philosophy in a New Key* (New York, 1942), and Ernst Cassirer, *An Essay on Man* (New Haven, 1944).

forbiddingly technical statement in simpler, albeit lengthier, terms: As man talks and uses other symbols, he not only crystallizes values in relation to social actions, but also endows himself with a self. Mark, however, that the mere taking over of a small bit of a single role (and for what may be just a moment or two at first, *à la* Bobby's internalized maternal discipline) yields only a *fragment* of a potential self. The child engages in social actions in the sense of assuming roles in and through significant symbols, but this does not necessitate an integrated self and a clearly differentiated other. He can be said to associate with and dissociate from others only when he can distinguish between self and other. At first he cannot do this; as Milne put it in " 'Round About":

> I think I am a Ticket Man who's selling tickets, please;
> I think I am a Doctor who is visiting a sneeze;
> Perhaps I'm just a Nanny who is walking with a pram;
> I'm feeling rather funny and I don't know *what* I am. . . .

As time goes on, a whole collection of such fragmentary roles accumulates: father-roles, sibling-roles, roles of intimates and acquaintances of every sort and description, roles of any number of differing organisms such as puppy-dog confidants or "Gallopoff, the talking pony," or even of inanimate objects such as dolls, taxicabs, or boats which are given the attributes of personality. Slowly, as various roles are played with greater or lesser dexterity, and as the child learns to skip from one role to another, his world begins to attain some semblance of order. That is to say, he knows what he is expected to do in the appropriate situations, and hence begins to achieve a relatively close-knit, unified self.[17]

In many parts of Western society,[18] one of the ways in

---

[17] Clearly, a thoroughly integrated self can appear only in adulthood, and there only in a society which is highly integrated, which has an accrete or fused rather than a discrete or scattered value-system. But more of this later.

[18] The reservation "Western society" is made because there are some simple nonliterate societies in which children apparently do not play games—if games are defined as activities having little or no relation to the ιuties and responsibilities of adult life. Children may be given little hoes, for example, and they "play" at gardening, but the play is not an end in itself, as it often is with us. Of course, play of this kind, modeled on the social actions of adults, may be an agent quite as powerful in the integration of the self as is the organized game.

which integration of the self begins to become manifest is when the child shows interest in and capacity to play organized games. In such games he is not playing with a projected aspect of his self, in thoroughly egocentric fashion—talking to his Teddy bear or his fairy godfather, Mr. O'Malley, and muttering the appropriate replies. Games force him to associate and disso- ciate with others as others, to take part in a set of sociative actions (sociation = [as]sociation and/or [dis]sociation). As a definite self develops, definite others likewise develop, and vice versa; sociation then becomes possible. By inducing the child to take part in a system of actions in which others are involved as others distinct from his self as a totality and not as a random assortment of roles, the organized game serves a highly useful purpose. Moreover, the game usually makes it necessary for the child to stay within the limits of his play role for a time sufficient to allow the whole set of actions to run its course; here again self-and-other development is furthered. *Sociative* social action is greatly facilitated by the game.[19]

[19] There are many definitions of social action, but those by Znaniecki and Weber are probably most frequently quoted. Recently I offered such a definition (in Georges Gurvitch and W. E. Moore, eds., *Twentieth Century Sociology*, New York, 1945, p. 78), but it stands in need of modification, and rather than quote it here I present the modified and expanded version. (It is retained, how- ever, in the essay on "Interpretative Sociology and Constructive Typology" in the present volume, largely because it is brief and good enough for the purposes of *that* essay; see pp. 198-199.) For all practical purposes the present version is a new definition or set of definitions:

The term "behavior" is to be used to designate those life processes engaged in by man as a merely biotic individual, and therefore is applicable to the other animals as well. In terms of the analysis presented in this chapter, it applies to: (1) raw needs ⇌ undefined values; (2) prepared needs ⇌ defined values; (3) habitual needs ⇌ attitudinally defined values.

The term "action," however, implies processes engaged in by man as actor, and hence involves role-assumption. This in turn is possible only in conjunction with a symbolic system or systems of some kind. Otherwise put: Action entered upon by any specific human being requires the participation, direct or indirect, of other human beings serving as culture carriers and transmitters. Action is therefore social and cultural. In the very earliest phases of child action, how- ever, roles may be assumed when as yet there is no clear-cut separation of self and other. Action may be meaningful in terms of symbols without awareness of an acting self set apart as self from the vague matrix of role action. Differ- ently put, the child may respond to his own actions as others respond to them without awareness of others as others and self as self. Action, then, may be de- fined as meaningful processes not oriented toward others as others; it applies to (4) meaningful needs ⇌ symbolically defined values not involving others as others.

The term "social action" comprises *both* "action" and "sociation." In the

Such games may at first be very simple, for instance, hide-and-seek. Here there are only two roles, hider and seeker; and when the child can learn to hide and stay hidden until caught, and then really to seek and keep on seeking in spite of the temptation to relapse into the hider's role, sociative action patterns are built up doing much to solidify the core of an organized self. Moreover, explicit norms of fairness-unfairness soon emerge; we can all recall the "King's X" and "No fair!" of our own childhood. As the child begins to take part in more and more complex games, the patterns of which are kept in force by the example and precept of other children, the more or less dependable, predictable sort of personality regarded as the desirable variety in our own society—and, with due allowance, in any society—distinctly appears.[20]

---

case of "action," the adjective "social" in "social action" means *only* that the symbolic system is imparted in processes of role-assumption necessitating participation with a human culture carrier or carriers. In the case of "sociation," the adjective "social" in "social action" means everything that it means in the case of "action," and in addition means association and/or dissociation with others *as* others.

For many purposes, the difference between "action" and "sociation" is not important; hence the general term can safely be used. In other words, "social action" is quite good enough in many contexts. In case it seems wise to make a sharp distinction, the writer should perhaps use "action" and "sociation" as indicated above or, going to the extreme of explicitness, should refer to action as "social action" and to sociation as "sociative social action."

Putting all this in outline form and recasting slightly:

LIFE PROCESSES OF MAN

I. Processes common to *Homo sapiens* and other animals:

		Needs		*Values*
		1. Raw	$\rightleftharpoons$	Instinctively defined, i.e., undefined where learning is concerned.
Behavior		2. Prepared	$\rightleftharpoons$	Interorganismically defined by learning.
		3. Habitual	$\rightleftharpoons$	Attitudinally defined.

II. Processes peculiar, in degree at least, to human beings as animals capable of speech and similar symbolic actions:

		Needs		*Values*
Social	Action	4. Meaningful	$\rightleftharpoons$	Symbolically defined.
Action	Sociation	5. Sociative	$\rightleftharpoons$	Self-and-other defined.

[20] Among hundreds of items of evidence, note the South Chinese villager's term for a rude or barbaric person: "an other-than-expected fellow." And does our term "shifty" indicate approval? Do we ordinarily praise the person who "makes up his rules as he goes along"?

V. CONDUCT IS ALWAYS NORMATIVE

Call to mind, now, the fact that the play of children is not a matter of entire indifference to parents or other representatives of an older generation.[21] Even if there is no positive approval of certain kinds of play, there must be at least tacit consent. Further, in those societies where children do not play organized games as we know them, there is still the effort to engage in adult activities without bearing adult responsibility, without being even potentially blamable for the certain failures, contradictions, or injuries that would result if adult standards were rigidly applied. Older persons therefore judge the permissibility of such juvenile activities; here again there must be at least passive toleration. In one society it may be quite all right for the merest toddlers to "play" at the sexual activities of adults whose close quarters they share, whereas in another the most rigid prohibitions against "genital rehearsals" may prevail; but in either case "older and wiser heads" maintain the controls. Organized role-taking (of which play is a subvariety) therefore runs its course under the more or less watchful oversight of culture carriers whose greater age has given them a head start in defining the proprieties.

Moreover, those phases of juvenile conduct escaping the oversight of the guardians of the general proprieties of the society as a whole still tend to be patterned by the example of older age-groups. The six-year-old youngster who becomes a tag-along member of a delinquent gang is doing his best to take over the roles so impressively played by the "hard guys" who feel their chins hopefully for excuses to shave. Among the various roles to which he aspires is that of loyal gangster; he absorbs a moral code the reverse of that enjoined in his home circle, but still a moral code. The "rat" or "squealer" is loathed; the "tough egg," on the contrary, stands only a little lower than the angels. Note, at this point, that the "hard

---

[21] Clearly, the "other representatives" need not be kin, however kinship is defined, and the "older generation" may be only a few years older. In peasant families where the number of children is great, siblings only a little senior may be assigned the task of bringing up the junior, and in many societies these child mentors need not be siblings.

guys" and "tough eggs" are in no way indifferent to what goes on among the smaller fry; they see to it that gang virtues are inculcated—if not systematically, at least steadily. Here again the older members of a functioning group point to or provide the models of approved personality, and also label the unworthy or despised in unmistakable ways.

Whether in a given society as a whole, or in an imperfectly integrated aspect thereof, it can consequently be said categorically that under all circumstance the web of childhood experience is woven out of strands spun by forerunners. The personality patterns that slowly take form, the selves that gradually integrate, have their models approved or at least tolerated in the more intimately surrounding sociative clusters. Among these models those most important, those exerting the most powerful impress on the child's personality, have to do with standards of conduct, with social actions defined, in all essentials, by elders mindful of the proprieties peculiar to the cluster in question. When at last Bobby has approximated the conduct of the approved models,[22] he has become, in ordinary sociological parlance, a socialized personality: he is the product of processes of socialization.[23]

[22] By "model" I do not mean anything of which *I* necessarily approve, but rather something of which the representatives of the society in question approve. As far as the sociological analyst is concerned, the chemist's model of a carbon ring is a good illustration; it is a useful tool but does not evoke praise or blame on moral grounds.

[23] This is not the place to present in detail the theories of G. H. Mead with relation to the parts respectively played by the "I" and the "me" in the socializing process. Here it need only be pointed out that the "me" represents those roles which are taken over with a degree of success regarded as within the bounds of normality as judged by a given society or functioning unit thereof. In other words, that phase of the personality called the "me" represents conformity to the personality models held relevant. The "I," on the other hand, is a kind of residual category, used somewhat carelessly by Mead to cover a number of aspects of conduct not assignable to the "me." For example, *all* conduct has an "I" aspect at the beginning; it is at first impossible to tell whether or not conformity will be achieved, and hence the very tip of the advancing action, to speak metaphorically, enters into the "I" category. Then, when the action has run its course, it may be found that the degree of success or failure was much greater than normal; this too is therefore "I" action. The reason for the extraordinary success or failure may be discovered in unusual propensities of primarily biological derivation—in our terms, raw needs, primarily, that pass beyond the ordinary means of definition. Or, a different reason may be revealed in a life history of altogether deviant type; a number of developmentally crucial needs may have

Crucial to this whole presentation is the fact that social actions in general, and a fortiori sociative actions in particular, are rarely if ever mere mechanisms devoid of "moral" or "normative" content. Praise and blame, in stronger or milder forms, are woven into their very fabric. Learning to eat properly, toilet training, playing with other youngsters, and a hundred and one other childhood activities are charged with normative meaning.[24]

Here has been the great contribution of Freud and the other exponents of functional psychiatry; through their efforts we have learned how the most apparently insignificant muscle-twitch, such as a facial tic, may be inseparably and essentially bound up with inner conflict arising from failure to play adequately the roles required by a given value-system.[25]   When

been defined in ways that transcend the confines of "everyday" life. In either case, "I" action is the result.

It will be readily seen that Mead's use of the "I" category enables him to avoid a complete socio-cultural determinism. If there were only "me" actions, there would be entire correspondence, at every point, between the total value-system of a society and its component personality structures. The "I" makes novelty, innovation, deviation, and similar breakaways possible. Mead doubtless should have been more careful in the specification and use of the category, but in one form or another it is theoretically essential if we are to account for the empirical evidence.

[24] The school of thought at present centering about Abram Kardiner—*The Individual and His Society* (New York, 1939), *The Psychological Frontiers of Society* (New York, 1945), etc.—makes much of all this. In my estimation, excessive emphasis is given to prepared and habitual needs, and far less than enough to social actions and their "vocal gestures," but that is another matter to be considered, by implication, later in the present chapter.

[25] Brief comment on psychoanalysis of Freudian extraction, particularly with reference to the trinity of Id-Ego-Superego, may be in order here. I quote an earlier formulation, with interlarded additions:

"The Id may be thought of as man in his unsocialized, relatively unmodified biological aspects, as a bundle of desires and impulses that have merely been overlaid, not transformed, by culture. [In other terms, used in the present study, the Id represents primarily the raw and prepared needs, although some of the habitual and other needs may on occasion enter into it.] When cultural controls disintegrate, or are relaxed in the dream, etc., the Id steps forth to achieve the gratifications denied it by the watchful Ego and Superego. Although the extreme behaviorists scout any such theory, it seems clear that the phenomena of release, as analyzed by Teggart and others, bear witness to the probable correctness of this part of Freudian doctrine. Men, even the best of men, are but imperfectly socialized, and under stress sufficiently great will follow patterns much more elemental than those prevailing in any organized society. . . .

"The Ego is a bit more difficult to characterize. It is the conscious self, yes, but in a peculiar form. Perhaps the best brief characterization is to say that it

Bobby grows up to a "normal" man assuming successfully the roles appropriate to his walk of life, he will *ipso facto* be free of such gross external evidences of "maladjustment" because all his needs and values, and the situations helping to define them, are relatively harmonious. Tensions not readily noticed either by Bobby or others will exist within him, to be sure, for no personality ever completely fits the models of the surrounding society,[26] but he will still represent the "man as he should be" in *his* social world.

is that part of the bundle of Id-cravings which has been woven into some sort of unity and is acceptable in the light of prevailing cultural standards. In a sense it is the more or less precarious subjective balance between unregulated animality on the one hand and the objective rigidities of social constraint on the other. What distinguishes the Ego, however, is its relative integration, persistence, and continuity. In some respects it is like the 'looking-glass self' of Cooley and the 'me' of Mead. . . .

"The Superego replaces what Freud once called 'the censor'; it may be thought of as the whispering of social control that has not been sufficiently incorporated in the Ego to be regarded as the voice of self. 'Conscience,' 'the demands of society,' 'decency,' 'propriety,' and all other demands that represent an imperfect introjection of social imperatives make up the Superego. Herein lies a marked resemblance to Durkheim's *conscience collective*, with its two criteria of exteriority and constraint. A strong Superego means that its possessor, or better, its possessee, lacks identification with the social patterns within which he has developed. A strong Ego, on the contrary, means that the degree of correspondence between the ensemble of social imperatives entering into the person's socially real world and his individual impulses is high—in other words, that there is a stable equilibrium between Id and Superego, and the result is an Ego relatively free from conflict" (Harry Elmer Barnes and Howard Becker, *Social Thought from Lore to Science*, Boston, 1938, II, 930-931; hereinafter cited as *STLS*).

Restating and oversimplifying for brevity's sake: the Id corresponds to the primarily biological phase of the "I"; the Ego to the "me," and the Superego to the value-system in so far as it is felt to be external and constraining.

[26] Speaking figuratively, and barring all theological finalities, it may be said that man is always and everywhere afflicted by "original sin." Unless the society in question is so thoroughly disorganized that it really is not deserving of the name of society at all, it cannot possibly give scope to the manifold potentialities of even its most ordinary members. Raw, prepared, and habitual needs are never fully provided for in the approved social actions. Consequently, "man is born to evil as the sparks fly upward"; all societies, from the simplest to the most complex, necessarily limit the range of approvingly defined situations. No matter how free and easy the life of a given people may seem to be, it will be found, on examination, that restraint is placed on certain types of conduct. Sin, crime, disloyalty, immorality, and the like are everywhere present, just as virtue, respectability, loyalty, and morality are everywhere present. The content may of course vary vastly: in one society the eating of pork brings about permanent ostracism; in another it is the publicly preferred food. The labels likewise differ radically: not only are languages divergent, but in addition the near-impossibility

VI. MEANS OF FOUR KINDS

Which social world? Obviously we could distinguish a great many, but for the purpose of setting a context for the analysis to follow just two major varieties will be presented: sacred and secular societies. Before discussing these constructed types, however, it is necessary to characterize the means and ends they embody—or rather, which their interwoven members embody.

This reference to "members" is intended to call once more to mind the fact that *only out of the ceaseless shuttling to and fro of social actions do societies take form.* Families are woven of familial conduct, states of political conduct, and so on. There are no societies that exist over and above their constituent members, like those "brooding omnipresences in the sky" to which Justice Holmes so bitingly referred. Convenience alone prescribes the use of "society" as a noun.[27]

It therefore seems wise to continue for a bit longer the essentially social-psychological method of presentation followed thus far. In order to make clear what is meant by "sacred" and "secular," attention must first be focused on four types of means followed by the members of any society in attaining their ends. This done, attention will then be directed to four types of end. Now for the means: more than four types can doubtless be distinguished, but for present purposes these are enough: (1) expedient rationality, (2) sanctioned rationality, (3) traditional nonrationality, and (4) affective nonrationality.[28]

---

of getting precise equivalents for the translation of normative terms is notorious. Nevertheless, every society has its saints and sinners, and every personality has saintly and sinful potentialities.

And to repeat, my assumptions are naturalistic: I speak "barring all theological finalities" in this context.

[27] Howard Becker, *Systematic Sociology on the Basis of the* Beziehungslehre *and* Gebildelehre *of Leopold von Wiese* (New York, 1932), pp. 78-93; hereinafter cited as Wiese-Becker.

[28] In earlier presentations I have used "irrationality," but its connotations cause misunderstanding. For example, *Webster's Dictionary of Synonyms* (Springfield, Mass., 1942) has this:

"Irrational may imply mental derangement or a temporary loss of mental control (as, the patient was *irrational* during the course of his fever) but, more often, it suggests a lack of control or guidance by the reason, or direct conflict with reason's dictates: it therefore comes close to *absurd, foolish, preposterous,*

(1) Expedient rationality is that kind of conduct in which the actor seeks to attain values by any means regarded as conforming to the principles of economy of effort, efficiency, and absence of undesirable consequences. "Doing things in the way that is thought to be easiest in the long run" is a useful paraphrase.[29] Social action may be termed expediently rational when it is completely centered upon means viewed by the actor as adequate for the attainment of ends which he conceives to be unambiguous.

From the standpoint of the detached observer looking at what the actor is doing, and possessing greater knowledge of the relevant facts, the means chosen to attain a given end may be wholly inadequate, and the end itself may be self-contradictory. So long, however, as the actor defines the means as sufficient and the end as consistent, the conduct must be called expediently rational. Here is an exhibit: A military commander—Rommel at El Alamein, let us say—may count on the certainty of victory if his strategy and tactics follow given lines and if his opponent meets his moves in the only ways defined as "possible" in the situation. The detached observer, studying Rommel's battle plan, would have agreed that within the range of the facts knowable to Rommel, his victory was certain. What Rommel could not know, given the limited range and penetration of his battle order intelligence, was that Montgomery possessed formidable shock troops—51st Highlanders "blooded" vicariously or actually at Dunkirk, and New

---

senseless, or *fantastic*. . . ." No such meanings are intended in my use of the term, and it therefore seems best to use *nonrational*, which conceals no value-judgments. See my "Interpretative Sociology and Constructive Typology," in Gurvitch and Moore, *op. cit.*, pp. 70-95 and pp. 189-247 of the present volume.

[29] From this it should be clear that "expedient" is being used in its original, etymological sense: "*expedire*, to free the feet, to release or extricate." It is here used as an approximate or, better, *partial* equivalent of *Zweckrationalität*, purposive rationality. See Rudolph von Ihering's *Der Zweck im Recht* (Leipzig, 1877-83) and Weber's adaptation. The recent connotation of "opportunism" therefore cancels out:

"Originally, and still occasionally, the word [*expedient*] and its derivatives carry no trace of derogatory implication. 'It is *expedient* for you that I go away: for if I go not away, the Comforter will not come unto you; but if I depart, I will send him unto you' (*John* xvi.7). 'The old man believed that the whip of shame and pain could drive her . . . into an appreciation of the *expediency* of morality' (Deland)" (*Webster's Dictionary of Synonyms*).

Zealand Maoris. Both these contingents were able and eager to use cold steel, and could be relied on to follow dangerously close, for themselves as well as for the enemy, to their own creeping barrage and tank attack. The detached observer, presumably knowing this, would have said that Montgomery's, not Rommel's, victory was certain, but that Rommel's plan was expediently rational in very high degree. No outworn traditions, no rigid *Oberkommando* doctrines, no outbursts of rage or jealousy distorted his plan. He simply did not have, and could not have, all the relevant facts. The Desert Fox was "outfoxed," *but he was a fox.* His final end, a *Wehrmacht* victory, would only have consolidated Nazi power, and even from a limited German perspective was not worth striving for, but the final end is here irrelevant. The means he chose were beyond doubt expediently rational.[30]

Let us now take heed of the fact that, as here defined, expedient rationality makes use of *any* means for the achievement of the end.

For example, if the social action is combat and the need is annihilation of the opponent, the value may be defined in such a way that, as it were, "no holds are barred." Anything from poison to terroristic inducement of insanity may be held suitable. Utter ruthlessness therefore may be the farthest reach of expedient rationality. *Why* the opponent should be destroyed is another matter, lying in the realm of ends. Once the end is accepted, however, expedient rationality may warrant the choice of the atomic bomb as means, for this lies in the realm of *how.*[31]

---

[30] Cf. Wiese-Becker, *op. cit.*, pp. 57-59.

[31] Another instance may be cited: Suppose a man wants to avoid being drafted for military service and carefully calculates "the best way" to do it. He was once divorced from his wife, but she is willing to remarry him and bear a child. This is done, the man is placed in a deferred category, and when the war is over, he divorces his wife again. The end was attained by the use of a given means viewed as satisfactory for that purpose, and regarded as having no undesirable aftereffects. Whether or not the later results and other aspects of this action are desirable for the future welfare of the major actor is, again, another matter; if he originally defined his needs and values in so thoroughly egocentric a way that the action was viewed as having no regrettable consequences, his conduct was expediently rational. *"Cold-blooded calculation" in the choice of means is therefore the hallmark of expedient rationality.*

The maxim, "The end justifies the means," is frequently invoked, even by

(2) Hard on the heels of this, we may single out sanctioned rationality as a type in which the principles of economy of effort and so on are followed as far as a certain limit; *this limit is set by the character of the end itself.*

A case in point is this: Although the action may be combat and the purpose the annihilation of the opponent, action and purpose may be integrally bound up with a code of sportsmanship. Many American soldiers when first encountering Japanese in World War II were themselves killed because of their readiness to "give the guy a break." Their conception of a fair fight kept them from plunging the bayonet into a Japanese groveling on his face—with the consequence that the groveler disposed of both his sportsmanlike conqueror and himself with one grenade. The value-system of the Marquis of Queensbury suffered speedy eclipse when the risks of observing it were fully realized. But while it lasted the restraint it imposed provided an excellent example of what we have here elected to call "sanctioned rationality," in indication of the fact that ends of certain kinds provide sanction for only certain means. "Strangleholds are barred," so to speak.

Charity, love, *agápē*, or *caritas*, the topmost value in the Christian scale, offers another illustration: "If you do not love

those who are not egocentric, in defense of this kind of conduct. As to whether or not the maxim is true we need not here concern ourselves; the plain fact is that many men, in effect, have echoed Cavour: "Ah, signor, we should be great rascals had we done for ourselves what we have done for Italy." Expedient rationality plus allegiance to the national state was made the basis of the "ethic of responsibility" by Max Weber, whereas he based the "ethic of sentiment" primarily on sanctioned rationality of New Testament character. See "Politik als Beruf," *Gesammelte Politische Schriften* (Munich, 1921), pp. 396-450, esp. pp. 441-442, or the translation in H. H. Gerth and C. Wright Mills, *From Max Weber* (New York, 1946). The *plus* of course makes the "ethic of responsibility" a kind of sanctioned rationality; the national state furnishes the sanction. Some such final sanction in terms transcending the purely egocentric and hedonistic is always invoked by those claiming that the end justifies the means. The invocation may of course be insincere, but that too is another matter.

These comments on Weber indicate that expedient rationality as here defined does not wholly match *Zweckrationalität*. Weber overlooked the fact that even an elaborate bureaucratic machine may have many members working under sanction; the real or supposed welfare of the national state provides this. When, however, a high proportion of bureaucrats function egocentrically in terms of their own career possibilities, the machine undoubtedly furthers expedient rationality.

the Lord your God with all your heart, with all your soul, and with all your mind, and your neighbor as yourself, I'll cut your throat," has long been a classic example of the contradiction of means and ends. The contemporary Christian cannot consistently sanction violence as a means of reaching immediately Christian objectives. In "religions of the sword" such as Mohammedanism, however, allegiance to Allah may be induced by physical coercion, although deceit and some other means are excluded.

British and American efforts to persuade the conquered of World War II to adopt democracy as a way of life offer still other examples, for they operate under the express sanction of democratic values. Consequently, only truthful propaganda, free elections, and due process of law based on "natural rights" can sincerely be used. The Russians have not recognized *these* sanctions, for their endeavors are based on sanctions of a different type, namely, those clustering about the Marxian dialectic as they interpret it. In either case, sanctions are operative; rationality is limited in its scope; and consciences are clear if the respective value-systems are firmly imbedded. The properly socialized Britisher, American, and Russian has each conformed, in his own eyes, to his ideologically sanctioned model of the "man as he should be."

(3) As a counterweight, as it were, of expedient rationality and sanctioned rationality we may also distinguish traditional nonrationality. This is marked by the dominance of means over ends or, otherwise put, by a state of affairs in which actions formerly regarded as mere means become ends in themselves. Practices once of strictly utilitarian character are elevated to the level of ceremonials or rituals.

Witness the fact that the carrying of an axe with a number of rods lashed about the handle was once a vital aspect of Roman military discipline. The *lictor*, a sort of combined scourger and executioner, did not carry this bulky bundle about with him for mere ceremonial display; he expected to put its parts to use, and often did so. With the passage of time, however, this bundle, the *fasces*, became an emblem of unchanging justice. It is lavishly displayed, for instance, as a decorative motif in American law courts. Further, it is the central symbol of the "tails" side of the American ten-cent piece, although there it has in the background an olive branch intended to evoke the notion of mercy. In the latter role, to be sure, the *fasces* also serves as an embodiment of the conception of "many in one"; alongside the axe and rods our dime carries the motto *e pluribus unum*. To the ordinary American this imagery is probably not much more than a dimly understood artistic convention. To the erstwhile Italian Fascist, however, the tools formerly marking the lictor's trade became the revered sign of the corporative state. Under the aegis of this state violence for its own sake was widely practiced. Further, it was invested with the halo of a tradition which, although in part spurious from the standpoint of the detached observer, was nevertheless defined as genuine and worthy of supreme sacrifice by the blackshirted adherents of the Fascist faith. As Thomas and Znaniecki put it, "If men define situations as real, they are real in their consequences."

Traditional nonrationality is therefore not solely a matter of the remote, the faraway, the medieval, or the so-called primitive; the modern world affords many instances.

Indeed, the vital significance of tradition is often obscured because it is interpreted in antiquarian fashion as outworn, moldy, stuffy, decayed, quaint, ancestral, time-hallowed, crumbling—multiply the adjectives! Actually, *traditio* means merely to carry over, to transmit. Bobby was "traditioned" by his mother as to the "right" way to feed himself. We get language by tradition, manners by tradition, morals by tradition.

What was said earlier about the activity of older culture carriers, or bearers of tradition, in socializing the child is also relevant here. The imparting of a system of social norms, of symbolically stated values amalgamated with social actions, is a universal process, beginning afresh in every generation but always channeled by the example of persons who themselves have been "traditioned" within essentially the same system. Ranging the whole world over we can nowhere find a society that does not develop basic agreements about alternative ways of acting and pass them on by tradition. A "fact" of social life in any society, however small and however "primitive," is the defining of approved and disapproved modes of conduct. The roles of hero and villain, so to speak, are traditionally delineated, and every youngster is told, and told repeatedly, that he is expected to be a hero.

Usually only certain members of a society are responsible for setting the models of good conduct, for assigning the traditionally approved roles, and their choices are made in the light of what they think or feel to be for the best interests of all concerned. Beyond doubt they make mistakes, but so great is man's capacity for self-justification that these mistakes are rarely admitted. Instead, they are draped in the same ennobling veil that is cast over genuinely beneficial decisions. Depending on the foresight, special privileges, and dispassionateness of the controlling group, the limits of what is thought to be for the good of all may be broad or narrow. Nevertheless, no matter how greatly such limits may favor those who have staked them off, with the lapse of time the favoritism is forgotten or obscured. The "boy as he should be" and "girl as she should be," to name no other members of the society, become so deeply etched in tradition that they seem to have endured from all eternity. Those whose personalities are shaped in accordance with such models necessarily take the inequities of tradition for granted; traditional nonrationality lies at the very base of a large proportion of social actions even among the "enlightened" members of any society.

Further, it must be borne in mind that tradition is not always inequitable. The young are often shielded from the disastrous consequences to which the uninhibited pursuit of imperfectly defined needs and values would inevitably lead—"inevitably," given the standards of the society in question. Realizing this when maturity is reached, those who have been thus "traditioned" come to feel a reluctance to depart from the ways of the tradition-bearers. Such reluctance powerfully reinforces the unwillingness or inability to change which the taken-for-granted always carries with it. "It was good enough for father, and it's good enough for me"—here again there is traditional nonrationality.

(4) Another counterweight of the rationalities is what may be called, for lack of a better term, emotional or affective non-rationality. It is definitely a catchall, including as it does everything from outbursts of love or hatred to the unquestioning, emotionalized acceptance of a leader who proclaims, "Ye have heard it said by them of old time . . . but I say unto you. . . ."

Let us begin with the outburst variety. An angered Alaskan prospector chopping in two the boat with which he and his partner had planned to voyage down the Yukon, because the partner had kicked the prospector's favorite Malemute, is indulging in an emotional discharge, to speak popularly—more precisely, in an affective release. Manifestly it is virtually impossible to find examples of the *purely* affective, for as we have seen, very little if any human conduct, in our sense of "human," is empty of symbolic reference. The purely affective would be the nonsymbolic; i.e., it would not be social action in any sense. After all, the fact that the chopping was done on the boat rather than on the head of the partner responsible for the howls of the anguished dog means that a way of expressing temper permitted by the given society was followed; in that sense, then, the action had a definite symbolic content. Hence the empirical manifestations of affective nonrationality usually occur in close conjunction with one or more of the other three types: expedient and sanctioned rationality and traditional nonrationality. It may be said, however, that when it is encountered as the *chief* phase of an action, it represents fairly complete fusion of means and ends; even analytic separation is often impracticable and impractical.

Affective nonrationality is also evident in the phenomena of the "mania," revival, fad, style, and so on. The Dancing Mania which followed the Black Death gripped a large proportion of the peasantry and townsfolk of Central Europe, but it soon passed away almost everywhere, leaving behind only the phrase "Saint Vitus's Dance," thereafter applied to a radically different but similarly uncontrollable manifestation. The Tulip Mania of seventeenth-century Holland left multitudes impoverished and vaguely wondering what evil spirit had caused the obsession with mere tulip bulbs and the heaps of gold they supposedly represented. The Great Kentucky Revival of 1800 led to scenes in which crawling circles of men "barked the Devil up a tree" and women "had the jerks" so violently that "their long hair cracked like a whiplash," but only feeble traditional traces have remained. The zoot-suit fad of the early 1940's caused riots in many parts of the United States; today it is well on the way to becoming a remote memory. The Fanny Hatrack style of woman's dress prevalent in the United States during the middle 1920's has silently slipped away, but what impassioned oratory, for and against, it called forth while it was still with us! The sudden fanatical attachment to an innovation, and the surging emotions that attachment calls forth, can properly be placed among the manifestations of affective nonrationality.

Still another aspect of affective nonrationality is that of charismatic leadership, of the "grace-endowed" capacity to evoke awe, devotion, and unquestioning obedience. The Greek word from which *charismatic* derives means "grace" in the New Testament, but it has now been expanded far beyond its narrower theological meaning, and in present sociological usage denotes simply the possession of extraordinary qualities.[32] These qualities may be many and varied; Mohammed owed a large part of his grip on Abu Bekr and other early disciples to his terrifying ability to "throw fits" and recount the visions he had seen while out of the flesh. Joseph Smith was a prey to hallucinations which he took for reality, and these plus his oratorical powers dragged in his train men such as Brigham Young, whose sober good sense in other matters is abundantly attested. Illustrations of this kind should not be taken to mean that the charismatic leader is always a religious leader—far from it. He may exercise his sway in many other fields: Jeb

[32] The range of literature on this topic is vast. Here, therefore, I cite only one of my own recent studies, "Proclamation: 'He Spoke as One Having Authority,'" *German Youth: Bond or Free* (New York, 1947), chap. iv.

Stuart, Custer, and Patton in the military; John McGraw, Leo Durocher, and Knute Rockne in the athletic; Sylvia Pankhurst, Susan B. Anthony, and Carrie Chapman Catt in the feminist; Hitler, Mussolini, Stalin, Churchill, and Roosevelt in the political.

The minimum definition of charisma, in effect, has already been stated: it is an extraordinary quality of an individual which commands the emotionalized obedience of others. The most pressing problem of a charismatic leader is to verify and perpetuate his charisma, whether through miracles, the cult of hero-worship, feats that regenerate trust in his leadership, or by otherwise gratifying the impulses of his followers.

While it endures, the relation between leader and led is a personal one based on belief and confidence in "extraordinariness." A leader having this quality needs no administrative aides, no officialdom in the usual sense, relying as he does on his band of personal disciples or henchmen held together by the affective intensity of their belief in his charisma.

In contrast with both sanctioned rationality and traditional nonrationality, this kind of affective nonrationality is not only extraordinary but also, in its implications at least, revolutionary. The famous "Ye have heard it said" formula of Jesus, quoted earlier in the chapter, typifies the innovative, iconoclastic character of charismatic authority. "Charisma is the great revolutionary power in traditionally engulfed epochs."[33] Old value-systems are shattered, and out of the fragments, with a few pieces added, new ones are formed. Needs and values are redefined, but the historical cleavage is never as complete as the innovators originally intended. Why? Because, to reiterate, it is virtually impossible to find examples of the *purely* affective. As I have put it elsewhere:

> Occasionally, of course, there comes some great image breaker. . . . Even these "extraordinary" or "uncanny" men, however, never make a clean break with the past; Mohammed and Buddha, to name no others, proclaimed their teachings with the sounding board of tradition behind them. . . . The charismatic leader must derive his . . . "gift

[33] Max Weber, *Wirtschaft und Gesellschaft* (Tübingen, 1922), p. 141.

of grace" from a source regarded as legitimate by . . . [those who follow] in his footsteps. Joseph Smith without a Biblical tradition and Protestant sectarianism is simply unimaginable, but given these and like essentials, the Book of Mormon finds its martyrs and its triumphs. Eventually, to be sure, all-powerful routine makes sedate ceremonial out of ecstatic deliverance, and tradition, temporarily set in second place, resumes its ancient sway, changed in outward seeming but inwardly the same.[34]

Many charismatic phenomena, therefore, have a heavy traditional or sanctioned content; one can say only that in some cases the affective element plays the preponderant part in the social actions of leaders, followers, or both.   There is a striking resemblance to certain aspects of what Mead has called "I" conduct (see n. 25), for here too there may be a large proportion of affective nonrationality.   Further comment on this correspondence, however, would carry us far beyond even the elastic confines of the present essay.

Leaving the topic of affective nonrationality, and epitomizing: (1) Expedient rationality is unrestricted in the means adopted; (2) sanctioned rationality has ends of sorts that inevitably bar certain means; (3) traditional nonrationality elevates means to the rank of ends; and (4) affective nonrationality manifests a coalescence of means and ends.

VII. THE FINAL GOALS

What human beings really want in life has been the subject of debate from time immemorial, and the debate shows no signs of diminishing in intensity.   "One man's meat is another man's poison" is occasionally all too true.   Broad uniformities within given societies can readily be detected, and even between one society and another there is frequently more agreement about essentials than we ordinarily suspect, but the difficulty of getting unity on the ends men *should* pursue is still notorious. Those who merely try to say what ends they *do* pursue have trouble enough.

Moreover, there is very little common ground when the

[34] Howard Becker and Reuben Hill, eds., *Marriage and the Family* (Boston, 1942), p. 11.

question arises as to *why* men seek certain ends. One thinker may say that the ends are fixed by God, and that man simply uses his natural reason in choosing the good and abhorring the evil. Another will agree that God has fixed the ends, but that man has nothing to do with choosing the ways in which he will strive for them, or whether he will strive for them at all—predestination takes care of that. Still another rejects God and all his supposed works, and pins his faith on Evolution or Nature or Progress; man blindly struggles for survival, or follows his biological impulses, or automatically seeks to move onward and upward.

Singling out just one capacity through which ends may be sought, there is still no consensus. Reason, for example, may be regarded as a divinely implanted principle, or as a weapon in the struggle for existence, or as a mere veil covering obscure urges that would be victorious in any case, or as the outcome of an evolutionary process of which Man the Reasoner, *Homo rationalis*, is the final culmination, or as itself a supreme end rather than a mere capacity.

This is no inconsiderable array, certainly, but it could be very much longer.[35] Whether or not we put them in words, in one way or another we all hold beliefs about the "why" of man's supreme ends and his struggles to attain them which in most if not all instances are quite as arbitrary as any in our list. It is impossible to carry on even the ordinary affairs of life without some kind of reference, implicit though it may be, to what Wells called "first and last things."[36] Those of us who think otherwise simply deceive ourselves.

To choose a trite but searching illustration: Life can be

[35] A brief discussion of these and related "philosophies of history" or "theories of the total course of the historical process" is to be found in my essay, "Historical Sociology," in H. E. Barnes, H. Becker, and F. B. Becker, eds., *Contemporary Social Theory* (New York, 1940) (hereinafter cited as *CST*), chap. xv, pp. 491-542, reprinted in the present volume under the title of "Prospects of Social Change as Viewed by Historian and Sociologist," pp. 128-188. As reference to this will show, it is only a readily available summary opening up for the student a vast range of problems. Nothing short of a bibliography covering every aspect of intellectual history would do justice to the topics so hastily touched upon.

[36] H. G. Wells, *First and Last Things: A Confession of Faith and Rule of Life* (New York, 1908).

brought to a slow or sudden halt in a thousand and one ways. These may range from prolonged fasting to jumping off a plane without a parachute. Most of us prefer to live, however, and hence consciously or unconsciously act in accordance with this preference. An inquiring reporter asking "Why do you want to go on living?" would ordinarily get only the mouthing of platitudes, blank stares, or impatient brushoffs in reply. (Gertrude Stein asked in turn, "Why shouldn't I?") That life *is* worth living is so deeply rooted an assumption for most of us that talk about it seems utterly superfluous or even ridiculous. Nevertheless, with sufficient persistence our reporter could certainly extract enough from his victims to fill a column, and when analyzed everything in it would be found to bear upon the "why" of man's supreme ends and the pursuit thereof.

Reading such a column, stuffed full of pros and cons as it would inevitably be, few of us could avoid taking sides. If we succeeded, it would be only because of an interest in scientific detachment.[37] Such an interest is highly specialized, hard to acquire, and hard to maintain. Indeed, only as we take over the role of scientist, together with *its* value-system, can such detachment be successfully practiced, and then only for short periods of time. Doing the scientific handstand is a part-time job.

This being true, there is no intention of denying the fact that scientists walk and sit and lie down like other people most of the time. Each of us decides, in one way or another, what the "chief end of man" is and why it should be sought. While we are carrying on our professional roles, however, no such decision need be made.[38] The "good" scientist is merely the man who succeeds in doing his handstand as well and as long as others who follow his calling. He succeeds in predicting, time after time, what happens next in his chosen field of re-

[37] Usually miscalled "objectivity." This word has now acquired so many contradictory and epistemologically dubious meanings that it should never be used when its precise bearing cannot be specified in the same context.

[38] Here again the literature is voluminous. A sketchy presentation, having only the merit of reasonably full illustration and a viewpoint in conformity with what has been said above, is to be found in my "Supreme Values and the Sociologist," *loc. cit.*, reprinted in the present volume, pp. 281-305.

search, and in systematizing his method so that others can use it regardless of the final ends they may pursue.[39]

Hence, in discussing the ends of human conduct there is, in this presumably scientific essay, no faintest idea of saying why they are ends—if and when they are. Nor is there the remotest suggestion as to whether the most prominently mentioned human capacity through which ends may be sought—namely, reason—in any of its forms *finally* governs man's activities. Contrariwise, there is no assertion that man is *basically* irrational or even nonrational. The most that can be said is that in some ascertainable situations rationality seems to govern and in others it does not. Beyond this, the scientist as scientist, like Pilate—and perhaps uncomfortably so—washes his hands of the whole matter. How long they stay washed or how often they have to be washed present interesting *psychological* and *sociological* problems, but they have little to do with the *logical* demands of the pursuit of science.[40]

As the scientist sees him, man's strivings for his supreme ends are classifiable as search for (1) security, (2) response, (3) recognition, and (4) new experience.[41] Moreover, these strivings, classified in this *general* way, are inseparable from the ends themselves; no useful working distinction is possible here, and none will be made elsewhere in this book. "End" will be used to signify both.

VIII. EVERYTHING FROM BREAD TO HEAVENLY REST

Security as a supreme end may mean that "eternal peace in God" of which Goethe spoke, or it may mean simply a state of affairs in which men know where their next meal is coming

[39] Expansion of this is to be found in my "Constructive Typology in the Social Sciences," *American Sociological Review*, V (Feb., 1940), 40-55, and in the chapter of the same title in *CST*, pp. 17-46, reprinted in the present volume, pp. 93-127.

[40] Cf. "Typology, Constructive," in H. P. Fairchild, ed., *Dictionary of Sociology* (New York, 1945).

[41] As is well known, these old categories of Thomas and Znaniecki have had a long and checkered sociological career as "wishes," "attitudes," and "tendencies," with the result that they have often been confused with raw, prepared, and habitual needs and their correlated values. This, however, is not the place for a bibliography of the problem; a good starting-point is to be found in Florian Znaniecki, *Social Actions* (New York, 1936), chaps. i-iii, and accompanying bibliographies.

from and have roofs over their heads. Not only is there this wide latitude in the meaning of security within Western culture, for example, but there is in addition the great variety introduced by the highly diversified meanings peculiar to the other cultures now extant, to say nothing of those which have passed off the scene. Nevertheless, security as one term in a fourfold classification will serve our purposes well enough as long as we do not place upon it a burden heavier than it was intended to bear.

To be avoided, for instance, is the use made of it as an implied universal goal in Adler's "inferiority complex." *All* human beings supposedly lack security, however much they may strive for it, and therefore suffer from a sense of failure and consequent inferiority that accounts for all their conduct. Barely distinguishable from this is Karen Horney's tracing of *all* mental ills (in her earlier writings) to basic insecurity. No such attractive but untrustworthy thesis is advanced here; social actions, with their symbolically defined values, are far too complex to admit of single-factor "explanations." If we can say with some assurance that in societies of certain types men seek ends more readily classifiable under the heading of security than under any or all of the other three headings, such a classification may prove to have predictive utility; if not, other analytic tools must be used.

Abstractions aside: Illustration of one kind of security as end is provided by the anxious efforts of contemporary (1948) Germans to build up defense against starvation. The mark as currency is regarded as utterly untrustworthy. Vivid memories of the inflation of 1923, when the mark was some 8,000,000 to the dollar, and rumors of the printing of unlimited quantities of present-day marks by the Russians, have made almost anything else more acceptable. Bars of chocolate, cigarettes, cans of lard, coffee, sugar, beans, and hundreds of other barter goods have almost wholly replaced the mark as a medium of saving.[42]

[42] Since the currency reform of June 20, 1948, this situation has altered somewhat—but the danger of fresh rejection of the mark is always present under today's conditions.

"Go to the ant, thou sluggard; consider her ways and be wise" is a Biblical injunction heeded by today's German just as an ant would heed it, namely, by restless scurrying to and fro in search of bits of food and other items to store up against the time of need when hunger, instead of being merely a gnawing insufficiency, might become the convulsively painful clutch of death. Families already half-starved refrain from eating part of the food that can be scraped together if it is of a kind that will keep; the desperate search for security overshadows everything else. Young and old alike busily collect cigarettes, which are then bartered, often after long journeys on foot, with grudging peasants for a few potatoes, a strip of salt pork, or a pocketful of rye. Other areas of starvation and famine the world over could be drawn upon; examples are unfortunately available on every hand. No one observing situations of this kind can be in much doubt as to the part played by security in human striving.

IX. THE SPAN FROM FLESH TO SPIRIT

Response likewise includes a great deal. The mystic ecstasies of Saint Teresa were centered upon the experiencing of divine love mediated through Christ as Eternal Bridegroom, and the patronage of Park Avenue pet shops rests in large measure on the assumption that life with a responsive Fido assumes meaning which it otherwise lacks. Response in these forms, of course, falls outside the realm of ordinary experience, but ties of kith and kin, friendship, courtship, marriage, and scores of other familiar relations have large—sometimes overwhelmingly large—response components.

In this connection also our use of the response category does not commit us to those supposedly universal explanations of human conduct offered, for example, by orthodox Freudians. Much use can be made of Freud's conceptions of the ends men seek without binding the sober social scientist to the more fantastic formulas of the psychoanalyst. Some societies demonstrably give larger scope to social actions focusing upon response than do others; this being the case, the use of the tool is warranted.

Take the fact that although beyond question security was and still is significant in Mormon affairs, the nature of the social organization of the Latter Day Saints between the 1840's and the 1890's gave response a very prominent place. This response, as the evidence clearly shows, cannot merely be labeled "lustful." The Mormons, apart from a few pathological members, seem to have been very much like the rest of mankind in their response strivings; mutual love, conjugal devotion, parental affection, and similar components of sociation in small, intimate human groupings were widely manifest. In other words, the family even when polygamous remains a major channel for practically all kinds of response.

It is highly relevant here to note that the Mormon family by no means represented the common caricature of a dominant male lording it over a herd of subjugated females who were all on the same level as over against their master. On the contrary, there were many tacitly recognized ranks and grades: the favorite wife (who was not necessarily the most responsive sexual partner), the oldest wife, the newcomer, the hardest worker, and a variety of others were all accorded the affection, respect, seniority, or precedence respectively due them.[43]

X. MANY WAYS TO GET ATTENTION

As the above reference to ranks and grades should indicate, recognition may not only be closely intertwined with other ends, but also ramifies in many directions. Shifting from the Mormon example, Napoleon's single-minded pursuit of military fame is in point, as is likewise the notorious striving of American clubwomen for space in the society columns.

Here Adler's focus on a gnawing sense of inferiority is directly relevant. No matter how high the status of a given person may be, it is always possible for him to regard others as at least potential rivals. Spurred by such a threat, human beings may enter upon courses of conduct which would be quite incredible if ample documentary evidence did not compel belief.

[43] The favorite wife, for example, could often be recognized by the fact that it was she who had charge of her husband's Sunday-go-to-meeting suit; we may perhaps suppose that some of the other wives occasionally yielded to feelings, where she was concerned, not altogether classifiable as response.

Historians make more use of the recognition category than do most other social scientists, and this is entirely understandable in view of the types of "famous" events and personalities with which they have traditionally concerned themselves. The sociologist cannot make such sweeping use of recognition as a goal of social action, but it must undeniably be granted a prominent place.

A well-known example is that in which parents face the problem of how to handle the family show-off. Youngsters not only want to be recognized as worthy of affection or attention, but also sometimes insist on getting much more than their share—to the point, indeed, where the other children, if there are any, may make common cause against Papa's pet or Mama's little darling. If parents are unwise or wishy-washy, animosities may be built up which make for family discord throughout the entire lifetimes of its members.

Occasionally it is possible to link show-off traits directly with sexual exhibitionism à la Freud, but for a large proportion of cases the connection is difficult to demonstrate to anyone not already orthodox. Most of us would be more inclined to accept interpretations laying at least equal stress on the competitive character of Western society in general, or on the strong demand for continuing evidence of affection that contemporary family instability calls forth, or on the effects of differing age levels within the family pattern, or on the expectation that one sex will automatically be more favored than the other.

At any rate, show-offs are to be found everywhere, even though the unkind term may not be used. What would military organization be like without the stripes, the brass, the hardware, the fruit salad, the bars, the stars, the hash-marks, and the rest of the display paraphernalia? Americans and Russians seem to besprinkle themselves more liberally with such decorative devices than do the French and British, for example: does this mean similar contrast of *innately* exhibitionistic traits? Yes? But what of the relatively sober and restrained academic garb of the American scholar as over against the almost gaudy attire of French academicians? Is it not apparent that recognition must always be interpreted as a component, and in a context, of social actions which are not attributable to any single instinct or raw need?

XI. THERE ARE NOVELTIES AND NOVELTIES

New experience is the last of our four pigeonholes. Apparently somewhat more limited in range than the first three, it is nevertheless a kind of end clearly evidenced in societies of every type. The restless adventurer may have little in common with the scientist persistently extending the frontiers of knowledge, but the ends they seek are in some ways remarkably similar. Of course, new experience may be found at a quite different level: the gourmet forever on the lookout for novel recipes and the fashion devotee incapable of resisting the temptation of "the very latest" fall in the same category.

Oddly enough, no body of psychological, psychiatric, or social-psychological theory has been built around the indisputable fact of the lure of novelty. Discussions of sexual varietism, to choose only one instance, lay stress on "sexual" rather than on "varietism," whereas it is plainly evident that there may be highly varietistic conduct in which the sexual element as such is quite insignificant. Further, there has been little attention to the ever-present human interest in "luck" as a source of novelty; only Sumner and Thomas among sociologists have thought it worth extended investigation. Yet we all know how largely games of chance, gambling, racing, and dozens of other evidences of interest in the novelty arising from the relatively unpredictable have figured in human life the world over.[44] New experience is a useful albeit unexploited category in the study of ends.

[44] Paradoxically, "luck" as a focus of interest goes hand in hand with the fact that most persons would regard new experience as the end most readily compatible with the belief that man is distinguished by his power of reason.

Having noted the paradox, the implications of which cannot be dealt with here, let us focus on the main point, namely, the relation of new experience and rationality. The mathematician, ceaselessly searching for new ways of dealing with his subject, is held to be the epitome of rational conduct. In only slightly lesser degree, the natural scientist, forever seeking for better ways of grasping the phenomenal world, is regarded as "cold-bloodedly rational." Even the handicraftsman or the practicing technician, preoccupied with novelties of improved workmanship and not infrequently disregarding immediate utility, is viewed by

For example, who has not been impressed by the eager interest of the child when taken on a visit to the zoo, and who has not been struck by the rapidity with which that interest wanes when the experience is too frequently repeated? Judicious spacing of the visits so that some charm of novelty can be generated afresh is a technique that many parents soon acquire. Such techniques for making old experience seem new are part of the repertory of anyone who has learned his way about in the social world.

Some persons, to be sure, are so strongly attracted by novelty that they will not put up with substitutes. Travel agencies of every kind flourish accordingly, to choose only one example, and for many persons it soon becomes a case of "We went to the Grand Canyon last year; let's go to Bermuda this time."

Further, vicarious new experience of this kind is eagerly sought by those who must stay at home or are otherwise compelled to accept a substitute "just as good as the original." Travel authors such as Richard Halliburton and H. V. Morton, with their personalized tales of the strange and the faraway, attract their myriads of readers.

From these more or less sedate kinds of travel experience, vicarious or otherwise, the path leads by degrees to that lust for roaming thus expressed by Kipling:

> For to admire an' for to see,
>   For to be'old this world so wide;
> It never done no good to me,
>   But I couldn't stop it if I tried.

XII. SINGLE-MINDEDNESS IS RARE

Like all of the other ends, however, new experience may lead or be mixed with polar opposites. The fictional adventurer who struggled his way into a remote nook of what may have been Tibet found intense gratification in the new experi-

---

himself and others as primarily devoted to reason. In the pursuit of no other end, with the possible exception of security, is the connection with rationality so entirely taken for granted—at least in Western society. In contradistinction to this, response and recognition, together with security in some of its aspects, are viewed as pre-eminently nonrational ends.

Why all this should be so is another matter; that it is so seems open to little if any question.

ence of Shangri-la, but when that queer but idyllic community had been left behind and the road of return had unaccountably vanished, Shangri-la became the "lost horizon." The man who had shared in the security, response, and satisfying though odd recognition to be found in a place removed by far more than distance from Western civilization sacrificed everything in the effort to return.

In this piece of fiction, then, new experience as an end had become so intermingled with or even transmuted into other ends that the combination exerted strong appeal for the readers of James Hilton's book. Summer cottages, vacation camps, and similar retreats all over the United States bear witness to this fact; a day's drive in "resort territory" is almost certain to lead to the discovery of at least one sign marked "Shangri-la."

In these pages, however, Shangri-la leads to this point: few if any social actions are classifiable with reference to any single end. Recognition laps over into response or new experience, and even new experience may have a bearing on security. The most that can be said, where concrete instances of end-seeking activity are concerned, is that greater emphasis is laid on one end as over against another. Unless this is clearly realized, fruitless and essentially unscientific argument will be the only outcome. *If, in a given context,* a high proportion of social actions can be successfully predicted by directing attention toward demonstrable concentration by the actors upon certain ends, to the relative neglect by those same actors of other ends, the purpose of the classification has been achieved.

XIII. THE ENSHRINING OF THE SACRED IN SOCIETY

"If, in a given context. . . ." With perhaps wearisome frequency, the analysis of needs, values, means, and ends thus far presented has referred to societies as contexts. Further, we have specified those contexts as interpretable in terms of "sacred" and "secular" value-systems and the other social phenomena inextricably bound up with such systems. The point has finally been reached where the closer characterization of "sacred societies" and "secular societies" becomes possible. Only when this has been done can the bearing of the present chapter on the analysis of other social structures and institutions be clearly seen.

Foremost is the fact that societies are simply larger networks of sociation within which other groupings as smaller networks find their appropriate place. Moreover, it must be recalled that sociation is a shorthand way of designating association and/or dissociation with others *as others*[45] in and through role-taking involving the use of significant symbols. Less technically expressed, sociation is a label for social actions in which selves and others intercommunicate. This means, of course, that societies as networks of sociation take form only out of the continual interweaving of social *actions.*[46]

"Sacred" likewise refers to conduct, for it points to inability or unwillingness to respond to the new, particularly at the symbolic level peculiar to the *human* being. For us, social action has sacred traits when an aversion to change is manifested. True, this aversion is more strongly marked in some circum-

[45] This point is crucial for a clear understanding of the difference between the general study of culture and the more specific study of sociation. Only by means of such differentiation can there be set up a workable division of labor between, let us say, "social and cultural" anthropologists, on the one hand, and social psychologists and sociologists on the other. If it seems necessary and possible for anthropologists who define their science as "the study of man" to take in *everything* having to do with needs and values (see p. 16, n. 19), well and good. Sociologists will then become specialized "anthropologists" restricting their efforts to the analysis of sociation.

Of course, the tone of the above remarks should make it quite clear that I, for one, am a little skeptical about the far-flung claims of some contemporary American anthropology. These claims, if taken seriously, stake off *all* the life processes of man as the anthropologist's three-ring circus, with the sideshows also included.

Even if the field of action alone is claimed, that is in all conscience large enough. Social action, it will be recalled, subdivides into action and sociation. Action, bound up with meaningful needs and symbolically defined values, includes *all* of man's cultural activities, from digging sewers to the Fifth Symphony of Beethoven, in so far as they are not directly self-and-other defined. Any university faculty, with its various departments, has a wide array of specialists dealing with action. Are they all anthropologists?

It should be noted, in fairness, that sociology, defined *merely* as the study of sociation, also takes in too much territory. Closer delimitation is badly needed, but the problem is too difficult to be dealt with here. Cf. Wiese-Becker, *op. cit.*, Part I.

[46] See Wiese-Becker, *op. cit.*, pp. 78-93. Recent popular interest in the atom perhaps makes this cited passage more intelligible than when it was first written. Few indeed are those who do not now know that "matter" is convertible into "energy," and that the basic category of modern science is *process.*

stances than in others, and there are certain kinds of non-symbolic and imperfectly symbolized behavior in which the explicitly sacred aspects are very slight although much resistance to change is evident.[47] Omitting further discussion of this qualification, however, let it be repeated that societies which impress upon their members modes of conduct making for a high degree of resistance to change are for us sacred societies.

From this it should be clear that *sacred* is here being used in an entirely warranted but precise and limited sense; it simultaneously means somewhat more and somewhat less than do *religious* and other words frequently thought synonymous with it.[48]

[47] This of course refers to raw, prepared, and habitual needs. Note, however, that such needs are not "merely mechanical" in their expression. Cf. pp. 13-14, n. 15.

[48] "*Sacred* as meaning having such a character that it is protected by law, custom, tradition, human respect, or the like, against breach, intrusion, defilement, or profanation. *Sacred* implies either a setting apart for a special and, often, exclusive use or end (as, among civilized peoples, property is regarded as *sacred* to its owner; a fund *sacred* to charity; the study was *sacred* to the father of the family) or a special character or quality which makes the person or thing held sacred an object of almost religious veneration or reverence (as '[Louis XIII] saw that things which happened increasingly strengthened the Royal Office which was sacred to him'—*Belloc*. . . .

"[Analogous words] Protected, shielded, defended, guarded . . . : revered, reverenced, venerated . . ." (*Webster's Dictionary of Synonyms*, pp. 721-722).

Authority, then, supports the present use of sacred as distinctly different from religious, holy, divine, spiritual, supernatural, sacrosanct, blessed, and related terms. True, it is *possible* to use sacred in senses roughly equivalent to many other words, but here the "roughly equivalent" will not do. Science advances as its instruments are perfected, and among these instruments is language.

It may seem odd thus to refer to language, but there is at least one way in which it does function as an instrument—in this case, of observation. Disregarding here the moot question of how thought and speech are tied together, the history of human activities shows that only when certain terms were invented to characterize certain relations, processes, and even objects was it possible to observe accurately those relations, processes, or objects. Some of the simpler peoples have no words or other symbols for numbers greater than five, ten, or twenty. Beyond these limits the term is simply "many." Can such peoples really *observe* 136.927? Or take the words for color: if "purple," "violet," "magenta," "cerise," and "crimson lake" are not available as vocabulary resources, how accurately can differing observers report what colors they have seen? Can they really *see* magenta as a color distinct from cerise without having had the difference between them nailed down, so to speak, by the differing words?

Such questions might make material for lengthy debate, but here we have other fish to fry. Most of us would agee that words and like symbols make a difference, and that agreement is enough. We want to look at the societies most important in weaving the contexts of social actions, and in order to do this most

Sacred societies imbue their members with ends most readily classifiable under security, response, and recognition, with security in many cases uppermost. The means by which these ends are sought are chiefly of traditionally nonrational and sanctioned rational types. This skeleton-like statement needs meat on its bones, and this can best be provided by describing, first, what have long been called traditional or folk societies,[49] and second,

effectively we must use special terms.

These special terms, however, must be used scientifically, i.e., without connotations of praise or blame. "Sacred" already has praiseworthy connotations for many if not most persons; these must be resolutely excluded if analysis is not to be perpetually hampered. It therefore seems wise to use "secular" instead of "profane" as its polar opposite. Not only does profane have its own highly colored connotations, but by contrast it heightens the coloring of sacred. Secular, on the other hand, is relatively colorless, and it therefore diminishes the irrelevant contrast effect.

The essential colorlessness of the sacred-secular antithesis, as it occurs in these pages, may perhaps be underscored by the statement that if certain other terms did not also have irrelevant connotations of character potentially quite as misleading, or did not too sharply limit the range of phenomena to be observed, these other terms could well be used. We might speak of traditive and transitive, conservative and conversive, retrospective and prospective, immobile and mobile, perpetuative and alterative, hallowed and hedonic, prohibitive and permissive, conventional and sophisticated, lore-holding and law-making, customary and innovative, usage-limited and utilitarian, venerative and varietal, ceremonial and functional, neophobiac and neophiliac, and so on and on.

Further, there are many antitheses in the literature of sociology that seem, at first glance, to point at identical phenomena. Primitive and civilized, established and adaptive, component and constituent, folk society and urban society, primary group and secondary group, community and society (*Gemeinschaft und Gesellschaft*), societies with "mechanical solidarity" and societies with "organic solidarity," constraint and normlessness (*anomie*), traditional and rational, ideational and sensate, cumulative and disintegrated, status-maintaining and contractual, preliterate and literate, ancient and modern, static and dynamic, "residues of the persistence of aggregates" and "residues of combination," organic and critical, organic and atomic, particularistic and universalistic, kinship society and political society, societies with "custom-imitation" and societies with "mode-imitation," *yin*-state and *yang*-state, and other explicit or implicit distinctions of the same general character abound.

Nevertheless, the qualification, "seem, at first glance," must be held in view. For example, Redfield's folk-urban dichotomy is *not* identical with sacred-secular, for many urban societies are strongly sacred in either "folk" or "prescribed" senses, or both. Moreover, folk, as just indicated, is only one of the subdivisions of sacred. Similar comments might be made about the other paired terms. See the lengthy footnotes, charts, and discussion in chap. v, "Sacred and Secular Societies: Retrospect and Prospect," of the present volume.

[49] Robert Redfield has provided, for his folk society course at the University of Chicago, a mimeographed bibliography of nearly one hundred titles on this topic.

what may here be designated as sanctioned or prescribed societies.[50]

XIV. THE FOLK VARIETY OF SACRED

The best examples of folk societies are to be found in the old-fashioned, backward, or even primitive parts of the world. Regions where the "cake of custom" is thick are of course likely to be remote from the highroads of commerce and the hum of communication—that is, folk societies are ordinarily isolated. To be sure, the isolation is not merely a question of the land under the feet of the folk in question; i.e., it is not exclusively "geographical" in any legitimate sense of that overworked word.[51] But even at the merely geographical level, the absence of disturbing changes may enormously enhance the effect of isolation. When occasional natural catastrophes such as flood, fire, or drought do not interrupt the even round of events, conduct readily becomes stereotyped. Feast days come and go, planting and harvest seasons succeed each other, birth and death replenish and diminish the ranks of the members, and routine is lord of all. From the fish racks of the Faeroes to the yam plots of the Trobianders, folk societies show a startling uniformity of essential function; the more obvious patterns are so diverse that the unwary may be deceived, but the weave is fundamentally the same.[52]

But as the inhabitants of Iceland discovered not so long

[50] This is the first use I have made of the "folk-prescribed" subdivisions of sacred, and, so far as I know, it is the first explicit systematic use by anybody.

[51] In elementary schools, the description of the earth (geography in the etymological sense) necessarily takes in everything covered, at more advanced levels, by most of the specialized sciences. To this inclusive coverage there can be little if any legitimate objection *at the elementary school level.* It is quite another matter, however, when the college and university geographer tries to deal, even descriptively, with literally everything on the face of the earth. To attempt to be simultaneously economist, political scientist, archeologist, botanist, zoologist, geologist, meteorologist, anthropologist, sociologist, comparative linguist, and so on and on, leads only to wasted effort.

But more specifically, geographic location properly refers only to man's relations with the earth as such, not with other men.

[52] "The same," that is, within the limits of constructive typology. See "Typology, Constructive," in Fairchild, *op. cit.*

A summary of the main features of folk life is to be found in Robert Redfield, "The Folk Society," *American Journal of Sociology,* LII (Jan., 1947), 293-311. See also Wiese-Becker, *op. cit.,* pp. 222-226 n. 6; Barnes and Becker, *STLS,* chap. i, *et passim;* and chap. v of the present volume.

ago, an island once remote in the purely geographic sense may suddenly become a bustling crossroads when man's ways of traveling change. What really constitutes the isolation of a folk society, in other words, is the lack of relations with neighbors, a point aptly made by Semple when, taking her cue from the French *vicinage*, meaning neighborhood, she spoke of *vicinal* isolation.[53]

Over and above this sheer absence of effective contacts with peoples representing contrasting or even distinctly differing ways of life, folk societies are likely to be *socially* isolated. When a straying neighbor "gets outside his own bailiwick," he sometimes[54] finds that barriers to social intercourse may be higher than mountains and deeper than seas even though folk meets folk face to face. Just a few little differences in accent or dress or hairdo or gesture may put the newcomer in a world as socially remote as that of our familiar man from Mars, and perhaps even colder.

To vicinal and social isolation must be added a third kind, namely, *mental*. The members of different folk societies think and feel differently. Granted, the patterns of logic are not entirely arbitrary,[55] and neither are man's emotions, but the combinations of mental processes functionally effective in the conduct of one folk may contrast so radically with those characteristic of another that the unschooled observer may wonder which if either of the two is "really human."

The contrast of course derives from the fact that vicinal and social isolation have furthered the development of strongly contrasting symbolic systems that may initially have differed from each other in only slight measure.[56] The absence of inter-

[53] Cf. my article, "Vicinal Isolation and Mental Immobility," *Social Forces*, XI (March, 1933), 326-334.

[54] "Sometimes" is inserted because of the fact that strangers are *welcomed* by certain peoples—primarily, however, because they are held to be quasi-divine: "Who entertains a stranger entertains a god unawares." In other instances, strangers who are not *too* strange are hospitably received because they are bearers of news and the like. See Margaret Mary Wood, *The Stranger* (New York, 1934), and Wiese-Becker, *op. cit.*, pp. 325 *et seq.*

[55] This is the nub of the entire discussion *re* sociology of knowledge. See H. O. Dahlke, "The Sociology of Knowledge," in Barnes, Becker, and Becker, eds., *CST*, pp. 64-89; see also pp. 892-893.

[56] Divergence, the opposite of Goldenweiser's concept of convergence.

course with other peoples permits small variations to increase in something almost like a geometric ratio, until finally once mutually intelligible dialects of the same language, for instance, may pile up differences to the point where only the skilled philologist can discover that they were ever related. Language and logic are closely interwoven, and for this as well as for many other reasons sharply divergent folk mentalities may emerge.

The cumulative force of tradition, linguistic or otherwise, is powerfully aided by absence of the written word. Even when folk societies are not wholly nonliterate, the art of writing is often restricted to a select few who use it for quite limited purposes. Total or partial nonliteracy makes for domination by tradition in many ways. Everything regarded as important in the past of a given folk, for example, must be passed on by word of mouth, and this leads to the memorizing of long ballads and epics which by their combination of meter, alliteration, assonance, paired balance, acrostic pattern, rhyme, or whatnot, makes possible almost unfailing repetition. The grooves of language and of thought soon become so deeply channeled that it is virtually impossible to pass beyond their confines. Traditional oral transmission and folk mentality flow along together.[57]

Similarly contributing to traditional control is the prevalence of kinship bonds in folk life. Indeed, some writers claim that "kinship society" is prior to all other principles of organization, and their claims are in considerable degree borne out by the amazing intricacy of many kinship terminologies. Some dwellers in folk societies have as many as three hundred ways of labeling their various relatives, whereas in this modern day, with its small family units as over against the mammoth kinship clusters of earlier periods, we think that we are doing well when we can identify a few second cousins. Enmeshed in a maze of relatives, what wonder is it that the children growing up in folk societies acquire binding types of conduct in the form of codes of propriety, ceremonials, "Thou shalts" and

[57] See Barnes and Becker, "Social Thought of Preliterate Peoples," *STLS*, chap. i.

"Thou shalt nots," and a thousand and one other accustomed traditions? The inner countenance, so to speak, is wrinkled, creased, and seamed by the endless repetition of stock grimaces called for by the limited repertory of roles in the drama of sociation. Standard situations and scenes recur again and again, and the parts must be played in the traditional way or not at all. A folk society has many universals and few alternatives.[58]

This limiting of the range of conduct is also evident in the modes of gaining a livelihood. The minute division of function, ridiculed as "Man number 63 screws on nut number 807," characteristic of much of contemporary life, is significantly absent. To be sure, even the folk society has its specialists, as Sale[59] pointed out, but any folk specialist is "master of *one* trade *and* jack of all." He may be the wood carver or the flint flaker par excellence, but in case of need he can still wield the digging-stick or the spear. If he is a teller of tales or a "ghostly man" passing the time of day with familiar spirits, he may be somewhat set apart from his fellows, but except in extreme cases he is rarely so insulated as is the professional writer, cleric, or other member of the "learned professions" in our society. That is to say, the traits characteristic of the mentality of a particular folk are likely to be widely diffused among its members because occupational compartments are not watertight.

The power of tradition in folk societies is also enhanced by the necessity of what may be called apprenticeship. Learning the skills necessary in the struggle for sustenance requires long and painstaking effort. The modern expedient of going to school or of hiring a guide or instructor cannot be resorted to by a folk member when he wishes to learn stalking, fishing, tillage, or weaving. Technical handbooks or the ever-ready encyclopedia do not come within his ken. Instead, he must kowtow to the "old-timers," who are not slow to exact obedience and zeal and who are keenly aware of the duties owed by the young to the old. If the elders impart their cunning and sleight, they demand conformity; in many folk societies the

[58] Ralph Linton, *The Study of Man* (New York, 1936), pp. 272-287.
[59] *Ibid.* Linton of course does not refer to Chic Sale's folk classic, *The Specialist*.

rebel is an outcast, and the outcast quickly becomes a corpse. In short, those who resist tradition may simply fail to survive. Once the more or less willing conformist has mastered the mysteries of his craft, he has by the same token established action patterns of great complexity and persistence, and when these are adequately embodied in the symbolic standards of his society, and particularly in speech, the character and life policy of the economic man-as-he-should-be are clearly outlined. Once this result is reached, any disturbance in the traditional way of getting a livelihood, or in any other key practice, encounters stubborn resistance;[60] the member of a folk society is "set in his ways." A halo, as it were, encircles the accustomed procedures and prevents their profanation by change.

With this in view, it becomes relatively easy to understand the folk society's self-imposed social and mental isolation vis-à-vis the stranger; there is deep dislike of the person who concretely represents the forces of change. When he is genuinely a stranger on the human plane,[61] he is necessarily an "other-than-expected-fellow"—the Chinese villager's term for the outlander who as such is inevitably crude, disconcerting, barbaric. Any breach of the everyday routines is disquieting, for the mere sight of conduct in conflict with tradition tends to

[60] An apt illustration is provided by an island community recently studied:

"There is at least one very conspicuous trait in the life of the Tristan islanders, and that is the almost complete lack of any institutionalized forms of social inter-relationship. Actually, the institutional order, or formal laws, are only of a very rudimentary kind. . . .

"And yet the social order of this community is firm and consistent and constitutes another very conspicuous trait of the social life of the islanders. This firmness applies both to the specific codes of overt action and behavior and to the more general basic valuations and patterns of attitudes. In all aspects of life we are met with a very strong conventionalism and adherence to the prescribed forms, whether we are concerned with details of dress and housebuilding or with the general and specific attitudes and ideas by which the islanders meet their daily problems. Actual breaches of this social order very seldom occur and, if they do, always bring about a strong reaction on the part of the rest of the community in the way of a certain degree of *excommunication* [italics ours]. . . . Apparently the social codes of this community possess very strong coercive power, by which they have been able to produce a thorough adjustment and conformity of the individual characters, even under the consistent repression of certain rather basic appetites and inclinations" (Peter A. Munch, "Cultural Contacts in an Isolated Community: Tristan da Cunha," *American Journal of Sociology*, LIII, July, 1947, 1-8).

[61] Cf. n. 54.

call forth "upset" feelings of a kind that would seize upon any thoroughly "set" personality engaging in actions so blame-worthy in the eyes of his own folk. The homebody imagines himself doing the detestable things perpetrated by the "fur-riner," and "gets all stirred up inside."

This disapproval of the stranger of course extends far be-yond the realm of queer appearance and unfamiliar gesture. Strange speech, for example, is always striking in its oddity, its "outlandishness"; an old proverb has it that "Whoever speaks two languages is a rascal." This aptly represents the feeling of the custom-bound member of a folk society when "jabberers" or "people who just go bar-bar-bar all the time"— namely, barbarians—apply the wrong names to everything. Name and thing are identified; the use of other words is thought unnatural. To quote a classic instance:

"Why, Huck, doan' de French people talk de same way we does?"

"No, Jim. . . . S'pose a man was to come to you and say Polly-voo-franzy—what would you think?"

"I wouldn' think nuffin; I'd take en bust him over de head—dat is, if he warn't white. I wouldn' 'low no . . . [cullud man] to call me dat."

"Shucks, it ain't calling you anything. . . . It's only saying, do you know how to talk French? . . . Ain't it natural and right for a Frenchman to talk different from us? You answer me that."

"Is a cat a man, Huck?"

"No."

"Well, den, dey ain't no sense in a cat talkin' like a man. . . . Is a Frenchman a man?"

"Yes."

"Well, den! Dad blame it, why doan' he talk like a man? You answer me dat!"[62]

Not only is the stranger expected to "talk like a man," but he is also expected to have "common sense." In a folk society, common sense is sense because it is common, and an added war-rant of its validity is provided if it is couched in proverbial terms. The stranger who cannot pass out the coins of ancestral wisdom,

[62] S. L. Clemens (Mark Twain), *Huckleberry Finn* (New York: Harper and Brothers, 1896), chap. xiv, pp. 113-114.

worn smooth by centuries of use, is necessarily beyond the pale. "Stories are told to stupid children, but proverbs are taught to the clever" is a maxim that in substance guides the elders in folk societies.[63] Anxiously careful lest the painfully acquired lore that lends order and coherence to their little world be forgotten, they administer precious capsules of it to those who they think will hold place and power in the succeeding generation. The proverb is common sense raised to the nth degree, and to doubt this compressed wisdom, or even to be unfamiliar with it, is the mark of the witless or the wanton. Sages of folk societies coin new proverbs continually, but they are accepted as proverbs because their makers already bear the character of sages, and this character is acquired only by copious outpouring of traditional formulas.

The uninterrupted dominance of use and wont is made easier when the ties of familiar locality reinforce the bonds of vicinal, social, and mental isolation, kindred, livelihood, apprenticeship, tongue, and lore. Anyone socialized in a sacred society is subject to some degree of nostalgia when torn away from his familiar context; homesickness does occur. Men grow their way into landscapes, so to speak, and a severe wrench is felt when the native place is left behind. If our bearer of a folk personality tills the soil, he becomes with the passage of time so deeply rooted in the particular plot over which he labors, and which embodies so much symbolism, that shift to another with which he has not the same intimate relation brings with it the disturbance of deepset action patterns and a feeling of uneasiness or even distress. "For such a man, the neighboring valley, or even the strip of land at the other end of the village, is in a certain sense alien territory."[64] To speak with Granet, the "occasions" and "emblems" with which his personality is functionally interrelated are indissolubly linked with the "sites" of his lifelong surroundings.[65] Exploiting the once well-known play and the familiar song, it may be said that "the old home-

[63] Dietrich Westermann, The African Today (Oxford, 1934), p. 17.

[64] Robert E. Park, E. W. Burgess, and R. D. McKenzie, eds., The City (Chicago, 1925), p. 18.

[65] Marcel Granet, La Pensée chinoise (Paris, 1934), pp. 119, 127, 151-160, 173-208.

stead" is not simply so-and-so many acres, for the reason, among others, that "the old oaken bucket" is not simply a wooden pail.

XV. QUESTIONS WITH FOLK ANSWERS

Discussion of these and other general traits of folk societies might go on indefinitely. To be brief and still serve present purposes, however, it is enough to list a few questions almost certain to be asked by any sociologist trying to determine the frequency and intensity of folk traits (together with a few of "prescribed" variety) in certain smaller American communities:

I. Intensity of kinship bonds:

A. How many relatives can the ordinary member of the society readily list? What proportion is this of those that he actually has?

B. How strong is his genealogical interest? Can the name and place of birth of a large number of grandparents, great-grandparents, etc., be readily given?

C. What proportion of living relatives has the member actually seen in the past five years?

D. With what proportion of relatives are at least annual meetings (dinners, reunions, etc.) held?

E. To what extent is identity felt with blood kin? With in-laws, second cousins, and so on?

F. What are the attitudes towards divorce and illegitimacy within the family? To what extent do these attitudes rest on religious or related prescription?

G. How frequently are letters and gifts exchanged between relatives?

H. Are christening, baptism, confirmation, and like "rites of passage"[66] family affairs?

I. To what extent do children visit relatives? Is there any sense of family responsibility for orphans?

J. What degrees of relationship are in evidence at family marriages, funerals, and similar "rites of passage?" How great is the time-cost distance typically traveled? What is the defined significance of such travel?

[66] This Van Gennep term is better translated as "ceremonies of transition"— transition from one stage of the life-death cycle to another. Unfortunately, some literalist gave us "rites of passage" for "rites de passage," and now we must put up with it.

K. Is the practice of burial in the family plot maintained? Are the tombstones of traditional character? Of religiously prescribed character?

L. Do the members of the family (collateral and affinal relatives as well as lineal or blood kindred) belong to the same religious body? By explicit prescription?

M. Is there a family homestead, or are there commonly revived memories of one?

N. To what extent are names and birth dates recorded in Bibles or similar places of family inscription?

O. How large is the realm of family symbolism and family secrecy? How much does conversation turn on allusions understood only by family members?

P. Are relatives, friends, or banks most generally named as executors of wills?

Q. When money is loaned to relatives, is it loaned with or without interest?

R. To what extent is mutual aid practiced among relatives in moving, housebuilding, sewing, nursing, and the like?

II. Intensity of friendship and neighborhood ties:

A. All questions concerning participation in "rites of passage" are also pertinent here.

B. Are there many lifelong friendships between members of the same or opposite sexes in the locality?

C. Are money and property freely loaned back and forth between friends? As taken for granted, or by explicitly quoted prescription? Is interest or rent charged?

D. How frequent are visiting relationships between friends or neighbors?

E. To what extent are friendship and neighborhood mutual-aid practices in evidence?

III. Locality relations:

A. All questions concerning participation in "rites of passage" are pertinent here, as are also those pertaining to friendship, mutual aid, etc.

B. Within what area is the typical member of the society referred to by first name, nickname, or in similar familiar terms?

C. What proportion of the persons in the circle of acquaintanceship are "familiar-name acquaintances?"

D. What proportion of community members were born within it? In the case of those who are not native, from how far away did they come? How long ago? And why? What are the general attitudes toward them?

E. What is the range of calling or visiting relationships? To what extent does residence determine neighboring? With whom are social visits carried on? How?[67]

[67] The full outline should be provided, but sections iv-vii, given in this footnote, are of less direct relevance for illustrative purposes:

IV. Livelihood patterns:

A. How freely is family land alienated? Is there any communal opposition to the splitting up of ancestral land? Is there a nuclear or homestead parcel of land which would cause loss of status if sold outside the family?

B. What is the scope of the "cash nexus," i.e., how consistently can it be said that "everything has a price"? For what services are wages or fees ordinarily refused? If so, why?

C. In employment and trade, are community members disproportionately preferred as workers, merchants, etc., to outsiders? What is the general attitude toward the local banker or moneylender? Does his calling evoke any general approval or disapproval? What is the local significance of such attitudes?

D. What occupations yield high social status? Is the amount of actual or potential income a determining factor? Do certain occupations yielding low income carry high status? If so, by unspoken tradition or by direct prescription?

E. What proportion of young people voluntarily choose the occupation of their parents? During depressions is outside help or governmental relief freely sought? Do those who accept relief lose community status? If so, in what ways?

V. Political participation:

A. Are there determinable interrelations between stable family life, friendly and neighborly connections, approved economic activities, and community leadership?

B. Is any political party thought of as particularly respectable or the reverse? Why? By prescription, or as taken for granted?

C. How extensive is the attendance at community political and administrative meetings? What are the principal purposes in attending? Is there a contrast between purposes as verbally stated and as unverbalized? If so, what are the reasons for the contrast?

D. Is political officeholding generally acknowledged to be an indication of high community status?

E. What proportion of those eligible to do so cast votes? Can light or heavy voting, as the case may be, be attributed to community conflicts, special-interest groups, and so on?

F. Is corruption in political office in evidence? If so, how is it defined? How regarded?

VI. Educational institutions:

A. Are local schools preferred to those outside no matter what the differing extent of "educational advantages" may be? By pupils? By parents?

B. Are the models of leadership set before school children drawn from or illustrated by community members? Do school children define "what I'd like to do when I grow up" in ways approved by the community?

C. How zealous are local school boards in making certain that teachers have

Even those of limited social experience should be able to call to mind American societies almost poles apart in the answers returned to some such list of questions. Possum Trot in Alabama and Plainville in Missouri[68] show a high degree of inability or unwillingness to change, and this manifestation of sacredness is primarily of folk rather than of prescribed derivation. Many other folk societies of essentially the same character are still to be found all over the world—indeed, the great majority of mankind still sociates in sacred contexts of markedly folk variety. Even in centers of rapid secularization such as New York, Chicago, and Los Angeles, folk nooks and corners abound: orthodox Jewish communities on the East Side and on Maxwell Street, Molokan "pilgrims of Russian Town," Mexican "Jalopy Parkways" in California cities, and transplanted Deep-South villages in Harlem or along South Park Boulevard provide instances.[69]

Certainly the construct "folk society" as a subdivision of sacred is only one among the many tools necessary for a complete sociological kit; its use alone will not assure a finished job. Nevertheless, it serves a useful purpose in trimming away nonessentials, for recognizable shapes are thereby revealed. When we can see the rough outlines of one general

---

"correct," i.e., community-sanctioned, attitudes? Are "local products" preferred for teaching positions? Is honorific status accorded schoolteachers?

VII. Religious sanctions:

A. How wide is the scope of supernaturalistic controls? Are forms of recreation, dress, child training, etc., under specific religious sanction in the form of direct prescription?

B. Are nonchurchgoers subject to scorn, ostracism, or ridicule?

C. Are guilt-feelings manifest among those church members who do not follow the precepts of their religion? When was the last revival, retreat, novena, or similar manifestation of faith? How was it regarded by the community as a whole? Were local leaders identified with it?

D. What is the traditional attitude toward Sunday school, parochial schools, or similar types of religious education? The prescribed attitude?

E. Is old age held in special reverence? How does age-stratification in the religious organization compare with the proportion of persons in different age groupings in the community at large?

F. Is tradition of special religious significance? If so, by direct prescription, or simply as taken for granted?

[68] H. C. Nixon, *Possum Trot: Rural Community, South* (Norman, Oklahoma, 1941); James West [pseud.], *Plainville, USA* (New York, 1945).

[69] See the bibliography of this chapter at the end of the book.

context within which other social groupings function, we can refine our analysis considerably.

XVI. SACREDNESS BY PRESCRIPTION

Sacred societies, as already noted, have two subdivisions, and we have termed the second "prescribed." The clearest examples[70] of this variety of sacred sociation are to be found where sanctioned rationality operates to the fullest extent, namely, where a definite body of dogma calls forth, sets up, or maintains a totalitarian kind of social structure. The Geneva theocracy of Calvin, the Jesuit state of Paraguay, and, by intention at least, Fascist Italy, Nazi Germany, and Soviet Russia are among the most prominent of many instances.[71]

The sanctioned rationality marking the choice of means within these sociative networks may be placed in the service of radically differing ends—that is clear. Although both were presumably devoted to the "greater glory of God," the society of Geneva seems to have centered chief attention upon spiritual recognition and security, with economically individualistic ends playing a very large although at first subordinate part. In contradistinction, the society of Paraguay granted a very prominent place to spiritual response, but at the same time developed a collectivist economy stressing mutually rather than individually achieved security. How fundamentally Fascists, Nazis, and Communists have differed in their final ends is a question that might lead to hairsplitting, but it would appear that racial recognition has had little place in the Fascist and Communist mentalities.[72]

However this may be, the basic feature of sanctioned rationality is evidenced in all the cases mentioned, for the ends forbade the use of certain means. The devout Calvinist could acquire no spiritual recognition by indiscriminate charity, for

---

[70] "Clearest," but certainly not the only examples.

[71] Several other examples, beginning with Franco Spain, could readily be listed, but space forbids.

[72] Of course, ethnic sentiments, frequently on a linguistic basis, have played important parts. Pan-Latinism as represented by certain Fascist ideologists called for solidarity among all the peoples speaking languages primarily derived from the Latin. Pan-Slavism is almost certainly as important in current Russian ideology as is Communism, and Pan-Slavism carries a heavy linguistic emphasis.

58 THROUGH VALUES TO SOCIAL INTERPRETATION

the doctrine of stewardship directly barred means of this kind.[73] The Paraguayan Jesuits resorted to force only as a means of maintaining conditions regarded as necessary for the well-being and salvation of their Guarani charges. In resorting to it, elaborate religious sanctions were always invoked, and the spiritual mentors, at least, did penance.[74] Whatever else Fascists might do, no concessions could be made to economic liberalism or to parliamentarism, for corporative unity, the supreme end of mutually achieved recognition and security symbolized by the fasces,[75] would thereby be basically flouted. The genuinely fanatical Nazi really did keep himself free of "racial taint," for otherwise how could he have been granted recognition by his omniscient Führer? The convinced Communist sincerely thinks that he scorns the use of "bourgeois" means for reaching the ultimate goal of a classless society in which security, response, recognition, and new experience combine to fill the prescription of "From each according to his ability, to each according to his needs."[76]

Given the highly contemporary character of the Russian illustration, it is plain that prescribed societies must not be thought of as being of interest to antiquarians only. Indeed, the fact that the element of prescription in any such society stands in the foreground should not blind the observer to the large amount of tradition which can be brought up to date, as it were, by incorporation in a prescribed formula. The Fascists, to single out only one of our instances, made liberal use of symbols that had long been traditional;[77] they were simply infused with new life by appropriate sanction. The same could be said of Nazi Germany;[78] and Soviet Russia in recent years has certainly done much to incorporate every presumably "dia-

[73] See Max Weber, *The Protestant Ethic and the Spirit of Capitalism* (New York, 1930), *passim*.
[74] Lewis Hanke, *The First Social Experiments in America* (Cambridge, Mass., 1935), chapter on the Jesuit state of Paraguay.
[75] See pp. 26-27.
[76] Engels's famous phrase.
[77] Pp. 26-27.
[78] Becker, "The Accomplishment of Perversion," *German Youth: Bond or Free*, chap. vii.

lectic" and beneficial[79] tradition from the time of Ivan the Terrible onward into the prescribed ideology.

This is one of the chief reasons why the notion of geographic isolation makes little sense as the exclusive determinant of sacred phenomena. Of scant use even where sacred societies of traditional type are concerned, it fails utterly when confronted by the great sacred units operating under prescription in the modern world.

Vicinal isolation, however, may prove quite relevant, for restrictions on travel in the form of passports, currency regulations, and a host of other devices readily bring about situations in which near neighbors are separated as effectively as though impassable oceans lay between them.[80]

Social isolation likewise plays its part in generating prescribed mentality. Protestants may have as little access to the real intimacies of a Catholic community as do Jews, and conversely, the term "Jesuitical" carries with it a degree of reproach, in some outspokenly Protestant communities, reminiscent of the eighteenth-century ostracism of "the man in black."[81] By isolating the sacred stranger[82] of this type from effective contact with those addicted to contrasting prescriptions, unwillingness or inability to change is maintained in full force.

Part and parcel of social isolation, in most instances, is mental isolation, and in this regard prescribed society differs not a whit from folk society. Nazi totalitarianism in its heyday promulgated the slogan "We think with our blood," with such telling effect that the logical patterns evident among large sections of the German population—and not the most fanatical alone—made it very difficult for the outsider to establish any mutually intelligible universe of discourse. Anyone properly

[79] "Beneficial" in the sense of benefiting any effort toward the attainment of the supreme ends of present-day Russian Communism, i.e., useful to the Kremlin authorities, particularly the Politburo.

[80] It is said that Russian troops too much "infected" by close contact with Western ways of life are never returned to their home areas, but instead are widely scattered where they can do the least damage. Given the ends of Communist life, such tactics are shrewd.

[81] Cf. George Borrow, "The Man in Black," Lavengro (London, 1937), chap. xc. And what of passage after passage in The Bible in Spain?

[82] Wiese-Becker, op. cit., pp. 322-344.

schooled in the Soviet version of the Marxian dialectic thinks along lines that set his mentality widely apart from anything current in Western "bourgeois" circles. Because overt acts are never taken as they stand, but are always subjected to imputation of motives,[83] the amount of suspicion and hostility which may arise among those mentally isolated by prescription would be unbelievable if evidence of societal paranoia of this kind were not all too abundant.

Prescribed societies are frequently literate, hence the peculiar reinforcement of sacred traits stemming from absence of the written word is not always at hand. Instead, reinforcement may issue from the very fact that a *limited* kind of literacy is systematically maintained. Suppression of opposing doctrine can of course take place in societies that have no books to burn, but literary bonfires have unquestionably helped to hold many prescribed regimes in power. Extreme measures of this sort are not always necessary, for control of press, radio, and other means of mass communication may simply drown out the opposition. In any event, the formulation of a body of doctrine and its according-to-plan inculcation by creed, catechism, sermon, speech, editorial, "news" broadcast, and the like is of the essence of control technique in a prescribed society.[84]

Kinship in the ordinary sense plays little part in such control, but in broader meaning it may be highly significant. The "Pan-" movements[85] of every sort, from Pan-Germanism to Pan-Slavism to Pan-Hebraism (Zionism) stress unities which, although not necessarily of racial character, rely heavily on common religion, tongue, "political destiny," or culture. The racial dogmas of the kind involved in Nazism or Nipponism of course present a clearer analogy to the sacralizing[86] effects of kinship ties. No miracle, therefore, is the intense solidarity engendered by such aids in prescribed societies.

[83] See my chapter, "Interpretative Sociology and Constructive Typology," *loc. cit.*, esp. part I, reprinted in the present volume, pp. 189-247.

[84] The doctrine may be learned "at mother's knee," but it is still doctrine. Naturally, a great deal of the inculcation taking place in early childhood is traditional rather than prescribed.

[85] See Hans Kohn's article of this title in the *Encyclopedia of the Social Sciences.*

[86] See n. 96 if the meaning of this term is not self-evident.

Ways of gaining a livelihood are frequently brought within the scope of prescription by invoking the idea that a society is an organism in which the humblest cells (members) have functions necessary in the highest degree for the life of the whole.[87] The Fascists and Nazis unweariedly rang changes on this theme, and to a considerable extent succeeded in overcoming the splitting and splintering effects of the minute division of labor. "Strength through Joy" (*Kraft durch Freude*), and "After Work" (*Dopolavoro*) were used to make recreation meaningful in relation to labor and to give it the same organismic bearing, for under prescription even man at play exists for society and not vice versa.

In prescribed societies strangers are often physically in evidence to an extent far greater than in folk societies, but genuine intercommunciation on an intimate plane may nevertheless be rare. Conducted tours, whether commercial or government-sponsored, usually bring the outsider into only superficial touch with the people among whom he moves. The mutual lack of comprehension would be harmlessly ludicrous if it were not for the amazing confidence with which all concerned report on each other's "real nature," with accompanying damage to valid intersocietal knowledge. Where those dominant in a prescribed society carefully herd visitors along walled-in paths, there can of course be no penetration of the mental isolation of any of the subjugated—or of the herded either.

The use of unfamiliar language may not set the stranger apart in a prescribed society, but the use of *any* language to voice a disapproved ideology inevitably does. Hence we might change the already-quoted maxim[88] to read "Whoever is familiar with two *ideologies* is a rascal"; it simply does not do to quote with equal facility and relish from Adam Smith *and* Josef Stalin, or from Churchill *and* Goebbels. The wise man in a prescribed society is he who expounds orthodox doctrine with fluency and force, and quotes opponents only to refute their devilish designs. Common sense, in other words, is prescribed orthodoxy.

[87] Barnes and Becker, *STLS*, pp. 664-692.
[88] "Whoever speaks two languages is a rascal."

The bonds of locality, so powerful in sacred societies of folk variety, operate in a different way where the prescribed type is concerned. For example, there is a strong contrast between eras "when patriotism was a hearty parochial love of the native land rather than a reedy hurrah for a tinsel-bedecked, brand-new national state,"[89] and those when chauvinistic loyalty to the German nation put love for Westphalia in a subordinate place. In other words, the ties of territory are likely to be intertwined with abstractions: nation, empire, Fatherland, God's country, Worker's Homeland, or Celestial Kingdom.[90] Social actions evoked by reference to such territorial abstractions may be quite as fatefully decisive for other conduct as are those linked with the relatively tiny plots of soil for which homesickness in its more specific meaning can be felt. Few if any can dispense with the basis for loyalty which territory provides, even though the grand finale runs:

> Today we hold the Fatherland,
> Tomorrow the world is ours.

This sketching of the more prominent features of prescribed societies might go to much greater length, but our immediate purpose is to present only enough to provide meaningful context for the study of smaller social groupings. For example, it should take little effort to see that the family and marriage can never exist in their own right in certain prescribed societies;[91] they must always be subservient to the larger demands of the totalitarian structure. More members of the church, the nation, the master race, the international working class, and what have you—that, plus schooled and ready conformity, is frequently the objective. From another aspect, this appears as unwillingness or inability to change on the part of a population steadily stimulated by prescription to increase in number.

From what has just been said, it might be thought that prescribed societies are always exclusively dominated by traits to which, in particular, the ordinary non-totalitarian American

[89] Becker, *German Youth: Bond or Free*, p. 86.
[90] Cf. Wiese-Becker, *op. cit.*, chaps. xlii-xlv.
[91] Of course, not all prescribed societies stress population increase. The Shakers were celibate.

would strenuously object.[92] That this tends to be the case is doubtless true, but it must never be forgotten that we as Americans accept many prescriptions as beneficial. The Declaration of Independence, the Constitution (and especially the Bill of Rights), the oath of allegiance, and the Four Freedoms all have their prescriptive aspects.

Indeed, the later discussion of stable secular societies deals with the essential functions served by tradition or prescription, or both, in keeping these societies in that state of moving equilibrium which alone can be called stability in our rapidly changing world. Final, essentially unquestioned loyalties there must be if social change is not to issue in extreme social disorganization, and prescription has much to do with generating those loyalties in any modern society having a firm foundation of principle.

XVII. WHERE PRESCRIPTION COMES FROM

At this point there may well arise the question, "How are prescribed societies generated?" as well as the closely related query, "What antecedent conditions make the emergence of prescription possible?" Fully adequate answers would of course enable us to seize the elusive master-clues of history, "to get the feel of the fur on the tail of the world," but no such adequacy is hoped for, here or elsewhere. Moreover, the few hints that can be offered here are drastically limited by the space available, but even fragmentary hints may be better than nothing.

Prescriptions oftentimes are not much more than systematic verbalizations of tradition. Over long centuries a large stock

[92] It is too much to hope, in the present time of high political tension, and in my present function and location (Chief of Higher Education in the Hessian division of the American Occupation Zone in Germany, 1947-48), that I have preserved full detachment. The frequency with which I have referred to Soviet Russia, for instance, is probably direct evidence of failure to be wholly aloof from political preoccupations. Nevertheless, I have *tried* to maintain balanced judgment—more I cannot say.

Naturally, I regard the claims of the scientific ethic as uppermost where essays of this sort are concerned, even though my "value-polytheism" might lead me to set those claims aside when a limited range of alternatives in political action forces decisions that can never be scientific. See my essay, "Supreme Values and the Sociologist," *loc. cit.*, esp. the conclusion, reprinted in the present volume, pp. 281-305.

of proverbs and similar condensations of folk wisdom having sociative bearing accumulates. This lore is eventually put into some sort of order by patient systematizers, and may even be compressed into relatively brief formulas from which, by deduction, subsidiary doctrines running more or less parallel with prevailing social actions may be derived. In other words, prescription may arise in such a way that it does little more than underscore tradition. The priestly codes of the Old Testament are instances of exactly this sort of process.

In other cases, however, prescriptions break like volcanic eruptions out of traditional ground that has been turned into a "shatter zone," full of faults and fissures, by powerful shocks and pressures. Again the Old Testament provides illustrations: the eighth-century prophets proclaimed their doctrines under the stress of potential or actual catastrophe. The sway of tradition had either brought on crisis or proved unable to meet it, or both, and the prophets set themselves in conscious opposition to the established society of their day. That their saving formulas partook of what has been called "reactionary radicalism"[93] is of little moment here; significant for the present analysis is the fact that they attempted to make a clean break with the prevailing traditions of *their* times.

Such Old Testament examples can be matched, in all essentials, by many others, not excepting dozens drawn from the modern period. In every case there will be found a strong streak of affective nonrationality in both leaders and followers of the new prescription, and this can usually be characterized as charismatic. Extraordinary or even "uncanny" men are often the only members of a society who can crack its traditional crust.

The answers to the questions posed earlier, then, can be phrased thus: "Prescriptions may be the result either of gradual systematization or sudden charismatic reformulation of older conceptions"; and "Either societal continuity long enough to permit the rise of prescription out of tradition, or the threat of societal discontinuity issuing from crises of various kinds, are the necessary preconditions."

[93] Barnes and Becker, *STLS*, pp. 124, 314.

Finally, note that the impact of affective nonrationality necessary to break the cake of custom may be so great that the only persons capable of exerting it are those who in personality make-up are of a type unable or unwilling to formulate prescriptions of clear-cut character. Adolf Hitler provides an excellent example: only as systematic interpretations were provided by Goebbels, Rosenberg, and other subsidiary prescribers was the new creed brought into forms that could be readily imparted to the rank and file. Without an array of faithful disciples who put the aphoristic utterances of the master into easily intelligent form, it would be impossible for most charismatic leaders to exert any marked effect on the masses. That is to say, affective nonrationality is ordinarily transmuted into the sanctioned rationality characteristic of prescribed societies only by undergoing formulation and systematization at the hands of persons having deductive powers, inclinations, or opportunities greater than the man initially responsible for shattering traditional restraints.

For a time it often happens that the sanctioned rationality thus brought to the fore is belligerently anti-traditional where the *old* tradition broken up by the affective eruption is concerned. Sooner or later the sanctioned rationality of prescription calls to its aid a body of *new* traditions. Eventually the implicit or imperfectly verbalized controls of the new tradition may prove more powerful in sustaining the prescribed society than are the explicit, precisely worded doctrines and dogmas with which it began and which it continually improves and restates.

The history of Catholic Christianity roughly follows the drift of the foregoing analysis: Jesus, the charismatic leader, proclaiming in telling aphorism, metaphor, and parable a set of antitraditional prescriptions; John and Paul, disciple and apostle, taking the first steps toward interpretation and systematization; the Church Fathers, from Clement to Athanasius, deducing in minutest detail every prescribed item; Thomas Aquinas, acting as the great comprehensive systematizer of previous Christian systems; and eventually the perfecting of

Roman Catholicism as, in so many words, "the hallowed tradition of the Christian Church." The consequence in many countries, clearly enough, is that Catholicism is far more a total way of life on a traditional basis, deeply rooted in folk practice, than it is definite adherence by choice to prescriptions which are prescriptions only—and this is said in full realization of the fact that no organization anywhere devotes more attention to the adequate formulating and imparting of its characteristic prescriptions.

The conclusion to be drawn, for our purposes, is that prescribed societies never remain merely prescribed if they continue as societies for any length of time. What may be termed a folk-prescribed type is soon generated. Surveying societies the world around, moreover, makes it evident that, although nowadays the greater number which can be labeled as sacred are of folk-prescribed variety, most examples falling into this intermediate category have more folk than prescribed components. Further, although societies of almost pure folk type are occasionally to be found, it is nearly impossible to find comparably pure examples of the prescribed. After all, however, this is only what might be expected from what we know of the way in which human personalities are elicited and molded. Harking back: "Bobby was 'traditioned' by his mother as to the 'right' way to feed himself. We get language by tradition, manners by tradition, morals by tradition" (p. 27).

No society, prescribed or otherwise, ever starts from scratch.

XVIII. THE SECULAR IS ONLY THE RELATIVELY DISCRETE

Attention now turns to another main type of sociative network, already frequently mentioned but not yet adequately described or dissected, namely, secular society. It also subdivides into two varieties; these may conveniently be called unstable and stable—or, as in Chapter V, principled and normless.

Even when one is discussing the kind marked by extreme instability, however, there is a certain contradiction involved in calling it a secular society, for in terms of our analysis, a *completely* secular society would not be a society at all. That is to say, secularization would ultimately result in the appearance of a heterogeneous assembly of human units having no goals in common; instead of a value-system with ends in some respects accrete,[94] there would be only a systemless mass of utterly discrete ends pursued at random.[95] So entirely secular and disorganized an aggregate has not made its appearance anywhere and, we make bold to say, will not do so. The most that can be said of any society is that it is highly secularized or is secularizing rapidly,[96] for sacred components always remain, are regenerated, or are developed afresh in some form. Furthermore, the bonds that make a collection of mere human beings into a society—that is, into a coherent, continuing, self-perpetuative, and relatively self-contained social unit—are basically of sacred character. This means that a stable secular society could with almost equal warrant be designated as an adaptive sacred society,[97] a point of which more will be made later. As long as these and forthcoming qualifications are taken into account, however, no great harm is done by clipped terminology.

A secular society is one in which resistance to change is at a minimum or, to say the very least, where change in many aspects of life is usually quite welcome. In this special sense, then, "secular" is the photographic negative of "sacred," and therefore should not be taken as a mere synonym for "profane," "godless," or "irreligious," all of which mean consider-

---

[94] Accrete, in this context the opposite of discrete, is a botanical term meaning "fused" or "grown together." It seems permissible to borrow it for sociological purposes.

[95] Cf. Parsons, *op. cit.*, *passim*.

[96] Hence strict consistency would call for "a secularizing society" and "a sacralizing society," or "secularization" and "sacralization." The emphasis on *process* thereby resulting, moreover, would be advantageous.

Incidentally, note that "sacralization" is now an anatomical term meaning the fusion of pelvic vertebrae! Witticism aside, however, it seems that it may justifiably be used in a sociological sense as well, for the os *sacrum*—the fused vertebrae forming the posterior wall of the pelvis—was a bone offered in sacrifice. In other words, the sacrum had a function in a certain kind of sacred society. See chap. v.

[97] Elton Mayo has long made use of an "established-adaptive" dichotomy. His established society is quite similar to sacred society of both folk and prescribed varieties, and his adaptive is much the same as what is here termed stable secular society. He does not, however, pay much attention to *unstable* secular society, and there is no real place for it in his classification.

ably more *and* less.[98] Briefly, societies that endow their members with a high proportion of action patterns leading to readiness to change are secular societies.

The ends most frequently pursued by such persons are chiefly classifiable under new experience, recognition, and response, with new experience, obviously enough, dominant in most instances. The means furthering such ends are primarily of expediently rational and affectively nonrational character.

XIX. SECULAR SHIFTINESS

In order to make this abstract formulation reasonably concrete, let us begin by describing secular societies marked by much instability and its accompanying focus on expediency and affective appeal.

The clearest instances are to be found in centers of culture contact. These are very often sections of great cities standing at the crossroads of commerce and communication.[99] In other words, secular societies are ordinarily *accessible*—the antithesis of isolated.

This accessibility is by no means an affair of geography alone, for although sea, land, and air combine in various ways to further the antlike swarming of the metropolis, change in the technical culture may suddenly bring about accessibility where isolation previously prevailed. Iceland and air travel have already been mentioned, but for an earlier period the shift of Chicago from a remote fur-trading post to the world's greatest railway center is likewise relevant. Accessibility is largely of man's making, not nature's.

Clearly, however, the neighbors round about any given

[98] In particular, *secular* as used here does *not* have the blameworthy meaning which most Catholics and many Protestants assign to it when speaking of "modern secularism." See p. 68, n. 48 and the relevant sections of chap. v.

[99] This is of course the reason why Redfield uses "urban" as the antithesis of "folk." It must be noted, however, that certain varieties of the city show no high incidence of secularization. What of folk-prescribed cities such as Lhasa, Benares, and Mecca, or prescribed cities such as Fascist Rome, Communist Moscow, and Nazi Munich? Redfield obviously means only one type of city—namely, the highly secularized variety. This being the case, why not say "secular" instead of "urban"?

Further, it is not mere pedantry to point out that "rural" is the correct antithesis of "urban," and that some rural societies, past and present, show a low incidence of sacredness. Sacred-secular is a less ambiguous dichotomy. See chap. v.

people undergoing secularization must be so situated and disposed that vicinal accessibility prevails. This is tantamount to saying that highly secularized centers are almost necessarily cosmopolitan; all sorts and descriptions of people come together and succeed in communicating after a fashion. *Koiné* Greek, the *lingua franca,* pidgin English, Spaniola, "OK" American (otherwise known as Occupation English), or similar palavers flourish luxuriantly. Linguistic accessibility, as it were, comes into being.

Further, in a secular society the devices of communication have ordinarily advanced to the point where the roaring voice of Stentor, the herald, is not the only way of spanning the gap between groups. The knotted string quipu which aided in the uniting of the empire of the Incas, the Egyptian papyrus with its reed-penned symbols, the penny post, the far-writing telegraph, the telephone, and the radio, and television—all these methods have helped in varying degree to make possible or to increase vicinal accessibility.

Moreover, they have helped to generate social accessibility, which is another trait of a markedly secular society. Where it prevails in full measure there are no rigid social barriers cutting off one segment of the society from another. More specifically, there are no "untouchables"; ghettos and Black Belts, when they exist at all, do not determine the basic character of social relations, and gangsters and socialites mingle in the tolerant haven of the Stork Club, Number 21, or other modish hangouts.

The upshot is that vicinal and social accessibility come to be linked with mental. Any secular society is necessarily "open-minded," and if secularization is extreme, minds may be open, as one wit has phrased it, "at both ends." Otherwise stated, the open-mindedness may consist not only in easygoing disregard of matters once held sacred, but also in their ostentatious flouting. "Anything for a thrill"—which represents the fusion of means and ends characteristic of affective nonrationality—is often the outspokenly admitted maxim. Figuratively put, the walls of mental isolation have completely crumbled, and only rubble remains.

Secular societies, now everywhere in evidence, were quite rare in the remoter historical record, and nonexistent, it may well be assumed, among man's earlier clusters of sociation. It is for this reason, and for this alone, that secular here follows sacred, for as the discussion of prescribed societies may have shown, there is ample evidence that societies once strongly secular may be poured back into sacred molds. Recall the references to Nazi Germany; many others will readily come to mind.

Kinship, however interpreted, figures to an everdwindling degree in secularizing societies; the rapid shrinking of kinship vocabularies is a consequence. Along with this goes a decline in the social control exercised by kindred, for the household shrinks to the immediate marriage group and its scanty roster of offspring. The most effective of all modes of imparting tradition, viz., continual daily precept and example by a large number of intimately sociating tradition-bearers, no longer functions. Grandparents do not occupy a "west room" or gable end,[100] and the voice of Aunt Matilda, heard only during infrequent visits, goes unheeded. Instead of the reverent imitation of elders, ancestors, or other traditional models,[101] there is the prairie-fire spread of style among contemporaries. "Shirt-tail out" changes to "shirt-tail in" almost overnight, the switch from skirt to blue jeans and back overrides parental protest, and the Tubular Torso yields to the New Look. The social scene changes so rapidly that there are few standard situations; parts in the social drama cannot be played in traditional or sanctioned ways, and continual improvisation takes place under the sway of convenience and emotional pull. Reversing the sacred formula, a secular society has many alternatives and few universals.

The far-flung range of conduct thereby made possible is strikingly evident in the modes of gaining a livelihood. Competition has wide scope even when monopoly capitalism is well

[100] Here reference is to Irish and German examples: see Conrad Arensberg, *The Irish Countryman* (New York, 1937), and Howard Becker, "Peoples of Germany," in T. C. McCormick, *Problems of the Postwar World* (New York, 1945), section on Lower Saxony.
[101] See Barnes and Becker, "Age Discrimination," *STLS*, pp. 18-19.

to the fore, and minute subdivision of function is the rule. Specialties are uppermost, and the sage who incorporates all knowledge available in his society in his single person is replaced by the library which finds its only unity in its card catalogue. Technical vocabularies of mutually unintelligible character become so much a matter of course that it was possible for a cartoonist to play upon the theme for years in a "They Don't Speak Our Language" series.[102]

Moreover, although the skills necessary for economic survival presuppose special training, technical instructors, handbooks, and machines replace the guild masters and the graybeards. The action patterns that are established do not interweave with all portions of the personality; the technical man is distinct from the family man, the religious man, and so on, even though the same skin holds them all. The consequence is that action patterns which are of great importance from the standpoint of effective economic functioning, for instance, can be changed by the person concerned without a comprehensive change in his other conduct. To be sure, change of action patterns is difficult enough under any circumstances, but when action patterns are fractional, as it were, the principle of divide and conquer can readily be applied. Such segmental skills do not determine character and life policy; the man-as-he-should-be is not modeled by the mysteries of his craft, for craft callings are outmoded and there are no mysteries. The member of a secular society is therefore "set" in only some of his ways; for the rest, he has a high degree of "freedom from"[103]—that is, a minimum of specific social constraint. In such a society the normal personality, speaking statistically, is unintegrated; "the left hand knoweth not what the right hand doeth."

[102] This kind of cartoon, by "Tad," ran for a long time in the Chicago *Tribune*. It always had four sections. In the first, an outsider listened with some comprehension and a bland smile to a conversation between two technicians—engineer and fireman, let us say. In the next section, the outsider plainly is in great difficulty; his face shows that he understands little if anything of what is being said. In the third, he decides to make a bold front of it, and asks a question of the most naïve not to say stupid kind. In the fourth, the two technicians look disgustedly at the by now badly embarrassed outsider, and chorus, "They don't speak our language!"

[103] This comes from Nietzsche's aphorism: "Free *from* what? What is that to Zarathustra? Clear shall your eye tell me, Free *to* what?"

When secularization has gone a long way, the stranger becomes attractive to many persons, for the relative scarcity of over-all habits and the continual contact with new sensual values, made possible through "freedom from," lend charm to the exotic. This is particularly true of the leisured classes in a secular society, for they lack even the routine stabilizations of the time clock, the punch press, and the assembly line. Novel gesture, unfamiliar accent, "different" clothes and posture, have prestige value, and the cosmopolite is "intriguing." Instead of unwillingness or inability to respond to the new, there is frequently unwillingness or inability to *refrain* from responding to the new. Change of scene, dress, friends, and marital partners becomes virtually compulsive among that small proportion of a secular society which pays the costs—or if one prefers, reaps the advantages—of ultrarapid secularization.

Be it noted that the stranger is present not only in the more obvious form described above, but that everyone is in some sense a stranger. Anonymity is the rule: the subway patron, the ten-cent-store clerk, the one-arm luncher, the taxi driver, the newsboy, and the chain store manager are units, not names. The through-the-elbows social control exercised by intimates who knew one's whole family "way back when" is lacking, and Mrs. Grundy is strangely silent.

Silent likewise is the voice of the sage; his proverbs no longer pass as current coin. Instead, there appears the vendor of "wisecracks"—here today and gone tomorrow. The old turns of speech drop out of use; slang replaces them, and slang in turn occasionally yields to the studied novelty of "double-talk." If it does not so yield, it is in any case destined to be outmoded by still newer slang; what can be staler than the "twenty-three skidoo" or the "ishkabibble" of yesteryear? In secular society the old as such is despised, and the new as such is esteemed. Even the archaistic revivals are sponsored by self-conscious devotees of style; "Early American" and "Mid-Victorian" enjoy vogues, but these vogues may be as short-lived as the one-season "Empress Eugenie" hats of the early 1930's. When a style once drops out of sight, it drops with a thud.

Another significant aspect of secular societies is the importance of the written word. The unspoken understandings or tacit agreements, the eating of salt or the breaking of bread, the ceremonial utterances, are all replaced by the lawyer's whereases, the marriage license, the will with its witnesses and possible contestants, the passport, and the notary public's seal. The chanted ballad yields to the pulp thriller, and the long life histories of garrulous oldsters are supplanted by the "true story" and "confession" magazines. Heroic sagas are replaced by sacred books, and these in turn by increasingly secular commentaries on sacred books.

In a secular society the ties of locality diminish in importance; as Stephen Leacock wryly put it, "I remember, I remember the house where I was born" becomes "I wish I could remember the flat where I was born." In normal times May 1 and October 1 are not betrothal festivals or reapers' frolics, but moving days; the landlord must redecorate "or else." The upshot of this is that the home is increasingly hotel-like in character: it is a mere secular stopping-place changed without emotional reluctance—indeed, with gratification.[104]

Supernaturalism may be quite prevalent in a secular society, but the cults that promise the Limitless Whichness and All the Works, from eternal youth to painless dentistry, are not of *traditionally* religious reference. Affective nonrationalisms abound, but they must bear the saving label of "scientific." Genuine science of course has great power and influence, but among its practitioners few are called but many are chosen. That is to say, the prestige of science in a secular society is so great that scientific quacks flourish like the green bay tree, and that a religion of Science develops.

Here again it would be possible to go on for a long time. Secular societies in *our* civilization are chiefly urban,[105] and whole libraries have been written on urban sociology. If the reader will take another look at the outline at the end of the section on sacred society (pp. 53-56), reversing the implica-

[104] See Norman S. Hayner, *Hotel Life* (Chapel Hill, N. C., 1936), *passim.*
[105] But to repeat: not all urban societies are secular, nor are all rural societies sacred! See n. 99.

tions of many of the questions asked, he can lend more meaning to the impressionistic comments just presented.

XX. SECULAR BALANCE

Manifestly, what has here been said about secular societies has focused on the unstable extremes. Turning to the more stable, it can be said with some confidence that stability is directly linked with the functioning of both tradition and prescription, and that security, in particular, comes to seem an end more important than new experience. The misoneism, neophobia, or dislike of the new characteristic of extremely sacred societies may not be strongly in evidence, but the philoneism, neophilia, or liking for the new[106] which runs rampant in rapidly secularizing societies is held in check.

The source of the check is always some sacred practice, precept, or principle.[107] Democracy, to choose a highly relevant example, is "self-evident" only to the heirs of a transmuted Greco-Roman tradition, Christianity in certain versions, or the natural rights philosophy of the eighteenth-century Deists[108]— and frequently of all three together, with other sacred components thrown in for good measure. To say this is not to challenge the validity of democracy as a form of social and political organization, for its pragmatic workability may—and in the estimation of the writer does—justify most of the arguments put forward in its behalf. It may well be possible that democracy, as a kind of stable secular society in moving equilibrium, may sometime reach the point where the sacred elements which called it into being and which still sustain it will be left behind—but that point has not yet been reached. Moreover, when it is reached for any given generation, other taken-

---

[106] The three terms in each of these two sets are synonymous. The redundancy is solely for the purpose of calling attention to the fact that they all occur in the literature.

[107] See Carl Becker, *The Heavenly City of the Eighteenth-Century Philosophers* (New Haven, 1932).

[108] This is the essential reason why Sorokin found it necessary to insert an "idealistic" intermediary stage between his "ideational" and "sensate" societies. In saying this, however, there is no necessary agreement with his choice of "idealistic" periods—fifth-century Greece and thirteenth-century Western Europe. Unless societies wholly disintegrate—and this rarely occurs short of internal or external conquest—a set of "idealistic" factors is always operative.

for-granted traditions and prescriptions will lend to the new democracy whatever stability it may possess.[109]

In the field of family relations the same analysis seems to hold. Precisely why a family should be democratically organized, with family councils entered into by co-equal husband, wife, and maturer children, is not self-evident to persons outside the pale of modern Western European middle-class, and perhaps, more specifically *American* middle-class ideology.

That ideology takes for granted, among other things, the desirability of family harmony and, by the same token, family continuity. From the standpoint of the well-being of society as a whole, there can be little doubt that such harmony and continuity are of the highest value. But is it possible to talk about the well-being of society *as a whole* without making a host of unproved and as yet unprovable assumptions?[110] The married pair coming together merely for the purpose of legalized copulation and its attendant gratifications of response and new experience are expediently achieving these ends, which for them are discrete, well enough. To convince them of the desirability of rearing acceptable citizens for an ongoing democracy, or active participants in a humanitarian and partially Christian ethic, or contributors to the lofty final ends of science, music, poetry, and art, would necessitate appeal to ultimate

[109] To talk about the possibility of an "organized secular society," therefore, is to recognize that norms ultimately deriving from sacred sources provide the possibility of organization.

Here reference is to the article by W. L. Kolb, "The Objective Possibility of an Organized Secular Society," *Southwestern Journal*, II (1946), pp. 161-169. Kolb phrases his hope for an organized secular society in part as follows:

"If . . . the persons of a secular society share a system of relatively well-defined but flexible and non-specific norms, lawmaking becomes an attempt to define and control changes in action patterns in the light of these ultimate values. Recognizing that rapid change makes impossible the growth of specific tradition out of general tradition, attempts would be made to forge a common definition of the new situation of . . . varying individual group definitions, all of which, however, share a common orientation toward a system of ultimate norms."

What Kolb is saying is that rigid, narrow, traditional nonrationality provides no basis for stability in periods of rapid change, but that some kinds of sanctioned rationality may. Folk societies and hardshelled prescribed societies go under, but it is perhaps possible for societies having broad general prescriptions, plus secular adaptability, to survive. In short, they become principled societies. Agreed; there is no argument. See the further discussion of this in the section on principled secular societies in chap. v, especially n. 49.

[110] See Kolb, *op. cit.*

values which are perceived only by those trained to perceive them. The family can never be grounded on a self-contained companionship providing its own inherent justification;[111] if there is to be a genuine family—which is to say, a social institution[112]—in any society there must be functional reference to a system of accrete ends transcending the merely expedient and affective. Less technically, the form of the human family never rests on a purely biological basis, and all of its various forms, including the "democratic," are bound up with sacred considerations which to the social scientist are by no means self-evident. Here again there is no intention of calling into question the pragmatic warrant of the modern monogamic equalitarian family. The only purpose is the underscoring of the indispensable sacred traits of *any* normative aspect of a stable secular society.[113]

XXI. NORMLESSNESS IS UNCOMFORTABLE

Highly interesting in connection with both unstable and stable varieties of secular society are the functions exhibited by affective nonrationality. In the unstable type, the fusing of new experience as end with affective nonrationality as means not infrequently reaches the point where the sociation of some members becomes quite unpredictable at the empirical level.[114] The most that can be said about their conduct is that "anything can happen," or that they will "try anything once," or that "they don't know where they are going but they're on their way."

Such a condition of relative normlessness,[115] however, soon becomes intensely disquieting to other members for whom

---

[111] As E. W. Burgess and H. J. Locke seem to imply in *The Family: From Institution to Companionship* (Cincinnati, 1945).

[112] Wiese-Becker, *op. cit.*, pp. 401-407, 565-571.

[113] Which, as already noted, might quite as well be called an adaptive sacred society or a principled secular society. Cf. n. 97 and chap. v.

[114] Although almost entirely predictable in *type* terms of negative character, i.e., what they will *not* do is predictable typologically.

[115] This is an Anglicization of Durkheim's *anomie*. Webster's Unabridged has the English form "anomy," but this is now obsolescent. Nevertheless, even an obsolescent English word would be preferable to such unnecessary use of a foreign term as *anomie* represents. Fortunately, however, "normlessness," following the precedent of "lawlessness," provides an acceptable alternative.

future security, continuing response, and assured recognition also constitute supreme values. These other members, therefore, give expression to *their* affective nonrationalities in ways which simultaneously serve, although in varying degree, all four major ends. New experience as such is not sought, but rather there is an effort to achieve *new experience compatible with other goals*.[116] Normlessness calls forth demand for norms, although in most instances this demand is not fully articulate, and occasionally may not be put into words at all.

Using the Mormon example again: The society of part of rural New York State had undergone extensive secularization[117] by the time of Joseph Smith's boyhood. Freak gospels, clashing ways of life, and itinerant prophets made their disconcerting appearance even in quiet village communities. The countryside had undergone revivals so frequently that evangelists referred to it as "burnt out." Relative normlessness prevailed, and many persons longed agonizingly for a new way of life which would grant equal claim to "new" and "way of *life*."

Certainly the little cluster of followers around the charismatic Smith valued their new experience highly, but his teachings, in spite of their confused and fragmentary character, also provided assurance of fellowship and well-being within an ongoing community of the faithful. The successive migrations which that community underwent consolidated both the Mormon hope and the Mormon determination, and the United Order finally set up in the valleys of the Rockies testified to the fact that a highly sacred society may emerge from conditions of marked secularization.

The affective nonrationality finding vent in miscellaneous cults, sects, "intellectual" fads, and passionately espoused ide-

[116] Here is something remotely comparable to Sorokin's "principle of limits" without, it is hoped, any animistic overtones. It also bears some resemblance to certain Marxian ideas, without, let us fondly fancy, an unduly large trace of what Lundberg has aptly termed "dialectical immaterialism."

[117] In the early nineteenth century parts of New York State were still of semi-frontier character. Add to this the complications of Erie Canal hell-raising, Shakerism, vociferous civil war among the sects of Protestantism, the rovings of tramp printers and garrulous peddlers, the upheavals following the War of 1812, and many other occurrences, and it becomes plain that a rural society may manifest a considerable degree of secularization.

ologies may therefore serve both as (1) a solvent of remaining sacred traits lending a rapidly secularizing society whatever stability it still possesses and as (2) a precipitant of new sacred deposits around which stable structures rapidly crystallize. Normlessness, in short, tends to call forth its own antidote; "the most that can be said of any society is that it is highly secularized or is secularizing rapidly, for sacred components always remain, are regenerated, or are developed afresh in some form" (p. 67).

XXII. PERSONALITIES CHANGE THE WORLD
AND VICE VERSA

Time and again attention has been called to the fact that societies are woven out of social actions. A corollary of this is that social actions issue from actors whose personalities in turn are constituted by the socially assigned roles they play and the ways in which they play them. It follows, therefore, that additional light may be thrown on needs, values, means, ends, and the contexts of sociation into which they enter by viewing some of the personality types relevant to a crucial phase of the total analysis and description.

This phase may be limited, for present purposes, to personality types appearing in conjunction with change from primarily sacred to primarily secular society. Examples are abundant, for social and cultural anthropologists, social psychologists, and sociologists have in recent years devoted a large share of their attention to precisely these phenomena.[118] Suffering from too much material rather than too little, then, it seems wise for us to distill the essence of the voluminous data rather than to attempt to be unduly specific.

To begin with, change from sacred to secular ordinarily takes much more than one generation, but having registered awareness of this fact, we shall proceed as though in most instances only one or two generations are involved. The gain in

---

[118] See my article, "Processes of Secularisation," *Sociological Review* (*British*), XXIV (April-July, October, 1932), 138-154, 266-286. See also the articles on sociology appearing in the *Encyclopaedia Britannica Yearbook* from 1941 to the present, as well as in the special Britannica volume, *Ten Eventful Years, 1937-1946.*

brevity probably offsets any slight distortion. Further, there is no intention of setting forth more than a few prominent traits of each of the type personalities, and these will be sketched merely as types, not as "real" individuals.[119] Still further, only seven types will be presented, although it would be entirely possible to isolate several more. Here again space dictates the limits of our analysis, more especially as the chart on subtypes of secular societies, given in Chapter V, can readily be adapted by the reader to a survey of personality subtypes.

XXIII. THE UNSOCIALIZED

First in logical order, but not necessarily in actual sequence, is the amoral or unmoral personality exemplified in many slum, trailer camp, and "defense town" children. Frequently the offspring of parents themselves rooted in tradition and prescription, these children, as is often all too plainly apparent, "just ain't never had no bringin' up." They are like the child outlaws of postrevolutionary Russia, or many of the waifs and strays among the "displaced persons" left adrift after World War II, i.e., literally *wild* children. The rapidity of the societal transition has been so great that their behavior follows the symbolically undefined channels of raw and prepared needs. Lacking definition, their responses are erratic and frequently unpredictable. "Broken homes," when they have been broken early and completely enough to deprive children of adequate and socially approved formative influence on personality growth, often turn out similar products.

Such children are not disorganized or maladjusted; they are unorganized, unadjusted.[120] Never having been properly inducted into the web of self-and-other relations peculiar to a given society or important part thereof, it is difficult if not impossible to tell what they are likely to do next. Skill in predicting conduct—and everyone who "knows his way around" in a given society has this skill—in some degree depends on familiarity with standard situations and standard roles. If the person under observation has never learned his part in the

[119] See n. 52.
[120] W. I. Thomas, *The Unadjusted Girl* (Boston, 1923), *passim*.

societal drama, does not know what the general expectations of his fellows are, the observer in turn often finds himself unable to tell "which way the cat is going to jump." The raw and prepared needs of the moment are the only ones which govern; there is little or no power of postponement, of inhibition, and the child gyrates from one minute to the next very much on the basis of whether he happens to be hungry, sleepy, or whatnot, at this time or that. The unmoral personality is not really a personality, for the person, strictly speaking, is capable of playing social roles consistently,[121] and hence predictably.

XXIV. THE DESOCIALIZED

The second of our types is the desocialized, or, to use the more common term, the demoralized. Here there has been some incorporation of sacred controls, but the collapse of the old society, or the loss of its buttressing pressure through migration, tears up the props of personality.

The resulting conduct is, in some cases, almost as unpredictable as that of the wild youngsters just mentioned. The appalling traits displayed by juvenile gangsters who have undergone such demoralization are matters of common knowledge; callous torture, rape, and murder unfortunately occur outside the pages of Farrell's *Studs Lonigan*. Similar far-reaching demoralization took place among Thomas and Znaniecki's uprooted Polish peasants carelessly thrust into the stony soil of South Chicago. The conduct appearing among the demoralized frequently falls outside of all traditional and prescribed bounds. Incest, for instance, is a word frequently encountered in the social casework records of such areas.

The recent war and its aftermath provide other examples. Demoralization which would be unbelievable if not all too well documented was manifest not only among the brutalized keepers in German concentration camps but also among their unfortunate victims. Cannibalism did occur, and sexuality of the grossest imaginable kinds was commonplace. The "displaced persons" camps maintained by the Allies after World War II

---

[121] The Latin *persona* referred to the mask worn by the actor when performing any of the standard roles.

have not showed such utter demoralization, but there has been a surprising amount of fairly extreme type. Theft, counterfeiting, "black marketeering," and similar property crimes have become everyday affairs, even among groups which had formerly maintained reasonable standards of honesty.

Significantly enough, the expellees and refugees, who are not "displaced persons" in the technical sense, show relatively little demoralization, for they are Germans or are classified as such, and are not kept in camps on IRO rations. They must shift for themselves as a part of the German community, and because they are regarded by other Germans as such a part, in most cases, their privations do not ordinarily bring about the demoralization from which they would otherwise suffer. The DP's, on the other hand, have only the formless and unstable DP community as a source of social control and a few policemen to impose external restraint. In extreme instances, therefore, demoralization goes almost all the way; the result is often the attempt to maintain order, where the police are concerned, by ruthless use of force. This is usually met by frenzied, savage defense. There is now a maxim among occupation troops that runs as follows: "MP's hate DP's." The maxim also applies in reverse.

XXV. THE SEMI-SOCIALIZED

More frequent in human conduct is partial demoralization, which we may here call segmental. The person in question is held in leash in some segments of his personality by economic or military routine, let us say, but is almost wholly unchecked in other segments, and goes in for "wine, women, and song, without much song." The placing of various segments of conduct in watertight compartments, so characteristic of a highly secular society, of course increases the likelihood of uncontrolled segmental manifestations in some of them. When to this is added the impersonality and anonymity prevalent in big cities, often the focal point of secularization in modern life, there results a state of affairs in which "anything goes."

Even when some restraints remain, there is a large amount of conduct that takes the form of substitute release. For instance, there is much passive adventure, vicarious new experience:

reading about sports, big-game hunting; war; "spectatoritis," and being a "fan"; gambling on sporting events by means of . . . pools or "office pari mutuels"; "playing the market on a shoestring," and similar speculation; getting "thrills" via "human flies," "the talkies," novels, and detective stories.

Another kind of substitute release for segmental impulses is bound up with response in its more crudely sexual aspects; instances are found in:

["tired business man"] musical comedies and "burlesk"; "taxi-dancing"; the libidinous . . . postcard, short story, "unexpurgated edition," . . . "Art Lover's Magazine," and all the *erotica* that the little "arty" bookshops disseminate . . . and so on.

Still another variety of segmental release is found in vaguely expressive conduct in which the affective fusion of means and ends is plainly in evidence:

cults and sects that have no goal beyond that of giving "peace," "health," or "inspiration" to their members; aimless, restless movement such as rapid change of residence and "going for a ride just to be going"; petty crime, useless shoplifting; and many other [substitute] . . . activities practiced by the segmental man.[122]

Societies undergoing rapid change cannot maintain an accrete value system. Ends conflict with each other, and the means to them involve contradictions so serious that personalities are sometimes saved from going to pieces altogether only by resorting to compartmentalization and its segmental accompaniments. For instance, where family life has been defined in ways that cannot be made to fit the total situation, we may encounter the gangster who is a loving husband and father when at home and a coldblooded bombthrower when acquiring the money to keep his home going. The ordinary businessman resorting to cut-throat competition and still passing the plate on Sundays is a less extreme but even more apt example of the segmental man.

[122] This and the two previous quotations are from Wiese-Becker, *op. cit.*, pp. 340-341.

It is probably fair to say that in a society like our own the path of least resistance, in a great many cases, is the path taken by the segmental personality. The achievement of some degree of consistency as between the varying social roles thrust upon the participant in a rapidly secularizing social world is occasionally very difficult. It requires a considerable measure of reflection, ability to focus on essentials, and sincerity with others *and* oneself—all of them capacities not automatically provided by "nature."

It is perhaps because of this difficulty in achieving personal unity that highly secularized societies are shot through with affective nonrationality of cult and "ism" type. Where tradition has lost power and sanctions wane in strength, sheer expediency comes to seem terrifyingly futile as a means of reaching the chief ends of life. The result is a frenzied search for relief from the confusion of segmental conduct by almost any channel leading to adequate affective release,[123] satisfying emotional outlet. Charismatic leaders who provide such release, and promise even more, frequently make strong appeal to segmental followers.

XXVI. THE TRANSITIONALLY SOCIALIZED

Fourth in our list is marginal social action. Sometimes the transition from old sacred to new secular is of such character that a few members of the old society are, as it were, "left hanging in the air." Their accent, gestures, color, diet, or other easily noticeable traits bar them from ready acceptance in the new society, and yet they have wandered so far away from the old that return is impossible. Parents may find their marginal children so unaccountably strange, for example, that living together in the same family becomes impossible.

The possessors of marginal personalities are often highly self-conscious and alert; the equivocal position in which they are placed forces them to be planful, adaptable, and reflective. They frequently resort to sheer expediency in the attainment of their ends, and among these ends recognition and security often loom large. Response in forms suitable to stable family

---

[123] "Adequate" in terms of the situation.

life is often slighted, with the result that marriage either is not entered upon at all or yields satisfaction for only a short time. Relevant instances of marginal conduct are to be found in the "ex-colored man" who poses as white, the partially assimilated Jew, and many other persons living "on the margins of two worlds."

For instance, in cities where the aftermath of Italian immigration is still strongly evident, children may be encountered who talk about "my fadder, dat Dago." Such a child sets himself apart from the world of his parents and yet is not able, because of his own accent and other traces of his background, to find his way into the so-called "native American world." He shuttles back and forth, attaching himself first to one set of loyalties and then to the other, with the result that he never develops any allegiance to anybody but his own divided self.

If possessed of marked native ability, such marginal personalities sometimes achieve, in the battle for recognition and security, positions of considerable prominence. Moreover, they may occasionally develop charismatic traits and thereby secure mass reinforcement. Interesting, to say the least, is the fact that many of the leaders of the Nazi movement, from Hitler down, or up—as the reader prefers—were clearly marginal: an Austrian housepainter, a champagne salesman trying to crash into "society," a crippled art historian who failed to secure a professorial appointment, the son of a German businessman living in Egypt, a flier who had lost status because of drug addiction, and so on.

If the marginal man is not of a type finding relief in aggressive self-assertion, but has expressive ability, he may manage to get along reasonably well in secular society. Instance the fact that many great poets such as Dante, Heine, Burns, Shelley, and Poe have been marginal men in one way or another. Often, of course, the marginal man is unable thus to express himself outwardly, and he therefore develops a fantasy environment of daydreams. Eventually he may retreat so far into an inner world that he cannot find his way back.

His problems have been "solved" by insanity. Even when this final disaster does not come about, his marginal traits may become so firmly fixed that he could never adapt to the new society even if barriers were removed; he is then permanently marginal.

Such persons often do much to speed up social change, for their inferiority feelings demand it; they are permanent neophiliacs. There is not only inability to refrain from responding to the new, but also aggressive activity in furthering it. The permanently marginal are always among the outstanding advocates of "a new world tomorrow," i.e., of rapid and, if need be, violent social change. Hundreds of leaders of cults and sects—religious, economic, or political—have been fixated marginal men, and their followers have rarely doubted their charismatic gifts. Further, in so far as less vehement criticism of existing conditions may bring about peaceful change, albeit at a slow rate, marginal men have played leading parts, for they are likely to be vigorous, searching critics of both foes *and* friends. The sacred-to-secular shift is sometimes difficult to understand if the role of the marginal man is overlooked.

XXVII. THE UNCRITICALLY RESOCIALIZED

A fifth result of transition from sacred to secular is found in the regulated personality, of which the once-famous Babbitt and the 200 per cent American offer classic examples. The regulated person so wholeheartedly abandons his own standards, and so uncritically adopts the new, that secular patterns almost at once acquire sacred significance. Himself of rural background, he holds "hicks" in contempt; of south European stock, he nevertheless despises "Wops" and "Hunkies." Family life is remodeled along the latest "Amurrican" lines, and Momma must starve herself slim or witness the victories of the "gold digger." Perhaps she both starves *and* witnesses. For Poppa all is well; is he not even as other men? Is he not a "regular feller?"

The regulated man has simply exchanged one set of absolutes for another, although in many cases there has been an intermediary period of demoralized or marginal character. In

almost all instances, moreover, regulated conduct is also segmental. This arises from the fact that uncritical espousal of
everything thought worthy or advantageous in the new secular
world means that the segmental conduct which is one of its
most striking features is likewise espoused. "When in Rome,
do as the Romans do, and do it completely, irrevocably, without doubt or hesitation"—such is the regulated man's all-
sufficing credo.

XXVIII. THE SOPHISTICATEDLY SOCIALIZED

The decadent personality, sixth of the types presented,
manifests in well-marked form some of the more extreme consequences of secularization. In some respects similar to the
demoralized personality, or even to the segmental, the decadent
is even more strikingly akin to the unmoral. The chief difference is that decadence as here presented is chiefly found among
persons of the leisure class whose status shields them from
the more immediately disastrous consequences of their erratic
conduct.

Everything that was previously said about the compulsive
search for variety is applicable here, and we need not expand
much further. It should be pointed out, however, that unwillingness or inability to *refrain* from responding to the new
not only brings feverish, hither-and-yon restlessness, but also
is dogged by boredom. After all, the capacities of the human
organism for response to fresh stimuli are limited, and the
decadent readily grows "tired of it all." Marriage partners
may be changed with Hollywood frequency, but eventually
old experience can no longer be made to seem new. Children
may be welcome for a time as playthings, but when they turn
out to be as bent on new experience as are their parents, and
to be quite as indiscriminate in their choice of expedients and
affective thrills, they become too troublesome to be amusing.
The plain fact is that nothing is more elusive than the bluebird
of happiness if directly pursued, and a sense of baffled futility
and maddening monotony overtakes its too zealous votary. He
is in a mood to "try anything once"—anything from psychoanalysis to hashish to flagellation to "second religiosity."

This extreme susceptibility to change frequently means that the tempo and volume of change reach a crescendo. The more one is a beneficiary of change, so to speak, the more one *must* be a beneficiary of change. The more frequent the relief from boredom by new sensual or other stimulation, the more frequent *must* be the relief from boredom. The process is never-ending, and in many of the decadent personalities encountered we find a sense of maddening monotony, a feeling of futility, and a desire to do anything rather than what one is doing at the moment. Neophilia in extreme form dominates. There is no saving routine; there is no work ethic. The result, of course, is that history is a cemetery, not of aristocracies as such, as Pareto mistakenly thought, but of decadent personality types who, in particular, are utterly unable to carry on the duties of responsible family life and citizenship.[124]

XXIX. THE EMANCIPATEDLY SOCIALIZED

Seventh and last of these personality types epitomizing, as it were, various modes and rates of the shift from sacred to secular is what may be termed the liberated. It will be recalled that in the discussion of stable and unstable secular societies the statement was made that the stable kind might with almost equal warrant be designated as "adaptive sacred society." This warrant issues out of the fact that stability derives from a value-system which, in its essential aspects, is devoted to ends that are in some measure accrete, fused, in harmony with each other. Members of such a society do not, figuratively speaking, jump on their horses and ride off in all directions at once; they do not pursue, where the key phases of their personalities are concerned, a chance collection of discrete ends. In important respects, they are at one with themselves and their society. Note that the phrase is "important respects," and not "*all* respects." Any society that is not utterly totalitarian makes allowance for inconsistency. If inconsistency is too strong a term, let us then say that such a society permits the pursuit of ends which would be mutually exclusive if treated as absolutes rather than

[124] P. A. Sorokin, *Social Mobility* (New York, 1927), chaps. xxi, xxii, has some interesting remarks on decadent personality types. So also has Niles Carpenter, *The Sociology of City Life* (New York, 1931), chaps. vi-x, xiii, xiv.

as relative goals subject to considerations of balance, mutual adjustment, or the like. At bottom, this means that the liberated man is the sort of person who without serious loss of integrity more or less successfully "makes the best of both worlds."

Otherwise phrased, the liberated man possesses a stout set of working principles, or even prejudices; unlike the decadent personality, he refuses to "try anything once." He is "not the first by whom the new is tried, nor yet the last to lay the old aside." This is tantamount to saying that his key needs and values have been imparted in a sacred context of folk or prescribed variety, thus indicating refusal or reluctance to change in these crucial respects, but in these crucial respects only.

In matters which the liberated man regards as nonessential, change may not only be welcomed but actually sought for eagerly. Although basic family relations, friendship and intimacy, community life, religion, and even politics may all be tinged with conservatism, at the same time ways of getting a living, of dealing with nature, of conducting affairs with outsiders, may be marked by readiness to accept or bring about innovation. The new as such is not esteemed under any and all circumstances, but neither is it always scorned. Neophobia and neophilia balance each other, so to speak, which is one reason why the liberated personality has elsewhere been termed "the tight-rope-walker adjusted."[125]

The rapid transition from one value-system to another frequently brings with it, as William James and Teggart have pointed out, the release of latent or potential energies previously held in check. This release may accelerate the disorganizing tendencies that sudden change always calls forth, with resulting demoralization; but if the new value-system is more complex and/or adequate to the total situation than was the old, there may be genuine liberation in the sense of a surge of creative power. Accordingly, Thomas and Znaniecki's description and analysis of "the creative man" in most respects

[125] In my mimeographed radio lectures, *Man in Society* (Madison, Wis., 1941), p. 71.

coincides with the present treatment of the liberated personality type.

A point of much importance with regard to liberation is that the flood of energy is at least partially held within channels leading to the higher levels of achievement in secular society. The channels are rarely those of expediency alone, although certainly success in the modern world demands due heed to expediency. Beyond this, however, there must ordinarily come about a broadening of traditional or sanctioned channels which permits the use of the released energies in directions not deviating greatly from those first followed.

The result is that the liberated man, unlike the marginal, is more or less in accord with the new secular world. The marginal man either withdraws from a social reality too much in conflict with the ends to which he is devoted, or else attempts to master it by sheer expediency or shatter it by revolt. The liberated man, in contrast, is likely to follow a policy making full use of the opportunities existing in secular society for the attainment of his ends, or at the most to propose only modification of that society. The marginal man is inclined to be idealistically aloof, cynical, or revolutionary. The liberated man, although not necessarily lacking in idealism, works with what he has at hand, has confidence in the worthwhileness of his own efforts, and is an advocate of gradual change or, at the very least, does not engage in revolution for revolution's own sweet sake.

It sometimes happens, of course, that liberation is a temporary matter. Adaptation to the new society may be so complete that the energies of release are soon dammed up again, and a variety of regulated man makes his appearance—the type called the Philistine by Thomas and Znaniecki.

In those cases, however, where a balance between release and the reorganization of personality within a secular framework is achieved, the new equilibrium is dynamic, and the liberated man remains liberated. Such persons have acquired a value-system which is flexible without sacrificing supreme ends of essentially sacred character. In other words, they have become mentally accessible and mobile[126] without falling prey to normlessness; they have met the crisis which shift from the rigidly sacred to the secular always generates without becoming permanently disorganized.

It should be pointed out, however, that in the contemporary world, liberated men are not, typically speaking, likely to be great creative geniuses in the field of expression. Poetry, music, drama, the fine arts, and other manifestations of the expressive culture[127] are at present judged great only when they are the product of inner struggle. The marginal man or even the segmental man is therefore more likely to be expressively successful in modern secular society than is the liberated man. The latter, on the other hand, is better fitted to undergo the discipline of science, or even to be a secular "man of action," than is the marginal man or any of the other types. The reason for this seems to be that such pursuits demand personalities that are considerably individualized and mentally mobile, but that are not so markedly mobile in their affective aspects as are those suited to the directly expressive arts.

The liberated man is in a state of moving balance on a tight-rope twisted out of both sacred and secular strands. The other personality types have not effected the combination of sacred and secular—a combination that requires skill, good luck, and sustained effort. Apart from a few ventures, past and present, in liberal education, there has been no planned production of liberated men. This is not at all surprising, for there is little knowledge of how to produce them and little genuine demand for their production. Moreover, it is extremely difficult even to discuss liberation, for most of us like to fancy ourselves lib-

---

[126] See Barnes and Becker, *STLS*, *passim*, for discussions of mental mobility.

[127] Here reference is made to James W. Woodard's distinction between the expressive, the control, and the technical aspects of any given culture. Expressive: the arts of all varieties, plus much of religion, philosophy, recreation, and other activities which are directly related to their ends rather than functioning as intermediary steps. Control: the mores, laws, regulations, modes of domination, governmental systems, and so on. Technical: all the devices of the culture, whether nonmaterial or material, which serve to extend man's power over the world about him.

It should be noted, incidentally, that Woodard's tripartite division is somewhat more useful, for many purposes, than the material-nonmaterial distinction to which Ogburn, more than any other sociologist, has given currency.

erated. *We* never have blind prejudices, but only firm principles, and *we* never either stubbornly resist or carelessly welcome change, for *we* are always eminently reasonable and intelligently adaptable.

Nevertheless, it seems clear that the liberated man is not entirely a product of the imagination, even though the examples which can be found in real life usually have some marginal, segmental, regulated, and even decadent or demoralized traits as well. The fact that an element is rarely if ever found in nature except in mixture with other elements does not mean that it cannot be isolated by proper analysis.

The upshot of these considerations seems to be that the really Good Life, in any day and generation, and however defined, cannot be lived without a Good Society and the Good Personalities intertwined with it. If we are to be saved at all—and that is a large "if"—we must be saved both individually *and* collectively.

XXX. LOOKING BACKWARD AND FORWARD

We now have before us some rough indications of the ways in which human needs and values grow and intertwine, of the development of genuinely human conduct in and through sociation, of the means and ends of sociative endeavor, of the main contexts within which this endeavor may run its course, and of the kinds of personality that produce and are produced by the transition from sacred to secular. Let it again be noted that the path from one polar societal type to the other is not a one-way street; all around us can be seen evidence of the fact that societies, even "modern" societies, can journey from secular to sacred. Historical priority and ease of exposition and illustration alone have governed our choice of the sacred-to-secular route; we are not advocating such a route, much less drawing it on the social map as a philosophy of history.[128]

With our universe of discourse thus established, we can analyze social actions and groupings with some hope of seeing the forest as well as the trees. Rarely, however, will the

---

[128] See the chapter on "Prospects of Social Change as Viewed by Historian and Sociologist," esp. pp. 158-168.

pendulum reach the extremes of ultrasacralization or ultra-secularization. Most family affairs, for example, in most parts of the world represent a mixture of the contrasting kinds of sociation. Only when considered in its wider context can we hope effectively to estimate what the family's functions are—in a world that has been shifting back and forth between sacred and secular for a long time. These functions, in the ordinary American sociological tradition, are commonly held to be seven: (1) reproduction of population; (2) protection and care of the child; (3) economic production of family goods and services; (4) socialization of the child; (5) education of the child; (6) recreation; and (7) affectional interaction. If we ask ourselves this question: "What are the differences in the way each of these functions is carried on when a society is sacralizing and when it is secularizing?" we will have done much to organize our thinking about the family, at least, in a lastingly useful way.

The study of the family, of course, is only a single illustration of the possible analytical applications of our proposed frame of reference. The efficiency with which we analyze the state, the church, the political party, the pressure group, the religious revival, and the clique of Bohemian artists is determined, in great degree, by the simultaneous or prior analysis of the context of socially embodied values within which they appear. In the sense in which they have been discussed in this essay, values and value-systems are indispensable tools of sociological analysis.

CHAPTER II

CONSTRUCTIVE TYPOLOGY IN THE SOCIAL SCIENCES

I. A DILEMMA AS FALSE AS MOST

THE DILEMMA of the particular and the general has long plagued social scientists of every description. Even the inveterate "other-things-being-equal" generalizer can scarcely fail to be aware that the society he is examining at the moment is unique in spite of all resemblances to other societies. Dismissing Platonic and Nietzschean objections, it is quite safe to assume that the specific configuration of phenomena presented by any given society at any given time will never be repeated—literally, never. And yet we are seldom content with a collection of unrelated snapshots, however startling or otherwise edifying those candid camera glimpses may be. Unless we are intellectual kodak fiends, a particularized description of the culture of the Scottish Lowlands from January 16, 1738, to March 7, 1739, does not fully satisfy our strictly scientific cravings. Not only do we wish to apprehend the unique, but as social scientists we also want to make a few generalizations. (Under "social scientists" may be included all those who conceive their function in the division of labor to comprise some measure of generalization about social matters; certain heterodox historians,[1] and most socio-cultural anthropologists, economists, political scientists, and psycho-sociologists, as well as the out-and-out sociological generalizers, would therefore be listed.) If sociology, in particular, means anything at all, it means at least the ability to say wherein the society

[1] Here the reference is *not* to "the new history," for this much-praised innovation is a methodological tangle. A little psychiatry, a little Marxism, a little "social-mindedness," a little free thought—"and they all live together in a funny little house." No, I refer to earnest researchers such as Toynbee, Alfred Weber, Xenopol, and other persons interested in "facts of repetition" (within a definite frame of reference) rather than in "facts of succession." See the chapter on "Prospects of Social Change as Viewed by Historian and Sociologist," pp. 128-188.

in question is like other societies and wherein it differs from them.

More is involved here than is apparent at first glance. For example, even those cultural anthropologists who, still following the recent mode, have simply changed allegiance from Morgan to Boas, and who therefore justify their existence by pointing out intercultural differences rather than similarities, presumably proving thereby that comparison is impossible, are forced to keep their eyes tightly closed. If they did not, they would be compelled to see that no one can say wherein a society differs from others unless a background of likeness, however vague, is simultaneously presented or tacitly assumed. In other words, absolute anti-comparison is impossible, for assertions of difference inevitably involve comparison, and two entirely discrete entities cannot be compared. The specialists in cultural differentials who maintain that no intercultural comparisons can be made are therefore busily engaged in sawing off the branch on which they sit. After all, however, very few cultural anthropologists belonging to this school take their anti-comparative oaths of allegiance with completely straight faces; the extreme type of particularism is better and more legitimately represented in other quarters.

Instance the orthodox monographic historian sworn to Ranke's dictum that his task is to depict the past *wie es eigentlich gewesen*—"as it actually and peculiarly was."[2] He is firmly convinced, as he rightly should be, that the body of materials which he happens at the moment to be analyzing is *this* body of materials and nothing else. He holds that history does not repeat itself if it is history presented as the description of things and happenings in their full "thisness." More technically put, the historian correctly maintains that he

---

[2] *Eigentlich* has been translated as "actually and peculiarly" because nothing else seems quite adequate. If Ranke had simply said *wirklich*, then "actually" or "really" would have been sufficient, but *eigentlich* is another story. *Eigen* means "own"; *eigentümlich* means "peculiar" or "unique." *Eigentum* means "property," "attribute," or "its (or 'his' or 'her') own," as in Max Stirner's *Der Einzige und Sein Eigentum*, customarily translated as *The Ego and His Own*. *Eigentlich* therefore has a connotation of "peculiarly" or "uniquely" as well as its more obvious meaning of "really" or "actually."

is a specialist in idiography, in the description of the unique. As the Scholastics said, he deals with the "haecceity," the "this-and-no-other" aspect, of time sequences in human affairs. The vitally necessary function of the idiographic historian should be plain to every unprejudiced social scientist; the "thisness" of events *must* be made clear. Even when they merely suspect disparagement or allegations of generalizing tendencies, however, many monographic historians energetically rise to defend their particularistic function as narrators of "as it actually and peculiarly was," as expounders of *specific* configurations of men and their doings. Such prompt and vigorous defense is certainly warranted when the disparagement or allegations mentioned are real and not imaginary—although, to be sure, some historians have delusions that the indispensability of their task in the scholarly division of labor is not fully recognized. Under the stress of such delusions, and in the heat of conflict, the embattled historian frequently goes to the extreme of assuming that nothing but the unique, the particularized, can be dealt with in the entire field of the social sciences. His legitimate rejection of generalization for *his own* definitely assigned task may lead him to assert that no generalizations with regard to human conduct should ever be attempted—in short, that there can be no social *science*. He says, in effect, "I know Jock Elliott—intimately. In all the wide world there is no one like him, and consequently you cannot say anything about types of the Scottish Lowlander. The history of the stretch 'south of Tay and north of Tweed' is nothing but a collection of individual biographies, and must remain so."

This is certainly forthright enough, but as we shall see, the most orthodox monographic historian is usually compelled to deal with units much larger than the individual. He may single out a few "great men" or "climactic events" as most representative of the given culture and period, and deal with them more or less exhaustively, but he is forced to use highly general terms when laying in the background: medieval Papacy, Calvinism, Whigs, Jacobites, Highland clan organization, the national state system, or what not. Nevertheless, as contrasted with his polar opposite, the sociologist, this historian remains highly particularistic.[3]

The sociologist, on the other hand, sometimes becomes so engrossed in the forest that he cannot see the trees. He could not for the life of him tell you whether he is dealing with a pine forest or a fir forest, or a spruce forest; it is just a forest. This is not in and of itself a handicap; sometimes knowledge of the mere existence of a forest in a given territory, to continue a useful cliché, is scientifically worth while. Nevertheless, neglect of the constituent elements, of the pines, firs, and spruces in the interrelated whole which the forest represents, might make it impossible to say very much that is ultimately worth while—if the specifically scientific criterion of *prediction* determines worthwhileness—about what may happen to that forest in terms of dominance, invasion, succession, and similar ecological sequences. And so too with social life; witness the fact that knowledge of the distribution of population in rural Scotland, in terms of relative sparseness alone, provides very little aid when the immediate task is the prediction of success or failure, not only from the cash-crop standpoint but also from that of subsistence farming, long-term familial adaptability, and survival. Neglect of typical differences between Scottish Borderers, Lowlanders, Highlanders, and Islanders deprives the observer whose chief reliance is the telescope, so to speak, of almost every vestige of predictive power. In other words, the sociologist's general knowledge is sometimes so excessively general that it is of virtually no value in saying what may occur in certain type situations within the foreseeable future.

II. THE HISTORICAL AND THE SOCIOLOGICAL CANDIDES

Both directly and by implication the word "predict" has been used. This gives a clue to a definition of science, or of scientific activity, that may perhaps make it possible to bring together these considerations relating to the particular and the general in a somewhat more meaningful way. For the ends

[3] See the essays on "Interpretative Sociology and Constructive Typology," pp. 189-247, and "Prospects of Social Change as Viewed by Historian and Sociologist," pp. 128-188.

now in view, let us define science as *the systematic statement of the probability of the hypothetical or actual recurrence of phenomena that for the purposes in hand are regarded as identical*. Without attempting in this chapter to define sociology, it may be said that this definition can be fitted to any generalizing social science, well enough for present needs, simply by inserting the word "social" immediately before "phenomena." When quantitative precision seems possible, it is advisable to insert the word "statistical" just before "probability." The phrase would then run "the statistical probability[4] of the hypothetical or actual recurrence of social phenomena that for the purposes in hand are regarded as identical."

Let us now go on to analyze the various parts of this definition as they bear on the problem of the general and the particular.

It has been said, in effect, that the scientist is not interested in the unique *as such*. Fully to know Jock Elliott I must respond to him as a total personality whom I shall never meet again under any other guise. He must be responded to emotionally as well as intellectually; indeed, the element of evaluation, of praise or blame, is inevitably involved. But for the scientist *qua* scientist, Jock Elliott in his ultimate essence—perceived, as it were, by mortal eye—need not be known at all, still less judged on moral grounds. It may be enough to be able to place him at a certain point in a statistical distribution

---

[4] It seems wise to stress the point that "statistical probability" means just that, and *not* "degree of belief probability." The actuary uses the term in *our* sense when he says, "There is a greater probability that a man of age thirty will attain his fortieth birthday than there is that he will attain his fiftieth." Contrasting with this usage, we have historical statements such as, "There is a greater 'probability' [i.e., plausibility] that Caesar visited the site of the present city of London than that he visited the site of the present city of Edinburgh." In the latter case, the word is used by the historian as an indication of his "degree of belief" in the statement. This belief is based on the information available about Caesar's travels, and the statement deals with a journey believed to have been made by this very Caesar. Not this "degree of belief" *plausibility*, but "actuarial" *probability*, is the kind that concerns us throughout this chapter.

Incidentally, it may be noted that one of the reasons for distinguishing between Weber's ideal-typical method and the constructive typology set forth here lies in the distinction between "objective possibility" and "objective probability." See the chapter on "Sacred and Secular Societies: Retrospect and Prospect," esp. pp. 259-262.

of height or weight. Or again, he may simply represent a good specimen of *Homo europaeus*. Once more, Jock Elliott may have teeth that make a dental mold an object of enthralling study. There are many things about him in which the scientist, necessarily a specialist in greater or lesser degree, is professionally interested—but not because these things are identified with Jock Elliott as *this* person and no other. His "thisness" is not a matter of scientific concern.

And here a warning notice must be posted. *Interest in the unique is in and of itself worth while.* No derogation of such interest is intended by refusing to apply the scientific label. Life as it is lived by us as total human beings assumes final meaning only as a set of ineffable, deeply significant relations with other persons now alive or dwelling in a past that may be more "real" than the present. Yet, however keenly we may be aware of such ultimates, absorption in them is not justification for a specialized *scientific* activity. The scientist necessarily deals with the general, not the unique.

Take any object turned out in thousands by mass production methods—a Grand Rapids chair, let us say. In pursuit of the ideal of a full description of the unique, it would be quite legitimate to include a treatise on the structure of the cosmos. A full description would involve precisely that. To begin with, the observer would have to push beyond the externalities of the wood, its growth, and the soil and climate that nourished it, to its basic cell characteristics, and from there to the atomic structure of the elements making it up. Following this, the periodic table would have to be expounded, for each element can be fully described only in conjunction with its place in the "family" of elements, and behold, the atomic and subatomic "solar systems" loom before us as we gaze "at each other with a wild surmise. . . ." But the end is not yet. In analyzing the vagaries of electrons, protons, and all the other "-ons," questions of quantum theory and the nature of light arise, and we have arrived at the frontiers of the universe, "where dwell the three Grey Sisters who have but one eye and one tooth between them."

From here let us go back to Grand Rapids. Numerous special histories would be tied in with each stage of this fantastically impossible task of full description. For example, there is no compelling reason, if the goal of *"all* the facts" beacons to us from afar, why the biographies of the multitude of workmen who were engaged in the building of this chair should not be included. Genealogy is an enticing study, too; why not go back to Charlemagne, or at least as far as the records in the College of Heralds will permit? Further, a full description, with no limitations, of "as it actually and peculiarly was," would lead to the question as to how the particular chair came to be dealt with, and why the particular describer made contact with it at a given time and a given place, and at no others. What a lot of interesting details for the man who abhors "preconceived limitations" on the scope of his research, and who therefore says that he simply gathers all the facts and lets them speak for themselves! Yet all this is very clearly in the realm of the unique, and, quite as clearly, little if any of such a nonlimited description of "as it actually and peculiarly was" is of scientific concern.

Obviously, too, there are certain aspects of such a chair that can be isolated and dealt with from a specifically scientific standpoint. To refer to the definition of scientific activity presented above: *For the purposes in hand* there are certain things about this chair that can be regarded as identical with other aspects of other chairs. They are not precisely the same, and they never will be, but for the purposes in hand the scientist can regard the external form of chair number 2002 as the same as that of all the chairs in the 2000 series. Minute examination will show that the external form is far from the "same" in each case, that determinable differences between chair and chair are inescapably present. If, however, the purposes in hand are of sufficiently general type, it may be quite safe to say that chair 2002 is the same as 2003, even though in the ultimate and final sense it is not and cannot be.

Many persons will grant these conditions where inanimate objects are concerned, but they have mental reservations, to say the least, when human conduct is under scrutiny. It must be granted that some of these reservations are warranted. Neglect of the meaning attached to conduct by the persons engaged in it, because the sociologist supposedly analyzing that conduct really wishes to pursue fanciful analogies that liken societies to solar systems, organisms, or conglomerations of atoms, has oftentimes earned well-merited criticism for such sociologists. But in the researches of many of the more penetrating and sober workers (now happily increasing in number) the meaningful aspects of social conduct are never ignored. They would agree that certain aspects of the meaningful conduct of Jock Elliott can be isolated for study, that for the purposes in hand it is possible to say that what Jock Elliott is doing at the moment is the same as the conduct in which Louie Rosenblum is simultaneously engaged halfway around the world, or was engaged in two weeks ago, or two years ago, or two centuries ago—under certain typical circumstances. When the idiographic historian says, "Each human being is unique, and the social situations in which he has developed are unique, and history never repeats itself in any ultimate or final sense," the modern sociologist can reply, "I agree with you, quite. True, history never repeats itself. And yet, my dear fellow, for certain purposes, which are not those of the idiographic historian, it may be entirely legitimate to say that certain phenomena can be bracketed with certain other phenomena. Let us each play the part of Candide, each in his own garden, and each in his own way."

The dilemma of the particular and the general, then, boils down to a question of purpose. What are the purposes in hand? If you wish to appreciate to the full the characteristic essence of the culture of the Scottish Border, let us say, you steep yourself in the folk song, the literature, the poetry, the arts—and how much more!—of that culture. In so doing you acquire kinds of sensitivity and of learning that may enable you to communicate, to others less sensitive or less erudite, some notion of what it meant, and still means, to grow up an heir to The Debateable Land north of the Cheviots, to be born within sight of "three crests against a saffron sky, beyond the purple plain." To be sure, you come to *know*, in a final and irreducible sense, some things about the Border that you cannot communicate to anybody directly: only in the nuances of style, the overtones of the written word, can the reader sense the fact that in learning to know the Scottish Border you have yourself become akin to the hard-bitten "raiders and reivers" who once made eternal vigilance a necessity for Northumbrian cattle-owners. There is no need to justify such immersion in and absorption of the particular; the only thing to which legitimate objection may be taken is the sometimes-encountered assumption of the idiographic historian, of biographical persuasion especially, that we can never deal with anything but the unique. To such a forthright challenge the reply should be equally direct: "We as sociologists can deal with the general because, if you will, *we are going to construct the general.* You as an idiographic historian wish to saturate yourself in the lore of the Scottish Border and to communicate to others the insights you thereby gain; we want to be able to predict within the framework provided by constructive typology."

The possibility of prediction is in many respects limited, and yet the ultimate criterion of scientific generalization in sociology, at least, is whether or not the goal is the prediction of the recurrence of social phenomena. The purpose in hand must be geared to the problem of predicting what may happen under certain circumstances. There are many other valid purposes, and there is no need unduly to exalt the role of the scientist or of the sociologist in so far as he is a scientist. The scientific role is but one of many, and that man is poor indeed, where the essential resources of his total personality are concerned, who is and can be merely a scientist. In stating, therefore, that the purpose of prediction is the specific criterion of scientific activity, I do *not* assert that being a scientist is more desirable than being, let us say, a poet, an idiographic historian, or some other disciple of the unique. Is it a question of either—or? Must we choose between Weber and Ranke?

Between Adam Smith and Walter Scott?   Between Darwin and Shakespeare?

III. SOCIOLOGICAL FADS AND ORTHODOXIES

So much for purpose. The next part of the definition of scientific activity to which attention should be directed is the item of recurrence. It will be recalled that "the prediction of the hypothetical or actual recurrence of social phenomena" was the phrase used. Why is it necessary to speak of "hypothetical or actual"? Because much of the recurrence with which the sociologist deals is hypothetical only; certain types of social conduct recur *if and when* certain conditions are given, and those conditions may be impossible to reproduce at will. The recurrences of the conduct are hypothetically there, as it were, but they may never become actual. Could we make them actual whenever we wished, we could carry on sociological experiments, and only then.

But in spite of high-sounding phrases in graduate school bulletins about Harlem or rural Iowa or gang-land Chicago as "a sociological laboratory," most sociologists know full well that they cannot experiment, that they are not laboratory scientists, and that in the opinion of many competent judges they never will be. There has never been real freedom to experiment with human beings except in the inhumanly totalitarian states, and there only for limited periods. When we turn to treatises labeled *Experimental Social Psychology,* for instance, we encounter many patterns of analysis that are called "experimental," but that lack anything remotely approaching experimental control. Power to manipulate persons and social situations at will, for as long a time as may be necessary, is *perhaps* a desideratum, but it certainly is not in the possession of any sociologist. Almost any practitioner of a genuine experimental science would turn up his nose at the loose and haphazard way in which our psycho-sociological and sociological "experimenters" go about their work. They are not to blame for the conditions that make actual control impossible; they are to blame for the direct invitation to criticism which they offer when they talk about "experiment." They use experimental *logic*, if you will, but not experimental *manipulation*. To talk about statistical techniques, such as multiple and partial correlation, as "manipulatory," is simply the licentious use of language.

In likening sociology to other sciences, an analogy much to be preferred to that provided by any of the experimental sciences is afforded by geology. The geologist is indubitably a scientist. He attempts to predict where deposits of lead-bearing ore will be found, where oil supplies can be tapped, where earthquakes are likely to occur as results of subsidence or upheaval. The purpose is prediction, but there is no experiment in any manipulative sense. The geologist is confronted by a series of strata that were laid down, we may safely infer, with no thought that geologists would some day make use of them. Analogously, the sociologist may be faced by a socio-cultural structure in which Negroes, Poles, Mexicans, Italians, and a host of other peoples are piled together indiscriminately with no foreordained plan of interrelation. We are confronted with socio-cultural deposits, in other words, very much like the deposits with which the geologist has to deal.

An analogy that may be even more enlightening is presented by language—itself quite as much a socio-cultural as it is a physiological phenomenon. The comparative philologist cannot experiment with the grammatical structure of Greek; he simply knows, for example, that this language has a middle voice and a dual number and turns initial *s* into an aspirate. It represents one stratum, deposited long ago, in the thick crust of the Indo-European languages. Again, there can be no question of "experiment" where Finno-Ugric is concerned. In Europe one finds it wedged into Hungary and into Finland, and to study it *as functioning, meaningful Finno-Ugric* one goes into the field and the library, not merely into the phonetics laboratory. The meaning of words as significant symbols cannot be determined adequately apart from their interrelations with numerous other words *and* with the conduct involved; indeed, sometimes the larger aspects of the structure of the entire language and of the society using it must be taken into account. Here again there is no experiment, but there can well be science. Grimm's "law" of consonantal change in certain varieties of Indo-European speech is cast in essentially predictive form, and predictions based upon it have been amply verified.

Much of the vogue of sociological "experiment" is explicable in terms of—vogue. The natural science most popular at the moment provides the model: in one generation it is sidereal mechanics; in another, biology; in another, relativity physics. The sociologists who want to construct their science along lines presumably preordained by some other science are very much like the modern Thomists who assume that all phenomena are necessarily amenable to interpretation à la the dictates of "right reason." "Orthodoxy is my doxy, and heterodoxy is your doxy." Such essentially a priori methods of approaching the variegated, kaleidoscopic mosaic called the empirical world are barren.

Any science must develop from the interaction of the scientist's mental processes *and* the data involved. Disregard of the data leads to disregard of science in favor of uncontrolled speculation. The scientist is certainly more than a mere empiricist, but he must be empirical.

The sociologist wishes to predict hypothetical or actual recurrence. The test of the utility of his work is its predictive power, not its conformity to an "orthodox" pattern. Judged in this light, a great deal of current sociological effort is misplaced, to say the least, for the purpose of prediction is not held steadfastly in view. For example, what genuinely scientific purpose is served by Dodd in lifting a collection of definitions of concepts from a secondary writer of Eubank's type, and then restating them in algebraic terms? Confusion becomes worse confounded, and in addition whatever predictive utility that may have existed is almost eliminated. Far better than faith in this transubstantiation ritual, because more open to examination as an act of faith, would be frank avowal of belief in the miracle of the mass. Again, it may be "a lot of fun" to make elaborate diagrams and charts of the social structure of a small town. If, however, it takes three months to do the job, and three weeks to interpret the pretty pictures to anyone else, when in three days the local editor and a few of his "sources" could have given verbal sketches better suited, when properly analyzed, to predictive purposes, might it not have been just as profitable and more enjoyable to have spent the extra time in playing chess? Simply to restate, in more elaborate ways, what informed observers already know and on the basis of which they can successfully construct predictively usable types is not necessarily scientific activity. Topologists, sociometrists, field theorists, and "group dynamists" take note. Not only the form of research, but also its purpose, its focus on the prediction of hypothetical or actual recurrence, and the *pragmatic* validation of that prediction, determines its scientific character. Theoretical relevance it must have, but the internal consistency of a theoretical structure is not enough. The "damned facts" must be faced.

IV. SOME TOOLS OF THE TRADE

Faced as the sociologist is by data not susceptible of experimental manipulation, by time deposits analogous to those dealt with by the geologist or the comparative grammarian, his only recourse is to construct types of social conduct, of social organization, of personality—to *construct* them. This is a very far-reaching statement, involving an epistemological position into the analysis of which there is no present opportunity to go. The statement will simply have to stand as an essential part of the abbreviated record.

Even the idiographic historian, dealing as he does with the unique, and sometimes setting for himself the impossible goal of full description, is forced to make use of constructs. As already noted, he writes about the medieval Papacy, Calvinism, or the national state system. These are all constructed types; not one of them conforms exactly to any specific historical instance. Unfortunately, however, most of the historian's construction of types is unconscious. Scorning "schematism" and "rigid definition" as he does, he often takes over the general notions that happen to be present and, but one step removed from journalism, gathers "all the facts" within the fields thus bounded for him and sorts them into the baskets already provided. In the process the terms of common parlance with which he started slowly acquire altered meanings; new types have been constructed, but not planfully, not deliberately, not with full awareness—there lies the rub.

The historian's types should perhaps be called "dated and localized types" by way of contrast with those used by the sociologist, which are *relatively* "undated and nonlocalized." No socio-cultural types are wholly "timeless" or "spaceless"; as with those upon which the geologist operates, some determination by chronology and location is always present. Nevertheless, it is possible to speak of *relatively* undated and nonlocalized types; here the elements of time and space are not in the foreground, as in the case of dated and localized types.

Using his dated and localized types, few of them explicitly formulated, the historian proceeds with his evocative description of the unique. The absolutely unique is of course beyond his grasp, or at least beyond his power to communicate; and, as we have seen, complete description is an impossibility. It remains evident, however, that the historian's goal is the polar opposite of the sociologist's; here the particular, there the general, and therefore here the dated and localized type, there the undated and nonlocalized.

It has frequently been stated that the sociologist's effort is directed toward prediction. Let us now put it more exactly: The sociologist wishes to be able to say, "Given such and such circumstances, these consequences will follow." He may not be able to produce the circumstances—that is oftentimes a matter of accident. He nevertheless wants to have sufficient knowledge to assert that once there appear configurations of revolutionary phenomena, let us say, that closely approximate certain constructed types, certain consequences have a high probability of ensuing. Revolutions manifestly differ. The English revolution in which Charles I lost his head certainly was not the same as the French revolution in which Louis XVI lost his. This French revolution, in turn, was not closely similar to the American revolution that preceded it, although some revolutionary impetus was undoubtedly derived from the American example. Again, the German revolution of 1918 was in many respects different from the Bolshevik revolution of 1917. Each of these revolutions represents a configuration of events never again to be exactly duplicated. All that the sociologist has to operate with in this case, to use our geological analogy again, are earthquakes or, at the very least, those slippings and slidings of strata that make earthquakes likely. And when he observes given types of fissure, or given types of fold, or given types of volcanic activity, he says, "Given such and such circumstances, these are likely to be the consequences."

After such a preliminary, highly provisional hypothesis has been formed, the sociologist then proceeds to examine as many revolutions as he conveniently can, in the effort to construct a typical set of typical revolutionary personalities, processes, and structures. These constructed types will be the tools with which he will operate. No one of these types will ever be found concretely exemplified. The reason such a type cannot be found in "external nature" resides in the fact that it has been modified by the investigator in accordance with his special background and scientific purpose. It is a *construct*, and hence does not correspond exactly to any unique aspect of the French revolution, for if it did, it would be of no comparative value when the English revolution was to be examined. It is constructed along lines sufficiently general so that it can be set down on this or that portion of the given terrain without tipping over, so to speak, and it then becomes possible to survey that territory. The constructed type is merely a tool. Hence when the methodologically sophisticated sociologist talks about a type of revolution, his hearers can be very sure that it will never correspond exactly to any empirical instance, to any "real" revolution.[5]

[5] In so far as the antithesis "real-ideal" has any instrumental value, it may be said that the constructed type is an ideal type, somewhat similar to, although by no means identical with, the Max Weber model. I now prefer to avoid the use of "ideal" whenever possible, because in the minds of some positivistic sociologists it immediately evokes notions of Berkeleyan idealism, or of perfection in some final sense, or like irrelevancies that should be excluded from the discussion.

It is perhaps permissible to liken this constructed type to the sort of image of the "pure type" Airedale or Percheron that a judge of dogs or of horses carries around in his head as the basis of his "objective" system of scoring for points. He has never seen a "pure type" Percheron or Airedale, but he has seen numerous close empirical approximations of his constructed types. In fact, he has built up these constructed types on the basis of numerous observations. He has observed Airedales with the desired type of rectangular head, with straight front legs, with diagonal stance of the hind legs, with the required angle and length of tail, with curly coat of suitable color, glossiness, and crispness, with the elusive something called "spirit" or "vitality"—and yet no single Airedale has all these traits in the degree "called for" by the type. The judge combines them and many more, lays the stress peculiar to himself on certain "key" traits, and then has a constructed type in the light of which he judges any empirical Airedale. Now the same would hold for a horse. Our Percheron would have literally dozens of desired traits gleaned from close observation and refined up to the limits of the objectively probable, but the final configuration never corresponds to any real horse called Dobbin.[6]

These constructed types are the tools with which we must

In addition to this reason for avoidance of the term is the fact that my divergence from Weber steadily becomes greater. Specifically, my own work stresses "probability" in the sense that I insist on the necessity of finding close empirical approximations of constructed types. The "plausible" is insufficient (see n. 4). But in the present context it is possible to say that the constructed type is an "ideal" type in the sense that it does not exactly fit any single empirical instance. The "classical case" of the physician is "ideal" in this sense. The set of revolutionary processes and structures worked out by our hypothetical investigator is an ideal set. He constructed it on the basis of numerous observations of many empirical revolutions, but they never "exactly" fit the type. If they do seem to fit frequently, as a matter of fact, there may be something wrong with the type. It is probably too particular or, what amounts to the same thing, not sufficiently general. But this properly belongs in another context, too lengthy to present here, dealing with the problem of "objective possibility," "plausibility," and "probability." See chap. v, "Sacred and Secular Societies: Retrospect and Prospect," esp. pp. 261-262.

[6] Nordic, Mediterranean, Alpine, and like racial classifications are constructs. Ammon, for instance, examined thousands of Rhineland Germans, and never once saw "a real Alpine," although he found many close approximations of the construct.

work. Laboratory experimentation, as we have seen, is to say the least sharply limited in its possibilities. In many instances the "experimentation" must be mental or selectively comparative. The process begins with a vaguely defined problem, the framing of a hypothesis, selective observation (and *all* observation is selective in some sense) with reference to it, and eventual construction of a type, or a battery of them, that aids in further research. (Note the implicit distinction between hypothesis and type; they are all too frequently confused.) The construct may be a type of social organization, a type of personality, or the like. By implication, if not directly, this statement is made: "Under such and such circumstances, this type would probably behave thus and so." And then the researcher looks for cases that provide some kind of comparative checkup on his tentative generalization.

The procedure may be exemplified thus: The existence of contemporary anti-Semitism sets a vaguely defined problem, "What is the source of these 'Jewish' traits to which objection is taken?" The preliminary hypothesis may then be that a number of traits ordinarily regarded as specifically Jewish in the "racial" sense are not the result of biological transmission, but of a peculiar socio-cultural heritage. If the researcher turns first to the past in the quest for data, he may focus on the early contacts with the Phoenicians and other traders, as well as on the "caravaneering" facilitated by the surviving nomadic pattern.

Next, perhaps, he may concentrate on the "middleman" locations characteristic of the Jews before as well as after the Diaspora; they were splendidly placed for the development of extensive trade with many lands. Once more, he may direct his lens toward the dual ethic separating the members of the in-group from those of the out-group—on the one hand, "the chosen people"; on the other, the unclean Gentile. (Many other traits might be listed, but enough has been said to indicate the procedure.) Looking for like phenomena in near-by areas, our investigator may then discover that the Armenians are strikingly similar to the Jews. They too are a trading people with a long history of widespread culture contacts with other traders. Further, they occupied "middleman" positions for a long period, dwelling the while in ghetto-like seclusion from Arab and Turk. Again, they drew the line between ingroup and out-group—you treat the brother Armenian as you would be treated, and you skin the Turk alive, commercially speaking, and nail his hide on the family strongbox.

With two cases partially parallel, it then seems worth while to go about the construction of a type of "marginal trading people." With the Jews as a focus-setting point, certain traits regarded as providing adequate causation[7] for the characteristic conduct have come into view. The selected traits seem to be at least partially relevant to Armenian conduct, and they are therefore worked into a guiding pattern that gives some promise of other empirical approximations. Equipped with this device, the researcher finds that the Parsees on the west coast of India draw into focus. They too are traders with a "middleman" position. Also present is the ideology that cleaves the social world in twain: within the fold is the fire-worshiper who gives the corpse of his beloved to the fowls of the air after death, who has an elaborate Magian ritual, and who is a follower of Zoroaster; in outer darkness is the unclean Hindu on whom the Parsee looks down and whom he exploits whenever necessary. Our researcher looks still farther afield and finds that the Chinese rice trader in the Dutch East Indies represents a fairly close approximation of the construct. Rambling into the interior of Egypt, always on the *qui vive*, he there discovers another trading people with many of the traits usually held to be peculiarly Jewish. These turn out to be the Greeks who migrated into Egypt, beginning in force with establishment of the trading center of Naucratis about the seventh century B.C., filtering slowly southward, ceaselessly trading, maintaining the exclusiveness of the Greek culture in spite of surface assimilation, and feeling themselves infinitely superior to the natives. These Greek traders frequently "played both ends against the middle," and in general approximated the characteristics of a

---

[7] The problem of adequate causation, or causal attribution, is of highest importance, but space limits forbid any attempt to grapple with it here.

marginal trading people. In earlier times they scorned the zoölatry of the Egyptians and held to the Greek pantheon; in later times their faith was Greek Orthodox. At both periods religious exclusiveness was maintained, for even when the wily Greek operated among Christian Egyptians, the latter belonged to the Coptic sect who defined the relation of the Father to the Son to the Holy Ghost in a way quite different from his own.

These approximations are interesting, but an even more arresting result of the survey made possible by the construct is the light thrown on certain Scottish traits. Many Lowland and Border Scots were active in small-scale trade from an early period. They even traded sporadically with the Romans along the line of Hadrian's Wall where Pictish "spearmen and charioteers and bowmen charged, and were scattered into spray." And the Wall, to recall Kipling's graphic character-ization, was "one roaring, rioting, cockfighting, wolf-baiting, horse-taming town, from Ituna in the west to Segedunum on the cold eastern beach." Later the favorably situated Low-landers dealt with the Lords of the Isles, with Red Hugh of Ulster, with "the King of Norroway," with the hated South-ron on his fat acres, with the "uncanny" Hielandman, that "daft body o' the North," with the Dutch, the French, and other queer folk. Then the Reformation came, and Jock Elliott listened to Calvinist Knox, "dingin' the pulpit to blads." Elect, by God's irresistible grace, the Covenanters underwent persecu-tions that sealed their conviction of being dear to Him "who scourgeth every son whom he receiveth." Set apart from the Catholics to the north and the "King-Papist" Anglicans to the south, the Scottish Presbyterians recognized themselves as a chosen people even while droning, with Holy Willie, "O what were we, and what our station, that we should get sic' exalta-tion. . . ?" Trade with the worldly reprobate? Of course. Treat him as you would treat one of the elect, a fellow-Calvinist with the outward signs of inward grace? Doctrinally, "Aye"; in terms of rank-and-file mentality, "Pairhops." (Of course, no Calvinist "sure" of election would *consciously* hold a dual ethic.) Shrewd, competitive, rationalistic, an ascetic *within* the world, "principled," industrious, acquisitive, calling many lands his habitation but only Scotland home, the man from "south of Tay and north of Tweed" still retains, in the midst of the Empire, what Stevenson called "a strong Scots accent of the mind."

The "marginal trading people" type has enabled us to range over a considerable body of data looking for certain specific things. The traits with which we started seemed to be linked with others: high degree of expedient rationality, emotional aloofness where the out-group is concerned, and considerable measure of economic internationalism—not *ubi bene ibi patria*, but "Wherever my *economic* good is found, there is my country." All these traits are in some degree, *within the limits of the construct*, Jewish, Armenian, Parsee, Chinese, Greek, Scottish. The complex configurations from which they are extracted cannot be produced in the laboratory. They are geological deposits, the outcomes of the sedimentations, slippings, and slidings of the earth's strata, as it were. They are socio-cultural structures built up by the slow accumulation of folkways and mores, by rapid, catastrophic changes in the form of wars, migrations, and rise of charismatic leadership, by rational systematization of essentially nonrational values, and so on. And, willy-nilly, the social scientist must work with what he has. Instead of planning research in terms of a virtually unattainable ideal, the laboratory experiment, he must accept the data as they are and adapt his method to the chasms and outcroppings they present. In many instances he will eventually find that he can predict what is likely to happen when certain typical traits turn up in typical relation with each other. He has made one indispensable stride toward realizing his purpose, which is the prediction of the hypothetical or actual recurrence of phenomena that for the purposes in hand are regarded as identical. He does not say that a Scotsman is a Jew; he does say that the existence of certain Scottish characteristics can be predicted—retrospectively, at least[8]—by means of a

---

[8] Prediction in our sense, it will be recalled, may be "retrospective" rather than "prospective." See the chapter on "Supreme Values and the Sociologist," esp. pp. 285-290.

construct that takes the Jew as one of its points of departure, and that for the purposes in hand those Scottish traits can be regarded as identical with these Jewish traits. Jock Elliott and Louie Rosenblum, although widely differing in many respects, nevertheless draw close together in certain phases of their conduct when these are framed within the outlines of a constructed type, the "marginal trading people."[9]

The initial hypothesis that certain characteristics often regarded as "biologically Jewish" are in reality of socio-cultural derivation has in some measure been substantiated, and in addition the constructed type has revealed the possible relevance of traits other than those originally listed. As a means of more definitive checkup, it may next prove desirable to refine the hypothesis by constructing subtypes discriminating more sharply between various kinds of marginal trading conduct, and then to seek statistical demonstration of the varying empirical frequency of the conduct isolated as significant. Whatever method of testing the hypothesis is chosen, it should be clear that the constructed type is not itself a hypothesis, and that it is not self-validating. Facts are stubborn things, and constructed types must be drawn from them and continually thrown back upon them if empty speculation is not to replace sound generalization. Constructive typology offers neither aid nor comfort to wishful thinking. Further, it gives ample room for relevant *quantitative* procedure.

This "marginal trading people" type is well over toward the undated and nonlocalized pole; it is therefore of markedly sociological rather than historical character. It now seems well to consider certain other types which, although primarily sociological in nature, are somewhat closer to the dated and local-

[9] It should go without saying that this brief illustrative sketch of the "marginal trading people" is not intended to stand the fire of criticism. A lengthy monograph would be needed to meet the protest of Elliotts who do not like to be called Rosenblums, or of Rosenblums who do not like to be called Sergenians. (May I note that my maternal ancestry is Lowland Scottish, with a remoter Highland streak?) To forestall some of the clamor, let me say that any adequate typology of a "marginal trading people" would necessarily include subtypes manifesting traits not characteristic of the type most relevant for the purposes in hand. Further, *nothing* has been said about the *numerical frequency* of the type discussed. A really adequate job would involve extensive and complex statistical work.

ized variety with which the historian often operates; their greatest applicability lies within the Christian era. In addition to this element of chronological determination, these types are "spatially" limited; they are designed to aid in the analysis of religious conduct in the Western world. (Some such quasi-spatial limitation must be imposed because of the sharply differing culture base of many Eastern faiths.) In spite of restrictions in scope, however, it must be emphasized that the types to be represented are still sufficiently general to be called sociological; they are introduced here in order to show that particularity and generality are matters of *degree*. If everything is *absolutely* different, there can be no analysis; if everything is *absolutely* identical, there can be no analysis. Sociological types are *relatively* general, but the exact point at which the *relatively* general becomes the *relatively* particular can be determined only in the light of the purposes in hand. Since the purpose in formulating the types to be presented was prediction, not prophecy, they should be regarded as relatively general, and hence as sociological or at least as social-scientific. Quoting from one of the writer's earlier efforts at type construction, and remembering that we are not discussing the validity of beliefs, but merely problems of social process and structure:

In order properly to deal with this vast maze of [Western religious] phenomena, it will be necessary to distinguish several sub-varieties of the [construct] . . . of the church [in the narrower sense]; these sub-varieties are: (1) the ecclesia, (2) the sect, (3) the denomination, and (4) the cult.

(1) The social structure known as the ecclesia is a predominantly conservative body, not in open conflict with the secular aspects of social life, and professedly universal in its aims. The phrase "Come ye out from among them and be ye separate" has no place in the ideology of the genuine ecclesiastic; "Force them to come in" is likely to characterize his thinking. The fully developed ecclesia attempts to amalgamate itself with the state and the dominant classes, and strives to exercise control over every person in the population. Members are *born into* the ecclesia; they do not have to *join* it. It is therefore a social structure somewhat, although remotely, akin to the nation or the state, and

is in no sense elective. Membership in an ecclesia is a necessary consequence of birth into a family, folk, or similar structure, and no special requirements condition its privileges.

The ecclesia naturally attaches a high importance to the means of grace which it administers, to the system of doctrine which it has formulated, and to the official administration of sacraments and teaching by its official clergy. It is in a very real sense an educational institution which, when functioning properly, trains its youthful members to conformity in thought and practice, and thus fits them for the exercise of the religious "rights" they have automatically inherited.

The ecclesia as an inclusive social structure is closely allied with national and economic interests; as a plurality pattern its very nature commits it to adjustment of its ethics to the ethics of the secular world; it must represent the morality of the respectable majority.

Two main varieties of the ecclesia may be distinguished: international and national. The Catholic Church is the most outstanding example of the first, whereas the Lutheran and Anglican varieties illustrate the second.

It should not be supposed, however, that a sharp line can [empirically] be drawn between the two. Catholicism, nominally international, as a matter of fact is pervaded by a great many minor nationalistic rivalries that sometimes flare out in controversy. French Catholicism, for example, sometimes maintains an attitude of marked aloofness toward the Vatican; just before the Reformation it was so thoroughly detached from the papacy that one could justifiably speak of two Catholicisms: French and "other." When all the necessary qualifications are made, however, there is no doubt that the Catholic ecclesia is much more international in character than is any other.

Lutheranism and Anglicanism, to mention . . . two varieties of the national ecclesia, . . . have been extremely nationalistic; they are types which began to flourish when the isolated sacred structure of the Middle Ages began to give way to the new ethnic cultures born . . . soon after the Commercial Revolution shattered the agrarian basis of medieval life.

(2) The sect is in marked contrast to the ecclesia. In the first place, it is a relatively small plurality pattern that has abandoned the attempt to win the whole world over to its doctrines; the phrase "Come ye out from among them and be ye separate" is followed literally. It is readily seen that the sect is a . . . body which one must *join* in order to become a member; [it is elective]. At bottom, the sect is exclusive in character, appeals to strictly personal trends, and emphasizes ethical

demands; it frequently requires some definite type of religious experience as a prerequisite of acceptance. It therefore attaches primary importance to the religious experience of its members prior to their fellowship with the plurality pattern, to the so-called "priesthood of all believers." It frequently rejects an official clergy, preferring to trust for guidance to lay inspiration rather than to theological or liturgical expertness.

In many instances sects are persecuted, but this persecution only reinforces the separatist and semi-ascetic attitude toward the world inherent in the sect as a social structure. At times it refuses participation in the government, . . . rejects war and other resort to force, and . . . seeks to sever as much as possible the bonds which tie it to the common life of the larger . . . [society] within which it develops. In general, the sect prefers isolation to compromise.

Sects exist in great variety at the present time, but they were to be found even before the period of the Reformation, as evidenced by the Cathari, the Waldensians, the Wyckliffites, and others. Since the Reformation, of course, many such bodies have come into being: Anabaptists, Mennonites, Huguenots, Presbyterians, Baptists, and scores of others dot the pages of history.

(3) Denominations are simply sects in an advanced stage of development and adjustment to each other and the secular world. The early fervor of the self-conscious sect has disappeared, as a general thing, by the second or third generation, and the problem of training the children of the believers almost inevitably causes some compromise to be made in the rigid requirements for membership characteristic of the early phases of sectarian development. Thus, for example, the Presbyterians inaugurated the Half-Way Covenant in order that children whose "calling and election" was not yet sure could be held within the fold, with the consequence that in time the greater proportion of professing Presbyterians were those who had gone no further than the Half-Way Covenant. Similarly, the Baptists have gradually lowered the age of "adult baptism" so that at the present time, in some branches of the denomination, it is possible for children only twelve years old to be baptized. Similar instances can be gleaned from the history of almost any sect one cares to name; time inevitably brings compromise.

A further factor in mitigating the mutually exclusive tendency of sects in Western Christendom is the common opposition of all genuinely Protestant bodies to Roman Catholicism. In the early phases of the Reformation members of rival Protestant sects detested each other just as thoroughly as they detested adherents of "Babylon the Mighty"; the burning of Servetus by Calvin is a case in point. With the passage of time, however, opposition to the common foe has gradually drawn the Protestant sects, especially of the evangelical variety, into a vague sort of mutual adjustment; it is tacitly agreed that Protestants should engage in polemics with Rome rather than with each other. . . .

(4) Tendencies toward religion of a strictly private, personal character—tendencies fairly well marked in the sect—come to full fruition in the cult as here defined. The goal of the adherent of this very amorphous, loose-textured, uncondensed type of social structure is not the maintenance of the structure itself, as in the case of the church and sect, but is that of purely personal ecstatic experience, salvation, comfort, and mental or physical healing. Instead of *joining* a cult, an act which implies the consent of others, one simply chooses to believe particular teachings or follow certain practices, and the consent of other members of the cult is not necessary. . . . The religious mystic of the Catholic or Protestant varieties has marked leanings toward the cult, although his mystical practices may be later incorporated in the general body of sanctioned behavior.

The sources of emotional satisfaction for the cult believer lie wholly within himself; the injustices or good fortune which others may suffer affect him, to be sure, but the center of his cosmos is his "I".

Only a highly atomized and essentially secular social order gives rise to extensive cult belief. The frontier cities of Ionia, Athens in the famous fifth century . . . , the cities of the Italian Renaissance, and the urban centers of the modern world have been and are the fertile soil from which new cults arise in rank profusion. The cult is the most ephemeral of all types of religious structure—indeed, it is usually so loosely integrated and so transitory that the term "structure" is almost a misnomer.

Cults frequently are much like sects, and it is extremely difficult to draw a line between the two—just as it is difficult [empirically speaking], to draw a line between the sect and the denomination. At the same time, the following . . .[empirical approximations] of the cult are quite close: Spiritualism, Theosophy, New Thought, [early] Christian Science, Unity, Buchmanism, and the various pseudo-Hinduisms associated with Swamis and Yogis who consent, for a consideration, to carry their messages to the materialistic Western World.[10]

[10] Howard Becker, "Protestantism and Religious Differentiation," mimeographed "assignment" written for Sociology 4, Social Institutions, University of Pennsylvania, 1929. This was published in Becker, *Systematic Sociology on the*

Each one of the empirical groups mentioned above manifestly differs from the constructed types, even though I had not yet reached the stage of conscious, explicit construction at the time (1929) when the above passage was written. A good deal can be said, from the standpoint of prediction, when we have a suitable hypothesis and a set of constructs such as the ecclesia, the sect, the denomination, and the cult. It becomes possible, for example, to construct a hypothetical cycle, and to say that a sect often begins as a cult, later changes into a denomination, and finally becomes an ecclesia. This essentially predictive statement can then be verified, either through a search of the past for religious structures not taken into account when the type was formulated ("retrospective prediction")[11] or through examination of contemporary religious conduct. In the latter instance, we can say just about when Christian Science, for example, shifts from being merely a cult into the configuration called a sect, and that now it shows definite signs of becoming a denomination.

The constructed type, in conjunction with an appropriate hypothesis, therefore may have predictive power, but certainly not in the sense of enabling us to say positively that on June 28, 1960, this or that will occur. Being neither market forecasters nor prophets, we can never cast predictions in such unconditional terms. We can say, however, that "*If and when* these typical factors are given in this typical relation, these will probably be the typical consequences." That is oftentimes as far as we can or should go. The geologist, to analogize once more, will seldom if ever hazard an assertion such as this: "If you bore here, at 3182 feet below the surface you will find a deposit of oil totaling 4,182,692 barrels in amount, flowing at the rate of 76 cubic feet per second." After much investigation he may say, "The indications are pretty good, considering what is happening in comparable fields, that by boring somewhere within a half-mile radius of this point you may strike oil in paying quantities at about a three-quarter mile depth." And then the man who has been paying for the geologist's advice goes ahead, and verifies or refutes the generalization—and his own bank account.

The verification or refutation is always pragmatic; so too is the verification or refutation of a sociological generalization— when it is verified or refuted at all. Often preoccupation with orthodoxy of method leads to the neglect of the search for crucial checks. Many of us, for example, continue to follow the alliterative lilt of Ogburn's "cultural lag" as an all-sufficient explanation of changes in American divorce rates, blithely ignoring the fact that such changes were proceeding in *reverse* direction in pre-World War II Japan under conditions of even greater "discrepancy" between nonmaterial and material culture. But when we are careful constructive typologists we say, "Given such and such circumstances, these consequences are likely to ensue," *and* we then inspect the "historical" record and/or the record of "contemporary" events to find out whether our generalizations, necessarily cast in terms about as noncommital in particulars as those of the geologist, are pragmatically verified or refuted. In undertaking the pragmatic checkup, there is every reason to make use of quantitative procedures when they are relevant—and they usually are.

The constructed type is an indispensable tool of analysis in the social sciences generally, and in no science is it more useful than in sociology. It is indispensable when one deals with longitudinal sections or time-series, that is, with the "same" set of processes and structures followed over a dated period. It is also indispensable from the cross-sectional standpoint, i.e., the study of the interrelations of a number of processes and structures in a given cross-section of the "existing" and/or "realizable" record. Finally, it is indispensable when the phenomena concerned are relatively undated.

V. BUILD IT SO IT WILL WORK

But if the high promise of the future is to be reaped by constructive typology, potential "despoilers of the harvest" must be closely watched. Not only must we be on guard against misuse of the method by the well-intentioned but ill-informed, but also against the vulgar misunderstanding that sometimes arises from passive indifference or active hostility.

As a case in point, someone is always saying, "Your constructed type is no good because several exceptions to it can be found." The obvious reply is, "You can never expect anything other than exceptions. If construct and 'reality' exactly correspond, you are in the morass of the particular. You are talking about *this* thing at *this* time in such a way that explicit comparison with anything else becomes virtually impossible." The belief that the constructed type is rendered useless because exceptions to it can be found is childishly naïve. Exceptions *must* be found; in the realm of the particular, as our discussion of the Grand Rapids chairs may have done something to show, only "exceptions" can be expected. Virtually all of Chapter V, "Sacred and Secular Societies: Retrospect and Prospect," is devoted to elaboration of this point.

Present-day cultural anthropologists of Boas's type, now fortunately waning in prestige and numerically much in the minority, are the most frequent perpetrators of the methodological naïvete just mentioned, in part because some of them, deceived by the limited spatial extent and numerical scope of the societies they investigate, seriously attempt "full description" of the unique. This tendency is also furthered by the fact that preliterates have no written records that enable adequate investigation of long-term changes, and hence it seems possible to "gather *all* the facts." The resulting failure to focus on definite problems that conform to the criterion of attempted scientific prediction causes anthropologists of this school to bog down in the particularistic swamp and, unaware of their frog's-eye view, to deride all efforts at generalization by croaking, "Exception."

Another vulgar misunderstanding which predictions based on constructed types frequently encounter is that the conditional character of the generalizations is disregarded. All that the constructive typologist ever says is that "if and when" certain factors, which have been isolated as significant, recur in con-

figurations which can be regarded as identical for the purposes
in hand, then this in turn will probably ensue. He does not
say in advance, nor can he *ever* say in advance, whether the
factors which are essential for the results will *actually* recur in
the required configuration. Socio-cultural structures cannot
be concocted in the laboratory; Calvinistic Scottish society or
Frankfort Jewry cannot be made to order. The constructive
typologist, like the geologist, must depend on the accidents of
past "deposit" or future "stratification." If it is only clearly
held in mind that these generalizations are cast in "if and
when" terms, a considerable amount of misunderstanding can
be avoided.

Still another kind of misunderstanding arises from the belief that constructed types are all of equal generality. Nothing
could be further from the truth, as we tried to show in the
discussion of dated and localized as over against undated and
nonlocalized types, as well as in the presentation of the examples of ecclesia, sect, denomination, and cult. It is worth
stressing again, however, that constructed types in the social
sciences are of many forms. Problem, predictive range, hypothesis, data, and validating techniques determine what they
are going to be like.

It may be necessary, for example, to construct a type that
is highly relative, quasi-"historical," for the purposes of short-
term prediction. To wit: "the American Middle Western
state university" is a possible construct. Reference will not
be to "the University of Minnesota," or to "the University
of Illinois," but it will none the less be a highly relative and
regional type. The more limited the type, the greater the
degree of short-term predictive power, *and* the greater the
degree of error to be expected in prediction even with the "if
and when" proviso, for the problems posed oftentimes require
unduly prophetic answers. Nevertheless, it is possible to say
a great deal more about the immediate future of "the American Middle Western State university" if your type is constructed on the basis of relatively specific factors, and not with
prime regard to "the university in general." In the latter

case, you would be forced to include private institutions all over the United States and the rest of the world, and the national universities as well.

For some purposes, of course, the construction of a type that is not so relative would be in order; to be tied down to a construct based only on "the American Middle Western State university" would stultify the projected research. The goal in view is more general, hence "the Euro-American university" is constructed. On the basis of such a type, a number of far-reaching "if and when" generalizations can be made. This construct, however, is less relative, and the more general it becomes, the less detailed can be the predictions based upon it. Illegitimate and foolhardy, to speak mildly, would be a prophecy to the effect that "the University of Wisconsin" will soon champion a revival of the humanities, for the constructed type with which operations are being carried on includes factors gleaned from German, French, and English as well as American universities; and moreover, specific prophecy is not our business. The generalizations made with the aid of the more general constructed type are necessarily of relatively indefinite character. In a certain sense, generalization is omission. The more ground a type covers, the less adequately it covers it so far as minor humps and hollows are concerned. And yet for some purposes you will want to have your construct cover a great deal of ground.

As an analogy, suppose that the face of some hero is being carved on the side of a mountain. The engineer-sculptor did not determine the form and composition of that mountain, but he must nevertheless go to work. He begins by building a scaffold in order to reach the surface of the mountain with hammer, drill, and dynamite. For preliminary purposes the scaffold can be of very open construction, without a great many stages, because the first step is to remove irregularities and prepare suitable working areas; such a purpose is entire justification for a scaffold of highly general character. Later on it will be necessary to rough out the features, and later still, to chisel the delicate folds and lines surrounding the eye. When these phases of the work are reached, the scaffold must be built in such a way that it gives access to the precise points of importance. Eventually every facility of position must be provided for the workman who puts on the finishing touches. The scaffold, manifestly, becomes more intricate and detailed as the purpose it serves changes.

Although "no analogy will go on all fours," it may be said that our constructed types are often altered or revised to bring them into line with changed purposes. In terms of our earlier illustration: For some purposes it is enough to use a construct of the ecclesia predicated on the hypothesis that it tends to be identified with the *status quo*, with the ruling political and economic organizations, with the powers that be. For other purposes, however, it will seem desirable to know whether Calvinism in Scotland tended toward the ecclesia or toward the sect, and whether the constructed types usable in the ecclesia? ← Scottish Calvinism → sect? problem are also usable in the ecclesia?⇌*status quo*? problem. The precise way in which the constructs are delineated will make all the difference. In one case the side of the mountain is being hewed off, as it were; in the other the expressive folds about the eye are receiving their last strokes.

The purpose in hand determines how the type is to be constructed. That is the all-important criterion. There is no way of saying in advance of the setting of the problem and the framing of the hypothesis exactly what a constructed type should be like. You must know the purpose of the study, the empirical data, and what kind of pragmatic verification or refutation is to be sought. Statistics may be called upon for this checkup function, or data drawn from history may be used to shape crucial culture case studies of societies and cultural blocs *à la* Toynbee, or psycho-sociology, with its resources of personality study, may carry out the tester's task. In short, the data from which the type is distilled and on which it and its initiating hypothesis depend for validation may be drawn from many different sources. Only when the researcher knows clearly what his purpose is, and only when he has tested the possible utility of his constructs in the light of that purpose, does he know whether his generalizations are likely to be worth the effort of pragmatic validation. If he decides "to put them to the touch," the final question is, "Does the construct work, within the limits set by the purpose, on the whole and in the long run?"

William James is not yet buried, for his ghost still hovers close at hand.

VI. A FICTION MAY NOT BE FALSE

And under pragmatic influence, I am led to further utterances: Generalizations in constructive typology are not True, if by this is meant the controlling, ultimate, ineffable Capital T. All that the social scientist can mean by truth is some amount, however slight, of predictive power. Truth as insight into the essence of things, as apprehension of first causes or final reasons, cannot be delivered by the scientist. This is not to deny the existence (or subsistence) of such Truth; it is just not within the scientific range.

But after all, the scientist does not seek for Truth. His task is not to inquire into the "Why?" of things, but into the "How?" "*Why* should there be a cosmos?" is not a scientifically answerable question. "*How* has the cosmos changed throughout determinable time?" is certainly a large order, but the attempt to answer it does not carry us beyond the confines of science. These considerations, however, range too far afield; let us return to the near-by task.

"Common sense" to the contrary, it seems to me that the scientist in a very real sense operates with fictions—or, if that term is unpalatable, with planned modifications or simplifications or even accentuations of the "empirically given," i.e., of the configurations he first perceives.[12] The working fiction of

---

[12] Manifestly, the "empirically given" is not "raw fact"; indeed, we cook and season all our facts to taste. Strictly speaking, there are no facts as such; the very act of perceiving, if our perceptions are to be communicable, depends on articulate or inarticulate concepts. Nevertheless, we here provisionally draw a line between (1) facts "known as such" to all normal human beings who have undergone like general socio-cultural training, and (2) constructs planfully developed by specialists for their particular purposes. For discussion along related lines, see the essay on "Supreme Values and the Sociologist," pp. 281-293.

the scientist—any scientist—is often a construct of the type I have already characterized.

When the physicist works out a formula for the bending strength of beams, he posits a homogeneous beam of determinate cross-section, supported on fulcra at certain definite points. On the basis of a constructed type of this sort, grounded on empirical observation, but to which no single two-by-four or channel iron exactly corresponds, he develops a formula that may be of the highest utility, but which, again, no "real" beam ever fits. The physicist also makes use of working fictions in theories of atomic process and structure. As someone has put it, "On Monday, Wednesday, and Friday we use a wave theory of light, and on Tuesday and Thursday we use a corpuscle or particle theory." Both of these theories work for the specific purposes for which they were intended; they procure prediction. But what light *is*, in any final sense, is never revealed by a scientific theory; it merely tells how something called "light" acts under given conditions. Most of us tend to think in spatial terms, and the result is the construction of models envisaging either wave motion or the bombardment of minute particles, depending on which model works out best under the terms of the problem and the data confronted.

It is entirely possible that in the future someone will construct a theory of light that will reconcile the wave and the particle assumptions.[13] This reconciliation of present contradictions would be no warrant, however, for believing that the reconciling theory is finally and absolutely True. Attainment of such Truth would not be the purpose of the reconciliatory achievement; instead, the general principle of economy of effort would probably enter into consideration. It is much easier to use one theory in which apparent contradictions are reconciled than it is to keep one's mind in separate compartments, as it were, using one theory in one situation and the other in another. The scientist *qua* scientist has no yearning for Truth in this or any similar case; he is simply trying to get a tool that works better, more economically, with less effort and more

[13] A fairly satisfactory reconciliation has already been effected, and if Einstein's most recent work proves valid, the reconciliation will be complete.

precision, than the two somewhat awkward implements that he is now forced to manipulate. The reconciling theory is just as much a working fiction as were the two he was struggling with before—unless we wish to assume that on the day and hour when the discrepant theories are reconciled the scientist knows all that he ever can know, in the predictive sense, about the phenomena in question.

In the late nineteenth century, of course, some physicists did think that they had "the feel of the fur on the tail of the world"; one of them even said, "From this time on, all that will ever be done will be to introduce refinements into the already existing body of physical theory." And yet within twenty-five years that whole body of theory was revolutionized through the new "extra-dimensional" geometries and the work of mathematical astronomers. It is unlikely that the physicists will again think that they have a tailhold on the cosmos; it remains to be seen how the social scientists will conduct themselves.

In the search for Truth as the Last Word, the working scientist is merely a blood brother of Pilate.

Let it be shouted from the housetops, however, that the working fictions of which we make use are not "just any" fictions. They should not involve the social scientist in conflict with established principles in other sciences. For instance, no sociologist in his senses would follow Freud in postulating a phylogenetic memory, a "racial unconscious," based on the inheritance of acquired characteristics. (I say Freud advisedly; see *Totem and Tabu* and its 1939 revival in *Moses and Monotheism*. Jung has of course perpetrated similiar nonsense.) The long battle of the biologists has apparently entered a stage in which victory at least provisionally rests on the banners of the anti-Lamarckians. True, the paleontologists, among others, raise timid pro-Lamarckian objections now and then, only to see them crushed under the weight of countervailing evidence. Further, Lysenko has succeeded in getting his neo-Lamarckian genetics declared orthodox in Russia, but this seems to be a political rather than a scientific victory. Disregarding,

CONSTRUCTIVE TYPOLOGY 127

therefore, the Russian doctrine, it may be said that unless Western biologists eventually make discoveries that overturn what they hold to be one of their most firmly established generalizations, no construct that assumes the inheritance of acquired characteristics can be regarded as a usable tool. Certainly the foolhardy alone would attempt to build their scientific houses on rejected theories, more especially when they derive from fields where the word of the qualified specialist is the only trustworthy guide. Most of us will feel that the conclusions of these specialists stake off the plots within which our constructs must be built. Even when these limits seem relatively narrow, there is usually space enough to tax the constructive endurance of the most assiduous typologist.

Finally, note that the constructed type *as such* is not necessarily a statistical mean or mode, or even a homogeneous universe as ordinarily understood.[14] True, it *can* be constructed in such a way that it corresponds to any of these, but usually its utility will be sharply limited by such practices. The instrumentally valuable construct is like a Franz Hals portrait rather than like a composite photograph printed from a large number of superimposed negatives. We might even say that the construct may be as selective as a sketch. The ordinary stereotype affords an instructive contrast: it is an unconscious, unplanned exaggeration of the "empirically given," mixed with much that has not been observed at all, and includes a large emotional freight of praise or blame; the constructed type is a conscious, planned selection, combination, and accentuation of the "empirically given," relatively free from value-judgment. Most important of all, the stereotype ministers to nonscientific ideologies; whereas the constructed type serves scientific activity, which is nothing more and nothing less than "the systematic statement of the probability of the hypothetical or actual recurrence of phenomena that for the purposes in hand are regarded as identical."

The wheel has come full circle.

[14] See the chapter on "Prospects of Social Change as Viewed by Historian and Sociologist," pp. 171-174.

PROSPECTS OF SOCIAL CHANGE AS VIEWED BY HISTORIAN AND SOCIOLOGIST

I. THE SHAPE OF THINGS TO COME

THE MIDDAY SUN beats down on Pharos, that lonely island flecking the Middle Sea but a scant sail from Alexander's great city at the mouth of the Nile. Step softly over the monsters of the deep that share the slumbers of old Proteus, the shepherd of the flocks of Neptune, and lay firm hold upon him. Shout in his ear the questions answerable only by those who glimpse the future, and tighten your grip. Dreading his task of prophecy, Proteus twists and turns, but your clutching hands mock his strength, and lo! you wrestle with a lion, grapple with a bear, or grimly clamp your grasp still tighter to hold a writhing serpent. Fear not, for you have seized only the harmless Proteus, and in the end your will decides. His "strong enchantments failing," the old man of the sea yields at last, dons his wonted peaceful guise, and reluctantly shares with you his vision of things to come. Then, humbled by human courage, Proteus pipes retreat to his seaweed-trailing herds, and plunges into the cool green refuge that laps ceaselessly at the shore. You are alone on Pharos.

Or were, in Homer's time. Today we know not Proteus, nor any of the gods, but our straining gaze is still turned toward the future. *Savoir pour prévoir*[1] has survived the nineteenth century to become one of the chief maxims of the twentieth; the mood of Lynd's *Knowledge for What?*[2] is that

---

[1] This maxim we owe to Comte.

[2] Although we differ with many of the implications of Robert S. Lynd's book (Princeton, 1939), there is no essential disagreement with the main thesis. The social sciences *should* be "relevant to futurity." *Ultimate* value-relevancy cannot be escaped. It is one thing to say this, however, and quite another to say that questions of immediate social utility should dictate the choice of problem, the technique of research, or the role of scientist as scientist.

of the Greek who sought out the shepherd of Neptune. What does the future hold in store, and how can we prepare today for the events of tomorrow? is an ever-recurring question. The values it dimly symbolizes are the key values of much of our work in social science; our efforts are "relevant to the values of futurity"—in short, *wertbezogen*.[3] We cannot escape, even if we would, from the scales of value implanted or elicited by our rapidly changing culture.

To be sure, this orientation toward the future is in no sense peculiar to ourselves; Proteus has been badgered by inquisitors since time immemorial. Yet there may be a difference between the ancients and the moderns; the men of old oftentimes posed questions touching on personal destiny or the fate of fellow-clansmen and small communities, whereas we are steadily becoming more and more concerned about the ultimate lot of nations or even of entire civilizations. Certainly the sages of bygone days were similarly concerned,[4] but we may well doubt the existence of an uneasiness as widespread as that which grips the world of today. The very fact that the Great Society has come to seem a possibility on the surface of a globe crisscrossed by countless strands of communication knitting together Hottentot and Eskimo, Frenchman and Brazilian, Russian and American, presses home to the humblest tabloid reader the further fact that the parts of the potential whole may destroy each other before his own life has reached its allotted span.

II. THE PROTEAN QUESTIONS

Within the scope of this chapter, however, we cannot take account of the inarticulate yearnings of the masses; our task is to see "what thoughts of old the wise have entertained," and to compare them with the ideas held by whatever sages the world of our own time may have brought forth. Hence it

---

[3] For discussion of this matter, see Harry E. Barnes and Howard Becker, *Social Thought from Lore to Science* (Boston, 1938), Vol. II, chap. xxiii; hereinafter cited as *STLS*. Rickert and Weber are the key figures. Goldenweiser's chapter on the relation of the natural sciences to the social sciences in H. E. Barnes, H. Becker, and F. B. Becker, *Contemporary Social Theory* (New York, 1940; hereinafter cited as *CST*), pp. 93-109, is also important.

[4] Here a useful survey has been provided by J. O. Hertzler, *The Social Thought of the Ancient Civilizations* (New York, 1936).

is possible to say that the questions thrust at Proteus have taken and still take the following forms: (1) What was the earliest condition of the creatures we call human, and how are those conditions changing with the lapse of time? (2) Can there be discerned an all-encompassing drift toward a single goal, in spite of the baffling maze of changes? (3) Are there any sequences or stages in societal development that when discovered will enable us to estimate the varying speeds at which the differing sections of mankind have approached the goal? (4) Can it be said that "history repeats itself" in any fundamental sense?

Obviously, these questions have often been asked in the same breath, as it were; those who clutch the writhing Proteus find little opportunity for nice distinctions. Still, we may provisionally consider the first two apart from the others, more especially as their aim seems on the surface to be the probing of the past rather than the discovery of the future. As we go on to examine them more narrowly, however, we shall see that even preoccupation with "first things" carries with it, as an inseparable counterpart, the contemplation of "last things."

III. FROM MUMBO-JUMBO TO DARWIN

The problem of first things is often "solved" by preliterates in terms of a culture hero or charismatic leader who is sometimes a sort of trickster, sometimes a wise elder, sometimes a divine or divinely inspired lawgiver. Fully armed from the brain of the culture hero springs the society, together with the altogether admirable institutions wherewith it is clothed. Frequently a complete creation myth, a cosmogony, spreads an aura around Osiris, Gilgamesh, Yü the Great, or Shiva. Virtually all these stories share the traits of wonder-working power, disregard of the means-ends schema[5] enforced by the necessities of everyday life, and by the same token, a very slight measure of anything that can be called expedient rationality. Here, in other words, we are confronted by two or more differing sys-

---

[5] The index of Talcott Parsons's *The Structure of Social Action* (New York, 1937) will provide numerous references on the means-ends schema. Max Weber is the major source of Parsons's analysis; when possible, Weber's own disquisitions on *Mittel und Zweck* should also be consulted.

tems of logic: one which applies to that marvelous world veiled in the awesome mists of the past or beyond control in the present; the other, the logic of familiar materials, of accustomed manipulation, of ordinary person-to-person intercourse, of everyday things and events.

"Beginnings" are always arbitrary, but perhaps one of the earliest groups of thinkers who more or less rationally dealt with the problem of social origins and development were the Greek "tale-makers" and their successors, not least among them the Metics and Sophists who flourished as early as the sixth century B.C. These mentally mobile "strangers" in the sacred societies[6] of their day had been forced to develop what we may call techniques—and the Greek word from which technique is derived means indifferently art, skill, craft, trick, strategem, ruse. That is to say, there had developed at this period several bodies of methods or means by which certain desired goals or ends could be attained in step-by-step, "causal" fashion. The various forms of the means-ends schema thus elaborated in and through the necessities of trade, warfare, organized communal life, handicrafts, money economy, and so on, were projected into the past, and the charismatic culture hero[7] began to be displaced by the reasoning mind of man.

Very popular, for example, was the theory of an originally animal-like, lawless state of Nature,[8] from which men emerged "according to plan." The first society, said our Greek exponents of technique, emerged when men fashioned a governmental compact, agreeing to refrain from violence toward each other and depositing their concentrated power in the hands of a dispute-settling ruler. Vehemently opposed to these thinkers and yet in accord with them in some respects was Plato, who set forth, in Book III of his *Laws*, one of the best-rounded accounts of social genesis produced by the ancients. Interest-

[6] The writer first defined these terms in his article, "Processes of Secularisation," *Sociological Review* (British), XXIV (April-July and Oct., 1932), 138-154, 266-286. See also the essay in the present volume, "Values as Tools of Sociological Analysis," pp. 42-66.

[7] Barnes and Becker, "Charismatic Leadership," *STLS*, pp. 22-26. Note that I say above, "*began* to be displaced." Charisma is still with us, and may well remain.

[8] "Theories of the Natural State of Man," *ibid.*, pp. 423-458.

ingly enough, he asserted that "every man should understand that the human race either had no beginning at all, and will never have an end, and will always be and has been, or that it began an immense while ago."[9]   The aloof, detached Aristotle paid scant regard to his teacher's concern with vast reaches of time, and provided a brief "solution" of his own that was analytical rather than historical.   Engaged primarily in proving his initial assumption that man is a "social animal," he traced the progressive manifestations of essential human sociality in the family, the village, and the state.   If it be true that he studied more than one hundred and fifty city-state constitutions as the basis of his *Constitution of Athens*, we may hold Aristotle to have been the earliest known exponent of the method of historical comparison.   Beyond question, his *Politics* bears the impress of an extensive collection of empirical data, shrewdly marshaled into inclusive categories and made to parade at the generalizer's command.[10]

Continuing in the Greek vein, we may well point out the significance of one of the most neglected discussions of political and social development, namely, Polybius's anticipation of the later combat theorists through the doctrine, contained in the sixth book of his *History of Rome*, that the state originated in violence.   As if this foreshadowing of Ibn Khaldūn and Adam Ferguson were not enough, Polybius, like Herodotus before him, antedated Sumner by more than two thousand years in his championing of the "customary basis" of morality, and achieved priority over Spinoza and Adam Smith in his discussion of reflective sympathy as an essential foundation of stable societal structure.[11]   While we are engaged in this secondary task of pointing out that "there were great men before William K. Smith,"[12] we may also call attention to that Spencer of the classical world, the great Epicurean poet Lucretius, who endeavored to show that the whole cosmos, including its societal phases, developed spontaneously without aid from or interference by the gods.[13]

[9] Plato *Laws* VI. 781e-782a.   [10] Barnes and Becker, *STLS*, pp. 180-193.
[11] *Ibid.*, pp. 200-202.
[12] James Barrie, *Courage* (New York, 1932), p. 43.
[13] Barnes and Becker, *STLS*, pp. 200-202.

Lucretius, however, reached only a small elite for whom human "invulnerability" against the ills of existence constituted a supreme value in their disintegrating, decadent culture. More significant was Seneca, the eclectic Stoic philosopher who carried even further than his predecessors the notion of the idyllic life of early man.[14] It was Seneca's fortune to find his sounding board among the Christian Fathers. They identified his Golden Age with the state of man before the Fall, and held that the later period of misery, confusion, and disorder was none other than that which followed the expulsion from the Garden of Eden. This notion of social origins and development held the field throughout those centuries now vaguely termed the Dark and Middle Ages, although nearly all the writers had little to say about the Golden Age; they were chiefly occupied in stressing the miseries of existence before the coming of the new dispensation embodied in the Christian polity.[15]

Christianity, as we know, had rivals. Far beyond even the late medievalists in intellectual grasp and command of fact was the great Mohammedan scholar and statesman, Ibn Khaldūn. His contribution to historical sociology was the most remarkable in the entire era between Lucretius and Adam Ferguson. In his analysis of the interaction of pastoral nomad and tiller, his penetrating insight into the factors of personal and social disorganization, his isolation of a cycle of political rise and decline valid for many regions other than the North Africa with which he was familiar, and his empirically based study of the sources of social control, we have the most strangely modern-sounding theories that one could well imagine.[16]

Distinctly inferior to Ibn Khaldūn in many respects, and yet marking the emergence of views going far beyond those current in the Europe of his time, was Jean Bodin. This Frenchman, apologist and publicist for rising kingly absolutism, revived and expanded the geographical determinism of certain later Greek thinkers, echoed the Sophists in premising a lawless

[14] Ibid., pp. 207-211.   [15] Ibid., pp. 234-241.
[16] Barnes and Becker, STLS, pp. 265-279. Note that we say "modern-sounding"; after all, Ibn Khaldūn was a child of his time.

primitivism, followed Aristotle in his doctrine of the family origin of society, and paralleled Ibn Khaldūn in tracing the origins of the state to their source in combat. The net effect of his work was to prepare the ground for that type of historical sociology most prevalent during the seventeenth and eighteenth centuries, namely, the assumption that society and the state developed through a social and governmental compact.[17]

Of this revived Platonism we need say little, for its historical and psychological weaknesses were effectively attacked by three writers who were in the forefront of those restoring the historical point of view in historical sociology to the place it had held with Lucretius and Ibn Khaldūn. The most famous of the three, Vico, while not devoting himself exclusively to the demolition of social contract theories, strongly stressed the necessity of amassing historical knowledge as part and parcel of the attack on the problem of social origins and development. Hume, child of the Enlightenment, showed that the social contract theory was a philosophical monstrosity, a psychological contradiction, and a historical anomaly refuted on every hand by easily ascertainable fact.[18] Still more sweepingly "anti-contract" in viewpoint was Adam Ferguson's *Essay on the History of Civil Society*. Here was enunciated once more the theory that the state arose in and through violence, particularly in the form of conquest. Not only this; Ferguson foreshadowed Boas and like ethnologists by discarding preconceived notions as to the nature of "primitive man" and his institutions and studying the life of the so-called "simpler peoples" as nearly at first hand as he could.[19]

Vico was also an early exponent of the philosophy of history[20]—a label applied in the eighteenth century to a type of thought as ancient as Proteus. It provided the uniting thread on which the Italian strung, three upon three, the successive eras of his history of civilization. A sample of the more im-

---

[17] *Ibid.*, pp. 348-358.
[18] *Ibid.*, pp. 396-404. In saying "refuted," above, I do not mean to imply that Hume solved the apparently insoluble "problem" of social origins. He merely showed that the social contract theorists had not solved it.
[19] *Ibid.*, pp. 451-452, 545-546.
[20] *Ibid.*, pp. 445-446, 465-470.

portant French contributors to these fields would include Voltaire, Turgot, Condorcet, and Saint-Simon. The latter, with his isolation of "organic" and "critical" periods, represents a clear-cut anticipation of Comte, Tönnies, Spengler, and Sorokin—indeed, not only does he anticipate but in many cases surpasses these writers.[21]

Much French thought of the early eighteenth and nineteenth centuries was dominated by the rationalism, skepticism, and optimism of the Enlightenment, whereas in the works of Herder, Adam Müller, Hegel, and other German thinkers, one finds a curious mixture. Along with numerous rationalistic streaks there are evident several layers of traditional allegiance (national and/or ethnic), "oversoul" conceptions, absorption in historical continuities, and exaltation of the non-rational factors in human life and history. In this Romanticism, as it came to be labeled, there are undeniable deficiencies in clarity and even in logic of the usual sort, but it was nevertheless significant because of the historical interests it stimulated and the crushing blows it gave to hastily carpentered reconstructions of the past.[22]

In the work of Auguste Comte, rationalism and a French variant of Romanticism were incongruously wedded; the resulting progeny furnished the historical retinue for the first system of doctrine to bear the name of sociology. Several "laws" of social and mental development were included in this system, notably the famous unilinear formula of "from the Military-Theological, through the Critical-Metaphysical, to the Industrial-Scientific."[23] There can be little doubt that modern historical sociology differs radically in method, content, and conclusions from most forms of the philosophy of history—certainly from the Comtean. Nevertheless, in the attempt to find bases in the past for the projection of the future, the

[21] A. J. Toynbee, *A Study of History* (London, 1934 ———), V, 24, quoting Bazard, "Exposition de la doctrine Saint-Simonienne," *Oeuvres de Saint-Simon et d'Enfantin* (Paris, 1877), XLI, 171-174.

[22] Barnes and Becker, *STLS*, pp. 487-490, 531-532. This excessively brief mention of the Romanticists and, in particular, of their Hegelian variant, is grossly unfair, but unavoidable.

[23] *Ibid.*, pp. 568-594.

philosophy of history has been indispensable as a driving force, and we shall try to assess its current significance, in the later part of the chapter.

In this hasty survey of prototypes, we dare not overlook the rise of critical historical scholarship as exemplified in the work of Ranke and his contemporaries and successors in many countries.[24] His insistence on the study of the past "as it actually and peculiarly was" (see the discussion in Section II of the chapter on "Constructive Typology in the Social Sciences"), did much to establish the later differentiation between history as an idiographic specialty concerned with "facts of succession" and historical sociology as a nomothetic specialty analyzing "facts of repetition."[25] Stimulated by critical historiography, scholars worked up a vast amount of concrete material, of which only a small part has yet been utilized by historical sociologists. Tremendous storehouses of well-attested evidence still await exploitation; no one who has advanced beyond an elementary knowledge of history can subscribe to Lundberg's statement that there is little of scientific worth in the products of modern historical research,[26] although it may be granted that the data must often be placed in other frames of reference.

Thus far our focus has been essentially pre-Darwinian, and before setting the lens for the post-Darwinian foreground, we should note the initial interest in historical economics and economic history evidenced in the work of Heeren, Sismondi, Hildebrand, Roscher, and Knies. The genetic point of view which characterized the group led them to ask many Protean questions, and the data they amassed are utilizable by historical sociology even today.[27]

IV. EVOLUTIONISM AND THE WAYS OUT

Yet, for all the pre-Darwinian interest in the early condition of mankind and the changes it has undergone in the

[24] Albion W. Small, *Origins of Sociology* (Chicago, 1924), pp. 93-101.
[25] The distinction between "succession" and "repetition" comes from A. D. Xenopol. The terms should not be taken too literally. See Barnes and Becker, *STLS*, pp. 1089-1090, and pp. 102-109 of the present volume.
[26] G. A. Lundberg, *Foundations of Sociology* (New York, 1939), pp. 512-513.
[27] Small, *op. cit.*, pp. 105-107, 194-197, *et passim*.

course of time, it is nevertheless true that the most potent influence on historical sociology until the very recent past was the theory of organismic evolution. Here Darwin's "random variation, struggle for existence, natural selection, and survival of the fittest" were the rallying slogans, with Spencer's grandiose watchword of "homogeneity to heterogeneity" only second in importance.[28] Human society, as well as the strictly organismic realm, was held to be the product of evolutionary forces operating over an immense period of time. The historical sociology arising on the basis of this assumption flowed in two channels: one, the social Darwinism of Gumplowicz and other exponents of a revived combat theory; the other, the "classical anthropology" of Tylor, Frazer, Morgan, Lippert, Keller, et al.[29]

Holding, as we do, that the phosphorescent glow of evolutionary doctrine plunged historical sociologists into a veritable Slough of Despond, there seems little point in listing those who were led astray by its will-o'-the-wisp flickering. The reader who has not explored the marshland of social evolutionism will find trustworthy guides in Lowie's *History of Ethnological Theory* and in Goldenweiser's fascinating essay on anthropological contributions to social theory.[30] Here we need say only that the classical school assumed that there is an organismic law of development in social institutions and, as an inseparable corollary, a sequence of gradual and orderly changes, basically the same the world over, proceeding from confused and/or simple relations to complex and well-coordinated socio-cultural structures. The formulas developed were essentially prophetic, for it was believed that subsequent stages of societal development could be forecast, whatever the special conditions affecting a given society, on the basis of the "later evolutionary stages" already passed through by comparable societies—and all societies were thought to be *directly* comparable in their preordained course of growth.

[28] Barnes and Becker, *STLS*, pp. 664-742. Cf. also this reference for the bearing of the distinction between "organismic" and "organic."

[29] Robert H. Lowie, *History of Ethnological Theory* (New York, 1937), pp. 54-85; Barnes and Becker, *STLS*, pp. 748-757.

[30] In Barnes, Becker, and Becker, *CST*.

These evolutionary postulates led to a widespread use of the so-called comparative method—which, let it be noted, is not comparative in the sense to which we shall later restrict this term, but rather "preferential" or illustrative. Given a hypostatized sequence of stages, the illustrative investigator rambled over the face of the earth, hand-picking preferred specimens of conduct and institutions which he then tucked into his ready-made pigeonholes.

The first sweeping rejection of the illustrative method by a sociologist of repute appeared in the writings of Émile Durkheim. As early as the beginning of the twentieth century, he had begun to insist that valid conclusions as to social development must rest upon intensive study of one social institution in a single and well-demarcated culture area.[31] This procedure he later (1912) utilized in his study of *Elementary Forms of the Religious Life*, in which he selected for analysis the function of religious institutions in Australia. Although the transferability of his conclusions to certain other "cultural circles" is not so entirely impossible as was believed a decade ago, it is still true that modern ethnologists outside France are exceedingly critical of Durkheim.[32] The flight from classical anthropology has usually followed other paths which, speaking in broad outline, have been five in number.

First is the trail represented in the attempted buttressing of the old illustrative method by comparison of a simple statistical type—an effort most prominently identified with the names of Hobhouse, Wheeler, and Ginsberg, and by most critics held to be unsuccessful.[33]

Second among these byways may be listed that followed by the diffusionists, who attempt to explain similarities in culture on the hypothesis of spread from a common center, or centers, of origin. Only one center is "discovered" by the extreme English diffusionists of the Smith-Perry school; several centers, varying in number, have been isolated by Ratzel, Graebner, Rivers, Frobenius, Schmidt and Koppers, and Wissler.[34]

[31] In *L'Année Sociologique*, Vols. I-XII (1896-97—1912), *passim*.
[32] Lowie, *op. cit.*, pp. 196-216; Barnes and Becker, *STLS*, pp. 750-751.
[33] *STLS*, pp. 751-753.
[34] Lowie, *op. cit.*, pp. 156-195. See also Goldenweiser, *CST*, pp. 453-459.

Diffusionism has much to commend it but, when pushed to extremes, falls foul of the fact that "culture is not contagious." That is, the spread of even material culture cannot be explained by means of mere spatial contiguity; societies living cheek by jowl oftentimes fail to affect each other in any significant degree.

Third is the route offered by an essentially historical method having strong idiographic leanings. Although it has had many practitioners, Boas and his school in America have been its most prominent exponents.[35] They have assigned full credit to independent origin as the indispensable factor in many societal changes, but when historically demonstrable, have also granted a prominent place to diffusion. Particularly searching has been their analysis of alleged socio-cultural parallels; the result has been to show that many traits once thought to be directly comparable are actually of quite different functional significance. Of positive contributions to historical sociology, however, Boas and his followers have relatively little to show; their function has been critical and idiographic. In passages to follow later we shall try to show the *sociological* shortcomings inherent in this approach, which we label "extreme historicism."

Fourth is the avenue recently opened by the functionalists: Malinowski, Radcliffe-Brown, Mead, Benedict, and many more.[36] These ethnologists attempt to account for apparent similarities in social origins and development on the basis of man's biological uniformity and the fact that this uniformity "calls for" a relatively limited number of types of interaction, and that these generate their accompanying socio-cultural structures and institutions. Further, the interactions and their concomitants inevitably engender other manifestations which are functionally bound up with them. In investigating social origins and development, therefore, the assumption is that any given society is a functional unity in which each component simultaneously "calls for" and is "called for by" every other component. Diffused traits are accepted only when they can be functionally interrelated with those already present; simi-

---

[35] *Ibid.*, pp. 128-155.   [36] *Ibid.*, pp. 230-249.

larly, innovations arising within the society gain headway only when they can be integrally united with the existing "whole." Functionalism has stimulated much worthwhile research but has been drastically criticized because of its initial premise that every portion of a given socio-cultural aggregate is related to it in such a way that the "parts" constitute the "whole" and the "whole" constitutes the "parts." This premise is a wholesome purgative for those afflicted with the crude illustrative method, but it also renders genuine comparison difficult or even impossible.[37]

Fifth and most recently chosen is the highway followed by those ethnologists influenced by modern psychology, psychiatry, psychosociology, and sociology. Thurnwald,[38] Redfield,[39] and Linton[40] are among the most conspicuous, but many others might be listed. In general, little is said about origins; Proteus is questioned about processes of development. Further, orientation toward the future is plainly apparent in the concern with acculturation and like processes whereby preliterates and denizens of "cultural islands" are drawn within range of modern secularized life. Stress on minute detail, regardless of relevance to a particular problem—a stress characteristic of the Boas school—gives ground to interest in generalization on the basis of carefully examined empirical evidence. The method is basically analytical rather than idiographic; "facts of repetition" rather than "facts of succession" are in the foreground. At the same time, due heed is paid to functionalist warnings concerning the necessity of taking processes in their full context; hence although generalization is regarded favorably, it

[37] Florian Znaniecki, "The Object-Matter of Sociology," *American Journal of Sociology*, XXXII (Jan., 1927), 540 ff. See also Goldenweiser's critique in *CST*, pp. 471-475. Essentially, the difficulty lies in confusing the *psychology* with the *logic* of configuration (*Gestalt*).

[38] Lowie classifies Thurnwald as a functionalist, but this seems a bit strained. Cf. *CST*, pp. 242-249. Perhaps Lowie's term "tempered functionalism" indicates that he himself has doubts of the validity of his classification. Thurnwald's great work is his *Die menschliche Gesellschaft in ihren ethnosoziologischen Grundlagen* (Berlin, 1931-34), 5 vols. A number of his articles, in English, are conveniently grouped in the *American Sociological Review*, I (June, Aug., 1936), II (Feb., April, 1937).

[39] Robert Redfield, *Tepoztlan: A Mexican Village* (Chicago, 1931).

[40] Ralph Linton, *The Study of Man* (New York, 1936).

is insisted that a genuinely comparative method, markedly similar to that later described in this chapter, is an indispensable corollary. Ethnology of this variety—comparative, contextual, and issuing in analysis of processes—will probably effect a closer *rapprochement* with the social sciences in general and with historical sociology in particular than will any other type. Moreover, it has the merit of being able to include old problems in a new frame of reference, and therefore does not have to start from scratch.

v. ETHNOGRAPHY, SOCIOLOGY, HISTORY

Few sciences, however, can wholly extricate themselves from the marshes of error in one generation, and when the flight has been precipitate, the paths chosen may lead dangerously close to other quagmires. Even those most keenly aware of the mistakes of social evolutionism sometimes fail to see how harmful may be the consequences of drastic reaction. Many of the American ethnographers of the "critical school,"[41] and those "cultural sociologists" who have followed in their wake, illustrate this fact. We rightly reject the grandiose and fantastic formulas of the nineteenth century, but should we abandon the attempt to find methods of analysis that may ultimately yield predictive power and that may be applicable to widely varying cultures? Can we describe a given people with the minute and scrupulous accuracy of the run-of-the-mine American ethnographer, and stop there?[42] In short, are we essentially idiographic historians who rightly eschew all questions of comparability and devote ourselves to the depiction of some limited sector of human life in its characteristic particularity? Or does our special niche in the division of labor call for sustained effort toward generalization, modest though the possibilities of such generalization may be?

If the term "sociology" means anything at all, it should be clear that we must try to generalize. Here lies *our* task. More, we must try to generalize in such ways that we put

[41] Boas and a host of others fall in this category.
[42] Paul Radin, *Method and Theory of Ethnology* (New York, 1933), is a good illustration of the dogmatic idiographer.

crucial questions to Proteus if we work in that part of the sociological field called "historical sociology." This we cannot do if we follow the style set by those who, in flight from the bog of nineteenth-century classical anthropology, strike trails across territory quite as spongy. No paradox is involved when, in devotion to the task of historical *sociology*, we warn against extreme historicism, whether of ethnographic or of conventionally historical extraction.

Further, we perpetrate no paradox when we assert that we can successfully grapple with Proteus only when we arm ourselves with historical data. Frightened by the gruffness of some orthodox historians, who would have us believe that any body of social phenomena manifesting datable time-sequences via written record is in the exclusive possession of historical specialists, we have deprived ourselves of vitally necessary equipment. The same historians, moreover, have successfully intimidated us on many occasions because of their harsh insistence that historical data can be dealt with only idiographically. With even less comprehension of the nature of constructed types than is manifested by American sociologists under the sway of raw empiricism, these historians have chased us off their supposed preserves by shouting "Exception!" As we try to show in the chapter on "Constructive Typology in the Social Sciences," exceptions *must* be found; they do not *in and of themselves* invalidate constructive-typological generalizations. But we are just beginning to wake up to this fact; most of us walk in fear and trembling of the idiographic historian's scowl.

A similar neglect of the aid of history is to be attributed to the surviving reverence for ethnographic data. Some of this reverence issues from mind-sets not much more scholarly than "noble Red Man" romanticism; we are enthralled, as it were, by Pocahontas and Hiawatha. Another source is to be found in the example of ethnographers who are still in the grip of nineteenth-century notions of the "social protoplasmic character" of preliterate societies—and these notions are manifest even among those who are most avowedly in reaction against classical anthropology. Thus a famous ethnographer, Murdock, stated: "The Arunta and the Tlingit and the Hindu [*sic*] are as important to sociology as the experimental rat and the fruitfly are to genetics."[43] The upshot of this evolutionism is that we think we can dispense with historical data if only we can learn enough about the remote, exotic, supposedly "primitive" peoples. Well, let us see; just how much aid can data of this kind give us in answering our Protean questions?[44]

To begin with, the preliterates studied by ethnographers provide no reliable information about long-term social and cultural changes. The orally transmitted lores cannot be trusted, even when they are available, for time spans covering more than two or three generations. Further, and in spite of Murdock and others, we know that the contemporary preliterate does not represent the primitive in the sense of the simple or "social protoplasmic"; many features of their societies are more complex than our own. Again, the greater number of preliterate groups have no historically demonstrable continuities with the larger civilizations for which written records are available, and hence cannot be even indirectly related to the major courses of social change. Once more, the absence of written records means that "document" and "interpretation" inevitably derive from or through the same person, and hence description and analysis tend to coincide—not the happiest of scientific situations. To restate this last point: The contemporary ethnographer is dependent upon contemporary informants. The latter necessarily select and interpret the facts entering into the

[43] George P. Murdock, book review, *American Anthropologist*, XXXIV (Oct.-Dec., 1932), 704. It is much to be doubted whether Murdock now holds this view. There is little or no trace of it in his recent magnificent work, *Social Structure* (1949).

[44] The negative tone of the passages following this question is warranted *only* with reference to the study of time-sequences covering a *long* period. The writer is exceedingly friendly to ethnography when its data are usable—and that is gratifyingly often. No sweeping disparagement is intended, for the sociologist owes a great debt to the ethnographer. He has shown us, for example, that we cannot lightly toss about terms such as "human nature," "basic needs," "fundamental institutions," "masculinity," "femininity," "religion," and the like. If ethnography had done nothing more than break the crust of "civilized," "modern," and "Western" prepossessions, it would have deserved its present high standing.

descriptions they provide. Obviously, selection and interpretation always take place, but it is one thing to have this done by the scientist, and quite another to have it done by someone who has only a remote conception of the problems involved. The historian, on the other hand, frequently has access to written records which, although beyond question bearing the impress of time and place, have not undergone the peculiar "contemporary distortion" to which the ethnographer's materials are exposed. To illustrate: Is knowledge of eighteenth-century Methodism best gained through study of the extant documents or through interviewing present-day Methodists? Plainly no competent historian would choose the latter course; many ethnographers, in dealing with problems essentially similar, are forced to use it, for no alternative exists.[45] Still further, the language obstacles present among preliterates mean that very few contemporary ethnographers are likely to be able to check each other; in fact, the difficulty of mastering a given preliterate tongue may be so great that only one linguist may be said really to know it. Contrast this with the records of historical peoples in languages understood by literally thousands of present-days scholars!

Historical sociology, then, must pay due heed to history, not as a source of idiographic insight, but as a mine of data to be utilized for the answering of Protean questions by the method of constructive typology. We must cease to restrict our choice of data to the history-less preliterates on the one hand and to current events in our own civilization on the other. Twenty years from now it should be impossible to admit the truth of the statement that "In most sociological treatises there is an amazing gap between the *corroboris* of Australian natives and the Coronation of George the Sixth." Certainly the historical sociologist who fails to make the fullest use possible of the verified information provided by ethnography justly incurs the criticism of his colleagues, but it is also true that the historical sociologist who ignores the data of history is a brother of the animal that bore Balaam.

[45] It is interesting to note that these scientists sometimes contrast "field work" with "library research" to the disparagement of the historian.

VI. ILLUSTRATION VS. GENUINE COMPARISON VIA
CULTURE CASE STUDY

Thus having declared allegiance to historical materials, not only for the struggle with Proteus but for all the efforts of sociology, we inevitably face a fundamental problem in the logic of the social sciences: What is the relation of history and sociology? How can the data of history be used by sociology at all? In the chapter on "Constructive Typology in the Social Sciences," the terms idiographic and nomothetic have been liberally applied, and the reader might easily infer that we have been speaking exclusively in the Windelband-Rickert tradition, namely, that history depicts the unique, the nonrecurrent, the empire of *Alexander*, whereas sociology sets forth the "laws" of the general, the recurrent, the *empire* of Alexander and similar rulers. This is simple, clear, and persuasive, and so far as the idiographic pole of the antithesis is concerned, it is hereby expressly accepted. When we turn to the nomothetic, however, certain restrictions must be imposed—restrictions akin to those proclaimed by the functionalists.

Let us say, to begin with, that historical items, in common with other social data, cannot be wholly separated from their contexts. Speaking metaphorically, if we are so rash as to tear apart an intricately patterned tapestry and sew the fragments on a "timeless" background, we get nothing but a crazy quilt for our labor. While maintaining that the "whole-part" relationship extolled by some dogmatic functionalists involves numerous logical fallacies, we are nevertheless convinced that "timeless" classifications are nothing more than tools convenient for dissecting purposes. They reveal relevant problems, but if they wholly destroy the historical strata to which they are applied, they leave nothing but a scattered collection of meaningless fragments.

This fact is well exemplified in the illustrative method used by the classical anthropologists and those social scientists who followed in their train. It is possible to fill the pigeonholes in almost any a priori scheme of classification by judiciously choosing the illustrations to fit. Spencer, Morgan,

Briffault, and many others have been guilty of this error, and the consequences we know. The sociologists should not approach his data with the fixed intention of subjecting them to classification on a Procrustean bed of "timeless" categories that are all generalizable in advance.[46]   He *can* do this if he wishes, of course, but in every case he will find that the result yields no predictive power; he has gratified his need for symmetry and order, and that is all. Genuine prediction, "retrospective" or "prospective," must be couched in "if and when" terms (see the chapter on "Constructive Typology in the Social Sciences"), *and "if and when" always refer to situations bearing some discernible similarity to historical situations that either have already occurred or that can be envisaged in terms of what has already occurred.* The "geologic strata" of history cannot be arbitrarily juggled; if the constructed types of historical sociology are to have predictive power, they must be developed without *primary* regard to their generalizability. If they prove to be generalizable *in spite* of the fact that they are first of all designed to yield a shorthand description and analysis of the social processes and structures permeating a *particular* historical configuration, and in close relation with a clearly defined hypothesis, so much the better, but such generalizability must not be the all-controlling aim of the endeavor.

Here again we refer to the chapter on "Constructive Typology in the Social Sciences." It will be recalled that we there set forth constructed types intended to be of use in the sociological comprehension of a particular series of historical occurrences, namely, the development of Western Christianity.

[46] Lundberg's *Foundations of Sociology* is literally full of classifications of this ahistorical character. We are in no sense, however, advocates of Pure Induction. Why should we advocate the impossible? We all have our "hunches," and they enter into research in a vital way. All that we mean by our attack on "timeless" categories is contained in the examples cited: Spencerian evolutionism, etc. There is no remotest intention of denying the part played in research by deduction, "hunch," speculation, "through-the-elbows" knowledge of the field studied, or the influence of generalizations made by past thinkers. Researchers certainly do not think in a vacuum, and they vaguely know where they are going when they start. Nevertheless, the method of culture case study helps us to avoid the pitfalls of uncontrolled illustration of attractive "hunches."

The ecclesia, the sect, the denomination, and the cult were not planned with the purpose of explaining the genesis and interaction of all religious structures, much less of social structures in general. They are avowedly limited to specific Western European and American phenomena. Such limitation is the essence of what we call "culture case study"; dated and localized types must be accumulated before there is any thoroughgoing attempt to build types of undated and nonlocalized form. Some indication of what is meant by this may be gleaned from the analysis of Jew, Armenian, Parsee, Greek, and Scotsman in the chapter on "Constructive Typology in the Social Sciences," but it may be well to provide another example.

VII. CULTURE CASE STUDY: THE MINIMUM-MAXIMUM SCALE

The relation of culture contact to social change may set a vaguely defined problem. In examining the society of Sparta, let us say, with an eye to this connection, one is likely to be struck by the fact that there is little evidence, over a relatively long period, of either effective culture contact or marked social change in this socio-cultural configuration.[47] Turning to Athens of the same era, we encounter evidence of what seems to be a maximum of both culture contact and social change in certain datable and localizable sectors. Culture case studies affording such extreme contrasts provide an approach that seems likely to vouchsafe a valid basis for selection and comparison. When as the result of intensive culture case studies, both at the extremes and in the transitional zone, the processes correlated with transition toward one or the other extreme have been discovered, the problem has been solved. This result achieved, it may then be possible to restate the constructed types in "if and when" terms, and then to search the historical record for other cases that will provide a checkup on the validity of the predictions made.

Only when validation of this pragmatic variety has been

[47] Of course, there were many Greek societies, such as that of Arcadia, which apparently changed less than did the society of Sparta. The sources for the study of such societies, however, are too scanty to make research worth while.

secured can there be any talk of far-reaching generalizations, and even with such validation it is altogether too much to assume that these generalizations will hold for all cases whatsoever. Generalization, in a very real sense, is omission; the more universal the statement, the less is its predictive power in answering questions "relevant to futurity." We may, if we wish, ask Proteus an empty question like this: "Do human beings associate and dissociate at all times and places?"—but do we not already know the answer? Is the voyage to Pharos worth the trouble?

In the foregoing paragraphs reference to Sparta, Athens, and related cases has been made with definite intent, for the writer has already carried out such studies and has arrived at the conclusion that there does emerge a factor in the culture contact and social change therein evident that inevitably enters into any generalized statement about Greek society. Naturally we lack space to produce the proof in these pages;[48] let us simply assert that the phenomenon of mental mobility appears as one analytical element in all the Greek configurations studied. Now, it should be noted that reference to mental mobility as a *comparable* aspect of these cases does not necessarily mean that it is a *generalizable* factor when it appears in other cases that have not been so minutely analyzed. *We must face the possibility that in the latter instances mental mobility may be only the known outcome of a series of unknowns having little or nothing in common.*[49] At the same time, the fact that it has emerged as the result of focusing on the same problem in a number of historical cases ranged in minimum-maximum sequence renders it probable, although by no means certain, that the formula which explains such mobility, relevant variables taken into account, in each of the cases studied, may also explain it, *mutatis mutandis*, in other cases. Note, however, that we have said "probable, although by no means cer-

[48] See the writer's unpublished doctoral dissertation, "Ionia and Athens: Studies in Secularization," University of Chicago, 1930.

[49] This is an exceedingly important point, for it is the basis of our distinction between "comparison" and "generalization." We may *compare* socio-cultural "parallels," but, as has been shown by the critical ethnologists, these alleged parallels may arise out of radically differing contexts.

tain." The formula is worth a trial, and that is all that can safely be said.

Again pleading lack of space, we do not here present such an explanatory formula. Assuming that the reader will give us the benefit of the doubt, let us go on to say that the result of our labors is the construction of certain types resting firmly on particular historical subsoils, and yet transportable to other regions for the purpose of making test borings, at least. It should be clear that these constructed types are not "timeless"; the presence of some degree of "historical saturation" is indispensable.

Turning to another example: The historically relative character of constructed types is thoroughly demonstrated by the work of Max Weber, in spite of the fact that he rendered lip-service to the Windelband-Rickert theory. In point are his types of domination: traditional, charismatic, and rational.[50] Only in particular types of historical configuration are these manifested in *clear-cut* fashion, and the attempt wholly to eliminate their historical reference deprives them of almost every vestige of predictive power. Furthermore, Löwith has plainly shown that all of Max Weber's ideal types have the red thread of a theory of the total process of historical change running through them; not only is their significance bound up with particular historical configurations, but their ultimate bearing becomes apparent only when what Weber regarded as the total historical process is held in view.[51] (This point will again be mentioned when we analyze theories of the total process of historical change.)

VIII. A THEODICY AND ITS EMPIRICALLY VALID PORTIONS

Let us now turn to historical sociology of a closely related type. Successful culture case study, pervaded by a theory of the total process of historical change, is strikingly exemplified in the recent work of Arnold J. Toynbee. Six massive tomes of *A Study of History* have thus far appeared,[52] and although

[50] Max Weber, "Die Typen der Herrschaft," *Wirtschaft und Gesellschaft* (Tübingen, 1922), pp. 122-176.

[51] Karl Löwith, "Max Weber und Karl Marx," *Archiv für Sozialwissenschaft und Sozialpolitik*, LXVII (March and April, 1932), 59-99, 175-214.

[52] London, 1934-39.

the work will probably run to at least three volumes more, those now available are sufficiently self-contained to be dealt with by themselves.

Toynbee's enterprise has just been termed "successful," and the adjective undoubtedly is warranted where *culture case study* is concerned. Unfortunately, a number of flaws in other respects are evident, and we must take reckoning of these. Of these defects, perhaps the most serious is Toynbee's adherence to a theodicy, to a kind of universal and transcendent philosophy of history (one of the "rejected varieties" shortly to be discussed). Goethe's conception, set forth in the prologue of *Faust*, of evil as a force that in spite of itself makes for good, is given definite approval. This is but an echo of the far older belief that "All things work together for good for them that love God." This may indeed be true "under the aspect of eternity," but it has nothing to do with science as understood, rightly or wrongly, by the present generation.

Second among the blemishes is an all-pervasive mysticism that leads Toynbee to dally with terms such as *yin* and *yang* in ways that occasionally result in emotional exaltation rather than intellectual clarity. To be sure, Toynbee sometimes uses *yin* and *yang* as equivalents of changelessness and change, but the mystic tendency, like King Charles's head, perpetually intrudes.

Third is a shortcoming usual among historians who manufacture their theories of social change in ignorance of the relevant sociological literature. Witness the fact that some of Huntington's most dubious doctrines have been adopted, with a few minor qualifications, as part of Toynbee's treatise. In view of the fact that the merits of his analysis are largely independent of the truth or falsity of Huntington's teachings, this is the more regrettable.

Fourth, Toynbee wastes a great deal of energy and space in exploding racial dogmas that are not taken seriously by any physical anthropologist of repute; here again his lack of familiarity with the critical literature has led him to manufacture his arguments *ad hoc*.

PROSPECTS OF SOCIAL CHANGE 151

Yet in spite of these and other flaws, the profound significance of Toynbee's work is incontestable. Beginning with a forthright attack on extreme historicism, he proceeds to a very thorough and circumspect discussion of method. Not sufficiently acquainted with the literature, he nonetheless avoids many of the pitfalls of crude empiricism and apriorism. A plan of operations centering about several societies held to be "intelligible fields of historical study" is elaborated. Following this, he isolates twenty-one comparable entities to which what is essentially a method of culture case study can be applied: Egyptiac, Andean; Sinic, Minoan, Sumeric, Mayan; Syriac; Indic, Hittite, Hellenic; Western; Orthodox Christian (in Russia), Far Eastern (in Korea and Japan); Orthodox Christian (main body), Far Eastern (main body); Iranic; Arabic, Hindic; Mexic; Yucatec; and Babylonic. Toynbee makes good his case for the relatively unfamiliar groupings of the above classification, and sets for himself a problem that includes all four of our Protean questions, namely, "What are the causes of the geneses, growths, breakdowns, disintegrations, and rhythms in the histories of civilizations, and what are the prospects of the contemporary Western world in the light thereof?" This, to say the least, is a large order, but it must also be said that Toynbee comes nearer to being equal to his self-imposed task than any other thinker, past or present, with whom we are familiar.

He begins his analysis by considering a number of "possible positive and negative factors" which may help to account for the traits manifested by "civilized" groups[53] as contrasted with more "primitive" societies. His conclusion, apparently valid in spite of its moralistic overtones, is that the negative factors of "psychic inertia" and "inferior race" vouchsafe no satisfying explanations. Next in order, as a possible positive factor, is the natural environment, and through the skilful dissection of several culture cases he demonstrates that "favorable" natural environments do not necessarily call forth the phenomena of

[53] Toynbee's definition of civilization is sufficiently different from those customarily used to warrant the quotation marks, although we shall drop them in succeeding paragraphs.

civilization. Indeed, Toynbee does much to render plausible the theory that strikingly *un*favorable natural environments have in many instances been the indispensable factor in the transition from "primitivism" to "civilization." The challenge of drought for Egypt; trackless marsh·for Sumeria; flood for China; tropical forest for the Mayas; bleak climate and grudging soil for Andean culture; sea for Minoan; and so on for most of the twenty-one culture cases. Where challenges from the natural environment have been conspicuously lacking, there have been "civilization-eliciting" challenges from the human environment, particularly from what Toynbee calls external and internal proletariats (of which instances are respectively afforded by the Germanic barbarians and the early Christians).

Every informed American sociologist will be struck by the similarity between Toynbee's "challenge and response" and Thomas's "crisis." This is rendered still more striking by Toynbee's masterly survey of the "range of challenge-and-response." Hard countries, new ground, blows, pressures, penalizations—all these challenges and the responses thereto are analyzed with staggering acumen and with an abundance of comparable culture cases. So inclusive is Toynbee's knowledge of history that he frequently seems able to select cases in which only the crucial factors vary; controls are thus provided for many of his generalizations. The outcome is that the role of challenge-and-response in the *genesis* of civilizations is attested in a rather convincing way.

The adequacy of Toynbee's researches with regard to the *growth* of civilizations, however, stands in grave doubt. He carries conviction, to be sure, in his analysis of arrested growth, although this may in part be due to the adroitly chosen cases of the Eskimos, the Mongols, the Janissaries, and the Spartiates. Yet we need not be hypercritical; even without Toynbee's evidence most sociologists would agree that antlike or machine-like perfection of adaptation acts as a check on change. When he turns to the positive factors in civilizational growth, Toynbee is much less convincing, for the mystical motif that merely confuses the first volume of his treatise becomes so loud by the end of the third (dealing with civilizational growth) that it almost drowns out the systematic-empirical theme. He operates with two conceptions at this point: "etherialization" and "withdrawal-and-return." By the first of these he means a process whereby a dominant minority meets internal or external difficulties by developing some saving formula. Solon's response to the challenge of the Athenian internal proletariat, a response in the form of abolition of debt slavery, currency revision, and so on, is one among many instances provided by Toynbee. In other words, the culture shifts to a higher level of complexity, is rendered more "ethereal" through the intervention of some especially gifted leader, who is usually representative of an advanced minority. "Withdrawal-and-return" is a process closely linked to etherialization. The leaders or the elite which they represent go into seclusion, either by actual physical withdrawal or "ivory tower" retreat, and in this seclusion develop the etherializing plans that make growth at a more complex civilizational level possible. The possibility is rendered an actuality through the phenomenon of return; the leaders or the elite come back to the common life from which they had temporarily absented themselves, bearing the saving formula. To the present writer it seems that Toynbee may at times grant too important a role to single individuals or small minorities, but it cannot be denied that he has an amazing array of evidence to prove his point. Future research alone will show whether or not this evidence is of merely "illustrative" character.

The breakdowns and disintegrations of civilizations in a certain sense run the film backwards. Challenges are so overwhelming that the response, even when forthcoming, utterly fails; mechanical imitation of an idolized pattern leads to cultural sterility; dominant minorities become disorganized, both "personally" and "socially," before etherialization can be effected; external and internal proletariats overwhelm the decadent civilization; archaism on the one hand and futurism on the other are chosen as escapes from an ever more onerous challenge—and the end is collapse.

With only slight aid from modern psychiatry and psychology (Jung excepted), Toynbee has produced a striking analysis of the types of mentality that appear in civilizations that are breaking down or disintegrating. His presentation of what he calls "Schism in the Soul" should be read by every social scientist; without technical verbiage and with profound insight Toynbee arrives at many of the conclusions also set forth by our mental hygienists and clinicians. Studies of "split personality," "marginal men," "demoralization," and "civilization and its discontents" would profit immeasurably through cross-fertilization with his remarkable array of attested historical evidence. Of great interest, for the recent phase of Euro-American civilization, is Toynbee's analysis of the yearning for "the savior with the time-machine" that appears among the decadent elites of disintegrating societies. Salvation is sought through a "leader" upon whom the weary and thwarted can cast their burdens. Responsibility becomes a galling load; anyone who seems able to carry it for all rises to "omnipotence." As a by-product, Toynbee also shows that dictatorship of this kind is not simply a result of more adequate means of communication (press, radio, and so on), as some myopic interpreters of current events would have us believe.

In the volumes to come later, Toynbee promises like discussions of those problems of historical sociology that can be subsumed under the headings of universal states and churches, heroic ages, contacts between civilizations in space and time, and other vitally important matters already mentioned. No matter what reservations one may have as to the Christian value-judgments that pervade the treatise, there can be no question that Toynbee has given to sociologists a magnificent example of the possibilities of culture case study in historical sociology. Those who fail to profit by his example can never hope for answers from Proteus.

IX. REJECTED PHILOSOPHIES OF HISTORY

Many of Toynbee's value-judgments, issuing as they do in a kind of Christian theodicy, force upon our attention once more, and this time in relative separation from the others, the second of our Protean questions: "Can there be discerned an all-encompassing drift toward a single goal, in spite of the baffling maze of historical changes?" In other words, Max Weber's total historical configuration and Toynbee's Christian philosophy of history make it necessary for us to survey the many attempts that have been made to determine the general trend of the development of culture, or of "the historical movement" as a whole. Few of these attempts are of the scientific character we associate with historical sociology; what is currently called the philosophy of history includes a great deal that the critical sociologist must brusquely reject. Still, it is necessary to run over the list of rejected varieties before discussing the type of philosophy of history that offers some prospect of harmonious union with a sound historical sociology.

The universal and transcendent kind of philosophy of history has been and is exceedingly prominent, and is first among those marked for rejection. By "universal" is meant ultimate purpose of meaning or value toward which not only all mankind but the entire universe, as it were, strives—that one far-off divine event toward which the whole creation moves. "Divine" affords a hint of what is meant by "transcendent"; the universal purpose is to be attributed to God's Will, or to the realization of the Absolute Idea, or to a Beneficent Nature. The genealogy of this variety of the philosophy of history is long; it begins with the earliest cosmogonies and finds present exemplification in the Millennial sects (although we might also name some sociologists). Within our present limits it is useless to try to justify the exclusion we have announced; we can merely point out that in our scientific roles as currently defined theodicies are not for us, and that they are not likely to be in the foreseeable future.

Similarly, we must announce the shutting of the gate before the universal and immanent philosophies of history. As "immanent" indicates, transcendent sanction in a Divine Will is not explicitly sought, but it is asserted that there is a goal or purpose toward which the development of the universe and, by the same token, of human society not only *does* tend but *ought* so to tend.[54]   Now, we should be the first to grant that modern sociology is "relevant to futurity."   But it does not follow from this that the sociologist should permit himself to answer his own questions before he has *earnestly* come to grips with Proteus.   All too frequently the vision of the desired end blinds us to the prerequisite and entailed conditions that may make its attainment undesirable or impossible.   Even though we concede that "impossible" is a restriction that has been successfully defied time after time in the long annals of mankind, it may none the less be true that the modern sociologist is now in a position to provide estimates of relative probability, at the very least.   Faith has moved mountains, but only at terrific cost.   The end to be achieved, whether "national sovereignty," "Aryan supremacy," "a classless society," or "a warless world," may be worth the price that must be paid—but the sociologist has the duty of determining what that price will be.   If he allows his dream of the perfect society—and all men rightly have such dreams—to veil the stark realities that confront him and his fellows, he has betrayed his trust.[55]

Even "men of good will" must be professionally skilled if they are to provide trustworthy guidance into the future; bungling amateurs, no matter how excellent their intentions, must be shouldered aside.   And not only the amateurs; many earlier writers of high standing, and many modern sociologists, have mixed too many nonscientific "oughts" with their counsel—Marx, Ward, Hobhouse, Oppenheimer, and ' scores of others.[56]   Valuable leads can be taken from them, but they are

[54] Virtually all the social philosophies setting progress as a supreme end are of this type. See J. B. Bury, *The Idea of Progress* (New York, 1932); Barnes and Becker, *STLS*, pp. 458-506; P. A. Sorokin, *Social and Cultural Dynamics* (New York, 1937), Vol. II, *passim*; Vilfredo Pareto, *The Mind and Society: A General Sociology* (New York, 1934), pp. 6, 49, 77, 93, 112, 393, *et passim*.

[55] *Verantwortungsethik vs. Gesinnungsethik*. See Max Weber, "Politik als Beruf," *Gesammelte Politische Schriften* (Munich, 1921), pp. 396-450, esp. pp. 441-442. Cf. H. H. Gerth and C. Wright Mills, *From Max Weber* (New York, 1946).

For a fuller statement of a similar but not identical position, see the chapter on "Supreme Values and the Sociologist" in the present volume, pp. 281-305.

[56] For a fairly full list, consult Paul Barth, *Die Philosophie der Geschichte als Soziologie*, 3rd and 4th eds. (Leipzig, 1922), and Ludwig Stein, *Die soziale Frage im Lichte der Philosophie*, 3rd and 4th eds. (Stuttgart, 1923).

beyond the pale of historical sociology as a responsible science.

Next in the array of our rejected varieties is the relative but transcendent philosophy of history of which Troeltsch provides the most arresting instance,[57] but of which examples are to be found in Scheler, Spengler, and, in some phases, Sorokin. Limiting ourselves to the writer first mentioned, Troeltsch drifts close to the ground occupied by the extreme historicists in holding that there can never be any theories of socio-cultural process applicable, even within carefully guarded limits, to all mankind—because there is no such thing as mankind. To be sure, says Troeltsch, there are great cultural totalities, but each constitutes a whole having its own untranslatable value-system, and therefore possesses a fundamentally unique kind of interaction among the "parts" of that "whole." Here there seems to be a patent confusion between "facts of succession" and "facts of repetition," as well as a farrago of "whole-part" illogic, but inasmuch as these have already been discussed elsewhere—namely, in this chapter and the one on "Constructive Typology in the Social Sciences"—the passing reference must suffice. According to Troeltsch not only is there no way of determining what *ought* to be the universal or even the common-human trend of development, but there is no way of determining what *is* that trend. At best we can discover the meaningful sequences of the cultures in which we have been saturated, so to speak, and into which we therefore have insight—and that is all. This seemingly complete relativity of value-systems and their "whole-part" effects Troeltsch cloaks with a sort of transcendental sanction by echoing the assertion that "Every epoch is in communion with God."[58] The values of the Turks are not our values; hence their "inwardness" cannot be comprehended nor their course of change predicted. The Turks, however, are God's children even as ourselves, and God will know and reconcile, in His transcendence, the relativities of mortality. Our task as bearers of the great Euro-

[57] Ernst Troeltsch, *Der Historismus und seine Probleme* (Tübingen, 1922); Eugene Lyman, "Ernst Troeltsch's Philosophy of History," *Philosophical Review*, XLI (Sept., 1932), 443-465.
[58] An aphorism which he attributes to Ranke.

American value-system is to strive to realize to the full the possibilities inherent in that system, trusting that God will ensure their ultimate incorporation in the realm of the Absolute. To the present writer this seems an ill-digested conglomerate of extreme historicism and "the theology of crisis."[59] Science is grounded upon faith,[60] but not of this kind, and we therefore refuse to include Troeltsch and like-minded writers among the historical sociologists to be given serious consideration.

X. A USABLE THEORY OF HISTORY

Lest we should seem too "exclusive," let us now turn to those theories of the total historical process that can with some assurance be brought within the category of historical sociology. The use of the plural "those" points to our plan of organization; the difference between the excluded and included varieties is so great that we can perhaps regard the latter as subtypes, differing only in details, of one comprehensive genus.

This kind of historical sociology is not cosmically universal, for it does not assume a meaning or purpose or value toward which the cosmos "strives." Moreover, it is not socially universal, for it presupposes no overarching end, ideal, or norm for the attainment of which humanity as a whole should or does bend its efforts. Further, it is not transcendent, for it incorporates no revelation of nor insight into the workings of the Absolute, Beneficent Nature, or the Divine Mind. Finally, and probably most important, it is not subject to the criticism leveled against extreme historicism in this chapter and elsewhere, for its advocates demonstrate effectively that certain generalizations can be made that are not entirely circumscribed by particular historical configurations at particular times and places. In short, these generalizations are not of the rigidly dated and localized sort.[60a]

Two subvarieties of this nonuniversal, nontranscendent,

---

[59] Now identified with the names of Soeren Kierkegaard and Karl Barth.

[60] Namely, the faith that man can know and control his world and his earthly destiny, and that such knowledge and control are worthwhile. Proof? There is none—not in the atomic age—nor has there ever been. But without this faith science becomes meaningless. See pp. 293-298.

[60a] See chapter, "Constructive Typology in the Social Sciences," pp. 105-119.

and nonrelative theory of the total historical process can be distinguished. They differ only in the degree to which the postulates, methodology, and remoter consequences of such a theory are laid bare and structurally interrelated. The first division, comprising the less thorough formulations, includes the theories of Shotwell, Robinson, Durkheim, and more especially Tönnies and Teggart;[61] in the second may be placed the more highly integrated presentations of Max and Alfred Weber.

By and large, the historical sociologists in the first group hold that the trend of social development the world over has been and will be toward a greater measure of geographical (vicinal), social, and mental accessibility,[62] mediated by all those devices of transportation and communication that wind about the globe with ever-increasing intricacy. Along with this go more and more differentiation and secularization and, *pari passu*, a heightening of those personality traits ordinarily labeled individuation, compartmentalization, and expedient rationality. For example, Tönnies builds his entire theory of social development, as set forth in *Geist der Neuzeit* as well as in earlier writings, in terms of the transition from "community" to "society," joining to it, as an inseparable corollary, a shift from "essential will" to "arbitrary will"—or in the terms used earlier in this chapter,[63] from mental immobility to mental mobility. A markedly similar trend is traced by Teggart, but the latter is more interested in the precise analysis of the processes involved than is Tönnies; he finds the chief clue in the breakdown of isolation following upon migrations and communication, for these precipitate conflicts of differing idea-systems and start processes leading to release from traditional restraints.

[61] Émile Durkheim, *The Division of Labor in Society* (Simpson trans.; New York, 1933), esp. Bk. II, chaps. i-ii; Ferdinand Tönnies, *Gemeinschaft und Gesellschaft* (8th ed.; Berlin, 1935), *Fortschritt und soziale Entwicklung* (Karlsruhe, 1926), *Geist der Neuzeit* (Leipzig, 1935); F. J. Teggart, *Processes of History* (New Haven, 1918), *Theory of History* (New Haven, 1925).

[62] Howard Becker, *Systematic Sociology on the basis of the* Beziehungslehre *and* Gebildelehre *of Leopold von Wiese* (New York, 1932), pp. 222-241; hereinafter cited as Wiese-Becker.

[63] See also Barnes and Becker, *STLS*, *passim*.

Essential agreement with this can rightly be attributed to Max Weber, but his agreement is qualified by the stringency of culture case study[64] and ideal-typical method.[65] Initially trained in jurisprudence and history, Weber commanded a simply staggering array of empirical evidence and was accord-

[64] Of course Weber did not use this label, but one variety of *Idealtypus* is the *historische Individuum*, bringing the latter close to culture case study.

[65] Although noted elsewhere (pp. 97, 259, 261), it should again be stated that constructive typology and ideal-typical method are similar but by no means identical.

The reader will note that in discussing Weber I consistently refer to his use of "ideal types." After all, this is the literal translation of *Idealtypus*. Moreover, I have come to feel that "ideal type" should be used *only* to refer to the variety, or varieties, characteristic of Weber's work. Since he first began to use the term and to exemplify the logic and method associated with it, a good half-century has elapsed. We are now in the midst of a Weber vogue in the United States, but our linguistic ineptitude means that it is a vogue based on translations, notably the Henderson-Parsons, the Gerth-Mills, and the Shils-Finch. That is to say, we are now, in the evaluation of Weber, about at the point reached in Germany during the 1920's. We are abysmally ignorant of the vast body of critical literature that has since appeared; Kraus, Bienfait, Oppenheimer, and von Schelting, to name no others, should be appearing in our footnotes. (See the voluminous bibliography in the Gerth and Martindale translation, *Max Weber's "The Hindu Social System,"* University of Minnesota Sociology Club, Bulletin No. 1, 1950.)

If "ideal type" is used for Weber's work, and for his alone, then another term should be used to designate concepts (types being concepts of a special kind) that diverge in significant degree from his. For this reason, I consistently use "constructed type" to label my own tools. As is noted in chap. ii and in many other places throughout this book, particularly chap. v, I am trying my best to bring typological method into line with modern probability logic, and with the logic of experiment as well. Much of this is latent in Weber, but here and there I think that "something new has been added." More especially, I think that a few steps have been made toward bridging the gap between typology and quantification. Although I am not prepared to say that no valid scientific work can be done without elaborate quantification, I am quite convinced that a great deal more quantification, notably in the pragmatic validation of conclusions, should be done if we are to pass out of the realm of the primarily artistic and impressionistic so strikingly exemplified by Ruth Benedict. Sometimes, of course, numerical statements provide only spurious precision, but the mere fact that the uncritical are deceived by numerical halos is insufficient reason for arrogant rejection of number as such. We should use numerical symbols, and quantitative formulation, when we *legitimately* can.

Whatever "ideal-typical method" may be, then, let it be clearly understood that constructive typology is *not* dogmatically anti-quantitative. To oppose Dodd's vaporings, for example, is not to oppose the use of statistics by sober, theoretically sophisticated researchers.

If this were a two-color printing job, I should like to put the foregoing paragraph in the reddest of red ink. Having myself been a practicing mechanical engineer, using complex computations to earn my daily bread, I yield to no one in my respect for precise numerical statement when and if it can genuinely advance the science of sociology.

ingly skeptical of sweeping formulas. One of his earliest pub-
lications was an agrarian history of the ancient world; one of
his latest (posthumous, in fact), an analysis of Pharisaism.
From beginning to end he was an unflagging advocate of "coming to grips with the data," of intensive culture case study.
Oftentimes dipping his pen in iron and gall, Weber opposed
all efforts to find modern capitalism, for example, in the Greek
world, or to equate the Middle Ages with the era marking the
domination of the Athenian landed gentry, or to cull illustrations for a rigid sequence of stages of industrial evolution, as
Bücher[66] and Pöhlmann[67] tried to do, from the Greek household and slave workshop. Yet Weber did not topple over
backwards into the swamp of extreme historicism; he succeeded
in finding comparable aspects of ideal types primarily intended
to render possible the sociological patterning of particular historical configurations. Further, he was able to make some of
those comparable aspects generalizable through judicious extension of the ideal-typical method with which he consistently
operated. This method utilizes various personality types, types
of social processes and structures, and relatively self-contained
interactive units composed of such personalities, processes, and
structures. These are never found in "pure" form, but for the
purposes of isolating analytic elements and of scientific systematization are dealt with *as if* they so existed.

For example, Weber was quite as keenly aware as is any
"institutional economist" that economic activity is historically
conditioned, and that it oftentimes evidences but a very slight
degree of anything that we should call expedient rationality; he
was no naïve classical economist. Nevertheless, he constructed
types of "the rational man" for the purpose of being able to
assert definitely, in relation to particular time, place, and circumstance, what can be regarded as expediently rational and
what cannot. He saw clearly that whenever we call economic
conduct "institutional" we tacitly presuppose our own ration-

[66] Carl Bücher, *Industrial Evolution*, trans. from the 3rd German ed. by
S. Morley Wickett (New York, 1901).

[67] Robert von Pöhlmann, *Geschichte des antiken Kommunismus und Sozialis-
mus*, 2 vols. (Munich, 1893-1901).

ality as observers. Not only this: in calling conduct "non-rational" we set it over against a definite conception—which, to be sure, may be tucked away in an obscure cranny of our minds—of what rational conduct is like under a wide range of circumstances. How else can we pass judgments of "institutional molding" or of nonrationality? "If the salt hath lost its savor, wherewith shall it be salted?" The rational, or what is believed to be rational, is always the meaningful standard by which the nonrational is judged.

Weber went on to point out that what is regarded as rational differs widely from place to place and from time to time. There is ample historical evidence to show that religious devotees have often engaged in conduct that would lead to their confinement in an insane asylum if it had occurred almost anywhere in Western Europe or America during the twentieth century, but in their day and generation they were taken quite as a matter of course—in short, they were believed to be "normal" and even rational. True, says Weber, a Hindu mystic suddenly transplanted to a center of Catholicism would not be regarded as in any way rational; the value-systems of the contrasting civilizations are too far apart. Still, it is clear that within any given civilization the scope of rationality is always implicitly determined and is taken for granted in passing social judgments of every description. We have, as it were, a sort of secret yardstick by which we measure conduct, sometimes without any clear idea of what we are doing. Indeed, some raw empiricists boast that they are able to analyze "behavior" without making use of "theories." All too often, however, these apostles of Pure Induction overlook the fact that their own civilization has imparted to them a host of preconceived notions which they never stop to examine or of which they are not even aware. Among these notions one of the most common is the prevailing standard of rationality. Weber rightly felt that "the rational man" can never be other than a fiction, but that if grievous error is to be avoided, the component traits of this fiction must be isolated, arranged in a definite pattern, and explicitly set forth in "public" terms. Having himself done this, he demonstrated, to anyone who will take the trouble to read his analyses[68] rather than depend on second-hand statements,[69] that a great deal of power in prediction (whether of "prospective" or "retrospective" variety)[70] can be gained by operating with what is after all, to repeat, a fiction. Moreover, he was at pains to point out that such ideal types are likely to have little utility if they conform to an ordinary statistical mode or mean; a deliberate modification or accentuation of the average is frequently advisable if scientific prediction of social processes is to be attained.[71]

The ideal type is a device made of the particularity of history, shaped in such a way that this particularity becomes comparable and, in some instances, widely generalizable. To take our "rational man" again: Only in particular historical epochs can even relatively well-marked conduct of the kind he represents be found. *Without knowledge of the particularities encountered in those epochs we should not be able to build a useful type of rationality.* Once such a type (or types) has been constructed, however, it may be of great aid in revealing the presence and further ramifications of the conduct in other eras and cultures. Moreover, if our "economic man" has been well constructed, the fact that a particular culture does *not* reveal his presence is in itself of great importance—the "negative utility" of an ideal type may in some circumstances be quite as significant as its "positive utility." (A large part of Chapter V, present volume, is devoted to this point.)

In the present context the interesting thing about the ideal-typical method of Max Weber is that it serves and stands in the service of a nonuniversal, nontranscendent, nonrelative

---

[68] Contained in *Wirtschaft und Gesellschaft, Gesammelte Aufsätze zur Religionssoziologie,* and *Gesammelte Aufsätze zur Wissenschaftslehre* (Tübingen, 1921-23). We now have available the translations by Henderson-Parsons, Gerth-Mills, and Shils-Finch.

[69] Such as the book by H. M. Robertson, *Aspects of the Rise of Economic Individualism: A Criticism of Max Weber and His School* (Cambridge, 1933).

[70] See chapters on "Constructive Typology in the Social Sciences," and "Supreme Values and the Sociologist," pp. 112, 285-290.

[71] Weber, *Wirtschaft und Gesellschaft,* p. 10.

theory of the total historical process. For Weber, at least, the most readily discernible factor in social development is the growth of the rational habit of mind. This eventually leads to that abstraction from the concrete and personal which is so deeply ingrained in the habit patterns of "the economic man" and, to choose an instance equally apt, of "the scientific man."

But let it be strongly emphasized that although Weber devoted his life to the devising of types of rationality and the analysis of the resulting interactional systems, he set no supreme value on rationality as such. Indeed, he once trenchantly said:

> It is the fate of our time, characterized as it is by rationalism and intellectualization, and above all by tendencies to secularize the world, that precisely the most ultimate and sublime values have been withdrawn from the common life of every day. To those who cannot manfully bear the burden thus imposed we must say, "Silently return, without the usual self-advertisement of the renegade, but rather with the simplicity and directness of faith, into the open arms, widely and pityingly extended, of the old churches. . . . 'The sacrifice of the intellect' must be made . . . , but we will not reproach . . . [you] for this if it can be made sincerely." Such a "sacrifice of the intellect" for the sake of unconditional religious self-abandon is morally something entirely different from the evasion of the demands of intellectual honesty which becomes manifest when the courage is lacking to make clear to oneself one's own final position, and instead substitutes a sickly relativism that slips from under the demands of duty.[72]

From the context of these and other passages, it is plain that Max Weber could never himself make the "sacrifice of the intellect," but he cast no scorn on those who did. The vials of his wrath were saved to cast upon the heads of those who fondly fancied that they could retain full sincerity and yet "blend the best features of science and religion" in their presumably scientific work.

The growth of the rational habit of thought and of the concomitant secularization of society, then, was for Weber the strand upon which all sociological constructs must be strung, regardless of the religious or ethical value of the strand. This

[72] Weber, "Wissenschaft als Beruf," op. cit., pp. 554-555, my translation. Cf. Gerth and Mills, op. cit.

is clearly a generalization, but it is not universal in its bearings, for Weber took pains to point out varying rates in the growth of rationality, fluctuations and *reversals* in the trend, and peculiar distortions resulting from the conflicts within personality engendered by rapid or all-absorptive rationalization. The trend merely appeared as the most easily comparable and generalizable trait of all the manifold culture case studies upon which he had so successfully labored. Moreover, he was under no delusions as to the range of rationality, for he regarded many phases of life as quite beyond its reach and, as has been intimated, his ethical standpoint was that of unqualified individual autonomy and responsibility on a wholly *non*rational basis: "Let us go to work and meet the demands that the day imposes upon us—as human beings as well as professionally. [The ethical task] . . . is plain and simple when each of us finds and obeys the inner urge that gives consistency to *his* life."[73]   Clearly this is not the creed of an apostle of "the rational man" as humanity's Messiah; Max Weber used ideal types of rationality as tools of analysis—and that is all.

XI. "CULTURAL HISTORY AS CULTURAL SOCIOLOGY"

His younger brother, Alfred Weber, has incorporated these and like analytical tools in his "sociology of culture."[74] Although Alfred Weber fails to reach the high level of methodological finesse manifested by his brother, his work is well worth examination, for it deals wtih some matters not explicitly discussed elsewhere.

Connections with several of our "rejected varieties" of the philosophy of history are evident in Alfred Weber's studies, but this is no sufficient ground for rejection. Problems are problems, in whatever context they occur: Romantic, rationalist, or Marxian. These examples, be it noted, probably represent the chief influences in his "sociology of culture." Indeed, the latter can perhaps be fairly characterized as an attempt to apply

[73] Weber, *op. cit.*, p. 555. The informed reader will note that I have rendered the Socratic *daimon* as "inner urge." One might also use "genius," as in our ordinary references to "a man's good genius" or his "evil genius." Nothing could give the sense of Weber more inaccurately than "demon," considering the English connotations of that term.

[74] *Kulturgeschichte als Kultursoziologie* (Leiden, 1934).

Marxian formulas of class struggle, economic interest, and dialectic development to historical happenings, and then to point out their inadequacy in the explanation of the "cultural" achievements of man.

The special sense in which Weber uses the word "culture" shows how he has attempted to solve the problems posed by Romanticism. The uniqueness and mystery of genius, as manifested in music, sculpture, poetry, and other "cultural emanations," is unqualifiedly affirmed. Yet, the manifest *conditioning* of these achievements by other phases of the total historical process does not *determine* their basic traits. These can be idiographically apprehended and in some measure communicated, but they defy prediction, whether of "retrospective" or "prospective" kind. Moreover, culture does not "progress," and it has no necessary connection with the rational control of the situations encountered in every day experience. MacIver, who presents a closely similar conception, says: "There is no 'march' of culture. It is subject to retrogression as well as to advance. Its past does not assure its future."[75]

Unlike Spengler, whom we shall consider later, Alfred Weber does not regard the "cultures" of different peoples as in any sense homologous; each is necessarily unique. Accordingly, there can be no "morphology of culture" of the type Spengler proposes. "Cultural emanations" can be absorbed and at least partially comprehended *once they have occurred*, but they can never be predicted, much less prophesied.

Quite otherwise for Alfred Weber are the rationalistic strands of "civilization"—also a term he uses in a somewhat special sense.[76] The secularization and rationalization of life, most clearly apparent in natural science, is the aim of the "civilizing intellect." The growth of "civilization" is coherent, in spite of checks, reactions, and shifts of emphasis, and its products are transferable from people to people. This universality

[75] R. M. MacIver, *Society: A Textbook of Sociology* (New York, 1937), p. 275. See also his more extended discussion, "Civilization *versus* Culture," *University of Toronto Quarterly*, I (April, 1932), pp. 316-332, and "The Historical Pattern of Social Change," *Authority and the Individual* (Cambridge, 1937).

[76] Closely akin, however, to MacIver's usage.

of "civilizational" phenomena means that the great historical entities, though differing radically in their "cultures," are nevertheless potentially or actually interdependent. Means-ends rationality, particularly in its expedient form, is everywhere applicable and, given the right conditions, it *must* emerge.

These conditions are in part provided by the "societal" process—once more a special usage. Every "intelligible field of historical study" (to borrow Toynbee's phrase) is characterized by definite configurations of "societal" processes. Some of their structural consequences are castes, classes, and other groupings such as those based on age, sex, kinship, or territory. Here the problems confronted by Alfred Weber are essentially those set by the historical materialism of Marx. In tracing "societal" developments, he tends to agree with the Marxians in maintaining that they are chiefly of *immanent* character; the relations between "intelligible fields of historical study," brought about by trade, war, migration, and other means of diffusion, are of secondary importance in "societal" change.[77]

Alfred Weber goes on to say that the processes and structures making up differing "societies" tend to follow in certain sequences—although, to be sure, no unilinear schema that is *empirically* valid can be constructed. In other words, he maintains that intensive culture case study entered upon for *sociological* purposes justifiably issues in the building of societal types and subtypes that, to use our terminology, are not only comparable but may also be generalizable within the limits set by constructive typology. Such comparability and generalizability are possible, however, only for the "civilizational" and "societal" aspects of historical configurations. Again in our terminology, the "cultural" phases are in some respects functionally interdependent with the others, but they cannot be subjected to scientific analysis, namely, to the systematic statement of the

[77] The present writer would take issue with this position if there were sufficient space at his disposal; as it is, all that can be done is to note disagreement and to refer the reader to his articles on "Processes of Secularisation," *Sociological Review* (British), XXIV (April-July, Oct., 1932), 138-154, 266-286; and "Forms of Population Movement," *Social Forces*, XI (Dec., 1930, March, 1931), 147-160, 351-361.

probability of the hypothetical or actual recurrence of phenomena that, for the purposes in hand, are regarded as identical.[78]

A signal service to historical sociology, in our estimation, has been performed by Alfred Weber in setting out this three-fold classification. We seriously doubt, however, whether "cultural" happenings and products are so wholly beyond the range of prediction as he maintains; Toynbee's discussion of archaism and futurism,[79] to choose no other instance, seems effectively to controvert his thesis in some respects. Further, Alfred Weber does not distinguish properly between the peculiar contents of the "cultural emanations" as such, which of course can be apprehended only idiographically, and the constructed types within which, for predictive purposes, many of these "emanations" can be scientifically incorporated.

Nevertheless, in the analyses of the full sweep of historical change presented by Alfred Weber and Max Weber, some features of which, in less clear-cut form, are also to be found in Tönnies, Teggart, and several other writers, we have theories that are worthy of the earnest attention of the historical sociologist.

XII. WHAT ARE STAGES GOOD FOR?

Closely bound up with many theories of history, and especially with the varieties just surveyed, is the conception of stages of development—essentially, our third Protean question: "Are there any sequences or stages in societal development that when discovered will enable us to estimate the varying speeds at which the differing sections of mankind have approached the goal?"

In part following Ginsberg,[80] we may distinguish four ways in which the notion of stages has been employed. Each of these has a different background in the panorama of social thought, and each possesses very different value for a sound historical sociology.

---

[78] Discussed at length in the chapter on "Constructive Typology in the Social Sciences," pp. 96-102. Needless to say, Alfred Weber does not operate within the confines of this definition of scientific activity.

[79] Toynbee, op. cit., VI, 49-131.

[80] Morris Ginsberg, "The Conception of Stages in Social Evolution," Man, XXXII (April, 1932), 87-91.

First is the notion of unilinear stage-sequences attributable to social evolutionists such as Spencer, Morgan, and the like. This has been thoroughly discredited, as we have seen, and hence may be dismissed without further ado.

Second is the idea of stages as typifying general trends of development in the socio-cultural life of mankind taken as a whole. One of the chief nineteenth-century efforts along this line is exemplified by Comte's theological-military → metaphysical-legalistic → scientific-industrial succession. Another was Durkheim's view that the mechanical and restraining solidarity of group repression of individuality slowly gives place to the voluntary solidarity of the social division of labor and the functional organization of society.[81] DeGreef held that the transformation runs from regimes based on force to those marked by voluntary contract.[82] Novicow contended that the stages of change may be most adequately formulated in terms of the substitution of "higher" for "lower" forms of social conflict: physiological → economic-political → intellectual.[83] Closely paralleling this, Ratzenhofer and Small suggested that the shift has been from a "conquest state" to a "culture state."[84] Hobhouse maintained that the stages of social development are best characterized as those in which kinship, authority, and citizenship have successively been the bases of cohesion.[85] Giddings divided social development as follows: zoögenic, or animal society; anthropogenic, or the society of man in transition from animal to human tribal organization; ethnogenic, or tribal society; and demogenic, or the society of the period covered by written records. This last era he further divided into the military-religious, roughly corresponding to early antiquity and the Middle Ages; the liberal-legal, covering Greco-Roman and early modern developments; and the economic-ethical, comprising the period since the Industrial Revolution.[86]

[81] Barnes and Becker, STLS, II, 829-834.
[82] Ibid., pp. 867-873.
[83] Ibid., I, 730-734.
[84] Ibid., pp. 717-718.
[85] L. T. Hobhouse, Social Evolution and Political Theory (London, 1922).
[86] Barnes and Becker, STLS, p. 778. See also chart 3 in chap. v of the present volume, p. 260.

Social evolutionism doubtless has had much to do with the formulation of these stages, but their authors probably owe most to those philosophies of history already listed and *excluded* from the field of historical sociology. At the same time we may admit that such stage-sequences have a few features that are not entirely devoid of utility for the nonuniversal, nontranscendent, and nonrelative historical sociology which we have approvingly expounded. In the later discussion of constructive typology in this chapter we shall try to show how they may be of use. The major weaknesses of these theories are the complacent optimism (characteristic of the nineteenth century, but sadly unwarranted in the twentieth) and the illustrative method usually invoked in their support. We feel that we do not incur the charge of reactionary relativism when we assert that Sorokin has effectively exploded the optimism,[87] nor that we are guilty of extreme historicism in claiming that Max Weber has shown, through his use of genuine comparison, that the illustrative method is a thing of shreds and tatters.

Third among the varieties of stage theory are the sober and subdued attempts of those who outline patterns of change for one or more parts of a total social organization, using the method of culture case study. Theorists of this variety frequently confine themselves to the description and analysis of one culture case, although many of them admit the possibility that comparable sequences may be found to apply, within broad limits, to other cases. Schmoller[88] and Myres[89] provide instances: the former developed a series of stages of economic change chiefly applicable to Germany but usable, with modifications, elsewhere; the latter worked out sequences of political ideology in the Greek world in a way that affiliates him with culture case study arriving at comparabilities—although he gave little explicit attention to questions of method.

Fourth are those stage theorists who refuse to make the assumption that stages arise or "evolve" out of preceding stages,

---

[87] P. A. Sorokin, *op. cit., passim.*

[88] Gustav Schmoller, *Grundriss der allgemeinen Volkswirtschaftslehre*, Part I (Leipzig, 1900).

[89] J. O. Myres, *The Political Ideas of the Greeks* (Cincinnati, 1927).

i.e., they reject the postulate of genetic continuity *as postulate.* Virtually all of the theories discussed under the three earlier heads implicitly or explicitly presuppose it. Even the otherwise cautious Alfred Weber courts danger by restricting "societal" change to a principle of immanence that bears some of the earmarks of a priori evolutionism. Writers representing the fourth point of view leave the question of genetic continuity entirely open. The stages distinguished are not necessarily descriptive of sequences as they actually occurred; they are merely viewed as types aiding in estimates of rank or quantity, in comparison, and, when due caution is exercised, in generalization. The influence of Max Weber is once more apparent, for even the severest historical critic of ordinary stage theories, Georg von Below, himself adopted stages cast in Weber's terms.

Entirely warranted is the skepticism with which modern historical sociologists regard the first three kinds of stage theory. Old-fashioned unilinear evolution obviously is in outer darkness; theories outlining general trends of social development rapidly crumble into decay when built of the shoddy scraps raked together by the illustrative method; and stages based on only one culture case study provide, *in and of themselves,* no constructs that span the abyss of extreme historicism. Only the method of constructive typology based on genuine comparison enables us to arrive at stages including everything of sociological value in the other varieties.

XIII. CONSTRUCTED TYPES RE-EXAMINED

Although we have said a good deal about constructed types elsewhere in this volume, a fresh statement, adapted to the present context, may not be amiss. These types are heuristic devices, not definitions or averages.[90] In dealing with a historical configuration such as Western Christianity, for instance, there is no hope of grasping and embodying in an array of words the infinite variety and intricacy of the phenomena called to mind by the term. The idiographic attempt to unroll the "full historical reality" yields nothing which the sociologist can *directly* utilize. (Moreover, who can ever communicate the

[90] Wiese-Becker, *op. cit.,* pp. 22, 319.

"*full* historical reality?") A special twist must be given to selected strands of historical happening, and they must then be knotted together with others which may not always be thus present in empirical situations or which do not frequently take place in the "same" way. This is necessary in order that they may be woven into a coherent whole, into a constructed type, and eventually used for predictive purposes.

In working with the late medieval stage of Christianity, to modify our example, no sociological profit results from trying to bundle together the strikingly diverse and even contradictory beliefs, emotions, and modes of conduct of a gigantic congeries of persons alive at any one medieval date. When we talk about the fourteenth-century Church, do we mean the parishioners and functionaries of St. Ursula's in Cologne, as of March 2, 1376, *plus* like bodies affiliated with Chartres Cathedral as of the same date, *plus* the adherents of St. Mark's in Venice, same day and hour, *plus, plus . . . n* ? Obviously not; the only way out of formless historicism is the weaving of a type; the warp and woof is provided by culture case studies centering on promulgated beliefs, moral ideas, maxims of conduct, modes of action, and so on. These constructs are then checked by reference to other culture case studies, and the outcome may be a set of types showing that a certain measure of comparison is possible. Beyond doubt, the strands used in our weaving are all spun out of experience, and they are certainly intertwined in accordance with conceptions of adequate causation and objective probability.[91] Nevertheless, the resulting fabric is designedly a heuristic construct, a means of possible comparison and perhaps of generalization, and is never exactly duplicated in any concrete instance.[92]

[91] Weber, *Gesammelte Aufsätze zur Wissenschaftslehre*, pp. 266-290. Weber speaks of "objective possibility," but for reasons which cannot be discussed in the present space limits, we stress "objective *probability*." See chap. v, pp. 261-262.

The reader will recognize the fact that we have taken a little liberty, here and in the chapter bibliography, by treating Weber's "ideal type" as synonymous with the "constructed type." They are similar, as has been frequently noted, but by no means identical. For present purposes, which in this section are primarily illustrative, the use of one term to designate both does no particular harm.

[92] If it does seem to be duplicated, the fact should be borne in mind that no

The church or ecclesia is but one of the religious structures of Western Christianity. Others, set forth in the chapter on "Constructive Typology in the Social Sciences," are the sect, the denomination, and the cult. In some studies this battery of four types is well adapted to the purposes in hand, but in others either a lesser or a greater number may be necessary.[93] They are constructed *as needed* for the mastery of the otherwise confusing data, and are modified or discarded where the data change or the purpose of the analysis is altered.

When attempting to formulate any or all of the Protean questions, it is permissible—nay, desirable because sociologically necessary!—to construct a typological sequence and to use it as a means of estimating the rate and trend of the historical occurrences in question. These in turn provide one test for the validity of the constructed type. Instance the fact that if culture case studies of handicraft economies are made, it is then possible to build a type of handicraft economy, and from it to make deductions or "mental experiments"[94] which can be verified or refuted by reference either to the culture case studies on which the type was based or, preferably, to others made expressly for validating purposes. For example, we may deduce that in a social order of which such a type of handicraft economy is a component, the only source of capital accumulation is to be found in ground rent. From this we may infer that a transformation of the system would be effected by a limited

---

type can possibly include all the traits of a concrete instance. Imagine that a supposed empirical match were found for the perfect "Airedale" as envisaged by some judge. The "match" has all the desired characteristics, *plus* a dozen more which the judge regards as desirable but does not include in his type, and five others held undesirable but likewise excluded because seldom encountered. In addition, the dog's owner knows that his Airedale has been trained to "roll over and play dead," but says nothing about this, for it is irrelevant for show purposes.

[93] The writer, for example, finds that the Greek religious phenomenon known as Orphism requires a special constructed type, as do also the worships centering at Delphi and Delos.

[94] Weber, *Wirtschaft und Gesellschaft*, p. 5. It should be noted, however, that this procedure is not based on a type arbitrarily constructed; it must have some probability of close empirical approximation. Unfortunately, Weber does not make this clear, and sometimes makes statements which could be interpreted as disregarding it. Here again, therefore, we stress "objective *probability*."

supply of land, population increase, influx of precious metals, and so on.[95]

The deductions thus made must then be placed in juxtaposition with the ascertained facts, and if they do not fit (as they do not in the so-called Middle Ages, for instance), we must infer that the social order in question was not primarily based on a handicraft economy, and the investigation proceeds to a deeper level of analysis. Let us recall our earlier statement that constructed types may have "negative" utility as well as "positive"! If the deductions *do* fit the facts, the former may be legitimately transferred to other cases having comparable features for further checking, and if repeated transference proves possible, a constructed type having some measure of generalizability has been produced.[96] Our "marginal trading people" construct is perhaps a type having such "positive utility" (see the chapter on "Constructive Typology in the Social Sciences," pp. 109-113).

As long as a stage-sequence is not regarded as absolute, as long as room is left for changes made necessary by increasing knowledge, the conception of stages may therefore be a very useful one. With some hesitation, we advance the idea that it may sometimes be possible to make use ("negative" or "positive") of the stage theories formulated on the old illustrative basis, *if* great caution is observed and *if* they are repeatedly checked by culture case studies. In this way, researches into "what thoughts of old the wise have entertained" may help us to grapple with our old man of the sea; knowledge of the anticipations of historical sociology in bygone days may yield more than flatulent footnotes and the narcissism of the savant. Manifestly, Ibn Khaldūn or Adam Ferguson cannot provide us with hypotheses that are "relevant to futurity" as we *now* view that futurity. Suggestions about the best ways to interrogate Proteus may be worth while, however, and at any rate, they may save us from the overweening belief that our generation is the first to set foot on Pharos.

[95] Ginsberg, *op. cit.*, p. 88.
[96] *Ibid.*

XIV. SMALL-SCALE CYCLES

Many members of the present scientific generation are probably inclined to say, at this point, "All very well, but suited only for Toynbees and Webers—let us look at a kind of historical sociology that the modest scientist of ordinary ability can hope to handle." The present writer feels that such a position may on occasion be eminently reasonable, and is inclined to regard small-scale cyclical theories of socio-cultural change as most clearly falling within the confines of a historical sociology conforming to modern canons of science.[97] We can perhaps ascertain "the probability of hypothetical or actual recurrence" most readily when we limit ourselves to the fourth Protean question: "Can it be said that 'History repeats itself' in any fundamental sense?"

Questions well asked usually admit, when experiment can be practiced, of a direct "yes" or "no" answer. Certainly Galileo did not dump a cartload of stones out of the Leaning Tower; he had so carefully pondered his problem that the demonstration of his solution could be yielded by the fall of only a few stones of differing weight. Unfortunately, sociologists have as yet achieved no such precise formulations, but many small-scale cycles have been isolated and have yielded some power of "retrospective" or "prospective" prediction. Manifestly, these cycles, process-series, sequence-patterns, rhythms, and periodicities must always be cast in hypothetical or actual terms, and thus evade laboratory experimental control; nevertheless, they conform to strict rules of scientific method *if* the line between the constructed type and the empirical evidence is held steadfastly in view.

This conformity is rendered easier because they do not attempt to determine the trend of the *total* process of historical change; large-scale theories, cyclical or otherwise, are manifestly very difficult to subject to scientific treatment defined as "the systematic statement of the probability of the hypothetical or actual recurrence of phenomena that, for the purposes in hand, are regarded as identical." Small-scale cyclical theories

[97] Lundberg, *op. cit.*, pp. 211-215, 238-239, 514, 517, 531.

are in better case, for they can be more easily verified or refuted. Some of those that may be held relatively successful are Simmel's "conflict cycle,"[98] Bogardus's "race relations series,"[99] Park's "succession series,"[100] Hiller's "strike cycle,"[101] Edwards's "revolutionary cycle,"[102] some of the Marxian theories of revolutionary tactics,[103] and Pareto's "circulation of the elite."[104]

This last verges on the large-scale variety, to be sure, and there may be some legitimate doubt as to whether its verification has been even relatively satisfactory. Nevertheless, let us present it in detail as a possible example of valid and relatively small-scale cyclical theory, avoiding Pareto's recondite terminology whenever this can be done without falsifying the picture.

Both in the present and the past, says Pareto, social equilibrium is constantly being upset by the accumulation of spineless decadents in the upper classes and energetic upstarts in the lower. When the upper classes no longer possess leaders with the attitudes necessary for governing, and the lower classes have such leaders, revolution is the unavoidable outcome. No society can maintain itself by persuasion; oligarchies using force rule *de facto* if not *de jure*. When such an oligarchy becomes soft-hearted, squeamish, humanitarian, when it has lost the capacity and/or willingness to use force, the social order becomes unstable and can be put on an even keel again only when a new elite, rising from the underdog level, forcibly wrests power from the effete rulers and does the governing itself.

Upheavals of this kind issue from changes in the balance of prevailing attitudes. For analytical purposes these attitudes,

---

[98] Georg Simmel, *Soziologie* (Munich, 1908), pp. 247-336.

[99] E. S. Bogardus, "A Race Relations Cycle," *American Journal of Sociology*, XXV (Jan., 1930), 612-617.

[100] Pervading many of the monographs of the Chicago "ecological" school: Wirth's, Thrasher's, etc.

[101] E. T. Hiller, *The Strike* (Chicago, 1928), pp. 5-11.

[102] L. P. Edwards, *Natural History of Revolution* (Chicago [1927]), *passim*.

[103] Frances Bennett Becker, "Violence the Midwife," unpublished M.A. thesis, Smith College, 1934.

[104] Vilfredo Pareto, *The Mind and Society* (New York, 1934), ¶¶2060-2612.

says Pareto, can be placed in two pigeonholes. Personalities in which attitudes of "combination" predominate are innovators, experimenters, risk-takers, mentally mobile. His term for such persons is *speculators*; their income is variable and depends on their sagacity and scheming. Personalities in which attitudes of "group persistence" predominate are traditionalists, followers of routine, advocates of "sound methods," mentally immobile. His term for such persons is *rentiers*; their income is fixed, or nearly so, and does not depend on adroitness and manipulative skill. The society that best maintains a moving equilibrium is one in which these contrasting attitudes are best distributed. The leaders are strong in "combination," thus permitting necessary innovations; the followers are strong in "group persistence," thus consolidating the advantages arising from innovation.

The leaders constitute an oligarchy that manages to retain control by the clever use of force and by playing upon stabilizing attitudes, but unless there is a "circulation of the elite," this power cannot be retained. History, says Pareto, is "a cemetery of aristocracies," for, as generations succeed each other, nepotism and formalism close the ranks of the upper classes against able upstarts. The result is that the oligarchs become prevailingly of complacent *rentier* mentality, and the underdogs are led by embittered, excluded *speculators*. The old cycle is closed by revolution, and a new cycle begins.

Little hope can be entertained for the indefinite self-maintenance of any upper class, says Pareto, but there are two ways in which its life may be prolonged. One is the unshrinking use of force whenever necessary. The other is the absorption of lower-class *speculators* who represent a threat to the existing regime; they should be permitted to become "worthy" or to acquire other requisites of oligarchic membership. Eventually, however, the oligarchs become decadent. Force is frowned upon, and at the same time nimble-witted and energetic recruits from the lower levels are barred. These enterprising outsiders, encouraged by relative immunity from punishment, plot and preach against the hapless, feckless, upper crust, the masses are converted to a new myth, and in due course the longed-for overturn occurs. Therefore, we have a cyclical pattern, the "actual recurrence of phenomena that, for the purposes in hand, are regarded as identical."

Pareto's cycle, as already noted, has not yet been adequately verified, although there have been a few studies tending in that direction. But however this may be, there can be little doubt of the scientific legitimacy of such historical sociology. The problems involved are definite, and there are sufficient empirical data to make an adequate checkup possible. The same is true of the other cycles listed at the beginning of this section. Whatever the hardened skeptic may think of the more sweeping varieties of historical sociology considered elsewhere, he can hardly fail to give his support to the study of small-scale cycles, even though he may think that *attested* results to date are meager.

XV. LARGE-SCALE CYCLES

The scientific warrant of large-scale cyclical theories is much less certain. Here we classify those which take in all phases— e.g., "societal," "civilizational," and "cultural"—of all the processes sustaining and changing each and every "intelligible field" of history. The supreme test is always prediction, whether "retrospective" or "prospective," and it can be most readily applied to phenomena of limited scope in time and space, such as "strike cycles" and "circulations of elites." For one thing, there is some prospect of determining[105] whether or not the phenomenon which is supposed to have recurred is really the "same," i.e., whether or not it falls within the limits of the constructed type already established, whether or not it can be regarded as identical for the purposes in hand. In contrast with this, when entire continents and epochs are included in massive cyclical generalizations, any framework of problem, hypothesis, and constructed type that is strong enough to bear the burden thus imposed is likely to be hewn out of timbers so cumbrous that precise leveling and squaring are not possible.

[105] For the reason that historical contexts of relative completeness are more readily procurable; there are fewer gaps in the data.

Oswald Spengler's *Decline of the West*[106] affords an excellent instance of a cyclical theory of the large-scale kind. It has already been mentioned among the "rejects" of the philosophies of history, but must nonetheless be considered here as well. Spengler makes no effective use of distinctions such as Alfred Weber's "society," "civilization," and "culture," to say nothing of carefully delineated subtypes such as those of Toynbee and Max Weber. Every intelligible field of historical study is dealt with as a "whole" that is more and other than the sum of its "parts." Here the objections raised against extreme functionalism are relevant—and indeed, Benedict[107] has been much influenced by Spengler.

Basic to the Spenglerian "morphology of culture" is a sort of Hegelian idea of an "oversoul" of historical entities, complicated by crude organismic notions. Each of the great units he isolates—Egyptian, Chinese, Classical, Magian, Mayan, Faustian, Russian, and the like—has gone or will go through a cycle of birth, vigorous maturity, and senile decline that is the same for all and is determined by immanent, unalterable organismic "laws." The analogy between "mentality-organism" and biological organism is more than an analogy; it amounts to homology or even absolute identity. Each of these functional "wholes" has its own mathematics, science, religion, and art; there is no effective interaction whatsoever with other "wholes." To be sure, there may be temporary deformation or "pseudomorphosis," but the immanent "laws" of the original whole work themselves out in spite of the external influences that have temporarily constrained them. Further, nothing can either speed up or retard the inevitable ripening, withering, and decay. Moreover, time limits can be set on these processes, for they usually run their course, says Spengler, in about a thousand years.

The numerous specific errors and general distortion of history perpetrated by Spengler cannot be discussed here; space

[106] The first volume of *Der Untergang des Abendlandes* was published in 1917; the second, in 1922. A good one-volume English translation is now available (New York, 1939).

[107] Ruth Benedict, *Patterns of Culture* (Boston, 1934). See Goldenweiser's comments on this work in *CST*, pp. 482-489.

does not permit. Suffice it to say that, in spite of the praise bestowed on Spengler's work by Eduard Meyer, among others, few historians of repute have accepted his contentions. Still more damning is the fact that historical sociologists dealing with the same body of materials, among them Toynbee and Max and Alfred Weber, regard the *Decline of the West* as nothing more than a tour de force executed by a man of undeniable literary ability and considerable erudition. (When contrasted with Toynbee, however, Spengler's range of information, great as it is, dwindles to insignificance.) The importance that Spengler's work has for the sociologist does not lie in the antiquated organismic version of all-inclusive cyclical theory which it reawakens, but in the cogent analyses of peasant and industrial-urban cultures to be found in the latter part of his treatise. Spengler does not give the sources of any of his ideas, except for references to Goethe and Nietzsche, but plentiful internal evidence shows that he borrowed his basic conceptions from Danilevsky, Rückert, and, where the rural-urban analyses are concerned, from Tönnies.[108] But not to be unduly disparaging, it should be said that Spengler unquestionably adds a great deal to the already fruitful conceptions of *Gemeinschaft* and *Gesellschaft*.

Somewhat resembling Spengler's is a recent cyclical theory which its originator prefers to call a theory of trendless fluctuations, clustering about an "ideational-idealistic-sensate" triad. This, it will be readily recognized, is the basic schema of Sorokin's *Social and Cultural Dynamics*.

The method is essentially illustrative, and the categories Sorokin applies are not explicitly recognized as constructed types. In fact, it is perhaps fair to say that there are passages in the *Social and Cultural Dynamics* in which Sorokin handles his categories as ontological entities, i.e., as "really" existing. Other aspects of the method are "logico-meaningful" and "causal-functional" interpretation. What Sorokin means by the first of these is that certain parts of a given socio-cultural unit are "congruent" with each other, even though the "inde-

---

[108] Barnes and Becker, *STLS*, pp. 784, 1032-1033 and notes.

pendent-dependent variables" relationship cannot be established. One might say, for example, that the philosophy of Saint Thomas Aquinas, with its system of deductively linked propositions, is "congruent" with Gothic architecture and its systems of interlacing groins, pillars, and buttresses. Causal-functional interpretation, of course, fits into the "independent-dependent variables" mode of analysis.

The main fields of study are the Greco-Roman and Western European cultures during the past twenty-five hundred years, with forays into Egyptian, Arabic, Chinese, and Babylonian cultures. A great deal of careful research work has been done in these different fields, but in the writer's estimation the fields analyzed have been subjected to categories that are a priori generalizable, and hence open to all the objections raised in the earlier part of this chapter. Genuine comparison is not practiced, and the "quantitative" presentation (of which few statisticians speak kindly) chosen for many of the data tears the cultures studied into minute bits. The resulting mosaic presents no pattern that anyone following a method of culture case study proper would recognize.

Sorokin finds that the socio-cultural units with which he deals are tangibly integrated in both the logico-meaningful and causal-functional senses, and each of the isolable "parts" is also found to be integrated as a "whole" that forms a part of a larger "whole." This comes perilously close to extreme functionalism; Sorokin attributes a much higher degree of integration to the units he investigates than is found in similar units by Toynbee and Max and Alfred Weber.

Sorokin also maintains that the prevailing mentalities discoverable in the time span of twenty-five hundred years undergo immanently determined changes, and that even the phases of these changes are also immanently determined. But for each fluctuation in a given direction, whether toward the ideational or the sensate wholes, there is an endpoint, set by what Sorokin calls "the principle of limits," after which the trend is reversed. This "principle of limits" has a dialectic flavor (although elsewhere Sorokin scoffs at Hegelian-Marxian

notions), and to the writer seems to have a definitely a priori
character. Sorokin wastes a great deal of space in attacking
unilinear evolutionism via "the principle of limits"; evolutionism has already been so thoroughly riddled that there seems
no need for an a priori fusillade. The result of this immanent
limitation, says Sorokin, is an ever-new recurrence of the
"same" patterns: materialism—idealism; determinism—inde-
terminism; ethics of absolute principles—ethics of happiness;
realism—nominalism; ideational art—sensate art; and so on.
There is no contesting the fact of empirical diversity, but
whether the phenomena that are supposed to "fluctuate" are
really the "same" is at least an open question. Culture case
study and constructive typology might have helped to provide
some empirical checkup; as it is, many of the assertions are
supported by what seem to be hand-picked illustrations.

In fairness, we should note that Sorokin himself asserts that
the transformations ascertained by his mode of analysis are not
always quite the "same." Each current of culture ("part"),
being an immanently determined system, shows a margin of
independence in its movement, but at the same time all the
"parts" of whatever "whole" is studied change together where
long-time fluctuations are concerned. In this sense, therefore,
the various socio-cultural entities studied demonstrate their high
integration in "part-whole" terms, although this integration,
says Sorokin, is not perfect.

There is an endeavor on Sorokin's part to escape from extreme functionalism by introducing the notion of the "leading
and lagging" of cultural variables. For example, the music
of a given culture may change in a certain direction somewhat
earlier than painting and sculpture, and on other occasions it
may lag behind them. Nonetheless, the long-term trends are
of the integrated character noted above. It seems apparent to
those not wholly subscribing to Sorokin's method and conclusions that we have here something much like the Marxian ideas
of "accelerating" and "retarding." When confronted by evidence that no well-marked integration as between "parts" of
certain intelligible fields of historical study is present, the

Marxian can always claim that there is a temporary differential in the rate of movement but that in the long run it will cancel out. Awkward facts can thus be circumvented, to the satisfaction of the exponent of the theory at least, but the scope thus afforded loose generalization seems a bit too great for the advocates of more precise methods.

Yet, in spite of the "leading and lagging" qualifications that Sorokin introduces, his position is essentially functionalist, and even verges on the extreme. To quote:

All the essential "swings" of the currents of culture-mentality . . . (science, philosophy, religion, art in all forms, ethics, law, economic, political, social forms) . . . appear to be but a manifestation of the passage of these cultures from one of . . . [the main types—ideational, idealistic, or sensate] to another.[109]

Those "swings" of cultures as "wholes" Sorokin finds clearly exemplified twice in the Western world. First is the Greek shift (1) from ideationalism in the sixth century B.C. and before, (2) to the idealistic type, which is essentially a mixture of the ideational and sensate, in the fifth, (3) to the predominately sensate in the late fourth and thereafter. The second major "swing" is clearly manifested in the Christian world about the the sixth century A.D., when its ideational phase definitely becomes "monopolistic"; this endures until the end of the twelfth, when sensate forms reappear and through intermixture yield an idealistic phase in the thirteenth and fourteenth; thereafter the sensate phase begins and reaches its climax in the nineteenth. In the twentieth century, says Sorokin, there are unmistakable signs of ideational traits that will ultimately bring about a fresh cycle; they mark "the beginning of the long-time decline of our overripe Sensate culture."[110]

We have already noted the fact that Sorokin makes a few excursions into cultures other than those mentioned in the paragraphs immediately preceding, but it is nonetheless true that the latter alone are thoroughly analyzed. And this analysis, it will be recalled, (1) leans heavily on categories generalized in

[109] Barnes and Becker, *STLS*, p. 787, special statement prepared by Sorokin for that treatise. Cf. Goldenweiser's note in *CST*, pp. 487-488.

[110] Barnes and Becker, *STLS*, p. 786.

advance, (2) is propped up by an illustrative method, (3) is backed by a type of "quantitative" technique looked at askance by many statisticians, and (4) finally rests on only two "intelligible fields of historical study." Sorokin's conclusions sound much like those advanced by Spengler, even though he calls himself an "anti-Spenglerist."[111] The resemblance becomes still more striking when one takes account of the fact that Sorokin makes liberal use of an organismic analogy closely akin to Spengler's "flowering, ripening, withering, and decay."[112]

To many sociologists, the functionalism and organicism espoused by Sorokin will appear to be heavy liabilities,[113] but the author of *Social and Cultural Dynamics* rashly shoulders still another burden. He proclaims, as does Spengler, that "Even systems of truth and knowledge, including so-called science, are but manifestations dependent upon the type of culture." The fact that science operates within the schema of expedient rationality is ignored or brushed aside; consequently no distinction is made between "society," "culture," and "civilization" (to borrow Alfred Weber's terminology). We are therefore compelled to ask Sorokin, as we might ask Spengler, How do you know that what you say is true?[114] If science is relative to given cultural configurations, how can you analyze cultures other than your own? How can you even analyze systems of knowledge that differ from your own within your own culture? More, does not this "cultural solipsism" bring you perilously near to personal solipsism? Are you not reduced to the position of the Scottish humorist?

> "We meet and mix with other men;
>   With women, too, who sweetly chatter:
> But mayn't we here be duped again,
>   And take our thoughts for Mind and Matter?"[115]

[111] *Ibid.*

[112] *Ibid.*

[113] See Znaniecki, *op. cit.*, pp. 541 ff.

[114] All that is implied by this question is that the schema of expedient rationality is, in our estimation, demonstrably commensurable as between differing cultures; no absolutism is implied.

[115] Charles Neaves, "Stuart Mill on Mind and Matter," *The Edinburgh Book of Scottish Verse* (London, 1911), p. 709.

Using a homely figure, the present writer is inclined to say that Sorokin, in painting the floor of his study, has painted himself into a corner, far away from all the doors and windows. Max Weber showed that scientific systems are beyond question "relevant to value" (*wertbezogen*), but that this does *not* mean domination by value-*judgment*. It is entirely possible to make sociology "relevant to futurity," for example, without simultaneously thinking exclusively in terms of a Golden Age or a Day of Doom in either past or future. We can justifiably say, "If this is the end to be attained, these are the means by which to attain it," without in the same breath plumping for either end or means.

Social and Cultural Dynamics has fluttered the academic dovecotes, perhaps because of its polemic tone and the relative unfamiliarity, to many American sociologists, of the point of view it represents and the historical learning it incorporates. Sorokin has performed a signal if unlooked-for service, for in the effort to deal with him in his own territory we may acquire new standards of erudition, and we may learn to face issues squarely, instead of resorting to the familiar dodge of the timid reviewer: "In spite of all its shortcomings, this is a good book."

Moreover, Sorokin's use of historical materials will probably help us to escape from that stultifying preoccupation with preliterate data on the one hand and current events on the other already anathematized in this chapter. To assail theories of social and cultural dynamics that build their walls with the stones of history requires the use of historical missiles. In other words, we must meet Sorokin on his own ground. When the din of battering-rams and the clank of catapults has died away, we shall probably be thankful for the provocative cyclical theories, large-scale or small-scale, that let loose the dogs of intellectual war. In the realm of the mind, at least, "Conflict is the father of all things."

XVI. NO HISTORICAL SOCIOLOGY WITHOUT HISTORICAL DATA

The foregoing survey of the cyclical varieties of historical sociology has perhaps demonstrated that systematic sociology and historical sociology are *complementary*. Without the problems raised and the validating techniques provided by the former, the latter degenerates into the "rejects" of the philosophy of history or into antiquarianism, while without the check on "timeless" abstractions afforded by culture case study and constructive typology, systematic sociology sinks to the level of verbal jugglery and mathematical incantation.

Most American sociologists would render at least lip-service to this complementary function, but when dealing with small-scale cycles, rhythms, and so forth, we all too often gather data only from the present and the immediate past. This puts us in the paradoxical position of trying to generalize in what is at least one aspect of historical sociology[116] while almost completely disregarding the data of history!

Our weakness is in part an outcome of the general ahistoricity of American thinking. Descendants, for the most part, of migrants who severed their European roots, and oftentimes contemptuous of "the old country," we have little sense of or interest in historical continuities. This frontier frame of mind contributes to the widespread American belief that it is easier to check the present than the past, easier to view events "under the aspect of our own era." Hence, runs the inference, the good sociologist should strain every nerve to collect current events, and if historical sources are used at all, appropriate apologies should be made for dispensing something that is not really "just as good."

Shamefaced confessions are not necessary, for the substitute, so-called, is oftentimes superior to the fancied original. Stevenson quite properly said, "The obscurest epoch is today." What do we now know about the "causes" of our Indo-Chinese policy? About the plots and plans now in full swing for the Presidential campaign of 1952? Clearly, information indispensable for anything remotely approaching sociologically sat-

---

[116] We say this advisedly. Any cycle involves time-sequences and, in addition, must be compared with the past cycles if "the next phase" is to be predicted. Further, are we not just as dependent on the "documents" if we study the Chrysler strike of 1950 as we are if we study the Lawrence strike of 1912? To be sure, we are able to find eyewitnesses of the former more readily than of the latter, but must we not subject *any* eyewitness to what is essentially "the criticism of sources," so well-known to the historian?

isfactory knowledge of the present never becomes available until the present is the historical past. Think of the diaries, memoirs, confessions, autobiographies, secret archives, undercover diplomatic deals, and *sub rosa* trade agreements! These and countless other data, as yet inaccessible, must become available before we know what situations have really affected the present day and generation. Again, how great is the scope of "today" in spatial terms? If we hope to pass beyond home, office, and the route between the two, do we not have recourse to essentially historical sources? To traveler's tales, letters, the printed word? Does the fact that we get news "over the air" render it any less second-hand than the word-of-mouth of the Addisonian coffeehouses? Do newsreels bring us all the *significant* facts? And is not *Recent Social Trends* now a *historical* document? How long will the census of 1950 remain "contemporary?" Once more, have the social processes initiated today or yesterday run their course? Is it not clear that the hypotheses we now frame, concerning cycles and the like, cannot be subjected to verification by referring to the present alone? We must either wait for the processes involved to reach their endpoint in a unique time-series (which puts us in the same position as the business forecasters who so gloriously demonstrated their competence in 1929 and the equally renowned pollsters of 1948), or we must search the past for phenomena presenting comparable and generalizable similarities. In short, no matter how advanced sociology may become, materials drawn from the present alone will never provide bases sufficient for the validation of any but the most minute of cyclical hypotheses. Finally, we readily recognize the distorting prejudices of the much-berated Victorians; what about our own? Does it not follow that generalizations based only on contemporary data and guided by contemporary theories alone are likely to suggest the frog's-eye view of the hack journalist rather than the bird's-eye view of the historical sociologist? If Proteus is ever to answer our fourth question: "Can it be said that 'History repeats itself' in any fundamental sense?" we must be prepared ourselves to supply the content of that crucial word "history."

XVII. THE IMPORTANCE OF METHOD

Yes, we must be prepared ourselves to supply the content of that crucial word "history," and we must also be ready to lend that content scientific meaning by placing it in the right framework of theory and method.

This gives the sought-for key to the cryptic myth of Proteus! A question properly asked is, in a sense, already answered. If it is not properly asked, no amount of aimless fact-gathering or high-flown speculation will serve as a substitute. Methodology is not something separable from "real research"; it is the very heart of sound research. *Nothing is more practical than theory*; does not its etymology show that the theorist was "one who traveled to see men and things?" And methodology, as a branch of sociological theory, is, etymologically again, simply "the scientific way to go."

"The scientific way to go for those who travel to see men and things"—what could be more practical than that?

To ourselves and others, then, we can say this: When you have carefully envisaged your problem, intensively studied your culture cases, skilfully framed your hypothesis, soberly constructed your comparable types, cautiously generalized, and thoroughly validated your conclusions, you have successfully wrestled with Proteus.

Fear not, then; in the end your will decides.

CHAPTER IV

INTERPRETATIVE SOCIOLOGY AND
CONSTRUCTIVE TYPOLOGY

I. HOW THE TOTALLY DEPRAVED MAY YET AVOID HYPOCRISY

ONCE UPON A TIME a waggish occupant of a Presbyterian pew drew a startling conclusion from the rigidly orthodox two-hour sermon through which he had just suffered: "Gin we are all puir sinners, we maun juist sin. What else can we dae?" Tradition has delivered no account of the dominie's reply to this heretical query, but it can be taken for granted that the good man, after the first shock of dazed astonishment, succeeded in convincing both himself and his audacious hearer that the Divine Author of the Scheme of Salvation had made suitable provision for exceptions to the general rule.

Where the Sociological Dispensation is concerned, however, it is gravely to be doubted whether any exceptions to Interpretative[1] Sinning are possible. In fact, if I could find someone carrying out the role of minister among a gathering of the sociologically elect (and there are persons who sometimes come uncomfortably close to playing such a part), I should ask him, not jocularly, but seriously: "Inasmuch as we all interpret the conduct of our fellows, whatever our confession of faith, why should we not interpret with full awareness of what we are

[1] "Interpretative" is assigned a meaning somewhat akin to but by no means identical with "understanding" as it occurs in the writings of Max Weber and others. See especially Max Weber, *Gesammelte Aufsätze zur Wissenschaftslehre* (Tübingen, 1922), pp. 405-450, 503-523, *et passim*; Florian Znaniecki, *Social Actions* (New York, 1936), esp. pp. 1-34; Howard Becker, *Systematic Sociology on the Basis of the* Beziehungslehre *and* Gebildelehre *of Leopold von Wiese* (New York, 1932; reissued, Gary, Ind.: Norman Paul Press, 1950), pp. 57-59, particularly n. 10 (hereinafter cited as Wiese-Becker); Talcott Parsons, *The Structure of Social Action* (New York, 1937), pp. 84-86, 583-585, 588-589, 634, 635-639, 681, 765; Alexander von Schelting, *Max Webers Wissenschaftslehre* (Tübingen, 1934), pp. 325-329, 353-404; R. M. MacIver, *Social Causation* (Boston, 1942), pp. 263-265; Theodore Abel, "The Operation Called *Verstehen*," *American Journal of Sociology*, LIV (Nov., 1948), 211-218.

doing?" A professor of the strictly positivistic sect[2] thus inter-
rogated would roll up his eyes in holy horror, denying that he
had ever committed the sin of interpreting, of imputing motives, or of inferring what lies behind overt action. Almost
certainly he would mumble something about mysticism,[3]
electron-proton combinations,[4] fallacies of folk belief, animism,
and behaviorism. After listening awhile to this assortment of
words conveying blame or dispensing praise, I might attempt
to convince him that the kind of interpretation of which I spoke
has nothing "mystic" about it, but on the contrary is utterly
matter-of-fact and everyday. Indeed, I might even try to
seduce him from allegiance to his cherished dogma by using
a kind of illustration much in favor with the Hard-Shelled
Pearsonian Church into which, in all probability, he was baptized, namely, an illustration drawn from a game of chance.
Instead of citing a proof-text from the Pearsonian canon,[5]
which would deliver me into his hands, I should choose certain apocryphal utterances of Edgar Allan Poe:

"I knew [a schoolboy] . . . about eight years of age, whose success
at guessing in the game of 'even and odd' attracted universal admiration.
This game is simple, and is played with marbles. One player holds in
his hand a number of these toys, and demands of another whether
that number is even or odd. If the guess is right, the guesser wins
one; if wrong, he loses one. The boy to whom I allude won all the
marbles of the school. Of course he had some principle of guessing,
and this lay in mere observation and admeasurement of the astuteness
of his opponents. For example, an arrant simpleton is his opponent,
and holding up his closed hand asks, 'are they even or odd?' Our

  [2] Naming names is always risky, and is certainly no way to win friends and
influence people. Still, scientific integrity requires specificity; hence I mention
Lundberg, Bain, Ozanne, and Campisi, as among the most devout of recent times.
  [3] "Mysticism," to many persons, simply means "not orthodox Watsonian
behaviorism." It is probably wise to use the term only in the meaning assigned
to it by writers on comparative religion.
  [4] Here I have in mind presentations such as those of George A. Lundberg,
Foundations of Sociology (New York, 1939). See my critical review, "The
Limits of Sociological Positivism," *Journal of Social Philosophy*, VI (July,
1941), 362-370.
  [5] Karl Pearson, *The Grammar of Science* (London, 1891). Cf. George A.
Lundberg in H. E. Barnes, H. Becker, and F. B. Becker, *Contemporary Social
Theory* (New York, 1940), pp. 128-130, 138-140, hereinafter cited as *CST*.

schoolboy replies, 'odd,' and loses, but upon the second trial he wins, for he then says to himself, 'the simpleton had them even upon the first trial, and his amount of cunning is just sufficient to make him have them odd upon the second; I will therefore guess odd'—he guesses odd, and wins. Now, with a simpleton a degree above the first, he would have reasoned thus: 'This fellow finds that in the first instance I guessed odd, and, in the second he will propose to himself upon the first impulse, a simple variation from even to odd, as did the first simpleton; but then a second thought will suggest that this is too simple a variation, and finally he will decide upon putting it even as before. I will therefore guess even,' he guesses even, and wins. Now this mode of reasoning in the schoolboy, whom his fellows termed 'lucky'— what, in its last analysis, is it?"

"It is merely," I said, "an identification of the reasoner's intellect with that of his opponent . . . [and this] depends, if I understand you aright, upon the accuracy with which the opponent's intellect is admeasured."

"For its practical value it depends upon this," replied Dupin; "and the Prefect and his cohort fail so frequently, first, by default of his identification, and secondly, by ill-admeasurement, or rather through non-admeasurement, of the intellect with which they are engaged. They consider only their *own* ideas of ingenuity; and in searching for anything hidden, advert only to the modes in which *they* would have hidden it."[6]

Here, reduced to its barest, most obvious terms, is what is meant by interpretation, no more and no less. The interpreter puts himself in the place of the actor as best he can, and the degree to which he views the situation as the actor views it determines his success in *predicting* the further stages of the conduct. Even and odd is a simple game, as Poe says; shall we then consider the case of poker? We are all thoroughly familiar with the interpretative procedure on which depends our chances of going home with our winnings in a wheelbarrow, on the one hand, or with our lack of skill concealed by a barrel, on the other. Hence the phrase "a poker face" has come to apply to interpretation-baffling conduct not directly presided over by their majesties of the royal flush.

[6] Edgar Allan Poe, "The Purloined Letter," *Complete Works*, ed. James A. Harrison with notes by R. A. Stewart (New York, 1902), VI, 40-42.

Continuing in this vein: What successful salesman does not continually interpret the conduct of his prospects, with an automatic check on the success or failure of his efforts in the size of the commissions he amasses? He will adapt his approach, his arguments, his persuasive devices, and his "closing" techniques to what he infers about the controlling attitudes of those with whom he deals. His inferences about the "man inside," as it were, will be based upon what he can observe of the "man outside," *but he will and must infer*. When doing business with Horace Pennyfist, he wittingly or unwittingly notes querulous tone, shabby clothing, skimpy luncheon order, and failure to tip as cues to talk in terms of price rather than of prestige or reputation. The joke about "the farmer's daughter and the drummer" will be kept on the shelf when P. Snupe Upright, a former member of the Gideons, is the prospect. The loose lip and expansive gestures of Aloysius Flash will elicit an offer of a burlesque ticket and a mental memo to check on his credit rating. The mousy secretary and prissy manner of Henry F. Budget will call forth the petty details of the order, discount, and delivery date in which the fussy Henry so obviously revels. Homer K. Tremblechin's allusion to Mrs. Tremblechin's business ability will lead to a resigned decision to call another day.

Throughout all of these maneuvers our astute salesman, Samuel O. Slick, has been sizing up his potential customers and adapting his own conduct, not merely to the situation as he himself (presumably with a greater knowledge of the facts) may view it, but to varying situations as defined by these varying personalities. In other words, he is not dealing with a vague, abstract entity called *Homo sapiens*, or even *Homo Americanus* as exemplified in standard specimens of John Q. Public. On the contrary, he is dealing with relatively specific personality types[7] whose conduct he is endeavoring to interpret in such a way that the outcome of his negotiations can not only be predicted but also actually controlled for his special purpose.

In order to achieve this end, Slick has made use of certain interpretative devices, and among these is what we may tech-

[7] Or even specific personalities (omit the types) if he has known them long and intimately.

nically call the construction of models[8] of motivation in accordance with which his tactics are shaped. Going beyond Slick's particular manipulations, models of motivation are constructs in two senses: (a) the observer selects and combines, for the purposes in hand, certain criteria regarded as significant for the solution of his special problems; and (b) these selected and combined criteria go beyond the immediately perceivable sense data, inasmuch as certain other criteria, either not observed at the time, very infrequently observed within the limits of ordinary experience, or directly accessible only "within" qualified observers, are built into the combination in such a way that a coherent structure usable for predictive purposes results.[9] Granting that constructs of this kind include meanings not encountered at the level on which the physicist operates, it is nevertheless true that they are in many respects equivalent to the constructs characterized as follows by Bridgman, high priest of the operationists:

There are many sorts of constructs: those in which we are interested are made by us to enable us to deal with physical situations which we cannot directly experience through our senses, but with which we have contact indirectly and by inference. Such constructs usually involve the element of invention to a greater or lesser degree. A construct containing very little of invention is that of the inside of an opaque solid body. We can never experience directly through our senses the inside of such a solid body, because the instant we directly experience it, it ceases by definition to be the inside. We have here a construct, but so natural a one as to be practically inavoidable. An example of a construct involving a greater amount of invention is the stress in an elastic body. A stress is by definition a property of the interior points of a body which is connected mathematically in a simple way with the forces acting across the free surface of the body. A

[8] By "model" is *not* meant "*desirable* structure" or anything remotely similar, but something of which a chemist's model of a carbon ring is a good illustration.

[9] In his unpublished doctoral dissertation, a Wisconsin graduate student, W. L. Kolb, has put this very shrewdly:

"The specific overt act of murder (let us say) may be interpreted within many contexts of motive, but as the clues continue to pile up which point to other overt actions, it gradually becomes apparent that these series of actions . . . [can be interpreted] only through one context (which is a construct) of motive" ("The Peasant in Revolution: A Study in Constructive Typology," University of Wisconsin Library, 1943, p. 34).

stress is then, by its very nature, forever beyond the reach of direct experience, and it is therefore a construct.[10]

Without pushing the analogy off its feet—for biped analogies cannot be made to go on all fours without absurdities—it can nevertheless be said that the physicist's concept of stress bears some similarity to our concept of attitude or motive, more especially when we regard the latter as a sort of stress imposed on a given actor prior to the immediate situation in which his conduct is observed. If, however, practicing the asceticism proper only to an orthodox member of that conventicle of the positivist sect once presided over by Parson John Broadus Watson, we restrict ourselves to the sense data directly given in the immediate situation, we are unable to make predictions of any kind. Let us take as an exhibit a man who is chopping wood at the rate of forty-five strokes a minute, using a four-pound axe with a three-foot handle. Having recorded these and many similar data, and comparing the results with records of woodchopping gathered elsewhere, we discover that the actor concerned is exceeding the ordinary rate by about fifteen strokes. What are the reasons, if any, for this discrepancy between the "stimulus," whatever it may be, and the ensuing "response"?[11]

If we are not orthodox behaviorists, we may of course try to discover by inferential means the stress entering as an effective factor into the performance of the given task. In other words, we may try to find what the attitude of the man in question toward woodchopping is, and we may learn that he has certain ends in view with relation to which woodchopping is merely a means. Perhaps he has quarreled with his wife because the coffee was cold and is working off a fit of temper,[12] or a visit to his physician has convinced him that his waistline

[10] P. W. Bridgman, *The Logic of Modern Physics* (New York, 1932), pp. 53-54. For comment on the logic of operationists not as careful as Bridgman, see Franz Adler, "Operational Definitions in Sociology," *American Journal of Sociology*, LII (March, 1947), 438-444.

[11] Becker, "The Limits of Sociological Positivism," pp. 367-369.

[12] Be it noted, however, that if woodchopping is a means of affectively nonrational character (as it is in this case), means and ends are fused in such a way that even analytic separation by the observer has little practical value. A repetition of the clammy coffeepot may lead to an affective display of radically different type, e.g., the actor may use the axe on his wife.

is much too large, or the threatened coal famine he has read about in the newspaper has made him think of a cozy wood fire next December, or he is to get $25.00 a cord for red oak in stove lengths rather than the accustomed rate of eighty cents an hour, or he is obsessed by the delusion that he is battering in the heads of Russian soldiers on Point Barrow.

Having provisionally determined the end to which the action is directed, we may then, perhaps, predict the length of time the action will be pursued, this prediction serving as a check on the inference. If the woodchopper is merely getting the taste of cold coffee out of his bridgework and an excess of adrenalin out of his bloodstream, we may hazard the guess that fifteen minutes will see the end of the furious axe-swinging; and if our doughty axeman does quit his job within a time not too far away from our quarter-of-an-hour estimate, our construct is rendered more *plausible* than it was at the beginning. We have therefore interpreted, as we might say, with some degree of success, and the *plausibility* of the interpretation may be brought to a fair degree of *probability* by the analysis of other evidence made available to us after the burst of woodchopping is far enough in the past for the aggrieved husband to talk without gasping for breath.[13]

To be sure, we most certainly would not accept the actor's interpretation of his own conduct at face value, for along with the capacity for speech, the human being has also been endowed with the ability to lie, both to himself and to others. In short, deceit and self-delusion are always possibilities; other corroborative evidence would have to be sought and found before our fair degree of probability could become reasonable certainty.[14] Nevertheless, the basic necessity in this little piece of interpretation is the ascertaining, by whatever resources of observation and inference at our disposal, of the actor's "definition of the situation."[15]

Note, by the way, that definition of this kind does not

[13] See Wiese-Becker, *op. cit.*, pp. 57-59 n. 10.

[14] *Viz.*, a very high degree of probability.

[15] MacIver, *op. cit.*, prefers "dynamic assessment," but Znaniecki uses "definition of the situation" in his most recent writings, and it seems unwise to deviate from his well-established terminology now.

necessarily involve the element of choice[16]—at least, not of choice with full awareness of the alternatives. Situations may be defined by the actors concerned with varying degrees of clarity, and a considerable amount of additional data may have to be obtained and analyzed before the investigator can determine the end toward which the conduct was actually directed. Regardless, however, of whether or not the actor can put into words the purpose that governed his woodchopping or similar activity, it still remains true that the purpose is his own, that the end pursued is the end he envisages, no matter how dimly. If the investigator's constructs are to possess any degree of analytic utility, they must be constructs imputing a certain "state of mind"[17] to the actor which is meaningful in the light of the actor's own personality traits, the elements of the situation, and the over-all value-system (or systems) within which those traits and elements function and from which they derive their ulterior significance.

Returning to our woodchopping illustration: what was the fulcrum on which the interpretative lever rested? What would strike the casual observer as problematic in the conduct of our irate husband? What might bring even the extreme behaviorist to indulge in the collecting of sense-data in the hope that somehow an intelligible pattern might emerge from the jumble if only a sufficient number of similar cases could be tabulated and the right formula applied? Well, even the positivist doing his best to restrict himself to the immediate situation would probably contrast the rate of forty-five strokes a minute with a

[16] Not that we are trying to dodge the fact that choice frequently does occur. As choice, purpose, and related terms are used here, they have nothing to do with the debater's dilemma of "free will *versus* determinism." See MacIver, *op. cit.*, pp. 240-241.

[17] W. L. Kolb, in the dissertation previously quoted (p. 193 n. 9), says: "If we are to credit the positivists with any theoretical sophistication whatever, we must assume that when they state that man is a biological organism 'endowed' with a nervous system [here the reference is to those mentioned in n. 2], they are not implying that the origin of the nervous system is supernatural. It is not unfair to expect, then, that the positivists will be willing to allow that their opponents conceive of 'mind' as something produced in naturalistic fashion. If this is recognized, the utilization of the concept of 'mind' becomes a matter of recognizing the nature and limitations of scientific systems. For the purpose of a systematic analysis of social action it is unnecessary to go beyond the concept of mind" (pp. 48-49).

"normal" rate of about twenty-five, and would feel that an increase of 80 per cent was in some way "interesting." In thus regarding the conduct as worth further observation, our behaviorist has been indulging in a little covert interpretation— that is to say, he vaguely feels that here is something "abnormal" that should be looked into further. He may say to himself, as it were, "I never saw a man chop so fast. I wonder what he's up to?"

If he does thus lapse from the ascetic creed of his positivistic sect, he may be making use of an implicit construct, namely, the construct of "the rational man."[18] Indeed, he may mutter to himself, "That fellow surely isn't working for wages. No man in his senses would make the chips fly like that even if the boss were looking on." Aha! "No man in his senses!" The problem-setting although hitherto covert interpretation has here become more or less explicit. Our behaviorist has ingenuously admitted that he is using a construct of rational motivation as a measuring rod by means of which he imputes nonrational motivation to the woodchopper whose mighty swings he is watching. Should he beat his breast in an agony of remorse when his sinful deviation from the pure doctrine is called to his attention, he can perhaps be consoled by the remark with which this essay began, "We're all poor sinners."

Inasmuch as we all interpret, usually by drawing upon constructs of rational conduct, even though these are only of problem-setting and negative character, the way out of the impasse is simply to make such constructs definite, to devise them in accordance with sound rules of method, and to carry them beyond the realm of the merely plausible by searching for further corroboration and applying crucial checks.

Although this is not a suitable context for the exhaustive discussion of sound rules of interpretative method,[19] it may be

[18] Cf. on this point my essay, "Historical Sociology," in Barnes, Becker, and Becker, *CST*, pp. 519-524, and also the present volume, pp. 161-163.

[19] In my estimation, Znaniecki's *Social Actions* is the best single presentation of interpretative procedure in English. Parsons's *Structure of Social Action* is also excellent. It should be noted that Znaniecki's 1936 work is largely an elaboration of his *The Laws of Social Psychology* (Chicago, 1925 [printed in Poland]).

If I have any strong objection to Znaniecki's presentation in *Social Actions*,

said that among these rules should be included those governing (a) selective attention to social actions rather than to human actions in general; (b) preliminary focus on what seem to be the major features of the end or purpose held in view by the actor or actors concerned; (c) tentative characterization of the social situation plus analytic distinction between the chief factors in that situation; and (d) working specification of the salient aspects of the value-systems entering into the situation, the ends pursued, and the meanings assigned to the situational conduct by those involved in it. *Seriatim*, now:

(A) As Park so aptly said, "Man is not born human"; conduct defined as characteristic of man as man in any society of which we have knowledge is the outcome of the planned or unplanned inculcation of social meanings by other human beings. In this broad sense, therefore, all conduct is social, but we can nevertheless distinguish between those actions which are more or less specifically directed toward the actions of other persons and those which have to do primarily with technology, aesthetics, and similar systems, objects, or actions which are social only in a derived and secondary sense.[20] Following the general principle of scientific division of labor, it seems expedient to restrict our interpretative and predictive efforts to man in his social capacities rather than to man as a biological entity, physical object, or what not. Accordingly, our field of interest should be limited by defining it about as follows:

The term "action" is to be used to designate that kind of conduct to which those involved in it assign meanings communicable to others by means of symbols, even though these symbols may be nonverbal or implicit or both, and even though the actions focused on may not be outwardly observable or may consist only in refraining from a given course of

it has to do with his lack of explicit attention to *general* value-systems, although his inductive evidence abounds in relevant implications. In *The Social Role of the Man of Knowledge* (New York, 1940) he does deal with value-systems explicitly and at length.

[20] I owe this distinction to Znaniecki, in whose *The Laws of Social Psychology* I first encountered it, but Weber's essay, dating from 1913, contains the same distinction in so many words, and his earlier writings abound in differentiations that involve it. See also chap. i, present volume, esp. pp. 14-17.

conduct. The kind of action that we choose to call "social" conforms to these requirements, but in addition is determinably and intentionally directed toward the conduct of others by the actor or actors concerned.[21] In the foregoing sentence "determinably" is to be taken as "ascertainable through direct and inferential evidence," and "intentionally" has the meaning of "in accordance with a motivational model or construct of the actor's other-regarding purpose or end, regardless of whether or not the actor himself is fully aware of the goal pursued." Finally, we add the obvious proviso that the action under analysis must continue for a length of time sufficient to permit accurate identification of it.

(B) The ends or purposes of the action may be differentiated in several ways; the analytic utility of any or all of these ways depends on the aspect of the action which the investigator has singled out as problematic. For some varieties of problem it may be sufficient to set up a fourfold classification.

First, we may distinguish the pursuit of ends by any means regarded as conforming to the principles of economy of effort, efficiency, and absence of undesirable secondary effects. Following a well-established sociological tradition this might be called "purposive rationality,"[22] but the term seems ambiguous; "expedient rationality" would appear to be better fitted to designate such conduct.

Second, we may single out another kind of rationality in which the principles of economy of effort and so on are followed up to a given point, or as far as a certain limit; this limit is set by the character of the end itself. Rationality limited

[21] It will be recognized that this definition is much the same as that occurring on the very first page of Max Weber's famous *Wirtschaft und Gesellschaft* (Tübingen, 1922). I incorporated it, without, however, making full use of it, in Wiese-Becker, *op. cit.*, pp. 57-58. Elsewhere in the present volume (pp. 16-17) I offer a revised, expanded, and, it is hoped, more adequate definition.

Note, by the way, that social actions in their "dynamic" aspects are social processes; in their "static" aspects, social structures. Almost the entire Wiese-Becker treatise is devoted to the analysis of actions from the process and structure standpoints. Nothing that is said here is intended to supplant analysis of the process-structure type; indeed, interpretative sociology and constructive typology run parallel to and continually interweave with process-structure analysis.

[22] From Rudolph von Jhering or Ihering's *Das Zweck im Recht* (Leipzig, 1877-1883; translated as *Law as a Means to an End*) and Weber's adaptation.

in such a way has been called "value-rationality," but it perhaps might be better termed "sanctioned rationality," in indication of the fact that ends of certain kinds do not provide sanction for any means whatsoever of their attainment.[23]

As counterweights, so to speak, of expedient rationality and sanctioned rationality, we may also distinguish two varieties of nonrationality, the traditional and the affective. Traditional nonrationality is marked by the dominance of means over ends or, otherwise put, by a state of affairs in which actions formerly regarded as mere means become ends in themselves.

Affective nonrationality is a variety somewhat more "private" than the sort identified with the publicly accessible symbols of the traditional.[24] The irate husband blowing off steam on the woodpile is indulging in an affective release or discharge. Obviously it is virtually impossible to find examples of the purely affective;[25] empirically it may manifest itself merely as an accessory of the expedient or the sanctioned modes of rational conduct or as a component of nonrationality of primarily traditional character. It may be said, however, that when it is encountered as the *chief* phase of an action viewed from the angle we are now utilizing, it represents a fairly complete fusion of means and ends; even analytic separation is of limited scientific utility.

In brief, expedient rationality is unrestrained in the means adopted; sanctioned rationality has ends of a sort which permit the use of only certain prescribed means; traditional nonrationality elevates means to the rank of ends; and affective nonrationality manifests a coalescence of means and ends.[26] In each of these four, be it remembered, interpretation always follows the definition of the actor or actors involved in the given situation.

Turning now to the attitude, wish, tendency, or, better,

[23] This discussion of "means to ends" is overbrief; for a fuller treatment, see pp. 22-32.

[24] "Private" and "public" are here offered as terms less ambiguous than the notorious "subjective" and "objective." Please note the "here offered"; in other contexts other terms are likely to be necessary.

[25] Because the *purely* affective would be the nonsymbolic.

[26] This formulation does not occur in the writings of Max Weber; the fourfold classification does although with some important differences.

end, which becomes manifest in the action, what convenient pigeonholes can be devised for its preliminary analysis? Here it seems best to accept the well-established distinction between tendencies to achieve the ends of response, recognition, security, and new experience.[27] This classification can be used safely as long as it is clearly recognized that the four tendencies must stand at the beginning and *not* at the conclusion of the interpretative task. That is to say, they do not necessarily represent common-human or universal personal-social impulses, drives, or wishes that need no closer specification in terms of socially meaningful trend, means-ends patterning, situational orientation, and location and direction within general value-systems. When they are used as interpretative guides rather than as interpretative finalities, they are eminently warranted, but validation by any or all of the empirical checks applicable to them is absolutely indispensable if scientific method is to replace arbitrary speculation and dogmatic assertion.[28]

(C) The need for these classifications will perhaps become clearer as we turn to the situational and value-system aspects of these social actions. The situation, broadly considered, has at least four distinguishable analytic elements: the social object, the social method, the social instrument, and the social response.[29]

Again taking our salesman, Samuel O. Slick, as an illustrative device that is crude in perhaps more than one sense: his action is social inasmuch as it is directed toward the securing of a favorable response in the form of a fat order for Today's Gadgets and the accompanying commission from P. Snupe Upright. The end pursued by Slick, in accordance primarily with expedient rationality, gratifies Slick's tendencies toward both recognition and security, with the latter clearly upper-

[27] Thomas and Znaniecki, *op. cit.*, *passim.* After about 1925 Thomas disavowed the "four wishes" because of their all-too-frequent finalistic use by the smaller fry of sociology. Znaniecki retained them but rechristened them "tendencies" ("wish" and "attitude" had previously been used synonymously by both Thomas and Znaniecki). I have taken the risk of classifying them as pulls rather than as pushes, i.e., as goals rather than as drives, as ends rather than as impulses. See pp. 35-42 for fuller discussion.

[28] See Wiese-Becker, *op. cit.*, pp. 171-174.

[29] Znaniecki, *Social Actions*, chap. iii.

most. He defines the situation in salesmanship terms, generally speaking, and imputes to Upright a motivational model in which both sanctioned rationality and traditional nonrationality are operative, and in which the end-pursuing tendency falls into the recognition category—Upright likes to be known as a man embodying all the Christian and American virtues. (This is of course nothing against the virtues of Upright!) The situation breaks down thus: Upright is a social object from whom a response favorable to Slick is to be elicited by use of the appropriate social method and social instruments. The method in this case is one of persuasive flattery, using speech and other forms of gesture as tools. The other instruments are a luncheon club pin in Slick's buttonhole, "dignified" printed material stressing the reliability and ethics of the firm he represents, circulars and price lists in which quality of the product is strongly stressed—at least in the emphasis Slick can lay upon them—and other devices regarded as legitimate in the craft of the salesman. Briefly, social object, social method, social instrument, and social response are the analytic elements of this situation.

In other situations the actor may include the reflected self among the vital elements of his definition, e.g., he may try to secure a response from the object that testifies to the high regard in which he, the actor, is held, and thus experience a heightening of his self-esteem. In the present case, to be sure, recognition is subordinate to security; Slick really does not care very much what Upright thinks of him as long as he gets the order. It is expedient, of course, to elicit a reflected self of character praiseworthy in Upright's eyes; and, given the self-justifying streak[30] which most of us have, Slick may for a time at least share Upright's estimate of him as an honest, ethical "sales representative." Nevertheless, to engender a favorable impression and at the same time to fail in the job of selling a bill of goods would leave Slick with a bad taste in his mouth.

---

[30] This will readily be recognized as Freudian rationalization. We are rapidly nearing the point (if we are not already there) where the coining of neologisms will be absolutely necessary if ambiguity is to be avoided. I detest neologisms, but "needs must when the devil drives."

The reflected self therefore does not always enter in an essential way into the actor's definition of the situation. Inasmuch as the sociologist's interpretative endeavor deals with the situation defined by the actor as the inevitable starting point, it is sometimes possible to work with only four analytic elements rather than five.

(D) Let us now take note of the fact that any situation is a whole within the context of at least one larger whole. This statement holds good regardless of whether we are dealing with the situation as defined by the actor or as defined by the detached observer, although it must be granted that ordinarily the participant, and in many cases the observer, does not—yea, sometimes cannot—put the whole-within-a-whole state of affairs into words. Nonverbal symbols[31] may be the only clue to the situational context; facial expression, hand gestures, habitual modes of dress, postures, and the like provide the evidence. Parenthetically, moreover, it must be noted that any whole is a whole by definition only; if we take "definition" in a sense sufficiently broad, it may be said that no wholes are "given" without definition. Varying biological equipment and/or social experience radically alter the dimensions of wholes regarded by the naïve as "natural." Further discussion of this point would carry us too far afield; suffice it to say that for us wholes are always taken to mean wholes by definition.[32] The point of cardinal importance here is that more inclusive social frameworks impinge on social situations in the narrower sense, and that even though these frameworks are sometimes ignored or, more properly speaking, remain vaguely marginal to the situation as defined by the actor and,

[31] To which G. H. Mead, among others, pays insufficient attention. For suggestions that the concept of symbolism needs revision, see Suzanne Langer, *Philosophy in a New Key* (New York, 1942). Charles Morris, "Foundations of the Theory of Signs," *International Encyclopedia of Unified Science*, I (1938), 2, is also of the highest importance, although it relates chiefly to language. See "Bibliographical Appendix," in Barnes, Becker, and Becker, *CST*, pp. 890-892, 895-898.

[32] A point that seems worthy of earnest consideration by extreme functionalists who make liberal use of part-whole procedures. Cf. "Historical Sociology" in Barnes, Becker, and Becker, *CST*, esp. pp. 500-501, or pp. 139-140 of the present volume.

in all too many instances, by the observer, the interpretative sociologist must take them into his reckoning.

Our discussion has already reckoned with them implicitly, for the rationalities and nonrationalities we have considered can be regarded as aspects of value-systems as the latter are viewed from the standpoint of the actor, rather than as conduct congruent with interpersonal patterns within which a large number of actors play their social roles (this congruent conduct may or may not enter directly into their immediate definitions). Sanctioned rationality and traditional nonrationality, for example, can be regarded by us as modes of conduct manifesting the existence of a sacred society, that is, of an interpersonal network of relations having as its chief characteristic the eliciting from participants of a certain emotionally tinged unwillingness or inability to respond to the new. Expedient rationality, on the other hand, may be thought of as a manifestation of the interpersonal phase of a secular society, i.e., of a web of meaningful connections between persons unwilling or unable to refrain from responding to the new so long as their actions pattern and are patterned by such a structure.[33]

Over-all social frameworks of these contrasting types are of course never existent in unmixed form; only for analytic purposes can the sharp distinction between absolute conservatism and absolute innovationism be maintained. Granting all this, it is still of the utmost utility, in many instances, to be able to specify the extent to which the given society approximates one or the other of these polar extremes. No one who remains within the confines of what we call sanity can entirely dissociate an immediate situation from its ulterior bearings; the definition of the situation will inevitably although indirectly take in some of the societal fringes. Indeed, the fringes, paradoxically enough, may determine the way in which the strands of action interweave to form the central pattern.

For example, Japanese society in its larger dimensions was and still is unquestionably sacred, even though Western secularization has brought the nation to a reasonably high level of

[33] For fuller discussion of the bearing of "sacred society" and "secular society," see pages 248-280.

technical efficiency. Yet who can doubt that although technical situations such as those involved in modern warfare were woven by the Japanese on societal looms in many respects strikingly similar to those used by Americans, they nevertheless introduced that all-important differential twist of definition which imparted to the concomitant actions their fundamentally contrasting course and meaning? Defeated admirals who committed hara-kiri and cornered soldiers who deliberately walked into direct gunfire were, until the very moment of their self-destruction, making use of the weapons which a rapidly secularizing Western society had made possible. Does not the mere mention of such conduct make it clear that immediate situations cannot be analyzed and their outcomes predicted in disregard of the general value-systems lending these situations their crucially differential character?

In brief, interpretative sociology cannot dispense with the analysis of social situations as parts of larger wholes, and for many purposes, although not for all, a simple twofold classification of these encompassing structures can be utilized; appropriate labels are "sacred society" and "secular society."[34]

With this outfit of analytic tools at our disposal, we ought to be able to do a fairly workman-like job. As long as we must sin anyway, let us do it with our eyes open; even the totally depraved can follow the example of Lucifer—that is, we can shun hypocrisy.

II. HOW NOT TO BE A PROPHET

Continuing in the theological vein, the doctrine that the totally depraved can, by taking thought, eliminate hypocrisy is certainly unorthodox to all except adherents of Arminianism, but it is both elastic and encouraging. Perhaps further meditation will enable us to avoid still other occasions for stumbling. In particular, we may be granted light sufficient to see and step aside from the overweening presumption that claims possession of prophetic gifts. In short, we can perhaps learn how not to indulge in prophecy.[35]

[34] These have been drawn from and utilized in numerous concrete researches by my graduate students and myself, and of course have many antecedents and contemporary parallels. See pp. 254-261.

[35] For many of the moot points in this whole section and the one to follow,

It seems a fairly safe assumption that most of our scientific brethren would assert confidently that the Age of Miracles is over—if indeed it ever began. Last-ditch defenders of revelation might try to refute such assertions by twisting scientific scripture to their purposes; for example, they might try to quote Heisenberg in support of loaves and fishes or turning water into wine. Nevertheless, the informed scientist would smile indulgently and properly point out that the principle of indeterminacy has nothing to do with the miraculous.

Still, there is ample evidence to show that although scientists scoff at the Age of Miracles, they apparently do not think that the Age of Prophecy is forever in the past. Men who have spent their lives peering through microscopes and manipulating microtomes, or shooting beams of light through sliced tourmaline crystals, sometimes fancy themselves to be Ezekiels or Hoseas. When one of those scientists is dealing with his own special field, his conditional predictions are usually marked by the utmost caution; he will refuse to prophesy. But, when called upon to "discover the future" about affairs concerning which he knows no more than any reasonably intelligent person, he casts scientific scruples to the wind. As the recent past shows, without the flickering of an eyelash he will oblige the inquiring reporter by giving lengthy replies to "What will Stalin do next?" or "Will Churchill retire from public life?"

This incidental disparagement of physicists and biologists has been by way of illustration only, for many practitioners of the social sciences also drape the mantle of the prophet about themselves at the slightest provocation. Only a few members of the social-scientific fraternity feel upset when called upon to provide or witness prophetic displays; unfortunately, the greater number of social scientists can stomach almost anything. The minority members feel queasy because they have come to think that no single science, nor indeed any combination of sciences at the disposal of mere mortals, can successfully

---

I should like earnestly to ask the reader to refer to my chapters ii and xv in Barnes, Becker, and Becker, *CST*, as well as to my article, "Supreme Values and the Sociologist," *American Sociological Review*, VI (April, 1941), 155-172. These essays are available in the present volume, pp. 93-127, 128-188, 281-305.

prophesy the beginning, course, and consequences of any *par-ticular* action at any *particular* time.[36]

The reasons for this conviction are many and various. I mention two only: (a) the literally innumerable array of factors involved in any unique phenomenon; and (b) the vast range of the weights or intensities assignable to these factors on any empirical basis, even if the factors themselves were limited in number. In a slightly different context, this has been pointed out as follows:

. . . the theoretical physicist's world . . . is an artificially simplified realm in which lines are fictitiously straight, cylinders and spheres are of ideally perfect form, plane surfaces are without even microscopic irregularity, and friction is banished utterly. Nobody expects him to formulate a "law" (a shorthand statement of his observations) relating to the behavior of a particular knotty, unplaned, kiln-dried, yellow pine two-by-four when struck by a dull axe by the sweaty hands of a 150-pound Italian laborer who receives only thirty cents an hour for his work; [the typical] . . . and the empirical are never confused, either by the public or the physicist himself. The sociologist, on the other hand, is often expected unfailingly to prophesy concerning the future behavior of that particular Italian laborer, so to speak, and in the effort to vindicate his science in the eyes of a skeptical world, some-times attempts to do so, apparently in entire ignorance of the theory of probability and the fact that not even the sociologist, strange as it may seem, is omniscient.[37]

More explicitly, if the goal of the scientist's activity is "the systematic statement of the probability of the hypothetical or actual recurrence of phenomena which, for the purposes in hand, are regarded as identical,"[38] then *ipso facto* the scientist is for-ever barred from the effort to deal with the unique *as the unique.*

Among students of social affairs, only a few ever attempt to deal with the unique as such. Among these are ethnographers who, because they are doing field work in situations where

[36] Znaniecki, *The Laws of Social Psychology*, p. 69.

[37] Wiese-Becker, *op. cit.*, p. 22.

[38] See article, "Science," in H. P. Fairchild, ed., *Dictionary of Sociology* (New York, 1944). This is a condensation of the formulation in my "Supreme Values and the Sociologist," *loc. cit.* See also pp. 93-105 of the present volume.

scientific division of labor is difficult or impossible, and where the population to be studied rarely numbers more than one or two hundred persons having a relatively simple past (because in the absence of written records bygone days lose their complexity), therefore attempt the gathering of "all the facts." Ethnographers who try to do this are not necessarily naïve; in many cases they know full well that they cannot possibly achieve their objective, and are content to do the best they can. They realize that unless they collect whatever data their focus of attention makes perceivable at the time, such data may be forever lost in the hurly-burly of change thrust upon the simpler peoples by the impact of a ruthless Western civilization.

Also among those who try to amass all the information they can lay hands on are the historians, some of whom it is not easy to absolve from the charge of naïveté. Granting the presence of numerous honorable exceptions, it still remains true that many of those who traffic with what is called history[39] actually think they can pile up, single-handed, everything that can possibly be relevant about a given time, place, and people. They do not recognize that selection is inevitable, nor that facts are scientific facts only for those who are prepared by equipment and training to perceive them. Moreover, when they do establish a division of labor, they base it on content or chronology rather than on problem-choosing. Stated differently, historians often split the past along the lines of political history, social history, or intellectual history, regarding the lines as somehow given in the data instead of being arbitrarily imposed, or else they chop time-sequences into convenient chunks, ordinarily selecting these by country and century, e.g., eighteenth-century England or eleventh-century France.

Very seldom, indeed, and then only among historians tainted by contact with social scientists, is a specific problem singled out as a center about which relevant facts are systematically arrayed. Only the honorable exceptions mentioned

[39] Some historians apparently think that anything falling in the "past" should be enclosed in a field which is theirs exclusively. This may be, if any historian is a Diogenes Teufelsdröckh, a Professor-of-Things-in-General. May I point out, however, that the "past" begins *now*? The reading of that very "now" is irrevocably a "historical" fact.

Taking up, then, our postponed discussion of the extreme empiricist position, let us ask, Can "all the facts" ever be gathered? Can full particularity ever be achieved? To the writer, at least, the answer is, Manifestly not. Not only would the search for "all the facts" about even a simple physical object carry us to the outermost confines of the cosmos,[48] spatially speaking, but from the temporal standpoint we are likewise confronted with an infinite *regressus*. The historian properly insists on dating the events with which he deals, but there is no good reason why he should confine himself to a given year, month, and day. Why not hours, minutes, and seconds? And why stop at the second? Modern stroboscopic photography enables us to freeze events in divisions of one hundred-thousandth of a second and even less; where is the logical terminus if full temporal particularization is the task in hand?

All this is clearly nonsensical, but the reasons why it is nonsensical may not be so clear. Manifestly, the historian particularizes only up to a certain point; anything beyond that is superfluous. This superfluity resides in the fact that the *absolutely* unique is ineffable, incommunicable. Unless the historian wishes to be a sort of James Joyce raised to the nth degree, in which case he alone could understand himself, and then only in a kind of mystic union achieved in a single flash of awareness, he must make use of the ordinary devices of communication. His language may be poetically evocative at times, but nevertheless he attempts to communicate within a universe of discourse. In such a universe only the *relatively* unique is effectively present, and its presence is vouchsafed only by the simultaneous presence of the *relatively* general. All forms of significant symbolism—and all communication is necessarily symbolic—are of general character (although the generality may be limited to a very few instances). This is obviously true even of proper names, as Korzybski so wearyingly insists. We have long known that $Mary^{1950}$ is not the same as $Mary^{1941}$, although for ordinary purposes the two can safely be regarded as identical. Using the generalities of symbolic com-

[48] See pp. 98-99 of the present volume.

munication, the historian manipulates them in such a way that relatively unique description results. If the person, occurrence, or whatnot described is set against the background of other persons and occurrences so that characterization regarded as adequate is brought about, that phase of the historical endeavor which distinguishes it from the social sciences per se is made manifest.

Assuming that the foregoing analysis is accurate, we can now ask, What are historians doing when they prophesy?[49] Answer: They are indulging in illicit generalization. All too often unaware of the problem that has governed their selection of facts, or unable or unwilling to specify it, and so innocent, methodologically speaking, that they think it possible to particularize without open or covert reference to general contexts, they make guesses, lucky or unlucky as the case may be. Given the gullibility of the public and the elastic language in which the guesses are cast, most of them are lucky. When an eminent historian intones: "I said that something terrible would happen, and now look at the mess we're in," most of us forget that grandmother said that much.

No, they did these things better in Judea. Lacking prophetic inspiration, the scientist had better confine himself to the job of prediction; this, in spite of current misconceptions, has nothing to do with prophecy, forecasting, or foretelling. Strictly, it refers only to the "before-saying" (pre-diction) of certain kinds of recurrence. (In the concluding part of the present essay, an abridged example of retrospective prediction on a typological basis is offered, and in the final chapter of this volume, prospective and retrospective prediction are discussed at some length.)

Sociologists are not prophets, for they regard unique configurations and happenings as forever beyond scientific grasp. Nevertheless, by the use of techniques adapted to legitimate prediction, they hope to be able to state the limiting conditions under which any phenomenon, however unique, will in all prob-

---

[49] Sometimes historians make direct mention of "historical generalizations," or "what we learn from history." These same historians, however, are often the first to insist that "history does not repeat itself."

ability be placed. Moreover, explicit attention to the logic of prediction, which is essentially the logic of probability, lifts their analysis out of the vague, epistemologically ambiguous situations in which reference to "causal sequences" would otherwise place them. By pouring their results in the predictive mold, they make it possible for others to check the validity of their conclusions in ways which would otherwise be barred. With Whittier, the sociologist must say, "I know not what the future hath of marvel or surprise"; but with all due humility, the sociologist can also assert that some advance statement of the probable range of the marvelous and surprising can be provided.[50]

Neither attracted by Isaiah's bright visions of a glorious day to come, nor appalled by Jeremiah's somber forebodings of a day of judgment, the sociologist is resigned to the fact that the Age of Prophecy is over, and convinced that the Age of Miracles will come no more. In the depths of his total depravity he still knows that he is spared not only the sin of hypocrisy but also the sin of presumption.

III. HOW TO SIN CONSTRUCTIVELY

In detailing the exploits of Sam Slick, Incense D. Woodchopper, and others, I was directly contradicting some of my statements about prophecy, for it may perhaps be remembered that when I was later talking like a common scold about those who think they can foretell future events on the empirical level, I flatly asserted that the sociologist can say nothing about why any particular social action is entered upon at any particular time. If this is true—and I think it is—why did I venture to talk about Slick and Company? Waiving the fictional form, are not such persons, in ultimate essence, entirely unique?

Of course they are; everybody is unique, and so is everything. My apparent self-contradiction derived from the fact that I could not properly discuss constructed types until I had dealt, however sketchily, with interpretation and prediction.

---

[50] This topic has been discussed at greater length in my "Supreme Values and the Sociologist," cited earlier. See pp. 285-290 of the present volume. A briefer version occurs under "Prediction, sociological," in Fairchild, ed., *op. cit.*

We are now at the point where the launching of constructive typology can proceed without further delay, and instead of the hypothetical instances hitherto used as illustrations, I shall draw throughout upon my study of German youth movements for which various preliminary researches, undertaken from 1923 to 1943, had been completed when the present methodological essay took shape in 1944.[51] Thus I can perhaps demonstrate to the reader that I am not engaged in word-polishing for its own sake, but on the contrary have been sharpening tools that have already been put to use.

Any study which properly bears the label of one or another of the social sciences begins with a question, and even though this question may be so broad that it will admit of many different approaches in the search for an answer, it should be explicitly formulated at the very outset. Our question is essentially this: What are the connections, if any, between the older German youth movements and the Hitler Youth?

Such a question could naturally be expanded indefinitely, for many subquestions begin to make their appearance almost immediately after the initial problem has been stated. Each one of these succeeding subquestions would progressively sharpen the focus, but for the time being the vaguer but more inclusive outlines called into view by the less specific formulation will prove to be of greater use.

In the discussion of the ways in which the historian can approach his only feasible goal, the depiction of the relatively unique, I said that selective attention to the data of the "past" was the only way to escape from the futility of trying to seize the absolutely unique by gathering "all the facts." Such selective attention is necessarily directed toward the materials bearing on a problem of the kind just posed. Delineation of the *relatively* unique on an *explicitly* selective basis I have elsewhere termed "culture case study," for every case study, whether of a single personality or of a nation, must take account of the cultural margin that surrounds and interweaves with social actions.

[51] *German Youth: Bond or Free* (Gary, Ind.: Norman Paul Press, 1950), *passim*. No page references to this book will be given, for it is relatively brief and has a full index.

A general value-system is for our purposes the most important part of this cultural context, but the value-system must often be analytically extracted from language, music, the dance, the graphic and plastic arts, and other aspects of culture representing its less thoroughly formalized phases, as well as from law, religion, moral codes, and similar cultural products which have been more completely crystallized. It is frequently necessary, therefore, to make selective historical studies of relatively unique configurations and time-sequences out of which it may then become possible to distill a general value-system and other distinguishable parts of the cultural context that qualify or essentially modify the means used for the attainment of given ends, the ends themselves, and the various elements of social situations.

The harsh remarks about the shortcomings of historians in which I have already indulged do not apply to those students of the past—and many of them are historians by profession— who carry out what I have called culture case studies; one of the greatest drawbacks of contemporary American sociology, to name no other social science, is its almost complete lack of this kind of historical sophistication. The necessity for culture case study in sociology arises from the fact that basing generalizations on hand-picked illustrative fragments torn from their contexts is thoroughly unscientific and has long since been discredited. If the sociologist is really a scientist, his ultimate goal will be prediction, as already noted; and prediction, retrospective or prospective, must always be couched in "if and when" terms. Now, "if and when" always refer to situations that either have already occurred or can be envisaged in terms of what has already occurred. The "geologic strata" of time-sequence evidence cannot be arbitrarily juggled; if the constructed types of sociology are to have predictive power, they must be developed without primary regard to their generalizability. If they prove to be generalizable *in spite* of the fact that they are first of all designed to yield a shorthand description and analysis of the social actions, etc., permeating a particular historical configuration, in close relation with a broadly stated problem and its derivative hypothesis, so much the better; but such generalizability must not be the all-controlling aim of the endeavor.

In short, the initial conclusions of a culture case study are limited to the interpretation of social actions within the area and period studied, but the basic method used, namely, constructive typology, may enable these configurations to be transferred, after appropriate modification, to other areas and periods. Dated and localized types must be accumulated before there is any thoroughgoing attempt to build types of relatively undated and nonlocalized form.

Putting this less abstractly, let us note that changes evident in the social actions engaged in by German youth have set for us a hazily outlined problem. In examining German society of a period prior to the consolidation of the German nation (from about 1800 to 1870) it has been found, as we shall see later, that there is little evidence of that loosely organized assault of youth on age which came to be known as the youth movement. Turning to German society of half or three quarters of a century later (from about 1890 to 1925), we encounter evidence of what seems to be a considerable amount, and perhaps even a maximum, of these conflict phenomena in certain datable and localizable sectors.

Culture case studies affording such contrasts provide an approach that seems to vouchsafe a valid basis for selection and a genuinely comparative method. A study of the culture, in the essential particularity of its time and place, where the phenomena relevant to the problem—in this case, the sources of the conflict of generations—are at a minimum, yields in earlier German society a sort of control or marginal case. One point thus fixed, we set at the opposite pole a culture case study—later German society—in which the same phenomena are at a maximum. With two points of reference thus established, we have a determining orientation; between these two extremes any number of relevant culture case studies could be placed. If a sufficient number were available, it is within the bounds of possibility that a sort of empirical continuum could be built up, and if the number were very large, transition from one case to the other might be almost imperceptible. Yet in either direction would lie the limiting extremes, giving significance, in terms of the problem and hypothesis, to even the minutest variation.

The extremes, let us remind the reader, are on the one hand earlier German society in which the phenomena denoted by the problem, i.e., the organized conflict of generations, are at the empirically discoverable minimum so far as the particular time and place focused on are concerned; while on the other hand we have later German society in which the same phenomena are at the empirically discoverable maximum. When as the result of intensive culture case study, both at the extremes and in the transitional zone, the processes correlated with transition toward one or another extreme have been discovered, within the limits set by the constructed types developed on the basis of the empirical data, the problem has been solved, *but only for the cases examined.*

This result achieved, it may then be possible to restate the constructed types in "if and when" terms and to search the record for other cases that will provide a checkup on the validity of the retrospective or prospective predictions made. This constitutes a genuinely comparative method,[52] even though the initial comparison is only between earlier and later cultural configurations which the unwary might be tempted to think of as necessarily the "same" society.[53] Only when small-scale

[52] A generation or two ago social scientists made a great to-do over the "comparative method," for to this method alone they attributed the apparent success of the theory of organismic evolution. Following the vulgarized biology of that day, social scientists meant by the comparative method the collection of "facts" supporting a given "theory." In virtually every instance these "facts" were items torn from the web of relations which gave them whatever legitimate scientific meaning they might have had. Such items were then jammed into the framework of the so-called "theory," and the result was Spencer's euhemerism or Frazer's totemism and exogamy or Morgan's unilinear social evolution.

Strictly speaking, however, this was merely the illustrative method. A genuinely comparative method has since been developed, chiefly by functional anthropologists and historical sociologists, but it needs clearer statement.

[53] Wholes, it should be remembered, are for us wholes by definition only. To the man who sits on it, a chair is a whole, but to various natural scientists it may be a conglomerate of other wholes—cells, molecules, atoms, and whatnot. To students building a rally-day bonfire, it is just a minor part of a splendid heap of fuel.

validation of this pragmatic variety has been secured can there be any talk of far-reaching generalizations about youth movements the world over, and even with such validation it is altogether too much to assume that these generalizations will hold for all cases whatsoever. The sociologist predicts, but he does not prophesy.

On the foundation provided by culture case studies of this kind interpretation in and through the use of constructed types proceeds. That is to say, after the delineation of the relatively unique aspects of the datable and localizable configurations set up as the poles of an empirical continuum has gone as far as is necessary for particularization, the next step is the construction of types adequate to the interpretation and conditional prediction of "if and when" recurrences.

It is now high time to offer a clear statement of what is meant by a constructed type. Such types are made up of "criteria" (so-called elements, traits, aspects, and so on) which have discoverable referents in the empirical world or can legitimately be inferred from empirical evidence, or both. The construction of these types should always be oriented toward a clear-cut hypothesis; the type of highest usefulness is not merely classificatory.[54] Although not always constructed with sufficient care, and sometimes lacking close empirical approximations (referents) and precise validation,[55] constructed types abound in sociological research. It should be pointed out, however, that the construct and the empirical approximation are not the same thing; in this sense, therefore, nothing but "exceptions" to constructed types exist. If the sociologist is to

[54] At the risk of wearying the reader, let us say again that the conception of science underlying constructed types is that scientific activity is essentially predictive; even though predictions must often be cast in retrospective rather than prospective terms, and even though they are frequently hypothetical rather than actual, the logic of scientific prediction, which is at bottom probability logic, is consistently followed. This point needs stressing, for some interpretations of "ideal types" (of which constructed types represent a closely related offshoot) do not hold the basically probable character of the "ideal type" clearly enough in view. (It is for this reason, among many others, that "constructed type" may eventually become the preferred term. At present it is restricted largely to my own writings and to those of the graduate students who have worked with me.)

[55] The problem of validation is thoroughly dealt with, in my opinion, in only one study, W. L. Kolb's unpublished dissertation (previously cited, p. 193 n. 9).

predict rather than prophesy, he must work on the basis of constructed types derived from culture case studies.[56]

Now that the main features of culture case study and constructive typology have been sketched, let us see what light our polar case studies throw on the problem, and more especially on the choosing of a working hypothesis.[57]

[56] It must be borne in mind that constructed types are not necessarily averages, although every average, in the special technical sense of the mean (not the mode or the median) has some of the attributes of a constructed type. For instance, the "average graduate of a woman's college," who reputedly bears only six tenths of a child during her entire reproductive period, does not exist in the flesh; she is not an empirical instance but is computed from empirical instances. (The problem of the "empirical possibility" of the constructed type arises here, but space for its consideration is lacking.) The same nonexistence holds for the extremes of a frequency distribution as long as more than one item is found in the given cell; a frequency distribution can be thought of as made up of many means arranged along a continuum, each mean being computed from a cell including two or more items. This being the case, it is possible to maintain that the constructed type may deviate widely from empirical phenomena ordinarily encountered, and yet that it represents a mean of some empirical phenomena falling on the same continuum as do the ordinary kind.

To be sure, we must take heed of the fact that constructed types usually include many more criteria than go to identify items capable of ready manipulation by present statistical techniques. The German youth movement (a construct derived from the study of more than one hundred distinguishable subvarieties) as a constructed type has at least twelve main criteria, and in almost any empirical research problem it would have at least as many more minor criteria. Present methods of computing multiple and partial correlations become almost insuperably complex and time-consuming when more than four variables must be handled. (Here the new electronic computation machines may offer aid.) Further, the criteria of the constructed type are *structurally* interrelated and necessarily include the typical ends, means, and defined situations of the social actors whose conduct makes up the social processes and structures under investigation. It follows, then, that although constructive typology is based on the logic of probability, it is not yet strictly quantitative unless every statement made in "more or less" terms can be so regarded. In the great majority of the problems dealt with by the constructive typologist, it is not at present feasible even to attempt numerical statement and statistical manipulation where the constructed types themselves are concerned; *quantitative methods can and should be used in the pragmatic validation of the predictions based on the types, but that is another matter.* Perhaps small-sampling theory will enable us to get around this difficulty, but that remains to be seen. Just now it seems advisable to see how well constructive typology lends itself to prediction; it has already achieved excellent results when the predictions are of retrospective character. See Kolb's dissertation (p. 193 n. 9).

Since the above footnote was written, Robert F. Winch has published an article on "Heuristic and Empirical Typologies: A Job for Factor Analysis," *American Sociological Review*, XII (Feb., 1947), 68-75. It is an interesting example of independent origin, although, to be sure, many authors appear in the text and footnotes.

[57] I say "more especially" because of the fact that the construction of the

Beginning with nineteenth-century Germany in the days before the Franco-Prussian War, culture case study seems to show that, in the first quarter of the century especially, older and younger generations manifested no marked discrepancies of outlook. In spite and in part because of the struggle with Napoleon, Germany was still "a geographical expression rather than a nation," and the life that was lived in the many pocket-sized dukedoms and principalities was singularly lacking in "dynamic" and "progressive" traits.[58]

Furthermore—and this is of the highest significance—this early nineteenth-century German world was defined by many of the writers, artists, and musicians of the later Germany in terms of a sentimental nostalgia, of a longing for "the dear dead days beyond recall" that obscured the petty cares, the jealous bickerings, the tragic narrowness of the life led by the German Michel. A Golden Age of unspoiled, unaffected natural virtue, of communion with nature and with fellow-men, was created.

Altogether apart, however, from fantasies of an Age of Innocence, no matter how fatefully meaningful these fantasies later proved to be, there does seem to have been very substantial warrant, on the basis of evidence drawn from everyday life, for contrast between earlier and later Germany.

The pace of social change before 1870 was unquestionably slow. Handicraft home industry was still uppermost in all

---

types and the whole procedure of validation depends fundamentally on the way in which the initial hypothesis is formulated. *Types are not themselves hypotheses even though developed in close conjunction with them.*

[58] Madame de Staël's descriptions of the ordinary German as a sort of good-humored, simple-minded sleep-walker were unquestionably idealized caricatures, but nevertheless they contained a large amount of close observation, as comparison with the writings of her contemporaries unquestionably shows. These and many other sources were drawn upon by Gustav Freytag in his *Pictures of the German Past*; in these genre studies surprising continuities between the Germany of even the sixteenth century and the middle nineteenth are clearly apparent. The drawings of Ludwig Richter and Moritz von Schwind likewise capture the spirit of parochial, bucolic intimacy; virtues and vices are those of a "little world" drowsily unaware of the bustle and stir characteristic of many other parts of Europe. Goethe's *Hermann und Dorothea*, for all its idyllic flavor, also seems to be a fairly accurate representation of the same state of affairs. Again, as late as 1840 the folktales of Grimm could still be gathered in the spinning-room, the blacksmith shop, and the market place.

but the very largest cities, commerce was but little concerned with other than local trade, and clergy and aristocracy were still the recipients of fear and reverence. Parents exerted far-reaching authority, whether benevolent or otherwise, and children looked forward confidently to the establishment of families in which they in turn would lay down the law, mildly if possible, sternly if need be. Although moral contradictions were by no means absent, they were not sufficiently flagrant to cause the younger generation to doubt the wisdom or goodness of the representatives of the established order: "So it has always been" and "God has so decreed it" soon quelled most of the impious questioners.

Where peasant unrest existed, the safety valve of emigration relieved the pressure; those who remained held tenaciously to ways that had begun to pass into the discard in neighboring England a full century before. Not only was economic discontent thus alleviated, but emigration also served to allay religious dissatisfaction. Anabaptists, Mennonites, and other sects dating from the sixteenth and seventeenth centuries had long since been expelled or had voluntarily departed, and streams of migrants flowed from precisely those regions where sectarian ferment was still at work. In spite of Zinzendorf and Herrnhut, therefore, Germany never had anything remotely comparable to the mass evangelical movements, such as Methodism, which appeared in Britain and the United States during the late eighteenth and early nineteenth centuries.

In political matters it can be said that apart from the adjustments forced by Napoleon's short-lived conquests, subjects of local overlords in the earlier Germany willingly rendered allegiance as long as taxation was not too heavy and the traditional rights of peasants, artisans, and others were not too greatly infringed upon. A tremendous amount of social prestige attached to membership in the aristocracy, and even hate-filled underlings passively acknowledged the superiority of noble blood.[59]

[59] Rebellious spirits raised their unhallowed voices in the great towns and cities, of course, but even the direful year of 1848 saw no such upheavals in Germany as those which caused thrones to totter in other European countries even at that time regarded as backward.

Untouched by the Enlightenment except in regions such as Upper Saxony, little affected by the Napoleonic upheavals and their aftermaths, and indifferent to the winds of doctrine blowing from the quarter of political democracy, German doctor, lawyer, and merchant chief continued to jog along well-worn roads like sedate livery stable nags, occasionaly balking or shying but never running away.

In the realm of family relations a good deal of steadiness likewise prevailed. The erotic tendencies of the young male were fairly easily gratified, at least among the peasantry. The survival of old bundling practices, tolerated familiarity during the betrothal period, fairly early marriage, and the ready acceptance of a life of diligent although slow-paced labor at a low standard of living, along with the fact that numerous children were not only expected but were also economic assets in the working of peasant holdings, meant that peasant youngsters saw no reason to be restive except in ways that an occasional brawl, spree, or *Fest* would appease.

The family situations of the middle classes, although not so definitely in agreement with defined needs, were after all not in strong contradiction. Sons followed the calling of their fathers, generally speaking, and the fathers felt the obligation to finance the sons, even though married, in the early stages of their careers. In addition, dowries were taken very much as matter of course; and because of the fact that individual choice did not enter into the selection of marriage partners to an overwhelming degree, marriages in which dowry considerations had played a very large part nevertheless were not defined as "marriages of convenience" by husband or wife. Goethe's *Elective Affinities* and Schlegel's *Lucinde* reached only a small novel-reading contingent; the day of vicarious erotic experience among literate masses came much later. Women were on the whole satisfied with their traditional roles of bearers of children, housewives, and exponents of charity under religious auspices. If husbands were unfaithful or unkind, wives meekly resigned themselves to their lot. Divorce was so very exceptional as to be almost nonexistent as far as middle-class definitions of possibilities were concerned. The unmarried young man of the middle classes could readily exploit servant girls and other members of lower status groups without becoming a victim of intense moral conflict or resolving that conflict by a cynical adjustment. To "sow wild oats" was accepted as the way of the world made inevitable by man's originally sinful nature. Even the taking of a mistress after marriage was defined in a similar way. Prostitution of course existed, but it was not widespread or specialized, and was easily brought under the scope of sanctioned rationality by being defined as part of the static order of original sin.

The erotic life of the aristocracy was relatively free and easy, but wide differences of status made exploitation more or less a matter of course, concerning which no intense resentment was felt by those exploited—nor were any irksome moral obligations absorbed by the exploiters. Traditional prerogatives, in other words, were accepted without much question.

In this essentially conformist Germany the training of the younger generation was fairly simple and straightforward. For artisans who labored outside their homes the apprenticeship system almost exclusively prevailed, and in the home handicrafts children were of course instructed by parents and other near relatives. Peasants had begun to follow improved agricultural practices to some extent, but these practices had not become so complex that anything beyond a modicum of the three R's was required for their mastery. Reading was very largely confined to the Bible, devotional literature, handbills of one sort or another, and an occasional newspaper spiced with a dash of politics. The period of schooling was short, and there were no regulations affecting the work of children in such ways as to make it difficult to use them as field hands or home-industry helpers throughout the larger part of the year. Peasant girls received very little schooling, and in many instances that little was soon forgotten when baking, hoeing, and childbirth began to bear down with full weight.

Sons of the middle classes read law after finishing a humanistic education, received simple medical instruction, entered a counting house where no great demands on anything but persistence and shrewdness existed, and so on.

These being "the conditions that prevailed," the absence of an organized youth movement can occasion small wonder.[60]

If we turn now to Germany after the Franco-Prussian War, striking contrasts become almost immediately apparent. The earlier Customs Union and the easy wins over Denmark and Austria were now crowned by the consolidation of a German empire which could boast of victory over a France that little more than half a century earlier had been virtual master of the European continent. The Swiss-like ingenuity of German craftsmen and technicians had borne fruit in the needle gun and other successful weapons, but with imperial consolidation, the fruits of the French indemnity, and the example provided by heavily industrialized predecessors such as Britain, Germany burst into an age of economic activity and prosperity comparable only to the mushrooming of Japan after the Meiji restoration. Essen, Berlin, Leipzig, and countless other cities became great centers of industry and commerce almost overnight, and ports like Hamburg, Bremen, and Duisburg experienced unbelievably rapid growth.

The bureaucratic network previously exemplified on a less complex scale in Prussia spread over all of the new empire, and even during Bismarck's time came to control, sometimes behind the scenes, sometimes openly, the policies of the monarchy and the futile negative activities of what passed for a parliament.

"Progress" was the watchword not only in material life

[60] As Lütkens cogently asserts, it does no good to claim the literary Romanticism of the *Sturm und Drang* cult or the nationalism of the *Burschenschaft* students as the initial phases of the later youth movements properly so called. The Romanticists of the days of the young Goethe and Schiller never numbered more than a handful read by a few, and the students who swore by Father Jahn, although politically suspect to the ultraconservatives, either wound up in physical culture clubs and singing societies or espoused a nationalism that was in no sense contradictory to the political aspirations of their fathers, even though those fathers were reluctant to risk anything to see their aspirations realized. Of rebellion against a Germanic culture and society presumably "perpetrated by a corrupt older generation" there is not the slightest trace, and of the conception that youth as youth rather than as preparation for adulthood has its own peculiar merits there is likewise no evidence.

but also in the things of the mind. Architecture became flamboyant, grandiose, and banal; music brassily pompous; graphic and plastic arts cheaply sentimental, chauvinistic, or both; scholarship and science steadily more specialized—production lines for advanced degrees; and skepticism, relativism, and positivism flourished.

In family matters radical alterations took place. The peasants who flocked to the cities or whose small village and towns were sucked into urban eddies soon found that numerous progeny were no longer a blessing, economic or otherwise. Compulsory school attendance and a host of other devices of the Bismarckian state made it very hard for the working-class father to feed and clothe too many offspring. Further, the old bundling, betrothal, and early marriage customs proved impossible to transfer to urban life.[61]

Formerly, left-wing ideologies had been kept alive only by refugees living in Switzerland, France, or England, but now the rapid growth of a working class having little or no ownership of the means of production made the gospels of Marx and Lassalle intensely appealing. With the spread of the doctrines of class conflict and exploitation, workers grew resentful of the fact that their daughters were regarded as fair game by the middle classes and the aristocracy, whereas in earlier days attentions by condescending "betters" sometimes held an element of flattery not altogether unappreciated. Prostitution vastly increased in scope, and instead of being taken for granted as an outgrowth of man's sinful nature, gave rise to more and more economic and ethical questioning.

Among the middle classes family tensions, previously latent but in many cases unrealized, now took on the openly threatening character, figuratively speaking, of a bent bow or a cocked trigger. Sons no longer dutifully followed in the footsteps of their fathers, for the number and range of professions was rapidly increasing. Frequently this meant that the father

[61] Illegitimate children brought with them legal complications of a sort previously unknown, and with the waning of religious beliefs the existence of such offspring came to be defined as a "social problem"; previously it had been only a religious problem.

no longer felt the same obligation to support the son while his career was getting under way, for the son oftentimes chose a calling that because of its very newness carried a certain tinge of disrepute. Further, the newly arisen conception of the natural rights of children sometimes led sons arbitrarily to select callings other than those hallowed by paternal tradition. When a son did slip into the groove worn by his father, it was no longer with the feeling that "At last I'm doing what father did," but rather that the groove was a rut. Self-justification by the son for having chosen the easiest way frequently led to blatant exaggeration of the rut's importance, and to escape from boredom in the commercialized "amusements" of the great cities, with their pandering to all vices.

Flush living in competition with business and professional associates made it more and more difficult for fathers to provide dowries for their daughters, more especially as these daughters came to expect education in a finishing school or similar establishment. Even when the dowry system did not fall into the discard, changes in dwelling-place, neighbors, and ideas of the socially praiseworthy not only gave more scope to individual choice but also meant that bride and bridegroom began to contrast "marriage for love" and "marriage for convenience" in a way unknown to earlier generations. This, added to the ethical questions raised by the existence of the prostitute and the mistress, provided material for literary men like Sudermann, Heyse, and a host of others; tension and unrest were thereby increased.

Children found themselves confronted not only by parental insincerity—or, at the very least, uncertainty—but in addition were expected to become little replicas of conventionally stylish adults. It might even be said that the extent to which parents departed from what earlier generations had taken for granted was directly proportional to the insistence with which they demanded that their children fit into a new world in which "progress" in all departments of life had become fashionable.

In the realm of formal education the clamor for applied

science, the increasing use of modern languages in salesmanship, the introduction of elaborate systems of bookkeeping, and
a host of other developments led to a rapid expansion of the
school system designed for middle-class youngsters. The old
humanistic training became more and more unsuited to the
needs of the day, and schools offering combinations of mathematics, science, modern languages, and commercial subjects
in varying proportions were established by legislative enact-
ment in all parts of Germany. The length of the school day
was increased, and the pace of education was stepped up;
school attendance hence became a very heavy burden on many
children.

Smaller families, lack of near-by cousins, the greater extent to which girls were educated outside the home, and growing formality and impersonality of social relations even for
adolescents led to separation of the sexes during the teens and
early twenties to an extent far greater than had previously
been in evidence among the middle classes—even though Germany has long been a land in which the division between the
realms proper to man and woman has been sharply marked.
After twelve or thirteen, boys saw very little of their former
girl playmates, and when they did see them it was usually only
on Sunday afternoon visits or at parties presided over by hawk-
eyed chaperones. Nevertheless, novel literature was saturated
with gushy romantic love at the very time when the demands
of education, both informal and formal, made it almost impossible for youngsters to form individual attachments with
those of the opposite sex. Girls associated chiefly with girls
and boys with boys; "crushes" became more and more prevalent. As the younger generation grew older, Paragraph 175
of the German Criminal Code (STGB)[62] began to seep into
the "humorous" journals, and in cities like Berlin "high-class"
establishments catering to adults of doubtful gender or "unusual" proclivities plied their specialized business.

The strenuously competitive character of the professions
led to ever-greater deferment of marriage, with the usual

[62] This is the law dealing with the punishment of male homosexuality.

result. Because, as hitherto noted, so many of the delayed marriages were regarded as "marriages of convenience," the double standard carried over from the wild-oats stage into the life of the married man. The German woman, except when she joined the ranks of prostitutes and mistresses, did not follow suit to any significant extent, but she began to absorb doctrines of natural rights and ethical consistency; a woman's movement, although on a much smaller scale than that which appeared in some other countries of Europe, notably Britain and Sweden, began to get under way. In spite of the ostracism with which divorce was visited, it greatly increased in frequency among the middle classes, and thereby brought the moral contradictions in which it had its source into ever greater prominence.

Supernaturalistic religion, especially Roman Catholicism, retained its hold on the peasantry, but the proportion of peasants in the German population rapidly dwindled. Whereas in 1800 seven out of eight persons were engaged in essentially rural tasks, in 1900 only one out of three, at most, was so occupied. Once the walls of the parish, whether Catholic or Lutheran, were breached by strange ways and strange people, all but those in sheltered nooks and corners felt the chilling blasts of doubt. In the swollen ranks of the urban proletariat the coldness of official religion and its identification with a despised political regime led to ready acceptance of competing ideologies in the form of Marxism and the like.

The middle classes in earlier days had weakened in religious allegiance because of the vogue of Hegelianism and the pantheism of figures such as Goethe, but there was nevertheless no widespread defection from orthodox belief nor, indeed, any great loss in the effectiveness of that belief in the control of conduct. After 1870 the middle classes waxed fat, and with their fatness came conviction that this world is not a vale of tears in preparation for a better, but is rather a Rabelaisian Abbey of Thelème. Evolutionism and the higher criticism found hearing outside the treatise and the lecture room, and the notion that religion is "an opiate of the people" was tacitly accepted even by those persons who had most to gain if the continued administration of the opiate were assured. That is to say, many eminently respectable people came to feel that religion is a good thing because it keeps otherwise troublesome trash contented. Further, the Sunday morning promenade to church with paterfamilias in the van still carried a halo of solid social position; only "fellows without a fatherland," viz., social, political, and economic malcontents, ignored the comfortable duties of pew-warmers. Again, few churchgoers forgot the legal and other disabilities that failure to keep up membership in the official churches entailed. Profitable hypocrisy is rarely agonizing; hence, although orthodox belief steadily waned in influence, church membership and attendance notably diminished only where the "dangerous thoughts" of Social Democracy had wreaked havoc.

The claims of the monarch to rule by the grace of God sometimes evoked indulgent smiles from his bourgeois subjects, but as an alternative to a republic—of which France presumably provided a horrible example—even the flighty Wilhelm II received unswerving allegiance. But although the monarchy as an institution was not always worshiped without question, the bureaucracy unquestionably was. "Order is the first duty of the citizen" was visibly incorporated in the regulations of staid officialdom. The ordinary middle-class German gloried in the smooth running of an elaborate administrative machine that apparently foresaw every contingency, provided for every exception, regulated everything from buttons to balloons, and incidentally furnished the pattern by which the German army, ever to be victorious, mobilized, maneuvered, paraded, and appropriately impressed foreign observers. Efficiency, probity, calculability—what more could one ask?

What of the German youth whose fathers had lived through the triumph of the seventies, the emergence of Germany as a first-rate industrial as well as military power in the eighties, and the plush-upholstered comfort and respectability of the nineties? In particular, what did the sons and daughters of the middle classes, especially the sons, think of the brave new world the fathers had acquired and were ready to bequeath? Were they grateful for the warmth of Germany's place in the sun? Well, to put it mildly, they thought that the brave new world was brassy and that the brass was badly tarnished, that the warmth was not the warmth of sunshine but the enervating stuffiness of overheated, garishly furnished apartments filled with the reek of stale beer and the acrid fumes of cigar stubs. Specifically, they thought that parental religion was largely sham, politics boastful and trivial, economics unscrupulous and deceitful, education stereotyped and lifeless, art trashy and sentimental, literature spurious and commercialized, the drama tawdry and mechanical, the dance cheaply titillating or excessively formal, family life repressive and insincere, and the relations of the sexes, in marriage or out, shot through with hypocrisy.

Not only did German youth think all this and far worse of the parental heritage; it also outspokenly proclaimed its opinion to all who could hear. Not content with impassioned denunciation by word of mouth, German lads and young men (for it was first of all a male revolt) wrote screeds calling on those of their own age to reject what the older generation thought supremely worthy of transmission to the younger, and also summoning them to share in a great new experience.

This experience was *das Wandern*, best translated as "roaming." To break away from flabby school routine, insincere church attendance, flatulent concerts, boring parties designed for social climbing and display, nauseous student "jollifications" laden with the sluggish ceremonial and alcoholic conviviality of the paternal tavern table, and to wander at will through the fields, forests, and mountains, to pitch camp in a ruined castle or under the lindens fringing a little cluster of peasant houses where the simple life was still followed, to return to the hearty fellowship of roving scholars and journeymen, and in so doing to discover their essential selves—for this the *Wandervögel* came into being. By the early 1900's these "birds of passage" or, as we shall call them, Roamers, could be seen in every part of Germany; browned,

travel-stained fellows with soft felt hats, here and there flutter-
ing red, green, and gold ribbons, on their backs simple belong-
ings in knapsacks, and over the shoulders of at least a few, lutes
which they merrily twanged while wandering afoot and while
around the campfire.

By 1913, the centenary of the Battle of Leipzig, there were
so many of these demonstrative dissenters that thousands of
them could assemble at Hohe Meissner, a hill hallowed by
centuries of German history, there to pass through an emotional
experience of revivalistic nature that brought to them a tremendous sense of solidarity and confidence in their mission.
What was the mission? No one could really say; it was simply
felt, but a rationale of some sort there had to be, and thus it
ran:

Free German youth, on their own initiative, under their own responsibility, and with deep sincerity, are determined to shape their own
lives.[63]

This famous formula was Alpha and Omega. It neither
preceded nor followed a constitution, a program, or anything
else by which the youth *movement* (for such it had now become) could be bound to any given course of action or directed
toward any definite goal. To roam for the sake of roaming,
to experience the fellowship of companions on the road or in
camp, to escape from the repulsive world that adults had
created in their own image—this was enough. Leaders arose
as they felt "called" to leadership, gathered their followers
about them, saw other leaders challenge their supremacy and
flit away with a number of the early devotees or with fresh
recruits, and finally, growing older, were forced into the ranks
of the despised adults or remained among those "eternal ado-

[63] In this formula, attributed to Gustav Wyneken, the reference to "free German youth" is to a specific body, *Die Freideutsche Jugendbewegung*, but the
Hohe Meissner revival (the religious term is used advisedly) affected virtually
all the other conventicles. Traces of the formula finally appear in the pro-
nunciamentos of even the most conservative youth tutelage (*Jugendpflege*)
organizations. Incidentally, the earlier movement, for all the similarity of name,
has *no* connection with the *Freie Deutsche Jugend* of today. The latter is
Communist.

lescents" who for better or for worse tried to keep on living in the youthful world they loved so well.

By 1914 there had been many schisms, but the inner unity of the movement was not sadly impaired thereby. Then came World War I, and herewith this ruthlessly pruned culture case study comes to a close.

Before making another that will more directly answer our question: What are the connections, if any, between the older German youth movement and the Hitler youth? we shall set forth a hypothesis and construct types which can be subjected to validation.[64]

The hypothesis runs as follows: The German youth movement came into being because the ends and prospective situations of its adherents had been defined by adults in patterns which were intended to "bring up the young in the way they should go," but which were in violent contrast with the situations of adult life as defined by adults for adult purposes.

In less compressed form: However hypocritical parents and other representatives of the grown-up world may be where their actual conduct is concerned, they are seldom fully aware of it themselves. In the later Germany that we have been describing, there was a zealous effort to impart to children all of the traditional virtues, and given the mentality of the generation which founded families shortly after 1870, examples of these virtues were found in a German past just far enough away to have the roseate tint of "the good old days." When you add to this the fact that "the good old days" really did have many aspects strikingly different from those of a present which, no matter how glorious, still lacked the halo that hovered about grandfather's youth, it is easy to see why youngsters were told, quite sincerely, that to be good German men and women they need only look back to and faithfully follow the

[64] I should be the last to claim, however, that such validation has been rigorously carried through in these pages. The full-length book previously cited (p. 214 n. 51) makes a start toward it. Moreover, I regret and deplore the lack of quantitative data. Figures of any precision are very difficult to obtain, although the notes of the book, especially of chap. v, contain rough estimates.

example of their ancestors. In our terminology, children were told that expediency should have nothing to do with the choice of means, and that freely vented emotions, no matter how deeply felt, could lead only to evil consequences—expedient rationality and affective nonrationality were alike placed under a ban, for had not the virtuous Germans of bygone days lived sober, responsible, God-fearing lives? Were they not loyal to church and state? Did they not honor their parents and therefore live long in the land? Only those means sanctioned by those whom God had set in authority, whether spiritual or temporal, should ever be chosen by good little boys and girls who hoped to grow up into men and women of whom papa and mama could be proud. Even though the path of duty was not always clearly mapped by God's earthly representatives, it could always be found by looking for the footsteps of departed worthies and by listening to the tales of their loyal, pious, and kindly deeds. Where express sanctions were lacking, tradition provided a safe guide—sanctioned rationality and traditional nonrationality, then, were continually enjoined upon the children who later flared up in adolescent rebellion.

The reason for their rebellion should be already clear. No matter how closepacked the padding of cotton wool may be, children in their teens soon recognize the difference between profession and practice, between words and deeds. Parents and other once-revered exemplars were seen to practice expediency under the guise of sanction or tradition, and were also discovered to be following affective outlets for thwarted impulses in ways that they were the first to condemn when indulged in by social inferiors or those careless enough to be caught. "The fathers have eaten sour grapes, and the children's teeth are set on edge." Youthful idealism and impetuousness led to the root-and-branch rejection of adult life. The only way out was a return to a past of childhood dreams that simultaneously seemed to offer escape from an intolerable present and at least an indefinite postponement of a forbidding future. No longer could German youth bow the knee in Rimmon's house; the world had to be redefined.

In this process of redefinition the restoration of old sanctions was well-nigh impossible, for once the prescribed practices of orthodox faith were called in question, the faith itself had been shaken at the root. Further, the vogue of "progress" and the advances of science inevitably affected even those youngsters to whom material progress seemed incarnate evil and applied science the product of the devil's workshop. The old supernaturalism with its elaborate apparatus of rational proof no longer had any appeal, for such proof no longer carried conviction when confronted by a world manifestly out of joint. Youth's new way of life could not be pursued under the old sanctions any more than by sheer expediency; tradition and "self-revealing" emotion were the only means left.

Next, we must set forth our motivational model. In the first part of this essay it was stated that traditional nonrationality represents an elevation of means to the rank of ends, and that affective nonrationality is characterized by fusion of means and ends. With these hints and with the extraordinarily "goal-less" character of the youth movement in the phase we have been examining as primary warrant, we can impute to its adherents a type of personality in which tendencies are gratified on an nonrational means-ends basis of mingled traditional and affective character. With proper qualification, which the space at our disposal will not permit us to offer, all the activities of the youth movement thus far described can be seen to be congruent with this imputational construct.

Further, it can be seen that the situations confronted by youth were defined in ways that left social objects, social responses, and reflected selves very vague indeed, and social methods only slightly less so. In fact, only one of the five analytic elements of the social situation became stabilized, i.e., social instruments were defined in progressively sharper terms.

To take these up in order: Social objects were simply other youths, at first other males, later both sexes. Whether the responses expected of the males were defined in terms of ordinary maleness, however, there is considerable doubt; if one were to believe Blüher, male comradeship had a strongly homosexual tinge, even though homosexuality was latent rather than active in most cases. In the case of leaders, the responses expected from followers did not constitute adherence to a definite program, but rather emotional attachment and manifestation of loyalty. Followers expected leaders to respond to them by providing a sense of being in the presence of someone of extraordinary capacities and by manifesting deep comradely interest in their personalities. Followership was usually on a graded scale, but in general it can be said that as between follower and follower each one expected from the other a sense of warmth and intimacy, of solidarity and common purpose, of "understanding" and sympathy. In other words, social objects, expected responses, and reflected selves were closely intermingled. What Durkheim has called "crowd elation and surplus confidence," almost hypnotic leader-follower rapport, and emotional coalescence of the kind called unipathy by Max Scheler[65] prevented clear-cut distinctions by the actors themselves.

The social method was roaming, at once emotionalized symbol and expression of rebellion on the one hand, and traditionally grounded way of joining forces with the like-minded on the other. The Roamers acted in unison, with some semblance of planning in many cases, but to thwart spontaneity by adhering to a fixed time-schedule and itinerary was unthinkable. To plunge into new experience, to feel as "free as the birds of the air" was in itself a supreme end; and the means, tendencies, and social situations partook of the same nonrationality.

No social action, however, can be formless; there must be a fixed point somewhere even though the fixation is merely relative. The social instruments provided this fulcrum or nucleus. Costume, a combination of old-fashioned items gleaned from wandering scholars, foresters, peasants, and journeymen. Music, a mixture of soldiers' marching songs (frequently from medieval times), shepherds' lilts, folk ditties of love, comradeship, and parting—all accompanied by the lute

[65] See "Behavior, sympathetic" in Fairchild, ed., *op. cit.*, and my article, "Forms of Sympathy: A Phenomenological Analysis," *Journal of Abnormal and Social Psychology*, XXXVI (April-June, 1931), 58-68.

or similar archaic device for tuneful expression. Food and cooking utensils, a Spartan array of the utmost simplicity. Knapsack and "wander-staff," well-worn aids along the lines of those used by herdsmen, mountaineers, or pilgrims. Sleeping quarters, a straw-sacked corner in the peasant attic, the local inn, or in good weather in the open air, varied with increasing frequency by the use of hostels specially devised for youth purposes. Reading matter, inexpensive but artistically designed brochures and handbound books with content drawn from knightly adventures, American pioneer tales, German equivalents of Henty, German folklore, German culture histories, and descriptions of the lives lived by peasants and artisans in bygone days. "Local habitations," retreats called "nests" in the larger cities where in the dull winter season, when roaming was too difficult, a substitute for the campfire and the strawsack under the stars could be created. All these and many more "positive instruments" helped to give structure to what one French observer called "applied Bergsonism."[66]

Negative social instruments were at least equally definite; a partial list includes abstinence from alcohol and tobacco, refusal to participate in ballroom dancing, rejection of comfort in favor of "hard primitivism." These and a host of other self-imposed inhibitions lent a rigorous, ascetic quality to the youth movement; they helped to make its break with the adult world readily evident to even the most obtuse parent, school teacher, or pastor.

Even when the youth movement began to lose its spontaneous character, a development later discussed in detail, these positive and negative social instruments remained, lending at least the semblance and sometimes the only substance of continuity within and between the multifarious little conventicles that sprang up on every hand.

The general value-systems interweaving with the social actions characteristic of the youth movement were essentially what have been termed "sacred" and "secular." The sacred network twined chiefly about conduct of traditionally non-

[66] *Viz.*, expression of *élan vital* in contradistinction to "mechanized intelligence."

rational nature, whereas the secular patterns were those against which rebellion occurred and social instruments were directed, namely, ways of life pervaded by (1) expedient rationality and (2) affective nonrationality that represented grossly sensual escape from the frustrations of expediency. Conduct controlled by sanctioned rationality is also a frequent aspect of a prescribed sacred society, but inasmuch as the old sanctions had collapsed, the Roamers were thrown back on tradition and their own surging emotions.

Next to be considered is the "leadership principle." Most supernatural sanctions, including a great many ordinarily thought of as political, are in a very real sense the lengthened shadows of great men—if we take "great" in the sense of possession of extraordinary qualities (of whatever kind are yielded prestige in the particular society and culture) which evoke in others the willingness to follow "wherever the master leads." This extraordinariness has been termed charisma.

The charismatic leader, as has long been known, never presents a wholly novel message; he must speak with the sounding-board of tradition behind him, but although he uses the language of the prophets, to choose a familiar example, he may nevertheless proclaim: "Ye have heard it said by them of old time, but I say unto you. . . ." Otherwise put, he ordinarily asserts that he comes "not to destroy the law but to fulfil it." In the course of its fulfilment, however, novel features are introduced that may bring about changes far beyond those initially anticipated by even his most devoted followers.

So it was with the youth movement. Karl Fischer and many others like him became charismatic leaders, apostles of rebellion and rebirth who knew only that the old expediencies, sanctions, and emotional dodges held no promise for German youth. They provided no program beyond the simple dictum that the adult world was despicable and that youth should live its own life in its own way for its own sake.

These, then, were charismatic leaders of a peculiar kind; Mohammed, Joseph Smith, and John Brown, for all the intensity of the bonds existing between themselves and their followers, aimed at goals lying beyond a vague sense of intimacy, comradeship, and solidarity; and in their own lifetimes social methods, much less social instruments, did not completely overwhelm the larger and more directly purposeful phases of their own and their followers' activities. With the charismatic leaders of the youth movement the case was different. They helped to destroy old sanctions, but they never succeeded in setting up ideologies that led from youth to adulthood, from the "little world" of the charismatic conventicles to the "great world"[67] in which they would some day—barring the "eternal adolescents" already mentioned—have to take their places. They expressly rejected the expedient rationality of *Festlegung*, best paraphrased as "planning toward determinate goals." Depending only on their own charisma—which is to say, on continuing recognition by their followers of their leadership capacities—they continued to denounce corrupt adulthood, to praise the life of youth for its own sake, and to make loyal followership utilizing the appropriate social methods and instruments the all-important criterion of "belonging."

Eventually these leaders, who came and went as the vicissitudes of increasing age, rivalry, and the shifting of followership dictated, slowly established a value-system which, although enclosed within the larger framework of a German order at that time rapidly secularizing, represented *a society sacred to youth as youth*. The web of value-laden relations interweaving to form this society finally came to focus the tendencies and define the situations effective in the lives of the greater number of German adolescents, whether or not they were direct participants in a youth movement of the primordial Roamer type.

Not only did this sacred society vitally affect the social methods and instruments of German youth in general, but it also did much to govern the definitions of social objects, expected responses, and reflected selves. Traditional and affective nonrationalities became more and more standardized in their modes of expression. More important than all of this, however, was the fact that charismatic leadership, at first highly

[67] Here the references are to the *Faust* of Part I and Part II respectively.

spontaneous and unpredictable, became increasingly standardized and indeed virtually traditional. Various types of customary charismatic leader became distinguishable not only to detached observers but also to members of the youth movements themselves. Youngsters manifesting one or another of the combinations of standardized attributes were expected to become leaders whether they themselves felt a "call" or not, with the consequence that calls occurred with ever-increasing frequency.

Followers came to know in advance what the leader could be expected to do to, for, and with them, and even before World War I the little conventicles began to coalesce into larger sects divided along various lines. Among the more important differentiations were those of homosexual eroticism, heterosexual eroticism, or just plain eroticism.[68] ("Eroticism" is not used in an invidious sense. It simply indicates the fact that, at the very least, an erotic undercurrent or overtone pervaded many, although by no means all, of the varieties of comradeship and solidarity.) Numerous members of the youth movement were fully aware of the basis of these divisions and talked and wrote at length in justification of their particular preferences. It was not until 1917, however, with the publication of Blüher's notorious first volume of *The Role of Eroticism in Male Society*, that the matter came to be widely debated outside youth movement circles.

This new type of sacred society, then, represents the transmutation of the idealized phases of the older Germany into a pattern congruent with a means-ends schema giving primary place to traditional and affective nonrationalities and helping to define situations and to focus tendencies in ways making the course of the typical social actions concerned quite predictable. The old sacred Germany of course incorporated many sanctioned rationalities, but as we have seen, these fell by the wayside and were not effectively replaced. Instead, affective

---

[68] Some sects of the movement vigorously assailed proposals to permit girls to go roaming, others welcomed them but advocated "heroic asceticism" (Wyneken), still others openly championed promiscuity, and a minority seemed to practice eroticism in relative indifference to the sexes concerned.

nonrationality of the type manifest in the sense of "belonging," comradeship, solidarity, intimacy, and unipathy made its appearance, and this became fairly well standardized by the time the pioneer leaders began to be replaced by a fresh contingent.

We have said that the members of a sacred society are characterized by unwillingness or inability to respond to the new. How can such a construct fit the adherents of the youth movement before World War I? Simply because of the standardization already referred to; the patterns of the youth movement became fixed on a traditional-affective basis in which the traditional came to be more and more significant, until finally affective-charismatic manifestations were recognized as such only if they conformed to youth movement expectations or what they should be like.

In my estimation the task of constructing types adequate to the interpretation of this relatively unique set of sociocultural phenomena has now been completed—at least within the space at my disposal. I have blocked in rough outlines, some implicit validation in terms of retrospective prediction has perhaps been secured, and here the task might end if it were not for the question initially asked: What are the connections, if any, between the older German youth movements and the Hitler Youth?

Only a *drastically* foreshortened answer can be returned here, but it is worth returning not only for its own sake but also because of its importance for the general method here set forth. Let me quote from an earlier part of the present section (pp. 217-218):

. . . it may then be possible to . . . search the record for other cases that will provide a checkup on the validity of the retrospective or prospective predictions made. This constitutes a genuinely comparative method, even though the initial comparison is only between earlier and later cultural configurations which the unwary might be tempted to think of as necessarily the "same" society.

What is now proposed, therefore, is to take the emergence of the Hitler Youth as *another case* that will provide some check on the validity of the retrospective predictions implicitly made about the old youth movements.

Most readers are reasonably familiar with the general state of German society after World War I. Hence, little need be said here except to note that all of the contradictions and conflicts apparent at the beginning of the century were present in exaggerated form, and that over and above this the further crumbling of stabilizing sanctions and traditions had led to extreme disorganization.

The youth movements which had carried on in halfhearted fashion during the early part of the war began to revive by 1917, and in 1919 and 1920 reached the peak of their popularity and influence. The members of sects arising out of the old Roamers, and becoming aware of their "mission" at Hohe Meissner in 1912, numbered well over half a million; and if we take in youth tutelage organizations and the youth auxiliaries of political parties, the total figure would be in excess of three millions.

The inclusion of youth tutelage and political auxiliaries is eminently warranted, for by 1920 the general value-system representing what we may call a "sacred society of youth" had interwoven with virtually all the activities of young Germans. Moreover, the social methods and instruments adopted by the Roamers and similar bodies were so widely imitated that it was hard to find a German youngster between the ages of ten and eighteen in whose way of life there were not some traces of the youth movement. Hence, judged in terms of numbers, the apparently trivial proposals of Karl Fischer and his followers had met with astounding success.

But when a movement becomes traditional—and that, in spite of surface spontaneity, was exactly what had happened to the Roamers and their like—it may bear within itself the seeds of its own destruction, particularly if the traditionalism helps to engender conduct readily directed toward goals radically divergent from those initially selected. If, to speak in paradox that is only apparent, goals of relative "goal-lessness" were characteristic of the conduct in its earlier manifestations, then this destructive direction "toward goals radically divergent from those initially selected" is quite easy, for planning toward *determinate* goals perverts[69] the actions concerned. Instead of "Youth for youth's sake" there appeared "Youth for the sake of the German people," "Youth for the sake of the German nation," "Youth for the sake of Lutheranism," "Youth for the sake of Catholicism," "Youth for the sake of Social Democracy," "Youth for the sake of National Socialism," and so on and on. This is tantamount to saying that many of the old sanctions, oftentimes precisely those against which the Roamers had initially protested, began to elbow their way in alongside of the traditions of the youth movement as such.

The consequence was that youth tutelage and political auxiliaries experienced upswings in membership, for now that the social instruments of the old youth movement had become so well standardized that they could be taken over by almost anybody, youngsters who were actually being manipulated by priests, pastors, or party hacks began to think that they were after all very much like the original Roamers, and glibly spoke of themselves as belonging to the youth movement. So evident was this trend that in 1920 it was said that "the distinction between youth tutelage and youth movement is now almost meaningless." This utterance was perhaps a year or two in advance of the more easily discernible developments, but by 1923, when I had a chance to observe almost seventy of the more than four hundred clusters claiming to be parts of the youth movement, it had become well justified. A similar assertion substituting "political auxiliaries" for "youth tutelage" could also have been made; there was a Communist youth movement, and the younger National Socialists spoke of themselves as *jungbewegt* (*sic*).

Further, a number of the youth groups deriving from the Roamers began to be pervaded by a considerable degree of expedient rationality. In the face of competition from youth

[69] "Perversion" is here used in its general *sociological* sense—the functioning social structures are planfully altered in such ways that they no longer serve their primary purposes. Cf. Wiese-Becker, *op. cit.*, pp. 392-393. "Diversion" is probably a more suitable term.

welfare and political auxiliaries, membership in these "Youth for youth's sake" bodies failed to increase or actually declined, and in the struggle to maintain themselves they began to set up little bureaucracies of their own. These centralized and routinized office staffs usually drew personnel from among those who had begun to pass out of the movement because of age, and frequently these aging "youths" were of that personality type which several times previously we have called the "eternally adolescent." Unstable of purpose, diffusely emotional, dogmatically idealistic, intellectually fuzzy, and erotically fixated on leaders or followers, they found the gates of the adult world too high to scale or too forbidding to enter. Compelled to eke out a livelihood in one way or another—for even if the inflation of 1923 had not wiped out their middle-class parents, papa and mama sometimes tried to force their errant children to cease being "youthful" by withholding the monthly remittance—they came to form a sizable proportion of the officials upon whom the "spontaneous" youth movements eventually became largely dependent.

For a time, to be sure, things went well. New organizations with the prestige of old names behind them regained some of the ground lost to youth tutelage and political auxiliaries. Moreover, they were instrumental in getting favorable legislation passed, in setting up hostel chains, and in regulating and administering youth affairs in good bureaucratic fashion. But as might be expected, the needs of the central organization soon came to seem more important than the preservation of traditional forms, even though those forms had come to incorporate some prescribed charismatic features. *Ergo*, measures were often adopted that ran directly counter to the best interests of "Youth for youth's sake"; "Youth for the officials' sake" became the unadmitted maxim.

And the Hitler Youth? Youth nationalism had of course existed long before Hitler. Some of the traditional nonrationality evident in the very earliest phases of Karl Fischer's following, for example, had nationalistic streaks, and in the terrible Battle of Langemarck thousands of volunteers who had consecrated themselves to the youth movement of Hohe Meissner marched singing into a hail of lead from which few returned alive. Taking it for all in all, however, the older youth movement was never chauvinistic, and many of the manifestations were primarily those of devotion to native countryside and folk life.

Only after World War I did nationalism of pathological intensity sweep through parts of the youth movement, and these parts made up only *a small minority* of the whole until 1930 and even beyond. Nevertheless, this minority was aggressive and ably led, and it profited immensely by the uncertainties, expediencies, and empty traditions of the heirs of the Roamers and the outmoded or conflicting sanctions of their youth-tutelage and political-auxiliary imitators.

Added to this was the fact that the very efficiency with which the "Youth for the officials' sake" organizations secured government support for hostel chains (to take one striking instance) helped the Hitler Youth and other right-wing radicals greatly. They hated the Weimar Republic, but they made use of the hostels which the Republic did so much to extend, administer, and finance. Hostels were ideal centers from which systematic propaganda could be conducted among those members of the older movements who were becoming increasingly dissatisfied with the standardization that had been introduced.

Even for the Hitler Youth, however, the hostels did not serve as centers of spontaneity. These were to be found outside in street-corner fighting, Nazi demonstrations, Jew-baiting, and the like. For those who craved affective outbursts under charismatic leadership that had not become routinized, Hitler Youth members were regarded with envious eyes, albeit with concomitant misgiving and distrust.

In still another respect standardization profited the Hitler Youth; this lay in the fact that many forceful and thoughtful youngsters, who might well have become Roamers of the original vintage had they been born in the eighties, remained aloof from movements that had begun to show signs of sedate middle age. If they did find their way into them, they soon quietly withdrew, forming little clusters of their own which they often did not trouble to name. Consequently, these new and spontaneous youth groups did not appear in the official handbooks and directories—one of which, incidentally, had swollen to nearly five hundred pages by 1931.

Can it therefore be said that a growing proportion of German young people were experiencing, by 1927 or 1928 at the very latest, an increasingly sharp contrast between "Youth for youth's sake" patterns of social action and "Youth for the sake of almost anything else but youth" coagulations that were steadily stiffening or even rigidly crystallizing? If so, does this not permit a revival of the hypothesis from which the constructs interpreting the old youth movement took their point of departure? Assuming such permissibility, our next task is the application of this hypothesis to this new instance. Moreover, even though "if and when" requirements cannot be entirely fulfilled *or the precise ways in which constructs have been modified adequately stated here,* let us also extend our typology a little further.

German youth movements of all varieties marked time throughout the late twenties and early thirties, with the exception of the Hitler Youth and a few of their left-wing competitors. The early days of the Roamers and the youth of Hohe Meissner had by this time receded into a glorious haze of romantic tradition, but in spite of the fact that there were still many followers longing for an opportunity to chant, "Leader, we follow thee and shout 'Yea!'" no charismatic leaders of the stature of Karl Fischer were on the scene. And yet, was there not an altogether extraordinary man named Adolf Hitler whose followers, for all their brutality, vulgarity, and ignorance, were challenging an "effete" social order?

Questions like this ran through the minds of many young Germans, and although *by far the greater number* were unable to overcome the revulsion which actual contact with the Hitler Youth produced, they were nevertheless rendered hesitant, or even became disquieted and fascinated. The leadership principle! Was this anything more than the homage which genuine

charisma should receive?   Doubt, confusion, passive waiting for
ever newer, more startling manifestations of "the wave of the
future."

Then at last the seizure of power, the liquidation of all
youth movement officialdom other than that to which the
Führer's grace was imparted, hither-and-yon drifting of youngsters deprived of or forsaken by their erstwhile leaders, chances
for violence, spontaneity, and erotically tinged devotion within
a gigantic folk-community undergoing a revival experience—
need much more be added?   Reluctant and recalcitrant adherents of the pre-Hitler movements undoubtedly remained, and
their number should not be minimized; nevertheless, by the
time membership in the Hitler Youth and the League of German Girls had become compulsory for all young Germans
between the ages of ten and eighteen—which is to say, by
1938—the Pied Piper of Berchtesgaden was leading in his
train millions of youngsters who followed him gladly.

1944

The same motivational model?   Not quite, granted, but
strikingly similar.   To be sure, traditional and affective nonrationalities are now buttressed by sanctioned rationality deriving from a holy man and his book, but would anyone claim
that Adolf Hitler and *Mein Kampf* are in any sense intelligible
to those who lack the nonrational faith that moves mountains
and confounds the wise?   The answer to *this* question is not in
doubt.

Moreover, it seems incontestable that social objects, social
responses, and reflected selves are just as thoroughly interfused
among Hitler Youth as they ever were among the Roamers,
that social methods are still without sharp outline, and that
social instruments, from the stag-handled dirk inscribed "Blood
and Honor" to the Castles of the Order, provide the leverage
with which the very foundations of pre-Hitler Germany are
being pried apart.

Climax: Once more a sacred society emerges, incorporating

to the entranced eyes of its votaries all that is good in the German past, and all that is charged with the glorious promise of a world-community acknowledging with grateful tears the benevolent but firm decrees of a German future. There is the value-system; " 'tis strange, 'tis passing strange, 'tis wonderful."

Anticlimax: The charisma of the *Führer* has been delegated to other, "lesser" men; the fighting sect of 1933 has become, to continue the religious analogy, the great state church of 1944; in this very year a generation reaches adulthood which has known only the Hitler Youth and *its* increasing routinization; the intuitive rightness of the leader's decisions has been tried and found wanting; death and capture are thinning the ranks of those who remember the ecstasies of the seizure of power; "the twilight of the gods" draws nigh.

Clearly, the prophetic mood is hard to down. The sin of presumption beckons enticingly. No more, then, lest we cease to sin constructively; "if and when" must end the matter. In the scientific role, prophecy has no place; prediction alone must be our guide.[70]

[70] Since the completion of this essay in June, 1944, my book, *German Youth: Bond or Free*, has appeared. In all essentials it was ready in August, 1944, but did not come off the press in England until October, 1946, and in the United States until March, 1947. It has many features not incorporated in this preliminary "methodological note," but the basic method is entirely the same.

Much has changed in German youth matters since the dates mentioned, but I see no reason now fundamentally to alter anything in this essay written in 1944. Others may differ, but only similar studies will give a final check. The German adaptation, for which I wrote two new concluding chapters, brings the analysis as far as June, 1948, but changes nothing prior to 1944. In other words, my own postwar investigations did not lead to any modifications. A restudy by someone else is needed.

CHAPTER V

SACRED AND SECULAR SOCIETIES

RETROSPECT AND PROSPECT

> . . . the major contributions of . . . Sumner—the relativity of cul-
> ture and the still incompletely appreciated fact of its affective basis
> and its permeation with sanction and moral values.—MURDOCK

IF WE LACK theoretical tools, we cannot do much more than pile up masses of material that we are unable to put to any effective scientific use. Granting this, it is nevertheless true that the tools we now possess are in a sadly jumbled state; when we reach hastily for this or that item in the kit, we run some risk of cutting our fingers. Why not stop for a few minutes and do a little sorting?

Of all the tools we possess, among the most useful are the twofold classifications of societies, but they are also the most easily damaged and the most dangerous if carelessly or unskilfully handled. Let us try, then, to arrange them in some kind of order, paying incidental attention, in our charts, to a few threefold ones as well. In undertaking this task, let us also remember that there is a vast literature about these tools, and that much of what might be said in the text of a chapter like this can well be stowed in footnotes, not only for the sake of brevity, but also for the sake of uncluttered arrangement. If this seems to result in dogmatic, pedantic, excessively schematic, or unduly didactic treatment, let us console ourselves with the thought that the possible gain in clarity is worth the risk.

I. TERMS DEFINED

The writer has long worked with the sacred-secular dichotomy,[1] as all the essays in this volume will testify, and natu-

[1] First in term papers for Robert E. Park at the University of Chicago, 1927-28, and then in a dissertation, "Ionia and Athens: Studies in Secularization," written during 1929 and early 1930. This dissertation has remained unpublished, but essential methodological sections were used in the writer's augmented adaptation, *Systematic Sociology on the Basis of the* Beziehungslehre

rally is more familiar with its denotations and connotations than with those of similar paired terms.   In this penultimate chapter, therefore, it is perhaps permissible to deal with the sacred-secular in some detail and while so doing, to point out its likenesses with and differences from other current classifications.

Before saying what sacred and secular societies are, it may be wise to say, once again and quite flatly, what they are not. Sacred and secular are not synonymous with holy and profane,[2]

---

and Gebildelehre *of Leopold von Wiese* (New York: John Wiley and Sons, 1932, unaltered reprint with new preface, Norman Paul Press: Gary, Ind., 1950), pp. 222-227, 319-344, *et passim* (hereinafter cited as Wiese-Becker).   Other sections appear in the articles, "Forms of Population Movement: Prolegomena to a Study of Mental Mobility," *Social Forces*, IX (Dec., 1930, March, 1931), 147-160, 351-361; "Processes of Secularisation," *Sociological Review* (British), XXIV (April, July, Oct., 1932), 138-154, 266-286; "Vicinal Isolation and Mental Immobility," *Social Forces*, XI (March, 1933), 326-334; and in several other articles.   Further use was later made of the sacred-secular dichotomy, this time as the organizing principle of the writer's two-volume collaborative treatise (with H. E. Barnes and others), *Social Thought from Lore to Science* (Boston: D. C. Heath & Co., 1938); hereinafter cited as *STLS*; see index for numerous references.   Since then there have been many other uses of the dichotomy, the most recent being the writer's introductory chapter, "Interpreting Family Life in Context," in Becker and Hill, *Family, Marriage, and Parenthood* (Boston: D. C. Heath & Co., 1948), pp. 1-49, esp. pp. 19-40, offered in unabridged and revised form as chap. i of the present volume.

[2] This is one of the most frequent errors, and is chiefly the result of failure to consult original sources or lack of attention to finer shades of meaning in ordinary English.

Let us take up first the failure to consult original sources.   As one of the latest examples, consider A. B. Hollingshead's reference, "Community Research: Development and Present Condition," *American Sociological Review*, XIII (April, 1948), 144, to "Durkheim's sacred and secular."   Durkheim used *sacré* and *profane* in his *Les Formes élémentaires de la vie religieuse* and elsewhere. Swain, the translator, used "sacred-profane," which is loose English, but at least he did *not* use "sacred-secular."

Concerning the lack of attention to ordinary English usage, we may begin with the old standby, *Webster's*; "Sacred, not holy, is opposed to secular" (*New International Dictionary*, 2nd ed., Springfield, Mass.: G. & C. Merriam, 1943).

This does not carry us quite far enough.   Consulting another Webster source, we find this: "In more general use, *sacred* applies chiefly to that which one treasures as a thing apart, not to be violated or contaminated by being put to vulgar or low uses or associated with vulgar or low ends" (*Webster's Dictionary of Synonyms*, 1st ed., Springfield, Mass.: G. & C. Merriam, 1942, p. 145).

In other words, "sacred" covers *more* than "spiritual," "religious," "holy," "hallowed," "blessed," "sacrosanct," and like terms.   His father's old armchair may be sacred, in the general sense, to a belligerent atheist.   But let us explore further, this time in a widely recognized "non-Webster": "Holy is a stronger and more absolute term than any other of similar meaning.   That which is *holy* is of a divine nature, or has its sanctity directly from God or as connected with him; that which is *sacred*, while *sometimes* [italics ours] accepted as entitled to

folk and urban, rural and urban, nonliterate and literate, primitive and modern, folk and state, communal and associational, primary group and secondary group, etc., etc. In the course of exposition some justification of this negative statement will be offered in the text and charts; when this cannot readily be done, resort will be had to footnotes.

Now for a series of preparatory definitions and accessory statements of general sociological character:

A human society is a larger structure or network of sociation within which other groupings as smaller networks, also designable as societies, can often be discerned as functional parts.[3]

Sociation is that set of social processes involving association and/or dissociation with others *as others* in and through role-taking involving the use of significant symbols.[4] Hence sociation refers to specifically human[5] interaction, i.e., to social action.

---

religious veneration, may derive its sanction from man; hence we speak of the *Holy* Bible, and of one's *sacred* duty to his country" (*The New Century Dictionary*, section on Synonyms, Antonyms, and Discriminations, New York: D. Appleton-Century Co., 1940, p. 2319).

The upshot of these and many other considerations is essentially this: "sacred-profane," although not strictly incorrect, is loose usage in view of the fact that "profane" is a more absolute term than "sacred," and hence should be used as the antonym of "holy." "Sacred," a more inclusive and less absolute term, should be used as the antithesis of the similarly general term "secular."

In view of the fact that Durkheim was writing about the elementary forms of the *religious* life, the translator should have used "holy-profane," not "sacred-profane," and certainly not "sacred-secular." (Incidentally, it may be noted that in French *sacré* must perform many tasks, for the French language lacks the wide range of terms here available in English. "Secular," on the other hand, divides into *séculaire* and *séculier*, with *laïque* thrown in for good measure. See nn. 47 and 48.)

The whole matter of appropriate terminology for the designation of various aspects of value-systems is worthy of an entire chapter, not a mere footnote. See, however, the similar lengthy footnote, chap. i, n. 48.

[3] "Structure" and "function" are of course not absolute terms. What for one analytic purpose is "structure" is "function" for another purpose. On this point see Wiese-Becker, *op. cit.*, pp. 6-7, 53-55, esp. n. 7 (sections by Becker—see preface); *ibid.*, "Action Patterns in Their Functional Aspects," pp. 111-115; *ibid.*, pp. 119, 352, 415, 418, *et passim*.

The same is true of "part-whole." See *ibid.*, pp. 78-93.

[4] For this point, see chap. i of the present volume, pp. 11-17. G. H. Mead, Cassirer, Langer, and related theorists are here taken as fundamental.

[5] Hereafter the adjective "human" will be dropped, but may be taken for granted at every appropriate point.

Sociation involves orientation toward others as others, but this orientation may be fluctuating, discontinuous, or erratic.[6] Consequently societies, as networks of sociation, are not always well-organized societies; they may be marked by extreme disorganization. Differently stated: a society composes and is composed of persons in interaction, but not necessarily in *ordered* interaction. One society may be responsible for and sustain a social order, and another a social *dis*order. A social order or disorder is an aspect of a culture.

A culture is the relatively constant nonmaterial *content* transmitted in a society by means of processes of sociation. Material artifacts and the like represent only some of the necessary accompaniments of a culture. One of the best definitions, for our purpose here, has been given by a historian, J. L. Myres, in his *Political Ideas of the Greeks* (New York: Abingdon, 1927): "... 'culture' is not a state or condition only, but a process; as in *agriculture* or *horticulture* we mean not the condition of the land but the whole round of the farmer's year, and all that he does in it; 'culture,' then, is what remains of men's past, working on their present, to shape their future" (p. 16).

In the above senses, neither society nor culture has priority in time; they emerge concomitantly. The same is true of personality and culture and of personality and society.[7] Personality is from one perspective the interlinking of needs and values.

[6] This reference to the possibility of lack of sustained orientation is not in literal contradiction to the definition of social action given by Max Weber, *Wirtschaft und Gesellschaft* (1st ed.; Tübingen: J. C. B. Mohr [Paul Siebeck], 1922), p. 1; translation on pp. 56-57 of Wiese-Becker, *op. cit.* Nevertheless, Weber's treatment of *Ablauf* (literally, "run-off") or "course," in the phrase *daran in seinem Ablauf orientiert ist*—"is oriented thereto during its course"— takes little account of discontinuities in the "run-off," and hence he pays scant heed to social *dis*order.

In this regard Znaniecki's treatment of social organization and disorganization is definitely superior. Its superiority is evident in *The Polish Peasant in Europe and America* (1918—theoretically based chiefly on Znaniecki rather than Thomas), *The Laws of Social Psychology* (1925), and especially in *Social Actions* (1936).

[7] For any given personality, society and culture in the general sense are of course prior in time. With regard, however, to the special version of that society and culture developed in any given personality (and *every* personality has its special version), society, culture, and personality are concomitant emergents.

There are no human needs without values; there are no human values without needs. Needs and values are reciprocally defined in and through sociation.[8]

Needs and values constitute and are constituted by culture. It need not be assumed, however, that because sociation is responsible for cultural transmission, there is nothing in culture which is not determined by sociation.[9] This assumption would amount to complete sociological determinism of cultural *content*, and this in turn to a sociological variety of solipsism.[10] Needs and values are reciprocally defined, true enough, but the human being is not a disembodied spirit, and many although not all values are selected aspects of objects existing independently of any observer.[11]

Given these necessarily brief remarks, almost aphoristic in form, it is now possible to define our sacred and secular societies.

A sacred society is one that elicits from or imparts to its members, by means of sociation, unwillingness and/or inability to respond to the culturally new *as the new is defined by those members in terms of the society's existing culture.* Otherwise put, a network of sociation that develops, among the personalities weaving and woven by it, a high degree of resistance to change, particularly in their social order, is a sacred society.

A secular society is one that elicits from or imparts to its

[8] See chap. i of the present volume, pp. 14-21.

[9] To make this assumption would be to beg the whole question of sociology of knowledge, sociology of religion, sociology of art, sociology of music, and so on. There *may* be nothing in culture which is not determined by sociation, but that would have to be demonstrated, not merely assumed. See H. O. Dahlke, "Sociology of Knowledge," in Barnes, Becker, and Becker, *op. cit.*, pp. 64-68.

From another standpoint, the assumption has been challenged by George Em. Marica, *Émile Durkheim: Soziologie und Soziologismus* (Jena: Fischer, 1932), esp. pp. 151-163.

[10] As is pointed out in chap. i of the present volume, pp. 19-21, G. H. Mead avoids this by adding to the "me" his well-known "I." Even though it may be granted that "I" is a residual category, including everything from biological deviation to individual variation in life-history pattern, it serves a very useful purpose. What is now needed is refinement of Mead's analysis and empirical research oriented toward its proof or disproof.

[11] This bald statement, badly needing expansion, must nevertheless be inserted here in order to avoid any implication of solipsism, group and/or personal, idealistic, or otherwise. See also chap. vi of the present volume, pp. 282-283.

members, by means of sociation, willingness and ability to respond to the culturally new as the new is defined by those members in terms of the society's existing culture. Stated in another way, a network of sociation that develops, among the personalities weaving and woven by it, a high degree of readiness and capacity to change, particularly in their social order, is a secular society.[12]

II. COMPARISON WITH OTHER CLASSIFICATIONS

Formulated differently: a society that incorporates and sustains an impermeable value-system is sacred; one that embodies a permeable value-system is secular.

The impermeability of a value-system depends on the absence of effective intersocietal communication;[13] the permeability of a value-system depends on its presence. That is to say, isolation marks the sacred, accessibility the secular.

Isolation and accessibility may each be conveniently divided into three varieties: vicinal, social, and mental.[14]

Vicinal isolation and accessibility respectively denote the absence and presence of communication, at the level of sheer physical opportunity for culture contact, with persons from other societies. They cannot come into contact, or they can. The social variety denotes the absence or presence of effective communication, at the level of social relations, with members of other societies when they can be physically present. They do not transcend mere commensalism or symbiosis, or they do. The mental variety denotes the absence or presence of effective communication, at the level of a "common universe of discourse," with representatives of other value-systems who are "physically and socially present."

With this as background, it is now possible to say something about subtypes of sacred and secular societies, beginning with the folk-sacred, the prescribed-sacred, the principled-

[12] More extended but in some ways less precise definitions are to be found in chap. i of the present volume, pp. 42-44, 66-68.

[13] Wiese-Becker, *op. cit.*, p. 344.

[14] Cf. the writer's chapter, "Social Thought of Preliterate Peoples," in Barnes and Becker, *STLS*, pp. 3-42. This passage is part (pp. 4-10) of the unpublished 1930 dissertation mentioned in n. 1.

secular, and the normless-secular,[15] in relation to isolation and accessibility. Quoting from one of the most recent of the writer's statements, but interlarding comment and qualification for the purposes of the present chapter:

Folk

The best [but not the only] examples of . . . [folk-sacred] societies are to be found in the old-fashioned, backward, or even primitive parts of the world. . . . Folk societies are ordinarily isolated.

To be sure, the isolation is not merely a question of the land under the feet of the folk in question . . . as the inhabitants of Iceland discovered not so long ago, an island once remote in the merely geographic sense may suddenly become a bustling crossroads when man's ways of traveling change . . . the isolation of a folk society . . . is [in part often constituted by] the lack of relations with neighbors, a point aptly made by Semple when, taking her clue from the French *vicinage*, meaning neighborhood, she spoke of *vicinal* isolation.

Over and above this sheer absence of effective contacts with peoples representing contrasting or even distinctly differing ways of life, folk societies are likely to be *socially* isolated. When a straying neighbor "gets outside his own bailiwick," he sometimes finds that barriers to social intercourse may be higher than mountains and deeper than seas even though folk meets folk face to face. . . .

To vicinal and social isolation must be added a third kind; namely, *mental*. The members of different folk societies think and feel differently. The patterns of logic are not entirely arbitrary and neither are man's emotions, but the combinations of mental processes functionally effective in the conduct of one folk may contrast so radically with those of another that the unschooled observer may wonder which if either of the two is "really human."[16]

Prescribed

The clearest examples of . . . [prescribed-sacred societies] are to be found where . . . a definite body of dogma calls forth, sets up, or maintains a totalitarian kind of social structure. The Geneva theocracy

[15] The terms "principled-secular" and "normless-secular" here appear for the first time. The writer's earlier designation was "stable secular" and "unstable secular," in Becker and Hill, *op. cit.*, pp. 33-40, here offered in unabridged form as chap. i. See pp. 68-76.

It may be noted that "normlessness" is here used instead of *anomie* or "anomy," and "normless" instead of *anomique* or "anomic." Whenever familiar English forms can be used without liability, they seem preferable (see nn. 47 and 48).

[16] Becker and Hill, *op. cit.*, pp. 21-22; present volume, pp. 146-147.

of Calvin, the Jesuit state of Paraguay, and, by intention at least, Fascist Italy, Nazi Germany, and Soviet Russia are among the most prominent of many instances. . . .

. . . the notion of geographic isolation fails utterly when confronted by the great sacred units operating under prescription in the modern world.

Vicinal isolation, however, may prove quite relevant, for restrictions on travel readily bring about situations in which near neighbors are separated as effectively as though impassable oceans lay between them.

Social isolation likewise plays its part in generating prescribed mentality. . . . [An American in Paris, with his distinguishably different gestures, walk, and costume, may find that he is socially accepted only in "Harry's Bar" or some other place catering exclusively to American trade. French society is not totalitarian, but it is strongly nationalistic and ethos-centric. The middle-class Frenchman, in particular, lives behind a Chinese wall of prescriptions which the American rarely penetrates. As a wit has put it, "A Frenchman may introduce you to his mistress after a two-weeks' acquaintance, and to his wife after six months. You have arrived, socially, when after three years you meet his grandmother."]

Part and parcel of social isolation, in most instances, is mental isolation, and in this regard prescribed society differs not a whit from folk society. Nazi totalitarianism in its heyday promulgated the slogan, "We think with our blood," with such telling effect that the logical patterns evident among large sections of the German population—and not the most fanatical alone—made it very difficult for the outsider to establish any mutually intelligible universe of discourse. . . .[17]

Principled

[In a principled-secular society, which may have the bicycle-like stability of moving equilibrium, the] . . . misoneism, neophobia, or dislike of the new, which is characteristic of extremely sacred societies, may not be strongly in evidence; but the philoneism, neophilia, or liking for the new, which runs rampant in . . . [normless-secular societies is held in check].

The source of the check is always some . . . principle.[18] [This principle may have derived from folk or prescribed value-systems, but it is subjected to requirements of adaptability, utility in new situations, amenability to "reasonable" deduction, and so on.

The vicinal and social accessibility of a principled society may be

[17] Present volume, pp. 57-59.
[18] *Ibid.*, p. 74.

quite high, but as long as the governing principle remains in force, mental accessibility will not be complete. Certain alternatives remain fundamentally out of consideration. Traitorous conduct with regard to the State, for example, is barred by the principle of political loyalty.] *Normless*

[Excellent instances of both principled and normless societies, but particularly the normless,] . . . are to be found in centers of culture contact. These are very often sections of great cities standing at the crossroads of commerce and communication. This is of course the reason why Redfield uses "urban" as the antithesis of "folk." It must be noted, however, that certain varieties of the city show no high incidence of secularization. What of folk-prescribed cities such as Lhasa, Benares, and Mecca, or prescribed cities such as Fascist Rome, Communist Moscow, and Nazi . . . [Nürnberg]? Redfield obviously means only one type of city; namely, the highly secularized variety. This being the case, why not say secular instead of urban? Further, it is not mere pedantry to point out that rural is the correct antitheses of urban, and that some rural societies, past and present, show a low incidence of sacredness. [Where the analysis of value-systems in relation to societies is concerned, folk-urban and rural-urban are involved in manifold contradictions, and must be rejected as *major* classifications. They can, however, be used in some subtyping. For general purposes,] sacred-secular is a less ambiguous dichotomy. . . .

Clearly . . . the neighbors round about any given people undergoing secularization must be so situated and disposed that vicinal accessibility prevails. This is tantamount to saying that highly secularized centers [tending toward normlessness] are almost necessarily cosmopolitan; all sorts and descriptions of people come together and succeed in communicating after a fashion. . . .

Moreover, . . . [the devices of communication, even at this level, help] to generate social accessibility, which is another trait of a markedly secular society. Where it prevails in full measure, there are no rigid social barriers cutting off one segment of the society from another.

The upshot is that vicinal and social accessibility come to be linked with mental. Any secular society [tending toward normlessness] is necessarily "open-minded" [in extreme degree]. The open-mindedness may consist not only in easy-going disregard of matters once held sacred [or in "principle"], but also in their ostentatious flouting. "Anything for a thrill" . . . is often the outspokenly admitted maxim. Figuratively put, the walls of mental isolation have completely crumbled.[19]

[19] *Ibid.*, pp. 68-69 (including n. 99). It may be noted that Marshall B.

Secular societies . . . [of both principled and normless types,] now everywhere in evidence, were quite rare in the remoter historical record, and nonexistent, it may well be assumed, among man's earlier clusters of sociation. It is for this reason, and this alone, that secular here follows sacred, for as the discussion of prescribed societies may have shown, there is ample evidence that societies once strongly secular may be poured back into sacred molds. Recall the references to Nazi Germany; many others will readily come to mind.[20] [Consequently, sacred-secular must not be equated with primitive-civilized, preliterate-literate, ancient-modern, folk-State,[21] and other irreversible dichotomies. There are also other reasons why they should not be equated; some of these will later appear implicitly in our subtype illustrations.]

Clinard, following Redfield and Wirth, uses "urbanization" as a *very* general term. Cf. his "The Process of Urbanization and Criminal Behavior: A Study of Culture Conflict," *American Journal of Sociology*, XLVIII (Sept., 1942), 202-213, esp. 203 n. 3. "Since the term 'urbanization' as used here is not limited to cities, it is occasionally possible that a group of socially disorganized nomadic or frontier people, not living in cities, may exhibit a high degree of development of the characteristic features of urbanism. When incorporated into the relatively 'permanent' life of a city, it is possible for them to become less urbanized in the sense used here, and incidence of crimes against property to decline."

"Urban" then means "disorganized." The writer feels that this usage is loose, for reasons noted in the text above, and many more. If nonurban peoples conduct themselves in "urbanized"—i.e., disorganized—ways, is this the result of influence from an urban center? Or what? If not all urbanites are disorganized, to what is their state of organization due? What does *urbis* mean, if not city?

In short, "urbanization" can be made to serve as a general term only by fiat. It is at too low a level of abstraction. This is strikingly shown in the forthcoming book by Oscar Lewis, title not yet fixed, involving a restudy of Tepotztlan, the village where Redfield first used the folk-urban dichotomy.

[20] *Ibid.*, p. 70.

[21] These dichotomies may of course be useful for other purposes. This is particularly true of the Odum folk-State pair. It is oversimple, but it does not involve its users in the grave difficulties of the folk-urban (see text and n. 20 above). It fails to take account, however, of the fact that State structure and mentality can disintegrate to the point of normlessness, and it does not differentiate between the prescribed-sacred and the principled-secular aspects that the State society may manifest in varying degrees at various times. Moreover, there is not enough stress on reversibility; historically, we know that State societies have shifted over into folk societies of one kind or another. An example is provided by the folk societies of post-Roman times in many parts of Europe; they had once had much more State structure about them, but the collapse of the administrative system of the Roman Empire brought about a reversal. For a good presentation of the case for the folk-State classification, see Alvin Boskoff, "Structure, Function, and Folk Society," *American Sociological Review*, XIV (Dec., 1949), 749-758.

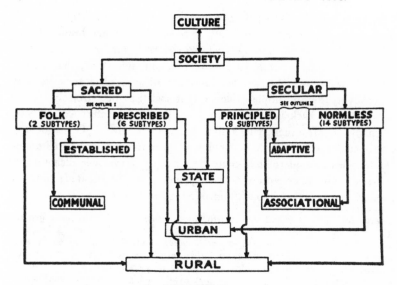

CHART I
RELATIONS OF SOME CURRENT TWOFOLD CLASSIFICATIONS

At this point the reader will find that Charts 1, 2, and 3 provide a useful conspectus.[22]

[22] The various twofold and threefold classifications appearing in Charts 1, 2, and 3 by no means exhaust the list, but the more important, in the writer's estimation, have been set down. The theorists with whom these classifications are most frequently identified are:

CHART 1

    Established—adaptive, Elton Mayo
    Folk—State, Howard W. Odum
    Folk—urban, Robert Redfield
    Rural—urban, nobody in particular, but widely used
    Communal—associational, Ferdinand Tönnies
        (this is only one of the many possible translations of *Gemeinschaft—Gesellschaft*; the writer personally prefers fellowship—affiliation).

CHART 2 (p. 259)

    Custom-imitating—mode-imitating, Gabriel Tarde
    Primitive—civilized, nobody in particular, but once widely used
    "Steady state"—"unsteady state," Gregory Bateson
    Equilibrium—disequilibrium, many, but especially Carleton Coon and Eliot Chapple
    Static—dynamic, nobody in particular, but frequently used by many English writers
    Non- or preliterate—literate, many, but especially Ellsworth Faris
    "Culture"—"civilization," R. M. MacIver and many German writers

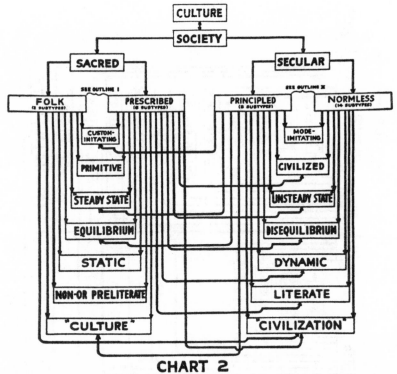

CHART 2
RELATIONS OF SOME MORE TWOFOLD CLASSIFICATIONS
(SIZE AND POSITION DO NOT INDICATE ANY ESTIMATE OF RELATIVE IMPORTANCE)

III. A LOGICAL FORMULA FOR TYPOLOGY

Sacred and secular societies, obviously enough, are constructed types.[23] Since we all use types in sociological inquiry anyway, they ought to be *explicitly* constructed if we are to achieve logical control over them.[24] If we are thus explicit, we

---

[23] Cf. "Typology, Constructive," in H. P. Fairchild, ed., *Dictionary of Sociology* (New York: Philosophical Library, p. 194). There is of course a large literature on "ideal" types, but most of it is irrelevant or inaccurate with reference to the present problem. There has been too much translation and textual exegesis, and not enough work on substantive theory and fresh empirical analysis. For a few of the reasons why the writer, after much earlier use of the term "ideal" type, now prefers "constructed" type, see pp. 107-108 and 160-218, present volume. See also the penetrating article by J. C. McKinney, "The Role of Constructive Typology in Scientific Sociological Analysis," *Social Forces*, XXVIII (March, 1950), 235-240.

[24] See present volume, pp. 160-205.

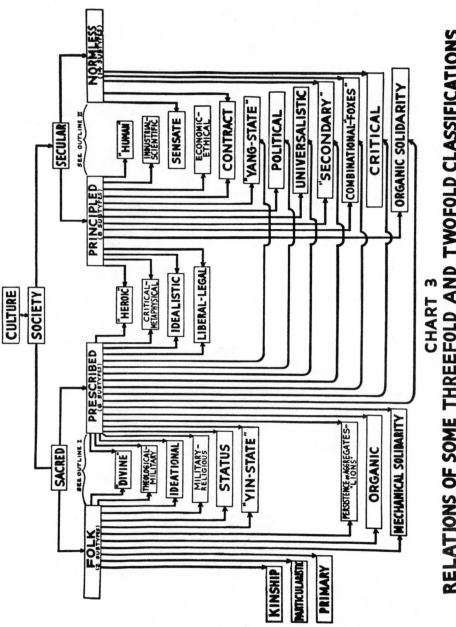

CHART 3

RELATIONS OF SOME THREEFOLD AND TWOFOLD CLASSIFICATIONS

(SIZE AND POSITION DO NOT INDICATE ANY ESTIMATE OF RELATIVE IMPORTANCE)

can better take heed of their presuppositions and note their roles in inquiry.

Of the many possible roles of constructed types, it seems best to give attention here only to their use as analytic tools in a rigidly limited special sense. *For other purposes* a different treatment would be possible, but present concern is exclusively with what may be termed the "negative utility"[25] of an array of sacred and secular subtypes. These types are distilled from empirical data, and are "objectively probable"[26] in the sense that reference to these data enables the distiller to say, "You see, it *could* happen." At the same time, such a type is logically

[25] *Ibid.*, pp. 119-120, 142, and 163, esp. the latter.

[26] "Objective probability" must be distinguished from "objective possibility." The latter can mean mere *logical* possibility; Vaihinger's fictions (*The Philosophy of "As If"*) are logically possible, but many of them have little or no empirical probability; i.e., they can never be even remotely approximated in real life.

Some of Max Weber's less guarded methodological statements sound much like Vaihinger's; his "objectively possible" occasionally sounds like the "purely fictional." His actual practice belies the inferences that can be drawn from his methodological statements; no one has ever taken more pains to insure the "objective probability" of his types as they are actually used. Nevertheless, Weber leaves the methodological door slightly ajar, and by stressing "objective probability" the present writer wishes to close it against the "pure fiction."

The accentuation or stressing of salient features of the constructed type, and its "closure," is fictional only in the sense of empirically "limited fiction." Examination of the empirical evidence must always enable the reseacher to say, "The probability that this type will ever be matched in reality is *very* slight, but the probability is not *inherently nil*."

As the writer has stated elsewhere, ". . . the working fictions of which we make use are not 'just any' fictions" (p. 126, present volume).

CHART 3 (p. 260)

"Divine—Heroic—Human," Giambattista Vico

Theological—metaphysical—scientific, Auguste Comte

Ideational—idealistic—sensate, Pitirim Sorokin

Religious—liberal—economic, F. H. Giddings

Status—contract, Henry Sumner Maine

"Yin-state"—"Yang-state," A. J. Toynbee

Societies pervaded by residues of the persistence of aggregates—societies pervaded by residues of combination, Vilfredo Pareto

"Lions—foxes," Niccolo Machiavelli

Organic—critical, Henri de Saint-Simon

Mechanical solidarity—organic solidarity, Émile Durkheim

Kinship society—political society, Aristotle and many others, especially Paul Vinogradoff

Particularistic—universalistic, Talcott Parsons

Primary group—"secondary group" (latter by implication only), C. H. Cooley

For other classifications, see Barnes and Becker, *STLS*, Vols. I and II, *passim*.

consistent with itself and is used as a "standard" by means of which empirical instances can be compared.

The general logical pattern for the testing of hypotheses is: If P, then Q, and, If Q', then P'. It is in this schema that we here place the type construction: If P (the type), then Q (the objective probability). Note, now, that the type itself is not the hypothesis; the former constitutes the premise or antecedent, P, whereas the latter includes *both* P and the consequent, Q. In the very nature of type construction,[27] however, the consequent seldom if ever follows empirically, and the antecedent is then empirically "false." If Q', then P'. The fact that the type is constructed in such a way that, in spite of possessing some degree of "objective probability," it is logically consistent with itself renders inferences logically sound. In the *difference* between what is inferred and what demonstrably occurs the constructed type here discussed assumes its "negative utility" and hence, one of its important scientific significances.

Why? Because the "falseness" of Q is not an accidental "falseness," but a specific one resulting from a necessary and not a chance difference between the type and the empirical instance. As the writer has put it elsewhere: "The belief that the constructed type is rendered useless because exceptions to it can be found is naïve. Exceptions *must* be found. . . ."[28] And again: ". . . types . . . are never found on land or sea."[29] As a result of this necessary difference, the constructed type plays up causal factors crucial to sociological inquiry.

Anticipating for the sake of illustration: one of the subtypes later to be discussed is the indigenous devised variety of prescribed sacred society, presented in detail in the writer's book, *German Youth: Bond or Free.*[30] A devised sacred so-

---

[27] *Ibid.*, pp. 106-107. The more subtle aspects of symbolic logic are not relevant here; an oversimplified formulation has been used in order to focus attention on the empirical evidence. Those versed in the refinements of notation will recognize this because of the absence of "   ", etc.

[28] *Ibid.*, p. 120.

[29] Wiese-Becker, *op. cit.*, p. 22.

[30] Recently issued in a German edition, with two new concluding chapters, under the title (taken from an old *Landsknecht* song), *Vom Barette Schwankt die Feder* (Wiesbaden: Verlag der Greif, 1949). The American edition (New

ciety must utilize folk values that are not explicitly incon-
sistent with the prescriptions it enjoins. As the result of an
elaborate culture case study preliminary to the construction of
the type under consideration, it was found that many items of
Germanic folk culture provided the indispensable bases of the
Nazi devised society. But had these items fulfilled the implications arising from their characteristics and from their combination into the type, empirically the resulting pro-Germanic
movement would *not* have developed into the Nazi hatred of
things non-German. This empirical difference, with others, led
the writer to the conclusion that in this *particular* devised sacred
society the unique personality characteristics of the "leaders"
were causally related to the perversion of the folk-culture combination out of which, and on the basis of which, the Nazi
movement emerged. If P, then Q—*but* Q'; Nazi prescriptions replaced folk-Germanic sentiments. From this, the special role of the Nazis could be more adequately assessed.

Conceptually, this is the general schema for the application
of the "negatively useful" constructed type. It is readily seen
that the type of "negative utility"—indeed, the type of any
variety—does not simply "photograph" or "reflect" empirical
instances. Any type "accentuates" the "facts"—if not by deliberate exaggeration, at least by the omission of "irrelevant"
data, so that the "relevant" stand out in sharp relief. In the
present context this can be taken to mean that the constructed
type creates a closed system. *The closure is deliberate.* Although for some purposes every effort is made to find "tight-
fitting" empirical approximations, there is never the imputation
that the system is "really" closed. On comparison with *any*
given empirical instance, we find that it is *not* closed. Constructive typology enables us to discover the specific factors
responsible for the difference between Q and Q', and, incidentally, between P and P' if they are not specifically known.
(That a general difference between P and P' exists is of course
presupposed.)

York: Oxford Univ. Press, 1947) is now out of print, but the English edition
(London: Kegan Paul, 1946) has recently been made available in the United
States (Gary, Ind.: Norman Paul Press, 1950).

Summing up: Constructive typology makes *planned* use of the proviso "All other conditions being equal or irrelevant" for the purpose of determining the "inequality" or "relevance" of the "other conditions." Full account is taken of the fact that societies rarely if ever can be studied under manipulatively controlled, "laboratory" circumstances; the *logic* of experiment, coupled with wide-ranging observation of the available "deposits"[31] of empirical evidence as the best available counterpart of the *practice* of experiment, is the bedrock of constructive typology.

IV. VARIETIES OF SACRED SOCIETY

Let us now proceed to describe the subtypes of sacred society (see Outline I), beginning with the folk variety. This splits readily into two, indigenous and exogenous.

OUTLINE I—SUBTYPES OF SACRED SOCIETY
If P, then Q (no change)

Subtype	Isolation	Q' (some important factors)
Folk-sacred		
Indigenous	vicinal, social, mental; maintained	inadequate traditional transmission; charismatic innovation
Exogenous	social, mental, preserved	dual role of new values
Prescribed-sacred		
Indigenous		
Articulated	vicinal, social, mental; preserved	specialization; "accidental" contact
Devised	social, mental; created	divergence of values out of which new social order is to be constructed, novelty of subsequent events
Exogenous		
Enforced	social, mental; enforced	inadequate control of communication
Transplanted	social, mental; maintained	inadequate control of communication
Imposed	social, mental; imposed	linguistic difficulty; inadequate contact agent
Quasi-nativistic	mental; preserved	dependence on the immediate situation
		Frequent result of Q', exendomorphism transitionally marginal persistently marginal

[31] Present volume, pp. 102-105, 118-121, 145-146. Naturally, actual manipulative experimentation is to be welcomed whenever it can be practical within humane limits.

Membership in an indigenous folk-sacred society occurs by birth, real or simulated. That is to say, it occurs either through indigenous kinship, however reckoned, or by some kind of adoption involving the performance of "rebirth" ceremonies in which exogenous kinship is stripped off and indigenous kinship donned.

Since birth is the only means of entering a society of this kind, the patterns of sociation are all structured along kinship lines. Among other things, there is close dovetailing of new-member roles with the roles of the actually or sociatively elder members; the only valid sources of sociative proficiency are to be found in those who have already passed through the "ceremonies of transition" (*rites de passage*). With mental isolation thus complete, social isolation concomitantly appears; the rare outsider is necessarily a stranger in the sociative sense. Vicinal isolation in high degree is also simultaneously present; this may result from anything ranging from actual sparsity of population to topographical barriers insurmountable because of rudimentary modes of transportation.

Communication is functionally at the nonliterate level; if writing is used, it is not regarded as an impersonal instrument. In other words, the elders control communication; the impermeability of the value-system is thereby assured. Individuality exists, but not individualism; the values of the folk-sacred society are supreme. The social order is never fundamentally challenged.[32]

[32] There are many other features of such folk-sacred societies that could be listed, but space forbids. Always remembering that a highly specific Q (exact kind of changelessness) often makes necessary a highly specific P, it is nevertheless true that the inclusion of everything that is known to occur with high frequency in empirical sacred societies is usually unnecessary. There is no way of telling exactly how a type should be constructed until the particular hypothesis has been clearly formulated. The nature of Q determines what must be included in or can be omitted from P. Cf. the references cited in n. 23.

Indigenous folk-sacred societies have long been the object-matter of folk-lorists, ethnographers, ethnologists, and sociologists, to name no other specialists. Omitting a host of the references that could be mentioned, let us merely say that since Sumner's day most explicit attention has been given such societies by Howard Odum and his students at the University of North Carolina, and by Robert Redfield and those he has influenced at the University of Chicago. Redfield, for example, offers a course on folk societies in which he uses a bibliography of well over a hundred titles. (A brief bibliography is to be found in Becker and

In such a society there is no room for basic change; it is logically closed: i.e., If P, then Q (no change). But we are working with a constructed type of "negative utility" at this point; the empirical evidence makes it clear that the most isolated societies we can anywhere find are not absolutely changeless. In short, Q' has followed instead of Q, and we are forced to infer that instead of P we have P'. By hypothesizing no change, and being led empirically to negate that hypothesis, we put ourselves in a position to search systematically for the crucial elements that intrude on the logical closure. We look for the specific difference between P and P' because we get Q' instead of Q.

Hence we may discover that (1) a biological and/or life-history deviate becomes a charismatic leader disrupting the smooth transmission of sacred controls by the elders, or we may find that (2) minor variations of culturally immanent type accumulate to the point where they precipitate a major variation, or we may note that (3) structural recombinations known to be possible but not provided for in the construction of the type result in slow but far-reaching alteration, or we may be faced by (4) a configuration of events hitherto unique in our scientific experience and hence not made part of the type, etc., etc. (This is the reason for the right-hand column of Outline 1: Q': some important factors.) By enabling us precisely to designate the element or elements that negate the hypothesis, the constructed type, "never found on land or sea," has rendered useful scientific service.

Turning now to the exogenous folk-sacred society: the ethnographic and historical literature abounds with instances of societies that have "reactively reified" their old social order. This frequently occurs in "culture contact situations," and such societies are ordinarily called "nativistic."

These reactively sacred societies result from contact that for whatever reason is unavoidable, and from its ensuing secularization. The generation of the elders observes the destruc-

---

Hill, *op. cit.*, pp. 47-48; another under the present chapter number, v, at the end of this book.) The source of the present writer's interest was Robert E. Park, who was Redfield's source also.

tion of the old ways of doing things, the old values; sacred
sociative patterns are being picked apart thread by thread. In
the effort to prevent this, old techniques of control are used in
modified form—for example, the indigenous secularizers are
given the same blameworthy name as the "foreign" and hence
inferior society, or brusque threats are used against them in the
hope of restoring at least the social and mental isolation that
once existed. Cleavage occurs; those who adopt the ways of
the foreigner split off from the old order; they become out-
casts. In terms of our logical closure, however, those who
have thus departed from the old ways are not parts of what
has now become a nativistic value-system.

It follows, logically, that with the establishment of reacti-
vistic nativism the society is oriented entirely around the indigenous culture, now somewhat reified. But in actual fact Q
seldom follows. Instead, we get Q' in ways like this: in Yap
a *modus vivendi* has been established according to which the
"nativistic chief" puts the society through its sacred paces under
some circumstances, whereas under others the "secularized
chief" holds the reins, particularly when negotiations with for-
eigners are to be carried on.

Rigorous application of the hypothesis to this and other
cases therefore suggests that at least two leaks in the typical
impermeability of a nativistic value-system may exist in actual
fact: (1) the leaders of the nativistic society can never regain
control of communication after culture contact has been effectively established; and (2) the new elements play a double
role—in so far as they are accepted as capable of being "in-
digenized" they help to buttress the nativistic system much as
do the old sacred elements, but in so far as they are new, they
inevitably modify the value-system they buttress! By directing attention to the differences between P and Q on the one
hand and P' and Q' on the other, the constructed type of the
exogenous folk-sacred society has shown its usefulness.[33]

[33] Roy G. Francis, instructor of sociology at the University of Wisconsin, is
directly responsible for the stress of the present chapter on the "negative utility"
of the constructed type, although the writer pointed this out in less systematic
form as early as 1932 in his chapter, "Historical Sociology," in L. L. Bernard,

The foregoing presentations of folk-sacred subtypes have certainly been sketchy enough, but because of space limitations we must be even sketchier in dealing with most of the subtypes of prescribed-sacred society. We use the indigenous-exogenous split again, and then split further into two kinds of indigenous and four of exogenous.

The first variety of the indigenous prescribed society is what may be called articulated. Preservation of isolation is the goal, and all the media and techniques of communication are directed toward it. Those versed in the sacred ways of doing things are explicitly charged with their transmission, and deliberate indoctrination follows. This is done by means of prescription; that is, everything of key sociative significance is linked into a system, and every item in the system is specifically enjoined. It is not a case of secular deduction from a supreme principle, for this leaves room for novelty; rather, the crucial sacred values are linked together, the links are sacred, and from the resulting system a supreme sacred prescription is induced that is then deductively used to intensify the sacredness of the subordinate prescriptions which have produced it. A prescribed value-system is like a house built of stones, boards, shingles, panes of glass, and the like that have accumulated over a long period. They must not be in any way cut or trimmed to fit, and they must all be used somewhere in the structure. Given sufficient ingenuity, a surprising degree of system and even of symmetry may be the outcome, and yet inspection will reveal the antiquity and essentially inviolate character of each unit. Think of the *Summa Theologica* of Thomas Aquinas; he articulated a medieval value-system in two senses—by joining its parts into a whole and by giving whole and parts adequate symbolic expression.

This leads to the next point: the prescribed sacred society of articulated type does not engender an "old oaken bucket" mentality among its bearers; it is not a nostalgic reference to a past long dead. *The past lives in the present*; the conjoined

ed., *Fields and Methods of Sociology* (1st ed.; New York: Long and Smith, 1934), p. 30, appearing in revised and expanded form as chap. iii of the present volume. See esp. p. 163.

and systematized prescriptions lead to such complete acceptance of the intrinsic superiority of the old sacred sanctions that the new simply is not a part of the system as defined by the participants. "The Church is a thousand years the same"—and the Church is by no means the only example; changes are either rejected or are regarded as mere redirections of attention to what has "always" been there.

From the example given, it should be clear that prescription of articulated kind develops crescively and continuously. Having been articulated, moreover, and particularly when *written* in a form controlled by experts only, prescription is given a degree of permanence ordinarily not attainable in the primarily oral tradition of a folk society. "Thus saith the Lord" has the ring of power when few can be certain just what the Lord did say, and when those few can point to chapter, verse, *and* interpretative glosses and commentary in an ancient holy tongue.

Logically closing the system, we must expect absence of change because of monopoly in the transmission of values. Culture case study may show, however, that the articulation defines only a limited number of items in the society as sacred—such as the Covenant in historical Judaism. What is omitted from the prescription is regarded as changeable. Or, a prescription may not be adequately related to unconscious motivations of conduct, and hence there may be a wide gap between the prescription and "what people really do." There are many other possibilities of discrepancy, as everybody knows, but the empirical inconsistencies may lead to important scientific results such as, let us say, a re-evaluation of the functional conception of society,[34] and in any event to greater precision in the analysis of supposedly totalitarian structures. $P \rightarrow Q$? No, $Q' \therefore P'$.

[34] "Functional" is here used in the sense of Radcliffe-Brownian functionalism. We may discover

> That nature still defeats
> The frowsty science of the cloistered men,
> Their theory, their conceits.

> —V. SACKVILLE-WEST

Coming now to the devised subtype of indigenous prescribed-sacred society already mentioned (pp. 262-263), let us note that we need not assume that articulation of the sacred sanctions always occurs crescively. There may be a determined effort to counteract the disruptive effects of accessibility—disruption that has broken the continuity of folk or prescribed tradition—by devising prescriptions for renewed isolation, for controls that go with it, and for sacred patterns that were once yielded full allegiance. The devising of the new but would-be-old value-system may arise because of a "crisis situation" and the resulting "normative reaction to normlessness,"[35] or out of less extreme conditions, but in any case the need for reasserting control is felt to be urgent by a significant proportion of the society's members.

Charismatic leaders representing themselves not as innovators but restorers may emerge (Hitler's many-faceted appeal included the prospect of restoration). When available, there is systematic use of (1) communicative techniques such as mass-meetings, songs, slogans, books and pamphlets, and a press that indoctrinates rather than informs, and (2) "counter-communication" such as censorship, book-burning, and ostracism or worse for skeptics and opponents. "When available" is of course an important qualification, for devised sacred societies have been many and various, e.g., the Calvinist theocracy of Geneva, Franco Spain, Fascist Italy, Imperial Nippon, Nazi Germany, Athens under the Thirty, Moslem Jerusalem under the Caliph Omar—and how many more![36]

If the new but would-be-old value-system is to prevail, the full range of values to which members of the society are exposed must be rigidly controlled. In the attempt to secure the acceptance of the devised value-system, not only the content of the values but also their structural relations are prescribed. That is, *who* makes the orations, tells the exemplary tales, uses the radio, is as much prescribed, among other things, as *what* the oration, the tale, or the broadcast conveys. And, ordinarily, there must be wicked, heretical, or traitorous oppo-

[35] Present volume, pp. 76-78.
[36] *Ibid.*, pp. 57-66.

nents against whom summary action can be taken—those who are not and cannot be members of the devised society are likewise prescribed.

Further discussion of this subtype—of contemporary importance, certainly—would lead us too far afield. Referring again to the writer's *German Youth: Bond or Free*[37] as one example among many detailed studies, let us now give heed to another variety of prescribed society.

This, the enforced, is the first of the exogenous prescribed-sacred societies in our outline. Exogenous here means that the isolation of a sacred society results from forces that, wholly or in part, stem from "outside" the society itself. A classic example is the Jewish ghetto, although, as Wirth points out,[38] the isolation was at first partially self-imposed. Later it was enforced, and rigidly so. Even this enforced situation, however, *plus* the ethnic-religious endogamy of the Jewish society, did not result in uniform conduct. Sephardic Jews differ in many striking ways from Ashkenazic, and among the Ashkenazic equally striking differences between, let us say, West German and Russo-Polish Jews are evident.[39] In other words, we get Q' instead of Q, and the discrepancy leads to a modification of P into P', or at least to fuller awareness of the limitations of P.

Next among the exogenous prescribed-sacred societies is the transplanted. There are some similarities to the enforced: relatively high noticeability,[40] segregation, incomplete participation in the "host" culture. At least one significant difference, however, is apparent: immediately before the transplantation, the society existed as part of a larger indigenous society. The key sacred elements of the larger society are thus transplanted as similarly key elements of the smaller. The contrast with the "host" society results in some measure of isolation which continues as long as the smaller society patterns itself along the

[37] See n. 30. Especially relevant here is chap. vi, "Tumult of the 'Twenties."
[38] Louis Wirth, *The Ghetto* (Chicago: University of Chicago Press, 1928), pp. 18-27.
[39] Arnold J. Toynbee, *A Study of History* (New York and London: Oxford University Press, 1934-37), II, 306-410. Toynbee's conclusions are open to question at many points, but for the matter here under consideration, i.e., diversity, they seem to be entirely valid.
[40] This is a further extension of Park's old term "high visibility."

lines of its earlier "home" culture. Examples are numerous: rural Norwegian, Belgian, Italian, Swiss, and Bavarian communities in Wisconsin, Chinatowns on the West Coast and all over the United States, Issei-Nisei Japanese centers (at least before World War II evacuations), and so on.

Again, if P, then Q. Our prediction would be that, if the isolation were complete, the Americanization of the Nisei, for example, would have been extremely limited. But Q'; the isolation was manifestly far from complete, as the amazingly good combat record of the Nisei regiments in World War II so plainly shows. Suggestions as to why Q' are, in sociological literature, so common that only passing reference need be made to them here. Since, however, most Americanization and like "acculturation" studies abound in "negatively useful" but *implicit* typology, it may be that more explicit use would still further demonstrate its value.

Following the transplanted in our list comes the imposed. An alien value-system is imposed on a society (ordinarily, but not always, as an aftermath of conquest).

Imposition necessarily brings with it destruction of the value-system of the subjected society, together with its nonmaterial and material props, and replacement by the value-system of the exogenous victors. Although imposition of the victor's language is not necessarily part of the type conditions, it frequently does occur. There may even be prohibition of the language of the subjects, destruction of their literary and historical documents, and the like. The leaders are usually exterminated, degraded, or humiliated in such ways that their effectiveness is minimized.

If, however, the subject's values can be interpreted in terms of the new values, this may be done in addition to or instead of eliminating the leaders. "Heathen gods," for example, may become Christian saints or, if this cannot readily be done, emissaries of that old Satan who goeth about seeking whom he may devour. Again, popular heroes of the past may be reinterpreted by the victors so that they can be invoked as "supporters of the new order if they were alive today." The Nazis tried to use the legend of General Boulanger, the French "man on horse-back" of the eighties, in this way—in spite of his notoriously anti-German pronouncements. His opposition to Third Republic parliamentarism and his advocacy of a French version of the leadership principle gave them their cue. The Japanese not only used the slogan of "Asia for the Asiatics" but also revivified the legends of rebels against Western domination in China, Burma, Indonesia, and elsewhere. They were represented as forerunners of Nippon's benevolent "co-ordination."

Methodologically closing the system, and searching for Q', we may ask, what actually takes place under conditions of "imposed diffusion"?

In one amusing instance, we find that natives of a hill tribe in British India gave up beer-drinking under a missionary's threats of hell-fire, and resorted to what they thought an innocuous substitute—namely, opium-smoking.[41] Typologically, this bit of evidence suggests that if an agent of "imposed diffusion" is compelled to accept, in whatever degree, the thoughtways of the subjects in order to express the values he is seeking to impose, the values will be modified and the imposition less complete.

Descriptions of difficulties of this sort are numerous, but they usually lack full cogency because the typological method that frequently underlies them is only implicit. Malinowski, among others, attempted to make the method explicit, but apparently never quite succeeded in saying just what he meant by his "zero point."[42] If P, then Q, but Q' would seem to be a step in the right direction.

[41] Related to Roy G. Francis (see n. 33) by Professor William C. Smith, sociologist at Linfield College, McMinnville, Oregon, who was for a time a Baptist missionary in India.

[42] Bronislaw Malinowski, *The Dynamics of Culture Change* (New Haven: Yale University Press, 1945), edited after Malinowski's death by Phyllis M. Kaberry. Since this book was compiled from notes, criticism may be unfair. But what Malinowski seems to suggest is that if we determine the precontact culture and the culture of the "imposer," we need only "subtract" the two knowns from each other. Some kind of reification of culture seems to be at work here, and the writer feels that if more attention were given to the native society and to the contact agents, the "content of the culture" might have more meaning. This, however, is not the place to present a detailed criticism of culture reification, even if, as may be doubtful, Malinowski was guilty of it.

Last among the subtypes of sacred society to be discussed is the "quasi-nativistic" or the "crypto-indigenous." A good contemporary analogy is to be found in the underground movements of World War II, and another in the secret Nazi enclaves to be found here and there in occupied Germany today.

Basically, this kind of sacred society results from a reaction to an imposed system of values, but differs from the similarly reactive nativistic society of indigenous folk-sacred type in that (1) it must be more covert than the true nativistic reaction, and (2) it is of prescriptive character. On the surface, conformity to the imposed values takes place, but uniform, genuine, spontaneous acceptance does not occur. Tacit acknowledgment of the validity of the symbols of the "new order" may seem to be in evidence, but actually the old prescribed values and their symbolic referents take on great intensity and undergo reification. "But since the color I must wear is England's cruel red . . . [green is the color I secretly wear] . . . and . . . please God, I'll stick, still Wearin' of the Green!" In addition to the Irish example, we have the famous Jacobite Scottish toast given in water instead of wine, "To the King (over the water)!" The crypto-Jews of Ferdinand and Isabella's Spain furnish another of the many possible instances.

Inasmuch as the quasi-nativistic subtype of sacred society is essentially a reaction, so much depends on the character of the imposition that it is extremely hard to frame a widely inclusive type. Instead of making the attempt, then, we shall merely remark that any such type must be based on a culture case study, or studies, undertaken in relation to a problem for which some kind of social-scientific solution is sought. Then it may be possible to say, if P, then Q, but Q'.

This concludes our survey of subtypes of sacred society. Other subtypes can doubtless be constructed, but the array presented is reasonably full. From this array, it should be obvious that "sacred" is *not* limited to the meanings of "holy," "religious," "spiritual," "godly," "blessed," "hallowed," "pious," "devout," "ecclesiastical," "churchly," "clerical," "divine," and so on and on. By a sacred society is meant one in which the new, when defined as new by the society's members, encounters opposition because the social actions involved in its acceptance are held not to be seemly, fitting, proper, congruous, decorous, meet, loyal, "good form," respectful, appropriate, in good taste, balanced—multiply these terms and add the "holy" ones too! Actions in violation of the sacred are felt or said to be unsettling, upsetting, unbecoming, distressing, irregular, illicit, unwarranted, disrespectful, "not done," traitorous, disloyal, outlandish, etc.,[43] and all the usual "moral"[44] and religious pejoratives as well.[45]

In a nutshell, a sacred society tries to maintain or reestablish an essentially unchanging social order.

V. VARIETIES OF SECULAR SOCIETY

High time it is, certainly, that we turn attention toward secular societies. As can be seen from Outline II, however, detailed description of the many subtypes would lead to a small book, or at least to another lengthy chapter.[46] The most that can be done is to make a few general remarks.

To begin with, let us say that the secular is not synonymous with the profane, unholy, infidel, godless, irreligious, heretical, unhallowed, faithless, or any similar terms. It subsumes them, but in a special way, includes a great deal more, and is in no sense pejorative. Hence the blameworthy connotations sometimes attached by religious leaders to "modern secularism" can-

[43] A look at any good thesaurus will show how ample is the stock of terms— in English alone—here applicable. Cf. *Roget's International Thesaurus of English Words and Phrases*, ed. C. O. Sylvester Mawson (New York: Crowell, 1924 and later eds.), Class VI, "Moral Affections."

[44] "Moral" is placed in quotes because in ordinary English its meaning is far more limited than in the "moral" which might be applied to Sumner's "folkways and mores." Perhaps mor*e*al would be a usable variant—but we have enough new coinage of doubtful worth already. "Sacred" of course also includes Sumner's "institutions" in their value-system aspects.

[45] Mawson, ed., *Roget*, Section V, "Religious Affections."

[46] Cf. the writer's old article, "Processes of Secularisation," *Sociological Review* (British), XXIV (April-July and Oct., 1932), 138-154, 266-268, or its abridged version in Wiese-Becker, *op. cit.*, pp. 319-344. It is now planned, following Outline II, to develop this further. Needless to say, the amount of comment on this programmatic outline offered here is utterly insufficient. It is hoped that the reader will be even more charitable than he has been hitherto, for such remarks must be *very* general and schematic indeed.

OUTLINE II—SUBTYPES OF SECULAR SOCIETY
If P, then Q (rate and kind of change)

Subtype	Accessibility and related matters	Q' (some important factors)
Principled-secular		
Indigenous		
Incremental change		
Eliminative	vicinal, social, mental; controlled	excessive or insufficient elimination
Substitutive	vicinal, social, mental; limited	substitute leads to new prescription
Mutational change		
Promulgational	vicinal, mental; selective	rate of change excessive, brings reaction or normlessness
Crisis-ensuing	vicinal, social, mental; transitory	social and mental accessibility never wide enough
Exogenous		
Incremental change		
Rationalizing	vicinal; restricted	old prescriptions survive in disguise
Adoptive	vicinal, social; unrestricted	new principles soon become prescription
Mutational change		
Conquest-ensuing	vicinal, mental; fragmentary	principles rapidly invalidate prescriptions
Defensive	mental; compulsively expedient	expedients destroy principles
Normless-secular		
Indigenous		
Incremental change		
Segmental		
Elicited	vicinal; severely limited	many folkways or prescriptions retained
Elective	vicinal, mental; channelized	enhanced status brings liberation
Decadent		
Residual	vicinal; status-limited	checked by status-striving
Distilled	vicinal, social, mental; status-facilitated	normative reaction to normlessness
Demoralized		
Interclass	vicinal, social, mental; antagonistic	develops or retains work ethic
Intraclass	vicinal, social, mental; fawning	class pressure limits
Nonmoral		
Familial-neglectful	vicinal; childhood-confined	some folkways imparted, or principles absorbed
Familial-impotent	vicinal, social; upper limit late adolescence	expedient considerations induce control
Mutational change		
Catastrophe-ensuing	vicinal, social, mental; "vicious circle"	new principles check
Mutinous	vicinal, mental; eruptive	minor concessions avert
Exogenous		
Incremental change		
Attritional	vicinal, mental; function of contrast	rationalization limits
Mimetic	vicinal; noncomprehending	principles learned
Mutational change		
Collisional	vicinal; function of sudden sharp contrast	folkways survive
Evocative	vicinal; social, mental; rigidly imposed	techniques of resistance found; principles survive
		Frequent result of Q', exendomorphism transitionally marginal persistently marginal

cel as far as we are concerned.[47] Moreover, secularization is not synonymous with social disorganization; there may be both organized and disorganized secular societies. Secularization, however, must not be merely equated with normlessness (*anomie* or anomy);[48] there are norm-structured or principled secular societies as well as normless ones.

Further discussion of what is meant by a principled secular society will perhaps serve to make some of the above points clear. Principle, as distinct from prescription, is highly flexible. Extending our previous illustration (p. 268), we may say that once the principle of shelter as such has developed, there is no need to follow any prescription of what a house should be like, and much less is it necessary to use, in one way or another, all the accumulated house materials that the past has piled up. The architecture is functional, as it were, rather than traditional. Any structure that shelters efficiently against extremes of heat and cold, facilitates the routines of daily life in the given society, accommodates the prevalent type of family, and so on, may be regarded as satisfactory. It is in principle an adequate shelter, regardless of any prescriptions as to what shelters ought to be.

In social terms, secular societies may have a wide range of organizing principles: natural rights, national welfare, humani-

[47] In French, *séculaire* means "coming or observed once in an age or a century; occurring in, or lasting through, a long process or period." Another term, *séculier*, is reserved for the meaning of "the secular arm," i.e., kingly or other political authority sometimes supporting, sometimes opposing ecclesiastical edicts. Still another term, *laïque*, is used to designate "the lay spirit" in educational affairs, for example, as distinct from the clerical. When the Pope or his *nuncio* denounces the public schools of France, he speaks of the evils of *laïcisme* or of *l'esprit laïque*, not of *sécularisme*.

Some of these meanings, and several others, are combined in the English term. For our purposes, however, secular can readily be used in a limited sense as roughly equivalent to mundane, everyday, common, ordinary, matter-of-fact, suitable, or optional, and then subspecified as tending toward principle or normlessness. In the latter case, pejorative terms are frequently encountered, but in sociological writing they must be treated as merely descriptive and/or analytic.

[48] DeGrazia (*The Political Community and Anomie*) and others use Durkheim's *anomie*; MacIver (*The Ramparts We Guard*) has adopted the old English "anomy." The Greek *anomia* from which Durkheim drew means, literally, "without convention," and this can readily be translated as "normlessness." We already have the long-standing precedent of "lawlessness," which fits into place as a special aspect of normlessness.

tarianism, free enterprise, socialism, "rationalism," "greatest good of the greatest number," "liberty under law," "functional efficiency," and so on. The essential point is that any of these principles admits of almost unlimited variation in the procedures involved in its application. The social order is vaguely outlined, but exact structural interrelations and precise details are not written into the specifications. They are left to be worked out as occasion demands.

Obviously, a *sharp* line between prescribed-sacred and principled-secular societies *cannot be drawn* except in the realm of the constructed type, and even there the difficulties are great.[49] One of the major difficulties is that the principle has to come from something, and that something is often a prescription or even a folk precept.

This can be seen when considering the incremental eliminative subtype of indigenous principled society (Outline II). Such a society has arrived at its guiding principle by the slow wearing away of the specificities of its prior prescriptions. Particularized local loyalties to "Little Rhodey" or "The Old Dominion" are gradually ground down to almost featureless State's Rights doctrines or rubbed smooth as sentimental memories in the mill of war and similar crises, until finally a universalized, "interchangeable" principle of Federal Union is turned out. An American citizen is first of all an American citizen; other political allegiances are secondary. The principle supersedes the prescription, but "in the beginning was"—the prescription.

Another general comment that should be made in this overbrief concluding section is that "primitive" societies can readily approximate the secular type. During the late eighteenth and the nineteenth centuries the Comanche, for example, developed a value-system of markedly secular character, in part fitting the

[49] This is one of the reasons why, in an earlier presentation, the writer said that "a stable secular society could with almost equal warrant be designated as an adaptive sacred society" (Becker and Hill, *op. cit.*, p. 33). It now seems clear, however, that insufficient account was taken of the difference between rigid prescription and flexible principle. Consequently, the writer now expressly aligns himself with the position taken by W. L. Kolb, "The Objective Possibility of an Organized Secular Society," *Southwestern Journal*, II (1946), 161-169.

collisional subtype of exogenous mutational change in the direction of normlessness, and in part fitting the crisis-ensuing subtype of indigenous mutational change in the direction of principle. This value-system was not merely transitional; for well over half a century the Comanche retained an ordered but significantly secular structure.[50] They were in fact closely similar to the "marginal trading people" type,[51] and consequently were simultaneously indigenous *and* exogenous. Their social structure being in a sense both "inside" and "outside," they were exendomorphic[52] (see Outlines I and II, bottom of Q' column).

Finally, let it be incidentally noted that normlessness, although often evoking a normative reaction, and although issuing in a society sustaining a social disorder, has not always called forth adverse value-judgments. Turgot, Teggart, Whitehead, and others[53] have even spoken approvingly, and Goethe, in Faust, lets the Lord assume responsibility:

> Man's efforts lightly flag, and seek too low a level;
> Soon doth he pine for all-untramelled sloth—
> Wherefore a mate I give him, nothing loathe,
> Who spurs and shapes, and must create though Devil!

We are all children of our time, and all philosophers of our time. Some of us are not inclined to cast our burdens and blame on the Lord; others are. Some of us find difficulty in imagining a Heaven and Hell Amalgamation Society, to speak with Carlyle; others are not only at their ease in Zion, but also in Gehenna.

With one thing, it is hoped, most of us will agree, namely, that at the beginning of the second half of the twentieth century, A.D., it is clear that we must proceed through values to

[50] Cf. the comments by Don Martindale, "The Variety of the Human Family," in Becker and Hill, *op. cit.*, pp. 60-62.

[51] Present volume, pp. 109-113.

[52] Simply combining, for our purposes, the petrographic terms "exomorphic" and "endomorphic." Such a neologism is of doubtful value, but is offered for what it is worth. One or another kind of "marginal" is probably more usable.

[53] Barnes and Becker, *STLS*, pp. 264 ff., 411-415, 470-474. See also pp. 158-168, present volume.

social interpretation. Social contexts, actions, types, and prospects must all be viewed from the vantage point of value-analysis if we are to be social scientists in substance as well as in form.

Whether or not we agree on the final ends of the conduct we analyze or in which we engage is another matter. This is the moot problem not only of sociology but of all the social sciences and humanities—indeed, of all men whatever their calling. The writer has not solved it even to his own satisfaction, but he has taken a definite position with regard to it in an essay written in 1940 when action rather than contemplation was called for, an essay that now appears as the concluding chapter of this volume. Our long journey is nearly over; let us, then, once more "sitting well in order, smite the sounding furrows."

CHAPTER VI

SUPREME VALUES AND THE SOCIOLOGIST, OR, OUR ROLES AND THEIR LOYALTIES

I. "THE STATE OF THE UNION"

WE ARE ALL familiar with the long-standing antithesis between the so-called "meliorists" and "purists" within our sadly *dis*-united sociological "union." This antithesis, which in its social rather than its logical phases might better be called a controversy, has recently begun to become even more definite because of an incipient parallel cleavage between "administrators" and "academicians."

Those of us who might otherwise be inclined to say, "A plague o' both your houses," have begun to realize that we cannot longer ignore the clamor.

Our concern, moreover, goes even beyond solicitude for the sociological enterprise. When, literally speaking, the destiny of the greater portion of mankind seems to be following courses of previously unimagined portent, it ill beseems the sociologist to remain on his pedestal.

Let us therefore re-examine some of the traditional issues, casting aside the pride of consistency, and with it all contentiousness.

II. "THE WORLD IS SO FULL OF A NUMBER OF THINGS"

The slogan, "No value-judgments in sociology," has been misused by its adherents (and here I make no exception of myself) and misunderstood by its opponents. Implicit or explicit assertions of final, irreducible preferences are absolutely inescapable. Only when a distinction is made between *ultimate* and *proximate* preferences and the values built upon these preferences can misuse and misunderstanding be avoided. But more of this later.

The same slogan has been taken to imply fundamental differences between "cold, hard facts," which are presumably the same for all "objective" observers, and moral interpretations of those "facts," which vary radically from person to person. There are differences, beyond doubt, between certain aspects of the phenomena with which men interact and of which they themselves are parts, but such differences are certainly not of this simple, so-called "objective-subjective" character. On the contrary, they seem to inhere in the differing preference-systems within which various aspects of the phenomenal world are incorporated. Again, more of this later.

Having hinted at this relevance to preference-systems, however, let us at once be on guard against the solipsisms,[1] of whatever sort, that such hints might seem to impose upon us. Certainly no one but the consistent solipsist raises doubts about the existence of a world "external" to ourselves, no matter how little we may know about the "real nature" of that world. Further, few of us would be willing to grant that our world is in the strict sense an "empirical chaos";[2] it seems to exhibit structural traits not wholly relative to the observer. So far forth, then, there may be said to be a world of "fact."[3]

Nevertheless, this world manifests for mankind distinguishable aspects of tremendous number and diversity. We perhaps need not champion Spinozism by insisting that "an infinity of aspects" is a more suitable statement, but we must maintain that there is no known limit to the ways in which the world may be related to observers. A pine forest is one body of preferred phenomena for a botanist, another for a hunter, another for a forester, another for a farmer, another for a geologist, another for an artist, another for a recluse, another for a lost child. Beyond question the forest *is*—but *what* is it?

[1] Here I have in mind not only the traditional solipsisms, but also the "solipsism of the response" implicit throughout George A. Lundberg's *Foundations of Sociology* (New York, 1939).

[2] Moreover, I am especially desirous of avoiding dualistic implications, for I have always thought of myself, rightly or wrongly, as a working pragmatist.

[3] This is what the constructive typologist is driving at when he says that his constructs must be "objectively probable" if they are to have any scientific significance. No judge at a dog-show is at liberty to "construct" an Airedale with cast-iron stomach and swivel casters for feet.

Not only does it have differing aspects for each kind of observer, but it has differing aspects for botanists A, B, . . . *n*, for hunters A, B, . . . *n*, and so on and on.

Further, the forest may be viewed by men who combine several observer-capacities within themselves; there may be botanist-hunters, forester-farmers, recluse-artists, and the like, throughout a stupendous range of permutations.

Running as a constant motif through these shifting patterns, moreover, is the persisting influence of the language in terms of which the observers take note of, arrange, and communicate their variously assorted "facts" (up until this point of our exposition the tacit assumption has been made that they all speak the same tongue). When we introduce the additional factors of linguistic diversities—syntaxes, accidences, vocabularies, and all the paraphernalia familiar to the comparative philologist—we may begin to feel that Spinoza's "infinity of aspects" comes discomfortingly close to the truth.

Our growing uneasiness is only heightened when we take account of the multitudinous moral, ethical, and religious interpretations to which this forest may be subjected. To the recluse the overarching pines make manifest the goodness of God or the benevolent spirit of Nature, and in contemplative mood he holds invisible communion. To the lost child the gloom of the deep woods and the utter stillness speak of disembodied but all-powerful Evil, and in terrified mood he cowers in near-collapse. To the artist, the uprooting of underbrush and the cutting of fire-lanes not only destroys beauty but violates Nature's moral code, and in indignantly righteous mood he fervently protests against such utilitarian desecration. To the geologist, the forest is simply an indication of the probable character of the strata that underlie it, and in dutiful mood he cuts down the giants of the forest in order to make test borings at strategic points.

Manifestly the forest is, in a sense, "all things to all men." Some of the "facts" it exhibits may be "colder" and "harder" than others, but what are "*the* objective facts?" And at precisely what points do preferences destroy objectivity? Is it not clear that the answers to these questions cannot be couched in terms of the old "objective-subjective" dualism?

III. THE SCIENTIST "KNOWS WHAT HE LIKES"

Science, including sociology, *prefers* certain aspects of the world to others, and may even be said to delineate or carve out those aspects because of such preference. Ever since the time of the Babylonian astrologers, and perhaps long before then, men have sought, in differing provinces of life, for "the systematic statement of the probability of the hypothetical or actual recurrence of phenomena that, for the purposes in hand, are regarded as identical."[4] In other words, they have sought for prediction. In this search they have, wittingly or unwittingly, disregarded all other aspects—aesthetic, ethical, religious—of the world of which they are parts.

What men have been willing to regard as successful prediction has of course differed tremendously in differing eras, but the end sought, it seems to me, has always been control. The magician seeks control even as does the scientist; the difference between their activities lies chiefly in the frequency with which the predicted results come about, *plus* the consonance of these results with verified predictions in other phases of life. Usually, although not invariably, this frequency and consonance has not been determined by careful comparison of data other than those included in the predictive act, but by sheer adaptive worth—oftentimes in terms of naked survival. The magician whose incantations against the plague have been highly prized himself succumbs; sacrifices before battle lose their accustomed efficacy, as testified by defeat; oracles foretell enduring rule for a king only to encounter a usurper; and the like. Isolated societies, shielded from the blunt "criticism" of culture contact, may for a long time preserve an inadequate predictive system, no doubt of that, but migrations and similar accessibility-producing events demonstrate the inadequacy of the old system and not infrequently introduce a new one that more closely fits "means" to "ends."

[4] See the chapter on "Constructive Typology in the Social Sciences," pp. 96-102.

Similarly, a scientific system, such as the Ptolemaic astronomy, yields predictions regarded as sufficiently accurate until a Copernicus breaks down the mental isolation of its upholders. The history of science shows that the first step in this breakdown is usually taken by calling attention to failures in prediction that cannot be explained away without introducing complications into the old system which its most skilled exponents cannot handle satisfactorily. The next and decisive step is achieved when it can be shown that the new system yields superior predictive power and is sufficiently simple to be within the capacities of ordinary scientists. Needless to say, the upholders of the old system do not yield without a struggle, for many of them are too advanced in years to make the shift, and others have vested interests in it represented by subsidiary theories, "authoritative" books, and like commitments. Hence science is a perpetual battleground in which victories are predictively determined. Scientific prediction is the ultimate test, and its momentum overcomes the inertia of the internal consistency of postulational systems. These systems are not destroyed so much as simply pushed aside; they no longer yield control, and hence *finis*. Their symmetry, logical perfection, persuasive power, time-hallowed prestige, aesthetic appeal, religious orthodoxy, and other "advantages" are dismissed as irrelevant; the scientist *prefers* control.

It will be noted that "prediction" and "control" have just been used interchangeably. This usage is warranted only if the peculiar nature of the control preferred by the scientist is kept steadfastly in mind.

To predict the recurrence of phenomena is, in a certain sense, to control that recurrence if it is possible to reinstate or reconstruct the conditions under which previous recurrences have taken place. The scientist may not have any interest whatever in bringing about an actual recurrence; he may be quite content to say that "if and when" certain factors are combined in certain ways, the results are predictable. The supreme test is experimental, but when a number of experiments suffi-

cient to diminish chance to insignificance have been performed—
and a small number of experiments, under some circumstances,
may suffice—the scientist as scientist has achieved all the control he seeks: When this is done, these—within a small range
of variation—*must* be the consequences.

Further, the scientist may get the control he is after even
when he is not able to reinstate the conditions of previous
recurrences, i.e., when actual, manipulative experiment is impracticable or impossible. He may, in other words, attain
hypothetical control through mental reconstruction and extension of such reconstruction.

Instance the fact that astronomers are able to say, because
of the study of certain aspects of the heavens over a long period,
that mass, time, and movement are in certain definite relations
with each other. They can therefore say that if the mass of
the moon were altered in a determinate amount, its orbit and
its cycle would also be changed in determinate amounts. Obviously the mass of the moon has not yet been added to or
subtracted from by astronomers; there has been no experimentation. Nevertheless, most of us are willing, because of
eclipse prediction and the like, to regard astronomy as an exact
science—indeed, as one of the most exact of all the sciences.
Now, this "if the mass of the moon were altered" is hypothetical control or, if you will, hypothetical prediction, on the
basis of previously observed recurrences of related phenomena,
of phenomena never before specifically observed.

A like instance is provided by language. Comparative
philologists have records of human speech that go back as far
as, or even further than, the astronomer's records of celestial
changes. Even though until recent times the philologist's
records are merely written, he is frequently able, through the
analysis of puns, meters, rhymes, alliterations, assonances, and
the like, to determine with a high degree of accuracy how a
given "dead" language was actually pronounced throughout
the greater part of its career. Moreover, he can often show
that the same thing could be done, if necessary, for a "living"
language, and in addition can predict the changes still to occur.

Many languages have been subjected to such analysis, and on the comparative basis thus afforded the philologist can therefore say that if he could rear a number of children in entire isolation from all other speech contacts and were given liberty to train them to pronounce a few key words in certain ways, all the rest of their pronunciation would follow a predictable though hitherto unexemplified pattern. Here again we have hypothetical control.

The varieties of control thus far discussed, whether hypothetical or actual, have all had an orientation toward the future, both with regard to the predictive act and with regard to the phenomena predicted. Putting it differently, I have tried to make clear the futureward implications of actual *prospective* prediction and hypothetical *prospective* prediction. There need be a reference to the future, however, *only in the predictive act itself*; it is not necessary that the *recurrence* of the phenomena under examination take place in the future.

Here is an appropriate example: paleontologists frequently reconstruct animals long extinct. They often carry out their task on the basis of fragmentary evidence: a jawbone here, a thighbone there, a shoulder blade elsewhere. Filling the gaps between these odds and ends may be data gleaned from apparently similar species alive today, from comparison with seemingly related extinct forms having a like habitat, or from specimens of the same species in earlier stages of development. Thus fortified, the paleontologist ventures an assertion like this: "If and when a complete skeleton is discovered, our reconstruction will be found to be substantially correct." This is *retrospective* prediction, for the skeleton which will provide the validation lies under strata deposited millennia ago. The only essential reference toward the future is in the "will," which is the inseparable component of the predictive act. There is no actual prospective prediction; the biology supply houses that stock our laboratories do not yet breed dinosaurs for the market, and Frank Buck does not "bring 'em back alive"—or dead. There is no hypothetical prospective prediction, for no living animal species known at present is evolving in the dinosaur direction; the phenomena in question have only an infinitesimal probability of future recurrence. The prediction is hypothetical in the same way as altering of the mass of the moon is hypothetical: If we found a fresh dinosaur egg or could produce a dinosaur mutant by X-ray bombardment of an iguana egg, and if we had proper environmental conditions, we could rear a dinosaur that would provide verification of our reconstruction. Finally, to repeat, the prediction is retrospective because the recurrence which will provide the validation presumably has already occurred; it is only the *validation* which lies in the future, and it is only to this that the futureward orientation implied in "before-saying," or "pre-diction," refers.

An example even more appropriate can be furnished by referring again to language. Hypothetical retrospective prediction may be achieved when linguistic data which do not have to be discovered at some future time, i.e., which are already available, are re-examined in the light of the given prediction. The comparative philologist knows a great deal about vowel shifts and like changes in speech patterns in certain Indo-European languages, but neither he nor anyone else has examined Old Prussian, let us imagine, with an eye to related vowel shifts. Nevertheless, he may say: "When Old Prussian texts now in the University of Dorpat library are examined, my prediction that vowel shifts demonstrably occurring in similar tongues have also occurred in Old Prussian will be verified." Old Prussian has not been spoken for centuries, and the texts are similarly ancient, hence the prediction is retrospective. It can be made explicitly hypothetical, *à la* our "mass of the moon," if there seems any point in so doing, by saying this: If a group of children could be brought up in entire isolation from all other speech contacts and if the earliest form of Old Prussian could be taught them, and if their descendants could be isolated from everything but the Old Prussian spoken by the original and succeeding groups, certain vowel shifts resulting from the immanent development of the language would clearly appear in the speech of a substantial proportion of the fourth generation.

Manifestly only the *validation* of hypothetical retrospective prediction is a matter of the future; *all else is past.*

Astronomy, geology, paleontology, archeology, zoölogy, botany, philology, ethnology, and several other sciences make much use of retrospective prediction. When the sociologists recover from the paralyzing fright they have suffered as a result of being roundly denounced as poachers by the idiographic historians, they too may profit by study of bygone days. As matters now stand, it is possible to find so-called sociologies of religion, for instance, that leap all the way from "our primitive contemporaries" in Polynesia to "our contemporary primitives" in Fundamentalia without so much as touching toe to ground in between. At any rate, it is one man's opinion that retrospective prediction in sociology has possibilities as yet unexploited and that if we are really in earnest about prediction and its inseparable corollary, control, we shall soon remedy our present shortcomings.

For one more point, the scientist as scientist does not necessarily covet *applied* control. In other words, he is not *ipso facto* a utilitarian because he is a scientist. When once a scientific elite has developed, direct utilitarianism in science wanes. The standards of that elite relate to hypothetical or actual control only in so far as such control provides selective criteria for and validation of predictive inference; once these are supplied, there may be no overwhelming interest in "putting science to work for the good of mankind."

To be sure, scientific activity receives continued support from the lay public, in this modern day, only because actual control is applied in socially approved ways by some sciences, or by the various technologies drawing upon these sciences. The scientific elite, however, usually presents a closed front to utilitarian probings, and in thus following the maxim of "One for all and all for one," sees to it that the lay public does not get a chance to single out a few of the members of this elite as conspicuously "useless."

In earlier periods, of course, each individual scientist had continually to justify himself, or at least to attempt to do so, by producing evidence that his control could be made actual and would be applied—generally by the scientist himself. The next step was to assert that apparently useless activities were designed to make eventual application of control possible—an assertion that in many cases was not the issue of whole-hearted belief. The final step is taken when a scientific elite develops solidarity, as was pointed out above; at present some scientific value-monotheists—of whom "more later"—proclaim the dictum "Science for its own sake." Regardless of what we may think of such value-monotheism, there can be little doubt that it has at least temporarily banished the utilitarian criterion of the "worthwhileness" of actual, applied control.

Hence the way in which "control" is used in these pages carries with it no suggestion of a utilitarian sanction for science.

But it is now high time that this digression cease; I must return to the main topic, namely, the scientist's special preference-system.

One striking peculiarity of the preference for control, the hallmark of science, is that it has no necessary connection with curiosity as ordinarily defined. Veblen's "idle curiosity" as the origin of science—as commonly interpreted—seems to me a half-truth that is worse than outright error. The members of a gaping crowd in front of a sidewalk pitch-artist are idly curious, so also are those rolling stones who roll "for to admire an' for to see, for to be'old this world so wide," or village postmasters who read postcards and hold up letters to the light, or poolroom loungers who saunter out to see a dogfight, or Peeping Toms. No, the *disciplined* curiosity of the scientist has definite historical origins as a culture pattern (most widely diffused since the Renaissance), and cannot be assigned to that old stand-by, "human nature."

In similar case is the "instinct of workmanship" stopgap. No one can successfully deny, of course, the importance of technology in relation to science, but technology is a far cry from workmanship. The Chinese ivory carver, executing unbelievably intricate fretwork, is a workman par excellence; so also is the tattooer who covers the skins of his patrons with swirls of geometric and naturalistic patterns, the butcher who can split the backbone of a beef with four strokes of his meat-axe, the weaver who after ten years of steady toil produces a marvelous Gobelin tapestry, and the old-fashioned cigar-maker whose pridefully cultivated ambidexterity dazzles the onlooker. These workmen may all be "curious" about better ways to perform their traditional tasks; they may take keen delight in demonstrating their skill—but they are not scientists, nor does science spring from such sources. "Human nature" again— what havoc that notion has wrought!

Likewise, the "urge to classify" must be dismissed in quite as cavalier a manner. The boy with a postage-stamp collection is a classifier; so also is the dilettante librarian who arranges books according to size and color; so also is the maid who "straightens" a study by carefully placing all loose notes and papers in the drawers and pigeonholes that fit them most closely. Granted, taxonomy is part of many sciences, but scientific taxonomy is not classification as such; it is oriented toward prediction and control, not toward order merely for the sake of internal consistency, aesthetic gratification, ready reference, or "tidiness." "Human nature" has failed us once again.

Moreover, it is apparently very difficult, to say the least, to explain the scientific preference for control by tracing it back to the "motivating" personality traits or proximate values of individual scientist. I should not wish to deny that there may be some such thing as a scientific temperament per se, or a few well-marked subtypes of such a temperament, but I can say that the historical record as I know it provides little satisfactory evidence. One biographer may say that his subject was attracted to science because of the prestige it promised to yield; another that the appeal for his subject lay in the privilege of demonstrating the wonders of God's cosmic design; another that feeble health in childhood made a quiet, regular, sedentary calling imperative; another that great family forerunners sounded the call of duty; another that rivalry with a brother gave the cue; another that a penchant for playing with puzzles was manifest early in childhood; another that mischief-making proclivities led to elaborate practical jokes involving much planning and manipulation of material objects; another that training for the bar was too expensive, and hence science, with attendant fellowship opportunities, was chosen as second best. Where is the least common "psychological" denominator?

In the light of all this (and much more which might be adduced if space permitted), many competent researchers are inclined to think that the scientific preference for those aspects of the phenomenal world that can be subjected to control arises or becomes dominant only in societies undergoing certain kinds of change. A convenient term, covering these changes fairly well, is found in "secularization."[5] The scientific preference is bound up with the "social role of the man of knowledge" (to use Znaniecki's apt designation) in secularizing or highly secularized societies.[6]

This means that the scientific preference is not generated from "within," as it were, but is imposed from "without."[7] Widely discrepant "motives" or proximate preferences may lead men to play the scientific role, but once that role is assumed, all preferences other than the ultimate scientific preference must be excluded. The scientist "knows what he likes" in the sense that he possesses hypothetical or actual control of those aspects of the phenomenal world which the scientific preference has defined as amenable to such control; that is, he prefers the "cold, hard facts," which are "cold" and "hard" because they are control-preference facts.

Plainly this is a circular statement. But we can break the

[5] See chap. v, pp. 275-280, and also H. E. Barnes and H. Becker, *Social Thought from Lore to Science* (Boston, 1938), Vol. I, *passim*, but esp. chap. iv; hereinafter cited as *STLS*.

[6] Florian Znaniecki, *The Social Role of the Man of Knowledge* (New York, 1940), pp. 113-199, esp. pp. 113-135.

[7] This is a mere figure of speech; I do not mean to subscribe without reservation to Durkheim's "exteriority" and "constraint." This much, however, may justifiably be said: the scientist is held in line by other scientists and their criticism as well as by his "scientific conscience." Further, he must *learn* to prefer control, although a modicum of this learning is oftentimes automatically acquired in a culture where science has prestige and is widely diffused.

circle by taking account of the historically demonstrable circumstance, mentioned earlier, that inadequate postulational systems are superseded, if at all, when their inadequacy is demonstrated by repeated or disastrous failure to predict, unmanageable complication, extinction of their adherents, or loss of influence on a dominant elite. Here, certainly, Goethe's maxim of "Die and develop!" applies. Of one thing the scientist can be sure, namely, that the working postulational system of today will be the museum piece of tomorrow.

IV. THE PRIESTHOOD OF THE SCIENTIST

Thus far I have tried, with how much success I cannot say, to refrain from introducing the question of the moral or ethical bearing of the scientist's preference-system. At this point, however, it must be confronted. "No value-judgments in science" is usually taken to mean that not only are scientific formulations ethically neutral, which is true enough, but also that the scientist who does the formulating is ethically neutral, which is arrant nonsense. Only the surviving assumptions of a faculty psychology which drew a sharp line between Reason and Passion, or the comic-strip inference that all scientists are completely schizoid or paranoid, could ever have gained currency for the myth of the scientist's personal impartiality.

To develop further a point which, although apparently extraneous, is not altogether so: It seems clear that science is basically dependent on control-preference. This preference for those aspects of the phenomenal world that offer promise of successful subjection to hypothetical or actual control seemingly does not arise out of innate propensities or special temperamental gifts, but is absorbed from or even imposed by general cultural patterns which make control paramount. Such culture patterns have definite ethical orientations. For whatever reason, the control-aspects of the phenomenal world must be thought important by some group which sooner or later comes to be tolerated by the powers that be. This means that due regard for the multifarious *other* aspects of the phenomenal world hinted at in an earlier section of this paper does not seem to be endangered by the control-preference group. At the very least, those noncontrol aspects are not decreed to be of such overwhelming significance for everyone that the tolerance of scientific activity is thereby rendered heretical or disloyal or immoral.   In other words, science is held to be permissible, and such permissibility is ethically determined.   How indifference or hostility to control-preference as nonethical or anti-ethical may prevent scientific development is shown in the following letter, quoted by William James and prefaced by this comment:

The aspiration to be "scientific" is such an idol of the tribe to the present generation, is so sucked in with his mother's milk by every one of us, that we find it hard to conceive of a creature who should not feel it, and harder still to treat it freely as *the altogether peculiar and one-sided . . . interest* which it is . . . the way in which it even now strikes Orientals is charmingly shown in the letter of a Turkish cadi to an English traveler asking him for statistical information. . . .

"My Illustrious Friend, and Joy of my Liver!

The thing you ask of me is both difficult and useless. . . .   I have neither counted the houses nor inquired into the number of the inhabitants [of this place]; and as to what one person loads on his mules and another stows away in the bottom of his ship, that is no business of mine. . . .

Listen, O my son!   There is no wisdom equal unto the belief in God!   He created the world, and shall we liken ourselves unto Him in seeking to penetrate into the mysteries of His creation?   Shall we say, Behold this star spinneth round that star, and this other star with a tail goeth and cometh in so many years?   Let it go!   He from whose hand it came will guide and direct it.

. . . I praise God that I seek not that which I require not.   Thou art learned in the things I care not for; and as for that which thou hast seen, I spit upon it.   Will much knowledge create thee a double belly . . . ?

O my friend!   If thou wilt be happy, say, There is no God but God!

IMAUM ALI ZADI"[8]

We smile at our good cadi and, as I think, rightly, but it must not be forgotten that, considered *merely* as one preference-

---

[8] William James, *Principles of Psychology* (New York, 1890), II, 640-641; italics mine.

system among others, his faith is as good or as bad as ours. It is only when we begin to define the ultimacy of values in terms of what we hold to be the possibility of their attainment that we can say which values "should" be regarded as "ultimate." If bitter experience had shown that preference for the control-aspects of the phenomenal world yielded no real control, hypothetical or actual, prospective or retrospective, there would be as little warrant for faith in science as there is for faith that all things happen by Allah's decree. This has been aptly put:

. . . though nature's materials lend themselves slowly and discouragingly to our translation of them into ethical forms, but more readily into aesthetic forms; to translation into scientific forms they lend themselves with relative ease and completeness. The translation, it is true, will probably never be ended. The perceptive order does not give way, nor the right conceptive substitute for it arise, at our bare word of command. It is often a deadly fight; and many a man of science can say, like Johannes Müller, after an investigation, . . . ["The work is blood-stained"]. But victory after victory makes us sure that the essential doom of our enemy is defeat.[9]

But we are not yet done with our cadi. He might say that the battle for control is not yet over, and that though the scientist, like Napoleon, may conquer a whole continent, one unsubjugated island still makes faith in final victory neither more nor less than a faith—and he would be right.[10] Moreover, the worthy cadi might point to the so-called "paradox of consequences," namely, that actual applied control in one phase of life may be the very reason why another phase gets out of control. We control the air and are faced by the bombing plane; we control chemicals and are faced by poison gas; we control conception and are faced by a "birth strike"; we control pneumonia and are faced by a steeply mounting old-age pension load; we control the Buffalo Plains and are faced by the Dust Bowl; we control atomic fission and are faced by the White Pillar of Doom. Such circumstances lead to the

[9] *Ibid.*
[10] He might also say that the difficulty of translating nature's materials into ethical terms is no reason why such translation should not be attempted and persisted in—and again he would be right.

scientific declaration of faith, "The remedy for the consequences of actual, applied control is more actual, applied control." And if the cadi then said, "I can't see that the defeat of the enemy is *certain*," again he would be right.

The upshot of these and like reflections is that mere preference for control cannot account for the persistence of the scientific enterprise. Such preference necessarily transmutes itself into ultimate value; the scientist becomes a priest of the faith in the possibility and supreme desirability of control. The secular society in which he has grown up and which sanctions his preference-system is endowed with sacred values by his enterprise; the quest for control becomes a quest for the Holy Grail. Nonrational? Yes! What ultimate values have ever been rational? Impartial? No! What priest was ever impartial?

Now we encounter something quite odd. The ethical partisanship of the scientist is precisely the reason why his scientific formulations are ethically neutral. Not only does his initial preference-system tend to preserve him from the seductions of other aspects of the phenomenal world, but in addition his faith in the desirability of control prevents him from being troubled by the skeptic's gibe, "Control for what?" Further, the fact that "Control for what?" can be asked at all shows how void of content control, in its scientific meaning, really is. Scientific control may or may not be actual, it may or may not be applied. This emptiness of control as a value-category permits it to be related to other ultimate and proximate values of the most divergent sorts and still to retain its own character as an ultimate value. Regardless of the end to be attained by a man acting in a given social role, he can, if he is also a scientist, view the means to that end in his scientific role and can say whether or not there seems to be any possibility of attaining it.

This of course can be done only by the man, who, as it were, is a "value-polytheist," i.e., who is a successful scientist in one role and a striver toward a different end or ends in other phases of his life. Such "value-polytheism," however, is not rare in the history of science, and in sociology we need name only Max Weber, Wiese, Thomas, Park, Znaniecki, MacIver, and Goldenweiser to establish the point. But, once again, more of this later. If "value-polytheism" within a single personality is not impossible, it should then be clear that there is a much greater possibility of treating control as an ultimate value in your own scientific role and at the same time treating it as mere means in the role of someone else.

In brief, "the systematic statement of the probability of the hypothetical or actual recurrence of phenomena that, for the purposes in hand, are regarded as identical" is an ultimate value, an end in itself, in the scientific role. Nevertheless, it may be merely a means to the attainment of another ultimate value in another social role, or even only a means for determining whether or not it is "worth while" to put forth the effort for the attainment of that other end in that other role.

The ethical neutrality of any formulation that can be called scientific is guaranteed as over against all ethical alternatives *other than the supreme end of control*. But with regard to the faith of science itself there is not and cannot be ethical neutrality; you are either a scientist in your calling or you are not. If you work on a different preference-basis, or if you refuse to project the control-preference beyond the "paradox of consequences" and thus refuse to accept it as a faith, you may be and, I venture to say, probably are just as good a human being, but you do *not* play the scientific role.

The slogan "No value-judgments in science" must therefore be expanded to read as follows: "No value-judgments in science which derive from sources other than *the supreme value-judgment that control is ultimately desirable*, are ethically permissible by the scientist in his specifically scientific capacity."

Scientists, when they are fully aware of the faith that is in them, form a Church for the preservation and propagation of the Supreme End. To continue the metaphor, they may not have a Pope, but they certainly have a College of Cardinals. Further, they have a doctrine akin to "the indelibility of the priestly character." As long as a scientist adequately carries out the functions of his office, his motives for performing those functions are irrelevant as far as the efficacy of his performance is concerned. Otherwise put, the personal motives or proximate preferences of the scientist are irrelevant; if his formulations further the supreme value of control, it matters not whether he is merely seeking a promotion, lusting for political power, trying to be of service to the "underprivileged," defending his nation, upholding his class, or demonstrating the omniscience, benevolence, and omnipotence of his God. The *argumentum ad hominem* has no place in science; the only question is, Does this formulation yield control we have not previously possessed?

The Church of Science, moreover, applies "pressures." If a scientist strays off the straight and narrow path by injecting other preferences and ultimate values into his supposedly scientific work, he will soon find that his books are no longer in the Holy Canon, his articles can be published only in journals which lack the Imprimatur and Nihil Obstat, and eventually he may discover that all his writings are in the Index Expurgatorius or even the Index Librorum Prohibitorum. Worse still, the institution with which he is identified may suffer Interdict, and he himself may be visited with Excommunication.

This is as it should be, if one has initially accepted the Scientific Faith. Absolute neutrality as regards all other criteria of "good" and "bad" must be maintained if control is to go on from victory to victory, as the Faith of Science necessarily assumes. If a formulation is mere wishful thinking, not only other scientists but the lay world as well will find it out, and the scoffers and skeptics will rejoice. The "sinews of research" and other conditions which make it possible for the scientist to strive for the extension of control will then be placed in jeopardy. Hence any measure, no matter how severe, that will deter heresy makes for the good of the Church and of the Scientific Faith it enshrines. *In hoc signo vinces.*

v. "VALUE-POLYTHEISM" AND "VALUE-MONOTHEISM"

Turning once more to the controversy between the "meliorists" and the "purists" which has furnished the occasion for this chapter, I am now prepared to assert that when once "value-polytheism" and "value-monotheism" are clearly distinguished,[11] many of the controversial issues disappear. Going further, I maintain that neither "meliorist" nor "purist" has any advantage if once the significance of social roles is clearly recognized. Let us see why this is so.

It is possible for certain key roles to exert great influence on the way the other roles are played, particularly if the key roles are infused with an absolute and strongly emotionalized ethics. Such an ethics is one in which personal (or proximate values) and ultimate values are in close correspondence.

Here are some examples. Not infrequently a social worker is encountered whose key values lead to intense sympathy with all her clients. The demands of her professional role, however, make it necessary to practice a certain emotional detachment *in that role* if the best interests of the client *and* of society at large are to be served. This detachment she is unable to effect; she cannot exercise "the ruthless kindness of the surgeon." Her value-monotheism finally leads to a far more serious condition, where both client and society are concerned, than existed when she first took over the case. A like instance is to be found in the judge whose political prepossessions are so strong that he is incapable of assuming the judicial role, and even goes to the length of passing on the question of his own impartiality (as did the notorious Judge Thayer in the Sacco-Vanzetti case). Once more value-monotheism wreaks havoc. Another exhibit is the scientist so wrapped up in his bacteriological or poison gas research that he will serve the ends of any master, Fascist or Communist, as long as his "liberty" to develop methods of mass destruction is assured. The scientific role usurps the place of all other roles—value-monotheism with a vengeance!

Personalities like this are of course continually carrying on

[11] These terms are metaphorical and internally redundant, but they serve present purposes. Usable neologisms would be "monoaxionomy" and "polyaxionomy." But who would use them?

an active conversation of roles, and may achieve a considerable degree of consistency in a limited range of conduct. The differing situations they encounter elicit differing responses, but nevertheless their Hamlet sounds strangely like their Ophelia, Laertes, and Horatio.

Some of these value-monotheists, to be sure, succeed in their key roles; the concentration of effort and the drive resulting from high integration are great aids. They may, however, be so limited by their preference-system and value-loyalty that their concentration and drive are self-defeating; initial errors are persisted in because nothing can shatter the internal consistency of their postulational structure and their conviction of being ethically infallible. Value-monotheism, then, yields unity of purpose but carries with it the danger of mental isolation and rigidity.

Many of our ardent "meliorists" and our extreme "purists" are adherents of value-monotheism. Where the "meliorists" are concerned, the key role is not scientific, but patriotic, democratic, humanitarian, or religious. This role tends to dominate all the others, and when the ardent "meliorist" attempts to respond scientifically, he literally cannot perceive the essential control phenomena. His preference-system does not work that way because his ultimate value-loyalty imposes another preference-system in which control is not paramount. Where the extreme "purists" are concerned, they sometimes think they have secured control merely because they have resisted the blandishments of other preferences and ultimate values both in the scientific role and in all other roles. Failure to predict accurately can always be "explained" by using the very postulational system from which failure resulted, by stressing good intentions and ethical integrity, and by the familiar "We need more research along this line." The Faith of Science is firmly held not only for the scientific role but for all conduct whatsoever, reminding one of Montaigne's character "who sought the quadrature of the circle even while he lay with his wife."

But even in an extremely sacred society it is difficult to find any one role that grants full scope to the potentialities and actual capacities of the personalities out of which the network of social relations is woven. The shaman, witch-doctor, or magician role perhaps comes as close to absorbing completely the full personality of the man who plays it as possibly can be conceived, but even the shaman may be a spouse, a father, a craftsman, a politician, an in-grouper, a beggar, or a spy. The number of defined and specifically assigned roles is of course less in a sacred society than in a secular one, but there is nevertheless a considerable range of "individuality"—meaning thereby that total personality and assigned role or roles coincide only roughly.

When we turn to secular societies such as those in which science has an opportunity to develop, we find that the range of possible roles is much greater. It becomes more and more difficult to find one that takes in an overwhelmingly dominant proportion of any personality which has developed in such a society. Personality and society being intertwined as they are, it follows that a complex and changing society bears and is borne by complex and changing personalities. The university professor may also be a citizen, a Democrat, a patriot, a teetotaler, a PTA member, a Rotarian, a Mason, a Methodist, a practical joker, a commuter, a Book-of-the-Month Club subscriber, a customer, a renter, a golfer, a woman-hater, a penny-pincher, and a tenor. (He may also be a scientist.) These roles are fairly easy to reconcile; our conventional professor can play all of them and still be free from advanced schizophrenia. But he cannot play all of them at once—what single situation can possibly elicit all the responses of which he is capable? When we turn to those unconventional persons of whom even a university community provides samples, the range of possible responses is much greater and the impossibility of eliciting a large proportion of them in any one situation more evident.

To be sure, the norms of success in a society marked by high differentiation make it imperative to play one role *well*. Again a quotation from William James:

Not that I would not, if I could, be both handsome and fat and well-dressed, and a great athlete, and make a million a year, be a wit, a *bon-vivant*, a lady-killer, as well as a philosopher; a philanthropist, statesman, warrior, and African explorer, as well as a "tone-poet" and a saint.   But the thing is simply impossible.[12]

Some potentialities that conflict with the key role, in other words, must be permitted slowly to dwindle—if, indeed, they were ever potentialities at all.   But not *all* roles are in deadly conflict—*there* is the taproot of value-polytheism.

It is entirely possible to be both humanitarian *and* scientist. There is danger, of course, that one preference-system will block out the other, that one ultimate value-loyalty will stifle the other, or that there will be a fateful mixture of both roles which will vouchsafe no opportunity of playing either well. Yet I should hesitate to say that the dangers of value-polytheism are greater than the dangers of value-monotheism. Always remembering the personal equation, I would even say that they are less.

Here, then, may be the remedy for "the state of the union." Value-monotheism we shall have, and little can be done about it, but let us also grant to our fellows the privilege of being neither "meliorists" nor "purists" only, but both.   There is no good reason why a man passionately convinced of the dire need for national solidarity should not devote his efforts to the pursuit of that ultimate value and still be a sociologist who subjects his work in his scientific role to the requirements of the Scientific Faith.   There is no good reason why a man passionately convinced of the dire need for actual, applied scientific control, whatever the end, should not devote his efforts to the pursuit of *that* ultimate value and still be a humanitarian who subjects his work in that role to the requirements of "the men of good will."   As John Buchan has so cannily said:

Wherefore to God the Father, the Son, and the Holy Ghost,
    Mary the Blessed Mother, and the kindly Saints as well,

[12] William James, *op. cit.*, p. 401.

I will give glory and praise, for them I cherish the most,
For they have the keys of Heaven, and save the soul from Hell.
But likewise I will spare for the lord Apollo a grace,
And a bow for the lady Venus—as a friend but not as a thrall.
'Tis true they are out of Heaven, but some day they may win the place;
For gods are kittle cattle, and a wise man honours them all.

VI. "UNITED WE STAND . . ."

What do these considerations mean in the everyday routine of the private or public research bureau, the classroom, the study, the statistics laboratory, and the field?

First, I think, they mean that we must insist on scientific freedom. If a man in his scientific role has reached conclusions that seem to him and his colleagues to yield control not previously possessed, he has the right to make them known through the established channels. If he fears that his formulations may be used for ends in radical antagonism to the supreme end of scientific control, he may justifiably take steps which will keep these formulations esoteric. Certainly he is under no compulsion to become a mere technologist who prostitutes the powers of science to political systems which kill at the source all scientific endeavor that conflicts with the ends of those systems. "We cannot remain free from the biases of lore if we do not foster a bias in favor of science."[13]

Second, it seems to me that we have a right to demand from the public and from our "meliorist" and "purist" fellows *freedom to practice value-polytheism.* In so far as our work is professedly scientific, it must be judged by scientific standards, not by patriotic, humanitarian, or religious standards. In so far as we have time, energy, and inclination to be patriots, humanitarians, or religionists, we have the right to play those roles up to the hilt. No protests about "public servants in politics" or "professors in politics," for example, should have the slightest weight with us. It is not our fault that legislators and journalists perpetuate the hoary myth that we should be indifferent to all save the advancement of our particular scien-

[13] Barnes and Becker, *STLS*, II, 1177.

tific specialties. Moreover, it is not our fault that the lay public grants to us in our nonspecialized roles prestige which properly belongs to us, if at all, only in our specialized capacities. The same unwarranted prestige attaches to the businessman, the minister, the artist, and the politician. Let the public learn to discriminate, and in the meantime let us mount our political platforms, our stages, our forums, or our pulpits, if we feel so inclined, and speak as free men and American citizens!

The "purist" may say, of course, that this demand for value-polytheism, this fight for freedom, is nonrational. But what of that? Is the fight for "pure science" rational? Have we forgotten our cadi? And even if "pure science" were a rationally demonstrable goal, can it be pursued when the scientist is chained to the chariot of political systems that deny the ultimate value to which, in his role, he is dedicated?

For myself at least, doubts are dead. The freedom to "travel any road, under the sun, under the stars, nor doubt if fame or fortune lie beyond the bourne" is for me the Heart of the Bruce and, I hope, for you as well. You will remember that the dying request of the Bruce was that his heart might be buried in the Holy Land. Accordingly, his faithful follower, the Douglas, together with many another doughty warrior, set sail for Palestine, but on the way thither, they heard that Alfonso of Castile was sore bestead. The Saracens were pressing him hard; hence the Douglas, to whom the Heart of the Bruce had been entrusted, decided that the fight against the enemies of Christendom need not wait until the Holy Land was reached. He and his men rode out and did battle; the issue was in doubt. Then the Douglas took "the casket with lions thereon wrought that shrinéd the heart of the Bruce," flung it far into the Saracen ranks, charged after it with his warriors, and scattered the heathen hosts. When the field was cleared of the living, the body of the Douglas was found, one arm outstretched in death. But upon that arm was a shield, and under that shield lay the golden casket. Thus was the battle-shout of the Douglas fulfilled: "Heart of the Bruce, I follow thee or die!"

Friends and fellow-workers, the enemies of freedom threaten, now as always. Let "meliorists" and "purists" forget their differences; let us be men who gladly do what must be done. Remember the rallying chant of the Douglas:

> Have down, have down, my merry men all,
>   Have down unto the plain!
> We'll let the Scottish lions loose
>   Within the fields of Spain!

CHAPTER BIBLIOGRAPHIES

(Supplementing Footnote References)

selected by

RICHARD L. HOPKINS WITH THE COLLABORATION OF JOE D. MILLS

Research and Teaching Assistants
University, of Wisconsin

These bibliographies are intended for general readers and students of the social sciences and humanities rather than for "professionals," although it is hoped that the latter will find useful hints here and there.

All foreign-language items have been omitted, but important translations are listed. The footnotes of the present book contain numerous references to foreign-language sources, but are not designed to be bibliographical. We have called attention to bibliographies in the articles and books we have included, and many of these give French, German, and other titles. To do more than this here would make our collection too bulky and of primarily "professional" character.

Beyond the limitation to materials in English, our bibliographies are not intended to be comprehensive; not only are they "selected," but they are also held within bounds fixed by what is likely to be found in smaller libraries. In most instances, therefore, we have given references to only a few journals, most of which have fairly wide distribution or can be easily obtained. Books have not been picked according to such rigid principles; if they are not obviously rare, we have included them, ordinarily choosing the latest edition or reprint rather than the scholarly "first." In many cases we have listed collections of readings or source books, in the belief that they are more likely to be available or more readily secured than the oftentimes scarce or inaccessible originals.

There is also a time restriction. In the case of journals, emphasis has been laid on articles published since about 1920. The same is true of books, although the exceptions are more numerous. The bibliographies we mention often list earlier items.

In one respect there has been no limitation, but rather the contrary Many selections have been included with which the author of these essays is not in agreement. We have followed his suggestion that we cover a wide range, for illustrative and other purposes, rather than se up an orthodox canon or favor a particular school of thought.   The footnotes of the chapters, *with which there is intentionally little overlap here*, give some indication of the author's preferences, but these have not controlled our selection.   Our motto is this:

WHATEVER MAY BE THE LIMITATIONS WHICH TRAMMEL INQUIRY ELSEWHERE, WE BELIEVE THAT THE GREAT STATE UNIVERSITY OF WISCONSIN SHOULD EVER ENCOURAGE THAT CONTINUAL AND FEARLESS SIFTING AND WINNOWING BY WHICH ALONE THE TRUTH CAN BE FOUND.—Report of the Board of Regents, 1894.

ABBREVIATIONS

(Titles of journals, etc., listed only once
are not abbreviated.)

AA .... *American Anthropologist*
AH .... *Agricultural History*
AJS .... *The American Journal of Sociology*
ASR .... *American Sociological Review*
PS .... *Philosophy of Science*
SF .... *Social Forces*
SJA .... *Southwestern Journal of Anthropology*
SR .... *Social Research*
SSR .... *Sociology and Social Research*
SSSQ .... *Southwestern Social Science Quarterly*
RS .... *Rural Sociology*

CHAPTER ONE

I

Bowman, C. C., "Role-Playing and the Development of Insight," *SF*, XXVIII (Dec., 1949), 195-199.
Goldenweiser, Alexander, *History, Psychology, and Culture*. New York, 1933. Esp. Part I, 2. Bibliography in footnotes.
Katona, George, "The Role of the Frame of Reference," *AJS*, XLIX (Jan., 1944), 340-347.
Sherif, Muzafer, *An Outline of Social Psychology*. New York, 1948. Esp. chaps. 7, 10.
Thomas, W. I., "The Comparative Study of Cultures," *AJS*, XLII (Sept., 1936), 177-185.

II

Dahlke, H. O., "Values and Group Behavior in Two Camps for Conscientious Objectors," *AJS*, LI (July, 1945), 22-33.
MacIver, R. M., and Page, C. H., *Society: An Introductory*

Analysis. New York, 1949. Esp. Book II, Part 1, 7. Good chapter bibliographies.

SUMNER, W. G., *Folkways.* New York, 1906. Chaps. 1, 2, 15.

WALLER, WILLARD, "Social Problems and the Mores," *ASR*, I (Dec., 1936), 922-933.

III

CHAPPLE, E. D., AND COON, C. S., *Principles of Anthropology.* New York, 1942. Part I, 3.

LINDESMITH, A. R., AND STRAUSS, A. L., *Social Psychology.* New York, 1949. Part III, 10.

NEWCOMB, T. M., *Social Psychology.* New York, 1950. Esp. Parts II, 4, and III, 9. Recent bibliography.

YOUNG, KIMBALL, *Personality and Problems of Adjustment.* New York, 1940. Part I, 9. Excellent bibliography.

IV

BALDWIN, J. M., *Mental Development in the Child and the Race,* 2nd ed. corrected. New York, 1903. Outmoded in many respects, but still interesting with regard to infant learning, esp. 332-348.

COOLEY, C. H., *Human Nature and the Social Order,* rev. ed. New York, 1922. Chaps. 5, 6.

MEAD, G. H., *Mind, Self, and Society.* Chicago, 1934. Esp. Part III.

PIAGET, JEAN, *The Moral Judgment of the Child.* New York, 1932.

YOUNG, KIMBALL, *Source Book for Social Psychology.* New York, 1927. Part II, 9. Excellent chapter bibliographies.

V

DAVIS, KINGSLEY, *Human Society.* New York, 1949. Part I, 3. Good bibliography.

HILLER, E. T., *Social Relations and Structure.* New York, 1947. Parts II, 4, and III, 6.

STOUFFER, S. A., "An Analysis of Conflicting Social Norms," *ASR*, XIV (Dec., 1949), 707-717.

VI

BAGEHOT, WALTER, *Physics and Politics.* New York, 1873.

BURNHAM, JAMES, *The Machiavellians.* New York, 1943.

DENISON, J. H., *Emotion as the Basis of Civilization.* New York, 1928. Of little current validity, but replete with examples.

EDDY, SHERWOOD, *The Kingdom of God and the American Dream.* New York, 1941.

KLAPP, O. E., "Hero Worship in America," *ASR*, XIV (Feb., 1949), 53-62.

PARETO, VILFREDO, *The Mind and Society,* trans. by Andrew Bongiorno and Arthur Livingston. 4 vols. New York, 1935. Vol. I, pars. 13, 147-52, 157, 161.

PARK, R. E., AND BURGESS, E. W., *Introduction to the Science of Sociology.* 2nd ed. Chicago, 1924. Esp. 879-881. Excellent bibliographies throughout.

PRATT, J. B., *The Psychology of Religious Belief.* New York, 1907.

RUSSELL, BERTRAND, *Why Men Fight.* New York, 1917.

TAWNEY, R. H., *Religion and the Rise of Capitalism.* New York, 1947. Part III.

WEBER, MAX, *The Protestant Ethic and the Spirit of Capitalism,* trans. by Talcott Parsons. New York, 1930.

VII

ADLER, FRANZ, "The Social Thought of Jean-Paul Sartre," *AJS,* LV (Nov., 1949), 284-294.

ATTWATER, DONALD, *Modern Christian Revolutionaries.* New York, 1947.

CABOT, R. C., *What Men Live By.* Boston, 1931.

HYDE, W. D., *The Five Great Philosophies of Life.* New York, 1928.

LEYS, W. A. R., *Ethics and Social Policy.* New York, 1941.

ROBERTS, W. H., *The Problem of Choice.* Boston, 1941.

RUNES, D. D., ed., *Twentieth Century Philosophy.* New York, 1943. Rich bibliographical source.

SARTRE, JEAN-PAUL, *Existentialism and Humanism,* trans. by Philip Mairet. London, 1949.

VIII

DEGRAZIA, SEBASTIAN, *The Political Community: A Study of Anomie.* Chicago, 1948. Good bibliography, but see review by Howard Becker, *AJS,* XV (Sept., 1949), 210-211.

HALLOWELL, A. I., "The Social Function of Anxiety in a Primitive Society," *ASR,* VI (Dec., 1941), 869-881.

FROMM, ERICH, *Escape from Freedom.* New York, 1941.

HORNEY, KAREN, *The Neurotic Personality of Our Time.* New York, 1937.

MERTON, R. K., *Social Theory and Social Structure.* Glencoe, Ill., 1949. Part II, 4. Bibliographies in footnotes and at end.

IX

BAIN, READ, "Sociology and Psychoanalysis," *ASR,* I (April, 1936), 203-206. Critical. Good bibliography in footnotes.

ELLIS, HAVELOCK, "Freud's Influence on the Changed Attitude Toward Sex," *AJS*, XLV (Nov., 1939), 309-317. Part of a symposium on Freud.

FREUD, SIGMUND, *The Basic Writings of Sigmund Freud*, trans. and ed. by A. A. Brill. New York, 1938.

HEALY, WILLIAM, BRONNER, AUGUSTA, AND BOWERS, ANNA MAE, *The Structure and Meaning of Psychoanalysis*. New York, 1930.

SALTER, ANDREW, *Conditioned Reflex Therapy*. New York, 1949. Contains critique of Freud.

X

ADLER, ALFRED, *Understanding Human Nature*. New York, 1928.

BENOÎT-SMULLYAN, ÉMILE, "Status, Status Types, and Status Interrelations," *ASR*, IX (April, 1944), 151-161.

COOLEY, C. H., *Sociological Theory and Social Research*. New York, 1930. Esp. the famous chapter on "Genius, Fame, and the Comparison of Races."

FARIS, R. E. L., "Sociological Causes of Genius," *ASR*, V (Oct., 1940), 689-699.

GOLDHAMER, H., AND SHILS, E. A., "Types of Power and Status," *AJS*, XLV (Sept., 1939), 171-182.

LASSWELL, H. D., *Power and Personality*. New York, 1948.

PARETO, VILFREDO, *The Mind and Society*, trans. by A. Bongiorno and A. Livingston. 4 vols. New York, 1935. Vol. III, pars. 2026-2059. Rich bibliographies in footnotes throughout.

XI

SAPIR, EDWARD, "Fashion," in *Encyclopedia of the Social Sciences*. New York, 1930-34. Vol. VI, 139-144. Extensive bibliographies and full index volume.

SUMNER, W. G., AND KELLER, A. G., *The Science of Society*. 4 vols. New Haven, 1929. "The Aleatory Element," II, 737-770.

THOMAS, W. I., "The Gaming Instinct," *AJS*, VI (May, 1901), 750-763.

XII

BAIN, READ, "Our Schizoid Culture," *SSR*, XIX (Jan.-Feb., 1935), 266-276.

BOWMAN, C. C., "American Culture and the Problem of Personal Organization," *SF*, XIX (May, 1941), 483-491.

JONASSEN, C. F., "Cultural Variables in the Ecology of an Ethnic Group," *ASR*, XIV (Feb., 1949), 32-41.

XIII

BARNETT, J. H., "The Easter Festival: A Study in Cultural Change," *ASR*, XIV (Feb., 1949), 62-70.

BOSSARD, J. H. S., AND BOLL, E. S., "Ritual in Family Living," *ASR*, XIV (Aug., 1949), 463-469.

FUSTEL DE COULANGES, N. D., *The Ancient City*, trans. by Willard Small. Boston, 1874.

MAINE, H. J. S., *Ancient Law*. New York, 1888.

————, *Village Communities in the East and West*. London, 1871.

SPENCER, HERBERT, *The Principles of Sociology*. 2 vols. New York, 1897. Vol. II, Part 4.

XIV

ARENSBERG, C. M., *The Irish Countryman*. New York, 1937.

BECKER, HOWARD, *German Youth: Bond or Free*. Gary, Ind.: Norman Paul Press, 1950. Chaps. 1, 2, 6. Bibliographies.

EMBREE, J. F., *Suye Mura: A Japanese Village*. Chicago, 1939.

FRANCIS, E. K., "Mennonite Institutions in Early Manitoba: A Study of Their Origins," *AH*, XXII (July, 1948), 144-155.

REDFIELD, ROBERT, *The Folk Culture of Yucatan*. Chicago, 1941. Esp. chap. 12.

WEST, JAMES, *Plainville, USA*. New York, 1946.

YANG, M. C., *A Chinese Village*. New York, 1945.

XV

BOSSARD, J. H. S., AND BOLL, E. S., "Rites of Passage: A Contemporary Study," *SF*, XXVII (March, 1948), 247-255.

CHAPPLE, E. D., AND COON, C. S., *Principles of Anthropology*. New York, 1942. Part IV, 20. Good bibliography.

REDFIELD, ROBERT, "The Folk Society," *AJS*, LII (Jan., 1947), 293-308. Bibliography in footnotes.

XVI

BECKER, FRANCES BENNETT, "Lenin's Application of Marx's Theory of Revolutionary Tactics," *ASR*, II (June, 1937), 353-364.

BECKER, HOWARD, "The Regimented Man: Interviews with German Officials under the Nazis," *SF*, XXVIII (Oct., 1949), 19-24.

HONIGSHEIM, PAUL, "The Roots of the Nazi Concept of the Ideal German Peasant," *RS*, XII (March, 1947), 3-21. Extensive bibliography in footnotes.

NEUMANN, F. L., *Behemoth: The Structure and Practice of National Socialism*. New York, 1944.

NIEBUHR, H. R., *The Social Sources of Denominationalism.* New York, 1929.

STALIN, JOSEPH, *Problems of Leninism.* Moscow, 1940.

TROELTSCH, ERNST, *The Social Teaching of the Christian Churches,* 2 vols., trans. by Olive Wyon. New York, 1931.

YINGER, J. M., *Religion in the Struggle for Power.* Durham, N. C., 1946.

XVII

BECKER, HOWARD, "Befuddled Germany: A Glimpse of Max Scheler," *ASR,* VIII (April, 1943), 207-211.

———, *German Youth: Bond or Free.* Gary, Ind.: Norman Paul Press, 1950. Chap. 6.

———, "Monuments: German Personality Types Foreshadowing the Collapse of the Weimar Republic," *ASR,* VIII (Oct., 1943), 525-530.

———, "Unrest, Culture Contact, and Release during the Middle Ages and the Renaissance," *SSSQ,* XII (Sept., 1931), 1-13.

———, AND BRUNER, D. K., "Some Aspects of Taboo and Totemism," *Journal of Social Psychology,* III (Aug., 1932), 337-353.

HERMAN, S. W., JR., *It's Your Souls We Want,* 3rd ed. New York, 1943. Esp. Part I.

HITLER, ADOLF, *Mein Kampf,* trans. by Ralph Manheim. Cambridge, Mass., 1943. Esp. II, 4.

SIMPSON, S. P., AND STONE, JULIUS, *Cases and Readings on Law and Society.* St. Paul, Minn., 1948. Book One, chap. II, sec. 3, "Divine Origin and Declaratory Nature of Early Codes." A very useful collection of readings, all too little known among sociologists.

XVIII

BAIN, READ, "Cultural Integration and Social Conflict," *AJS,* XLIV (Jan., 1939), 499-509.

DURKHEIM, ÉMILE, *The Division of Labor in Society,* trans. by George Simpson. Glencoe, Ill., 1947. Book I, 3.

PARSONS, TALCOTT, *The Structure of Social Action.* Glencoe, Ill., 1949. See pp. 59-60, 103, 123, *et passim* for "randomness of ends."

RIEMER, SVEND, "Damon Runyan—Philosopher of City Life," *SF,* XXV (May, 1947), 402-405.

XIX

CARPENTER, NILES, *The Sociology of City Life*. New York, 1931. Chaps. 6-10, 13, 14.

FRAZIER, E. F., "The Impact of Urban Civilization upon Negro Family Life," *ASR*, XII (Oct., 1947), 609-618.

SCHUETZ, ALFRED, "The Stranger: An Essay in Social Psychology," *AJS*, XLIX (May, 1944), 499-507.

SIMMEL, GEORG, *The Sociology of Georg Simmel*, trans., ed., with an introduction and a bibliography by Kurt H. Wolff. Glencoe, Ill., 1950. Part V, 3, 4.

SPYKMAN, N. J., *The Social Theory of Georg Simmel*. Chicago, 1925. Excellent bibliography of translations of Simmel's writings.

WOOD, M. M., *The Stranger*. New York, 1934.

XX

ANGELL, R. C., "Moral Integration and Interpersonal Integration in American Cities," *ASR*, XIV (April, 1949), 245-251.

BAUR, E. J., "The Functions of Ceremony in the Advertising Business," *SF*, XXVII (May, 1949), 358-365.

DURKHEIM, ÉMILE, *The Division of Labor in Society*, trans. by George Simpson. Glencoe, Ill., 1947. Book I.

MULLAN, HUGH, "The Regular-Service Myth," *AJS*, LIII (Jan., 1948), 276-281.

SIMMEL, GEORG, "The Sociology of Sociability," trans. by E. C. Hughes, *AJS*, LV (Nov., 1949), 254-261.

TOMARS, A. S., "Rural Survivals in American Urban Life," *RS*, VII (Dec., 1943), 378-386.

XXI

PARETO, VILFREDO, *The Mind and Society*, trans. by Andrew Bongiorno and Arthur Livingston. 4 vols. New York, 1935. Vol. I, pars. 827-833.

PARSONS, TALCOTT, *The Structure of Social Action*. Glencoe, Ill., 1949. Esp. 326-327, 334 *et sqq.*, 377-378.

SOROKIN, P. A., *Society, Culture, and Personality*. New York, 1947. Esp. pp. 699-701. Extensive bibliography in footnotes.

THURNWALD, R. C., "Cultural Rotation, Its Propulsion and Rhythm: A Contribution towards an Analysis of the Mechanism of Cultures," *ASR*, II (Feb., 1937), esp. 33-35.

WIRTH, LOUIS, "Ideological Aspects of Social Disorganization," *ASR*, V (Aug., 1940), 472-482.

XXII

CANTRIL, HADLEY, "The Effect of Modern Technology and Organization upon Behavior," *SF*, XV (May, 1937), 493-495.

GERTH, H. H., "The Nazi Party, Its Leadership and Composition," *AJS*, XLIV (Jan., 1940), 517-541.

LEOPOLD, LEWIS, *Prestige: A Psychological Study of Social Estimate.* London, 1913.

SCHETTLER, CLARENCE, "Personality Traits" (topical summaries of current literature), AJS, XLV (Sept., 1939), 234-258. Bibliography.

SEEMAN, MELVIN, "An Evaluation of Current Approaches to Personality Differences in Folk and Urban Societies," *SF*, XXV (Dec., 1946), 160-165.

WEBER, MAX, *From Max Weber: Essays in Sociology*, trans., ed., and with an introduction by H. H. Gerth and C. W. Mills. New York, 1946. Part II, 9.

WOODARD, J. W., "The Relation of Personality Structure to the Structure of Culture," *ASR*, III (Oct., 1938), 637-651.

ZNANIECKI, FLORIAN, "The Impact of War on Personality Organization," *SSR*, XXVII (Jan.-Feb., 1943), 171-180.

XXIII

DAVIS, KINGSLEY, "Final Note on a Case of Extreme Isolation," *AJS*, LII (March, 1947), 432-437.

SINGH, J. A. L., AND ZINGG, R. M., *Wolf-Children and Feral Man.* New York, 1942.

THOMAS, W. I., *The Unadjusted Girl.* Boston, 1927.

XXIV

LUNDBERG, G. A., KOMAROVSKY, MIRRA, AND MCINERNY, M. A., *Leisure: A Suburban Study.* New York, 1934.

SNYDERMAN, G. S., AND JOSEPHS, WILLIAM, "Bohemia: The Underworld of Art," *SF*, XVIII (Dec., 1939), 187-199.

THOMAS, W. I., AND ZNANIECKI, FLORIAN, *The Polish Peasant in Europe and America.* 2-vol. ed. New York, 1927. Esp. Vol. II, 1853-1859, 2240-2244.

XXV

BECKER, HOWARD, *Systematic Sociology on the Basis of the* Beziehungslehre *and* Gebildelehre *of Leopold von Wiese.* Gary, Ind.: Norman Paul Press, 1950. Chap. 25, sec. 2.

FARIS, ELLSWORTH, *The Nature of Human Nature*. New York, 1937. Esp. 46-60.

WIRTH, LOUIS, "Urbanism as a Way of Life," *AJS*, XLIV (July, 1938), 1-24.

ZORBAUGH, H. W., *The Gold Coast and the Slum*. Chicago, 1929. Chap. 4.

XXVI

CUBER, J. F., "Marginal Church Participants," *SSR*, XXV (Sept.-Oct., 1940), 57-62.

GREEN, A. W., "A Re-Examination of the Marginal Man Concept," *SF*, XXVI (Dec., 1947), 167-171.

PARK, R. E., "Human Migration and the Marginal Man," *AJS*, XXXIII (May, 1928), 881-893.

STONEQUIST, EVERETT, *The Marginal Man*. New York, 1937. Bibliography.

XXVII

GREEN, ARNOLD W., "The Middle Class Male Child and Neurosis," *ASR*, XI (Feb., 1946), 34-41.

HERMAN, THELMA, "Pragmatism: A Study in Middle Class Ideology," *SF*, XXII (May, 1944), 405-410.

THOMAS, W. I., AND ZNANIECKI, FLORIAN, *The Polish Peasant in Europe and America*. New York, 1927. Vol. II, 1853-1859, 2240-2244.

XXVIII

ROSTEN, L. C., *Hollywood: The Movie Colony, the Movie Makers*. New York, 1941.

VEBLEN, THORSTEIN, *The Theory of the Leisure Class*. New York, 1934.

ZORBAUGH, H. W., *The Gold Coast and the Slum*. Chicago, 1929. Esp. chap. 3.

XXIX

BURY, J. B., *A History of the Freedom of Thought*. New York, 1913.

MARTIN, E. D., *The Meaning of a Liberal Education*. New York, 1926.

MUNSON, GORHAM, *The Dilemma of the Liberated*. New York, 1930.

RUSSELL, BERTRAND, "The Role of the Intellectual in the Modern World," *AJS*, XLIV (Jan., 1939), 491-498.

THOMAS, W. I., AND ZNANIECKI, FLORIAN, *The Polish Peasant in Europe and America*. New York, 1927. Vol. II, 1853-1859.
WOLFE, A. B., *Conservatism, Radicalism, and Scientific Method*. New York, 1923.

XXX

GLICK, CLARENCE, "Transition from Familism to Nationalism among Chinese in Hawaii," *AJS*, XLIII (March, 1938), 737-740.
GROSS, NEAL, "Cultural Variables in Rural Communities," *AJS*, LIII (March, 1948), 344-350.

CHAPTER TWO

I

GOLDENWEISER, ALEXANDER, "The Relation of the Natural Sciences to the Social Sciences," in H. E. Barnes, Howard Becker, and F. B. Becker, eds., *Contemporary Social Theory*. New York, 1940.
DEWEY, JOHN, *Logic, the Theory of Inquiry*. New York, 1938. Part III, 15.
EUBANK, E. E., "Errors of Sociology," *SF*, XVI (Dec., 1937), 178-201.
McLAUGHLIN, I. C., "History and Sociology: A Comparison of Their Methods," *AJS*, XXXII (Nov., 1926), 379-395.
MILL, J. S., *A System of Logic*, 8th ed. New York, 1900. Esp. 207-324.

II

CROCE, BENEDETTO, *History as the Story of Liberty*. London, 1941. Part II, 2, and Part V.
DEWEY, JOHN, *Logic, the Theory of Inquiry*. New York, 1938. Part IV.
ELIOT, T. D., "Reactions to Predictive Assumptions," *ASR*, II (Aug., 1937), 508-517.
FAIRCHILD, H. P., ed., *A Dictionary of Sociology*. New York, 1944. See entries under "typology, constructive," "science," "culture case study," etc.
PARK, R. E., AND BURGESS, E. W., *Introduction to the Science of Sociology*, 2nd ed. Chicago, 1924. Chap. 1 and chapter bibliography.

III

BAIN, READ, "Sociology as a Natural Science," *AJS*, LIII (July, 1947), 9-16.

BALES, R. F., *Interaction Process Analysis*. Cambridge, Mass., 1950.

BECKER, HOWARD, "Distribution of Space in the *American Journal of Sociology*, 1895-1927," *AJS*, XXXVI (Nov., 1930), 461-466.

——, "Space Apportioned Forty-Eight Topics in the *American Journal of Sociology*," *AJS*, XXXVIII (July, 1932), 71-78.

——, "Sociology," in *Ten Eventful Years*, 4 vols., ed. by Walter Yust. *Encyclopaedia Britannica*. Chicago, 1947. Vol. IV, 113-116. Bibliography.

——, "Sociology," in *Encyclopaedia Britannica Yearbook*, successive issues 1940 to date, ed. by Walter Yust. Chicago, 1940—. Extensive bibliographical notations.

——, "The Limits of Sociological Positivism," *Journal of Social Philosophy*, VI (July, 1941), 362-370.

——, AND USEEM, RUTH HILL, "Sociological Analysis of the Dyad," *ASR*, VII (Feb., 1942), 13-26.

BIERSTEDT, ROBERT, "A Critique of Empiricism in Sociology," *ASR*, XIV (Oct., 1949), 584-592.

BROWN, J. F., "Individual, Group, and Social Field," *AJS*, XLIV (May, 1939), 858-867.

DODD, S. C., *Dimensions of Society*. New York, 1942. See Shanas, Ethel, "A Critique of Dodd's *Dimensions of Society*," *AJS*, XLVIII (Sept., 1942), 214-230.

LEWIN, KURT, *Resolving Social Conflicts*. New York, 1948.

LUNDBERG, G. A., *Foundations of Sociology*. New York, 1939. Bibliographical notes.

MORENO, J. L., *Who Shall Survive?* New York, 1934. Parts I and V. See also various issues of *Sociometry*.

STOUFFER, S. A., et al. *The American Soldier in World War II*. Princeton, 1949. 4 vols. See Shanas, Ethel, review, *AJS*, LV (May, 1950), 590-594.

ZIPF, G. K., *National Unity and Disunity*. Bloomington, Ind., 1941.

IV

EISTER, A. W., *Drawing-Room Conversion*. Durham, N. C., 1950.

——, "The Oxford Group Movement," *SSR*, XXXIV (Nov.-Dec., 1949), 115-124.

FOREMAN, P. B., "Negro Lifeways in the Rural South: A Typological

Approach to Social Differentiation," *ASR*, XIII (Aug., 1948), 409-418.

FRANCIS, E. K., "Toward a Typology of Religious Orders," *AJS*, LV (March, 1950), 437-449.

KLAPP, O. E., "The Fool as a Social Type," *AJS*, LV (Sept., 1949), 157-162.

LINDESMITH, A. R., AND DUNHAM, H. W., "Some Principles of Criminal Typology," *SF*, XIX (March, 1941), 307-314.

McKINNEY, J. C., "Constructive Typology in Scientific Sociological Analysis," *SF*, XXVIII (March, 1950), 235-243.

SPRANGER, EDUARD, *Types of Men: The Psychology and Ethics of Personality*, trans. by Paul Pigors. Halle, 1928.

STRONG, S. M., "Negro-White Relations as Reflected in Social Types," *AJS*, LII (July, 1946), 23-30.

———, "Social Types in a Minority Group: Formulation of a Method," *AJS*, XLVIII (March, 1943), 563-573.

WINCH, R. F., "Heuristic and Empirical Typologies," *ASR*, XII (Feb., 1947), 68-75.   Bibliography in footnotes.

WIRTH, LOUIS, "Types of Nationalism," AJS, XLI (May, 1936), 723-737.

V

BRIDGMAN, P. W., *The Logic of Modern Physics*. New York, 1932.

BURTT, E. A., *The Metaphysical Foundations of Modern Physical Science*, 2nd rev. ed. London, 1949.

JAMES, WILLIAM, *Pragmatism*. New York, 1943.

PEIRCE, C. S., *The Philosophy of Peirce*, ed. by Justus Buchler. New York, 1940.

POINCARÉ, HENRI, *The Foundations of Science*. New York, 1913.

PORTERFIELD, A. L., *Creative Factors in Scientific Research*. Durham, N. C., 1941.

VI

HINSHAW, V. G., JR., "The Pragmatist Theory of Truth," *PS*, XI (April, 1944), 82-92.

LANDECKER, W. S., "Fictitious Elements in the Theory of Social Dialectic," *SF*, XIX (Dec., 1940), 189-194.

OGDEN, C. K., *Bentham's Theory of Fictions*. New York, 1932.

VAIHINGER, HANS, *The Philosophy of "As If,"* trans. by C. K. Ogden. New York, 1925.

CHAPTER THREE

I

FLECHTHEIM, O. K., "Futurology: The New Science?" *Forum*, April and May, 1949, 206-209, 271-274.

SCHELER, MAX, "Future of Man," trans. by Howard Becker, *The Monthly Criterion*, London, Feb., 1928, 100-119.

SOROKIN, P. A., *Man and Society in Calamity*. New York, 1942.

II

BARNES, H. E., *Historical Sociology*. New York, 1948. Chap. 1.

COHEN, M. R., *The Meaning of Human History*. LaSalle, Ill., 1947.

CROCE, BENEDETTO, *History: Its Theory and Practice*, trans. by Douglas Ainslie. New York, 1923. Part I.

GUTHRIE, E. F., "Historical Materialism and Its Sociological Critics," *SF*, XX (Dec., 1941), 172-184.

KLIBANSKY, RAYMOND, AND PATON, H. J., eds., *Philosophy and History*. Oxford, 1936.

MANDELBAUM, MAURICE, *The Problem of Historical Knowledge*. New York, 1938. Excellent bibliography.

SPYKMAN, N. J., *The Social Theory of Georg Simmel*. Chicago, 1925. Book I, 5. Excellent bibliography of translations of Simmel's writings.

STERN, B. J., "Some Aspects of Historical Materialism," in Sellars, *et al.*, eds., *Philosophy for the Future*. New York, 1949.

TOYNBEE, A. J., *A Study of History*, abridged by D. C. Somervell. New York, 1947. Parts I and II. The original should be consulted, if only for the remarkable bibliographies in the footnotes and elsewhere.

III

BENEDICT, RUTH, *Patterns of Culture*. Boston, 1934.

BARNES, H. E., AND BECKER, HOWARD, *Social Thought from Lore to Science*. 2 vols. Boston, 1938. See esp. I. Bibliography in notes at end of book.

HEARNSHAW, F. J. C., ed., *The Social and Political Ideas of Some Great French Thinkers of the Age of Reason*. New York, 1930. There are seven other Hearnshaw-edited "social and political ideas" volumes, dealing with various periods. They contain many very useful chapters and bibliographies.

LÖWITH, KARL, *Meaning in History*. Chicago, 1949.

IV

GOLDENWEISER, ALEXANDER, "Diffusionism and the American School of Historical Ethnology," *AJS*, XXXI (July, 1925), 19-38.

MACIVER, R. M., AND PAGE, C. H., *Society: An Introductory Analysis.* New York, 1949. Book III, 27, 28.

RADIN, PAUL, *The Method and Theory of Ethnology.* New York, 1933.

LOWIE, R. H., *The History of Ethnological Theory.* New York, 1937. Esp. chaps. 4, 6, 7. Bibliography in footnotes.

WHITE, L. A., "Evolutionary Stages, Progress, and the Evaluation of Cultures," *SJA*, III (Autumn, 1947), 165-192. Extensive bibliography in footnotes.

V

BOAS, FRANZ, *Race, Language, and Culture.* New York, 1940. Esp. 243-311.

LINTON, RALPH, *The Study of Man.* New York, 1936. Bibliography.

MANDELBAUM, MAURICE, *The Problem of Historical Knowledge.* New York, 1938. Excellent bibliography.

MURDOCK, G. P., *Social Structure.* New York, 1949.

SCHMIDT, WILHELM, *The Culture Historical Method of Ethnology,* trans. by S. A. Sieber. New York, 1939.

VI

BECKER, HOWARD, "Culture Case Study and Ideal-Typical Method, with Special Reference to Max Weber," *SF*, XII (March, 1934), 511-526. Revised version of this appears in Barnes and Becker, *Social Thought from Lore to Science.* Boston, 1938, Vol. I, 760-763.

FAIRCHILD, H. P., ed., *A Dictionary of Sociology.* New York, 1944. See entries under "culture case study," etc.

KROEBER, A. L., AND WATERMAN, T. T., *Source Book in Anthropology,* rev. ed. New York, 1931. This is a source that covers a fairly wide range.

THOMAS, W. I., "The Comparative Study of Cultures," *AJS*, XLII (Sept., 1936), 177-185.

VII

BECKER, HOWARD, "Conquest by Pastoral Nomads," *SSR*, XV (July-Aug., 1931), 511-526.

———, *German Youth: Bond or Free.* Gary, Ind.: Norman Paul Press, 1950. Chaps. 1 and 2.

————, "Pastoral Nomadism and Social Change," *SSR*, XV (May-June, 1931), 417-427.

————, "Sargasso Iceberg: A Study in Cultural Lag and Institutional Disintegration," *AJS*, XXXIV (Nov., 1928), 492-506. Study of German peasant village.

WEBER, MAX, *From Max Weber: Essays in Sociology*, trans., ed., and with an introduction by H. H. Gerth and C. W. Mills. New York, 1946. Parts III and IV.

————, *The Methodology of the Social Sciences*, trans. and ed. by E. A. Shils and H. A. Finch. Glencoe, Ill., 1949. Esp. chaps. 1 and 2.

ZNANIECKI, FLORIAN, *The Method of Sociology*. New York, 1934. Esp. 246-248.

VIII

COULBORN, RUSHTON, "The Individual and the Growth of Civilizations," *Phylon* (1940), 3-58.

CROSSMAN, R. H. S., "The Mystic World of Arnold Toynbee," *New Republic*, July 14, 1947.

SUMBERG, T. A., "Toynbee and the Decline of Western Civilization," *SR*, XIV (Sept., 1947), 261-284.

TRINKAUS, CHARLES, "Toynbee against History," *Science and Society*, XII (Spring, 1948), 218-239.

TOYNBEE, A. J., *Civilization on Trial*. New York, 1948.

————, *A Study of History*, 6 vols. London, 1934-1939.

————, *A Study of History*, abridged by D. C. Somervell. New York, 1947.

IX

ATTWATER, DONALD, ed., *Modern Christian Revolutionaries*. Chicago, 1947.

BRYAN, G. M., "The 'Kingdom of God' Concept in Sorokin and Toynbee," *SF*, XXVI (March, 1948), 288-292.

BURY, J. B., *The Idea of Progress*. London, 1924.

EDDY, SHERWOOD, *God in History*. New York, 1947.

MORRIS, G. S., *Hegel's Philosophy of the State and of History*. Chicago, 1882.

NIEBUHR, REINHOLD, *The Nature and Destiny of Man*, 2 vols. New York, 1941-1943.

PARETO, VILFREDO, *The Mind and Society*, trans. by Andrew Bongiorno and Arthur Livingston. 4 vols. New York, 1935. Vol. IV, 13.

PARK, R. E., AND BURGESS, E. W., *Introduction to the Science of Sociology*, 2nd ed. Chicago, 1924. Chap. 14 and chapter bibliography.

RIGNANO, EUGENIO, "Sociology: Its Methods and Laws," trans. by Howard Becker. *AJS*, XXXIV (Nov., 1928, and Jan., 1929), 429-450 and 605-622.

SPENCER, HERBERT, *First Principles*, 4th ed. New York, 1896.

SPENGLER, OSWALD, *The Decline of the West*. 2 vols. New York, 1926-1928.

X

BENDIX, REINHARD, "Max Weber's Interpretation of Conduct and History," *AJS*, LI (May, 1946), 518-526.

TEGGART, F. J., *Prolegomena to History*. Berkeley, 1918.

———, *The Processes of History*. New Haven, 1918.

———, *Theory of History*. New Haven, 1925.

———, *Theory and Processes of History*. Berkeley, 1941. Contains all three previous items.

TÖNNIES, FERDINAND, *Fundamental Concepts of Sociology*, trans. by C. P. Loomis. New York, 1940.

———, "The Concept and the Law of Human Progress," trans. by K. J. Arndt and C. L. Folse, *SF*, XIX (Oct., 1940), 23-29.

WEBER, ALFRED, *Farewell to European History*, trans. by R. F. C. Hull. London, 1947.

XI

NEUMANN, SIGMUND, "Alfred Weber's Conception of Historicocultural Sociology," in H. E. Barnes, ed., *An Introduction to the History of Sociology*. Chicago, 1948. This symposium has numerous chapter bibliographies.

SALOMON, ALBERT, "The Place of Alfred Weber's *Kultursoziologie* in Social Thought," *SR*, III (1936), 494-500.

WEBER, ALFRED, *Fundamentals of Culture-Sociology*, trans. by G. H. Weltner and C. F. Hirschmann, WPA project supervised by C. J. Dittmar. Mimeographed. New York, 1939.

XII

GINSBERG, MORRIS, "The Conception of Stages in Social Evolution," *Man*, XXXII (April, 1932), 87-91.

WHITE, L. A., "Evolutionary Stages, Progress, and the Evaluation of Cultures," *SJA*, III (Autumn, 1947), 162-192. Extensive bibliography in footnotes.

XIII

BECKER, HOWARD, *Systematic Sociology on the Basis of the* Beziehungslehre *and* Gebildelehre *of Leopold von Wiese*. Gary, Ind: Norman Paul Press, 1950. Esp. Part I; see index also.

FAIRCHILD, H. P., ed., *A Dictionary of Sociology*. New York, 1944. See "culture case study," etc.

GERTH, H. H., AND GERTH, HEDWIG I., "Bibliography on Max Weber," *SR*, XVI (March, 1949), 70-89. Excellent collection; nothing approaches it.

GOODE, W. J., "A Note on the Ideal Type," *ASR*, XII (Aug., 1947), 473-474.

PARSONS, TALCOTT, *The Structure of Social Action*. Glencoe, Ill., 1949. Part III, 16. Discusses Weber from standpoint of a critical realist.

RIEMER, SVEND, "The Ideal Type in Criminological Research," in W. C. Reckless, ed., *The Etiology of Criminal and Delinquent Behavior*, Bulletin 50, Social Science Research Council. New York, 1943.

ROSE, A. M., "A Deductive Ideal-Type Method," *AJS*, LVI (July, 1950), 35-42.

WEBER, MAX, "The Theory of Social and Economic Organization," trans. by A. J. Henderson and Talcott Parsons, with introduction by latter. New York, 1947. Esp. introduction and Part I.

XIV

CARR, L. J., "Disaster and the Sequence-Pattern Concept of Social Change," *AJS*, XXXVIII (Sept., 1932), 207-218.

HERTZLER, J. O., "The Typical Life Cycle of Dictatorship," *SF*, XVII (March, 1939), 303-309.

HUNT, C. L., "The Life Cycle of Dictatorship as Seen in Treatment of Religious Institutions," *SF*, XXVII (May, 1949), 365-369.

MEADOWS, PAUL, "Sequence in Revolution," *ASR*, VI (Oct., 1941), 702-709.

OGBURN, W. F., *Social Change*. New York, 1923. Part II.

SIMMEL, GEORG, "The Sociology of Conflict," *AJS*, IX (1903-1904), 490-525, 672-689, 798-811.

SOROKIN, P. A., *Contemporary Sociological Theories*. New York, 1928. Chap. 13, 8.

XV

PARETO, VILFREDO, *The Mind and Society*, trans. by Andrew Bongiorno and Arthur Livingston. 4 vols. New York, 1935. Vol. IV, 12-13.

Sorokin, P. A., *Contemporary Sociological Theories*. New York, 1928. Chap. 13, 8.

———, *Social and Cultural Dynamics*, 4 vols. New York, 1937-1941. Esp. Vol. IV, Part II, 9.

Spengler, Oswald, *The Decline of the West*, trans. by C. J. Atkinson. 2 vols. New York, 1926-1928.

XVI

Bierstedt, Robert, "The Limitations of Anthropological Methods in Sociology," *AJS*, LIV (July, 1948), 22-30.

Destler, C. M., "Some Observations on Contemporary Historical Theory," *American Historical Review*, LV (April, 1950), 503-529.

Eliot, T. D., "The Use of History for Research in Theoretical Sociology," *AJS*, XXVI (March, 1922), 628-636.

Endleman, Robert, "The New Anthropology and Its Ambitions," *Commentary*, VIII (Oct., 1949), 284-291.

Meadows, Paul, "The Scientific Use of Historical Data," *PS*, XI (Jan., 1944), 53-58.

Tomars, A. S., "Some Problems in the Sociologist's Use of Anthropology," *ASR*, VI (Dec., 1943), 625-634.

XVII

Eubank, E. E., *The Concepts of Sociology*. Boston, 1932. Full bibliography, 395-539. Very useful.

Merton, R. K., *Social Theory and Social Structure*. Glencoe, Ill., 1949. Esp. Part I. Bibliography in footnotes and at end.

Parsons, Talcott, *Essays in Sociological Theory, Pure and Applied*. Glencoe, Ill., 1949. Parts I and II, 6. Bibliography in footnotes and at end.

———, *The Structure of Social Action*. Glencoe, Ill., 1949. Parts I, 2; III, 17; IV, 19. Bibliographical notes; very useful.

Thomas, W. I., and Znaniecki, Florian, *The Polish Peasant in Europe and America*. 2-vol. ed. New York, 1927. Esp. "Methodological Note." This note, and other theoretical passages, still the most important research-theoretical formulation in American sociology.

CHAPTER FOUR

I

Abel, Theodore, "The Operation Called *Verstehen*," *AJS*, LIV (Nov., 1948), 211-218.

ADLER, FRANZ, "Operational Definitions in Sociology," *AJS*, LII (March, 1947), 438-444.

ALPERT, HARRY, "Operational Definitions in Sociology," *ASR*, III (Dec., 1938), 855-861.

HARTUNG, F. E., "Operationism as a Cultural Survival," *PS*, XI (Oct., 1944), 227-232.

ISRAEL, H. E., "Two Difficulties in Operational Thinking," *Psychological Review*, LII (Sept., 1945), 260-261. Part of long symposium on operationism.

LUNDBERG, G. A., *Foundations of Sociology*. New York, 1939.

———, "What Are Sociological Problems?" *ASR*, VI (June, 1941), 357-369.

MACIVER, R. M., "Imputation of Motives," *AJS*, XLVI (July, 1940), 1-12.

———, *Social Causation*. Boston, 1942. Part IV.

MEADOWS, PAUL, "Science as Experience: A Genetic and Comparative Review," *ASR*, XIV (Oct., 1949), 592-599.

MITCHELL, E. T., "Metaphysics and Science," *PS*, XIII (Oct., 1946), 274-280.

REINHARDT, J. M., "Personality Traits and the Situation," *ASR*, II (Aug., 1937), 492-500.

ZNANIECKI, FLORIAN, *Social Actions*. New York, 1936. Esp. chaps. 2 and 3.

———, *The Method of Sociology*. New York, 1934. Esp. chap. 11. Bibliographical notes.

II

BENDIX, REINHARD, "Max Weber's Interpretation of Conduct and History," *AJS*, LI (May, 1949), 518-526.

GOLDENWEISER, ALEXANDER, *History, Psychology, and Culture*. New York, 1933.

HONIGSHEIM, PAUL, "Max Weber as Historian of Agriculture and Rural Life," *AH*, XXIII (July, 1949), 179-213. Extensive bibliography in footnotes.

LESSER, ALEXANDER, "Research Procedure and Laws of Culture," *PS*, VI (July, 1939), 345-355.

ROSS, E. A., "The Sociologist in the Role of Prophet," *ASR*, VIII (Feb., 1943), 10-14.

SOROKIN, P. A., *Social and Cultural Dynamics*. 4 vols. New York, 1941. Esp. Part II, 155-191.

III

ABEL, THEODORE, *How Hitler Came into Power.* New York, 1938. Excellent case material and informed analysis.

———, "The Pattern of a Successful Political Movement," *ASR*, II (June, 1937), 347-352.

BARNES, H. E., AND BECKER, HOWARD, *Social Thought from Lore to Science.* 2 vols. Boston, 1938. *Passim* for "sacred society," "charismatic leadership," etc. Bibliography in notes; full index.

BECKER, HOWARD, *German Youth: Bond or Free.* Gary, Ind.: Norman Paul Press, 1950. Extensive bibliography.

BELL, E. H., "Age Group Conflict and Our Changing Culture," *SF*, XII (Dec., 1933), 237-243.

CANTRIL, HADLEY, *The Psychology of Social Movements.* New York, 1941.

DAVIS, KINGSLEY, "The Sociology of Parent-Youth Conflict," *ASR*, V (Aug., 1940), 523-535.

MANNHEIM, KARL, *Diagnosis of Our Time.* London, 1943. Chap. 3.

———, *Man and Society in an Age of Reconstruction.* New York, 1940.

REUTER, E. B., MEAD, MARGARET, AND FOSTER, R. G., "Sociological Research in Adolescence," *AJS*, XLII (July, 1936), 81-94.

CHAPTER FIVE

I

BERNARD, JESSIE, "Observation and Generalization in Cultural Anthropology," *AJS*, L (Jan., 1945), 284-291.

HUGHES, E. C., "Personality Types and the Division of Labor," *AJS*, XXXIII (March, 1928), 754-768. One of the earliest analytic uses, resulting from Park's influence, of the sacred-secular dichotomy.

SEEMAN, MELVIN, "An Evaluation of Current Approaches to Personality Differences in Folk and Urban Societies," *SF*, XXV (Dec., 1946), 160-165.

SOROKIN, P. A., ZIMMERMAN, C. C., AND GALPIN, C. J., *A Systematic Source Book in Rural Sociology.* 3 vols. Minneapolis, Minn., 1932. Selected survey of rural communities in the past and present. Comprehensive bibliographies throughout.

TUMIN, MELVIN, " 'Culture, Genuine and Spurious': A Re-Evaluation," *ASR*, X (April, 1945), 199-207.

II

Boskoff, Alvin, "Structure, Function, and Folk Society," *ASR*, XIV (Dec., 1949), 749-758.

Durkheim, Émile, *The Division of Labor in Society*, trans. by George Simpson. Glencoe, Ill., 1947.

Sorokin, P. A., *Social and Cultural Dynamics*. 4 vols. New York, 1941. Vol. I, Parts II, IV; Vol. II. Extensive bibliography in footnotes and elsewhere.

Tönnies, Ferdinand, *Fundamental Concepts of Sociology*, trans. by C. P. Loomis. New York, 1940.

III

Ambrose, Alice, and Lazerowitz, Morris, *Fundamentals of Symbolic Logic*. New York, 1948.

Goldenweiser, Alexander, "The Concept of Causality in the Physical and Social Sciences," *ASR*, III (Oct., 1938), 624-636.

Miller, D. L., "The Behavioral Dimension of Prediction and Meaning," *PS*, XVII (April, 1950), 133-141.

IV

Bennett, J. W., "Culture Change and Personality in a Rural Society," *SF*, XXIII (Dec., 1944), 123-132.

Curwen, E. C., "The Hebrides: A Cultural Backwater," *Antiquity*, XII (Sept., 1938), 261-289.

Francis, E. K., "The Nature of the Ethnic Group," *AJS*, LII (March, 1947), 393-400.

Greifer, J. L., "Attitudes to the Stranger," *ASR*, X (Dec., 1945), 739-745.

Kollmorgen, W. M., *The Old Order Amish of Lancaster County, Pa.* Rural Life Studies No. 4. Washington, D. C., 1942.

Leonard, Olen, and Loomis, C. P., *Culture of a Contemporary Rural Community: El Cerrito, New Mexico.* Rural Life Studies No. 1. Washington, D. C., 1941.

Linton, Ralph, "Nativistic Movements," *AA*, XLV (April-June, 1943), 230-240.

Loomis, C. P., and Beegle, J. A., "The Spread of German Nazism in Rural Areas," *ASR*, XI (Dec., 1946), 724-734.

Miner, Horace, *St. Denis: A French-Canadian Parish.* Chicago, 1939.

Munch, Peter, "Cultural Contacts in an Isolated Community: Tristan da Cunha," *AJS*, LIII (July, 1947), 1-8.

PARK, R. E., AND BURGESS, E. W., *Introduction to the Science of Sociology*, 2nd ed. Chicago, 1924. Chap. 4, sec. 2, D, "Isolation and National Individuality." Chapter bibliography.

REDFIELD, ROBERT, "The Folk Society and Culture," *AJS*, XLV (March, 1940), 731-742.

————, "Primitive Merchants of Guatemala," *Quarterly Journal of Inter-American Relations*, I (Oct., 1939), 42-56.

SIMPSON, G. L., "Notes on a Definition of the Folk for Folk-Regional Sociology," *SF* (Oct., 1946), 31-34.

SIMPSON, S. P., AND STONE, JULIUS, *Cases and Readings on Law and Society*. St. Paul, Minn., 1948. Three vols. projected, one published. If one overlooks the evolutionary prepossessions of the compilers, it can be said that this is an admirable collection of readings.

TAX, SOL, "World View and Social Relations in Guatemala," *AA*, N. S., XLIII (Jan.-March, 1941), 27-42.

V

BECKER, HOWARD, "Processes of Secularisation," *Sociological Review* (British), XXIV (April-June and Oct., 1932), 138-154, 266-286.

BURGESS, E. W., ed., *The Urban Community*. Chicago, 1926. Chap. 1.

GIST, N. P., AND HALBERT, L. A., *Urban Society*, 2nd ed. New York, 1941. Chaps. 12-14.

HOFFER, F. W., "The Conditioning of Behavior through Structure and Function in an Urban Community," *SF*, XX (March, 1942), 316-321.

TISDALE, HOPE, "The Process of Urbanization," *SF*, XX (March, 1942), 311-316.

WOOLSTON, HOWARD, *Metropolis*. New York, 1938. Chaps. 2, 4, 14.

CHAPTER SIX

I

DEXTER, LEWIS, "Social Invention and Social Technology," *Journal of Liberal Religion*, IX (Spring-Summer, 1948), 135-142.

FARIS, ELLSWORTH, "Sociology and Human Welfare," *SF*, XVIII (Oct., 1939), 1-9.

GILLETTE, J. M., "An Examination of Criteria for the Determination of Normal Society," *ASR*, II (Aug., 1937), 501-507.

HARING, D. G., "Science and Social Phenomena," *American Scientist*, XXXV (Summer, 1947), 351-363.

HAUSER, P. M., "Are the Social Sciences Ready?" *ASR*, XI (Aug., 1946), 379-384.

HERTZLER, J. O., "Some Basic Sociological Postulates Underlying World Organization and Peace," *SF*, XXII (Dec., 1943), 125-130.

MERTON, R. K., "The Role of Applied Social Science in the Formulation of Policy: A Research Memorandum," *PS*, XVI (July, 1949), 161-181.

RIEMER, SVEND, "Values and Standards in Research," *AJS*, LV (Sept., 1949), 131-136.

TAYLOR, C. C., "Sociology and Common Sense," *ASR*, XII (Feb., 1947), 1-9. With discussions by Robert Redfield and S. A. Stouffer, 9-12.

II

BOWMAN, C. C., "Evaluation and Values Consistent with the Scientific Study of Society," *ASR*, VIII (June, 1943), 306-312.

———, "Must the Social Sciences Foster Moral Skepticism?" *ASR*, X (Dec., 1945), 709-715.

FOLSOM, J. K., "Changing Values in Sex and Family Relations," *ASR*, II (Oct., 1937), 717-726.

HART, HORNELL, "Factuality and the Discussion of Values," *SF*, XXV (March, 1947), 290-294.

———, "Value Judgments in Sociology," *ASR*, III (Dec., 1938), 862-867.

HERTZLER, J. O., *Social Institutions*. Lincoln, Nebr., 1946. Chap. 17.

HINSHAW, V. G., JR., "Epistemological Relativism and the Sociology of Knowledge," *PS*, XV (Jan., 1948), 4-10.

JAMES, WILLIAM, *Essays on Faith and Morals*. New York, 1943. Chap. 9.

KOLB, W. L., "Sociologically Established Family Norms and Democratic Values," *SF*, XXVI (May, 1948), 451-456.

MEAD, G. H., *The Philosophy of the Act*. Chicago, 1938. Esp. Part IV.

MILLS, C. W., "Methodological Consequences of Sociology of Knowledge," *AJS*, XLVI (Nov., 1940), 316-330.

MYRDAL, GUNNAR, *An American Dilemma*. New York, 1944. Appendix 2.

SHERIF, MUZAFER, *An Outline of Social Psychology*. New York, 1948. Esp. 48 *et sqq.* and 206 *et sqq.*

———, *The Psychology of Social Norms.* New York, 1936.

SPENCER, HERBERT, *The Study of Sociology.* New York, 1874.

WOODARD, J. W., *Intellectual Realism and Culture Change.* Hanover, N. H., 1935.

ZNANIECKI, FLORIAN, *The Laws of Social Psychology.* Chicago, 1925. Chap. 2.

———, *The Social Role of the Man of Knowledge.* New York, 1940.

III

FOREMAN, P. B., "Prediction in the Frame of Reference of the Single Case," *SSSQ*, XXIX (Dec., 1948), 284-292.

JAMES, WILLIAM, *Essays in Radical Empiricism.* New York, 1943. Esp. Vol. I.

REISSMAN, LEONARD, "A Study of Role Conceptions in Bureaucracy," *SF*, XXVII (March, 1949), 305-310.

RIEMER, SVEND, "Theory and Quantitative Analysis in Criminological Research," *AJS*, XLVIII (Sept., 1942), 188-201.

WOLFF, KURT, "The Sociology of Knowledge: Emphasis on an Empirical Attitude," *PS*, X (April, 1943), 104-123.

ZNANIECKI, FLORIAN, *The Social Role of the Man of Knowledge.* New York, 1940.

IV

GITTLER, J. B., "Possibilities of a Sociology of Science," *SF*, XVIII (March, 1940), 350-359.

MERTON, R. K., *Social Theory and Social Structure.* Glencoe, Ill., 1949. Esp. Part IV.

PARSONS, TALCOTT, "The Place of Ultimate Values in Sociological Theory," *International Journal of Ethics*, XLV (April, 1935), 282-316.

V

BLUM, F. H., "Max Weber's Postulate of 'Freedom' from Value Judgments," *AJS*, L (July, 1944), 46-52.

LUNDBERG, G. A., *Can Science Save Us?* New York, 1947. See review by Howard Becker, *AJS*, LIV (Sept., 1948), 170-171.

———, "Sociology vs. Dialectical Immaterialism," *AJS*, LIII (Sept., 1947), 85-95.

LYND, R. S., *Knowledge for What?* Princeton, 1939.

SIMPSON, GEORGE, "The Scientist—Technician or Moralist?" *PS*, XVII (Jan., 1950), 95-108.

WEBER, MAX, *The Methodology of the Social Sciences*, trans. and ed. by E. A. Shils and H. A. Finch. Glencoe, Ill., 1949. Esp. 1-47.

VI

BENDA, JULIEN, *The Treason of the Intellectuals*, trans. by Richard Oldington. New York, 1928.

CHAFEE, ZECHARIAH, *Free Speech in the United States*. Cambridge, 1941.

DAVIS, KINGSLEY, BREDEMEIER, H. C., AND LEVY, M. J., JR., eds., *Modern American Society*. New York, 1949. Esp. pp. 13-17, 23-26.

MANNHEIM, KARL, *Ideology and Utopia*, trans. by Louis Wirth and E. A. Shils, with an introduction by the former. New York, 1936. Introduction and chap. 3. Excellent bibliography.

MAX WEBER, *From Max Weber: Essays in Sociology*, trans., ed., and with an introduction by H. H. Gerth and C. W. Mills. New York, 1946. Chap. 4, "Politics as a Vocation."

NAME INDEX

Names occurring in the Editorial Note, Acknowledgments, and Chapter Bibliographies, and the author's name anywhere it occurs, are not indexed.

SUBJECT INDEX

Inasmuch as a very full Table of Contents has been provided, the Subject Index deals chiefly with topics not clearly recognizable in the section and chapter headings.